Policeman

Policeman

RICHARD RAMSAY

authorHOUSE®

AuthorHouse™ UK
1663 Liberty Drive
Bloomington, IN 47403 USA
www.authorhouse.co.uk
Phone: 0800.197.4150

Published by AuthorHouse 02/17/2015

ISBN: 978-1-5049-3603-3 (sc)
ISBN: 978-1-5049-3600-2 (hc)
ISBN: 978-1-5049-3604-0 (e)

Library of Congress Control Number: 2015900733

Print information available on the last page.

For my wife, Maureen

For my daughters, Amanda and Emma

Contents

Preface

This book is an account of my experiences as a police officer. Most of the narrative covers the period from 1964 until 1994, but some parts of the narrative will take the reader into more recent years. Although the central theme is my story, it is also a history of policing seen through my eyes during those years, and as such it includes the political and social background to a time of upheaval and change in British society. I have done my best to make the facts as accurate as possible; however, there may be a few incidents when the chronology is not completely correct. The names of informants and a number of other people have been changed. The backgrounds of three or four incidents have been deliberately altered to protect the identity of the people involved.

Acknowledgements

I should like to offer my thanks to the following people, who have given me a great deal of valuable information about themselves and events that they were involved with: Gil French; John Harvey, QGM; Michael Lyons, BEM; Norwell Roberts, QPM; Peter Spencer; and Chris Stanger. Sir Robert Mark's book, *In the Office of Constable*, proved a useful source of background information in respect to events involving the Metropolitan Police during the 1970s.

Glossary

ABH	An assault causing bodily harm
ACPO	Association of Chief Police Officers
Brief	Slang word used for lawyer
CO	Commissioner's Office, usually known as Scotland Yard
CPS	Crown Prosecution Service
DPP	Director of Public Prosecutions
Drum	Slang word for house or apartment
Flasher	Man who commits an offence of indecent exposure
Gamer	A person involved in illegal gaming
Grass	An informer
LOB	Police slang. Can be translated as 'a load of nonsense'
MO	Modus operandi. The method used to carry out a crime
Old Bill	Slang word for police
Pear shaped	A situation that goes wrong, often public-order situations
RCS	Regional Crime Squad
Skipper	Slang word for sergeant
Stickie	A member of the Official IRA

1

Central London, 1986

It seemed that the world was asleep, except for a few people on foot and in cars who were wearing dark-blue uniforms. Driving away from Gerald Road police station at that time of night I noted that the streets of Belgravia were mainly deserted and peaceful. As duty officer looking after two divisions, I spent a certain amount of my time driving between Rochester Row and Gerald Road.

There were always cases that needed my attention. Sometimes it was a matter of authorising the further detention of a suspect. By 3 a.m. there were few messages coming over the air, whereas three or four hours earlier it would have been the opposite, probably bedlam. It was possible to switch off a little bit, but as always, my ears pricked up when I heard the word Alfa, the call sign of units in South Westminster. Then I picked up on the other two key words – Chelsea Barracks.

Suddenly, the situation had changed. I had been feeling tired, but the radio brought me back to the real world with a jolt. Two cars were on their way to the barracks. Very little had been said on the radio, but my instinct was already kicking in. This could be something serious, I thought. The next call from Information Room was probably going to be for the duty officer, and I decided to save them the trouble of calling me.

'MP from Alfa Romeo One. On my way to Chelsea Barracks.'

The barracks were on Gerald Road's patch but just tucked inside the divisional boundary, with Chelsea division on the other side of the street. At that time of night, it would only take me two or three minutes to get there. For that short time, my thoughts went back to the IRA attack at the barracks five years earlier. The policy of the Provisional IRA was not to give a warning if they attacked a military target, and their bomb had left two people dead and forty injured. Would they attack the same place a second time?

In the first attack, the target had been a bus that was returning to the barracks, carrying soldiers from the Irish Guards who had been on duty at the Tower of London. At the end of its journey, the bus had to travel along Ebury Bridge Road, and that is where the bomb had been placed. When it exploded, the blast pushed its contents – coach bolts and six-inch – nails, in all directions. A couple of weeks later, I went to Westminster Hospital with one of my sergeants and visited two of the Irish guardsmen who had been injured. One of them had an empty whiskey bottle next to his bed that he was filling with bits and pieces of shrapnel that had come out of him. The skin, the largest organ in the body, does not welcome these unwanted alien intruders, and bit by bit it was expelling small fragments of metal and glass. We could see that the bottle was half full.

Some places seemed to crop up time and time again in my own story, and Chelsea Barracks was certainly one of those places. Sometime after the bombing, I had arrested an IRA man who was suspected of being involved in the attack. All of these thoughts were starting to bubble around inside my head during my short drive to the barracks.

'What's the story?' The words may vary from time to time, but this is the usual question that the duty officer asks at any incident. One of our PCs had spoken to a soldier at the guard house and then retold me the few facts known at that point. The soldier's job was to patrol the inside of the perimeter fence. He had noticed two men in Chelsea Bridge Road, close to the security fence, who were talking quietly and appeared to be doing something. He walked towards the fence and called out to them, asking them what they were doing. Their story was that they had just noticed two men acting suspiciously in the street outside the barracks and they wanted to tell somebody about it. The sentry moved a few metres away from the two men and used his walkie-talkie to call for assistance. When he walked back towards the perimeter fence, the two men had vanished.

Six or seven police officers had gathered close to the guard house; we could see that the army had started evacuating some of their buildings and soldiers were taking up positions at key locations within the barracks.

I asked the sentry to go back to the spot where he had seen the two men. Two PCs came with me, and we walked along Chelsea Bridge Road, keeping parallel with the guardsman who was on the other side of the perimeter fence. When he reached the place where he had seen the two men, he shouted to me and pointed. There was no sign of anything there, so we carried on walking for a short distance. Then I stopped, and it was my turn to point. We could see what appeared to be a metal box lying on the footway next to the perimeter fence.

It was something that was not easy to see unless you were looking for it. It was even more difficult because it was dark and the object was partly covered by leaves. Although the device was just outside the perimeter fence, its position was interesting – not too far from one of the main buildings inside the barracks. I had twinges in both legs. Not real pain but a little bit like a minor electric shock, a reaction that sometimes happened when I sensed danger. 'I don't like this one bit,' I thought. The priority in this type of incident is always the safety of the public, and my first thoughts were to work out an immediate plan for doing that as quickly as possible. However, as they say, first things first. The three of us were far too close to something that could be a terrorist bomb, and we moved away from it. I sent one of my officers about 100 metres north and the other one to the south of it. Their job was to stop any vehicles or pedestrians coming along Chelsea Bridge Road.

My position was still a bit too close to something that could be a bomb and I moved further away, in the general direction of Chelsea Bridge. The first call on my personal radio (PR) went to Alfa Romeo, the call sign for Rochester Row, with a request for an explosives officer. My next call was to direct every available officer from both divisions to make their way to the barracks.

Chelsea Bridge Road was sealed off at both road junctions, to the north and south of the barracks. The divisional boundary between Gerald Road and Chelsea ran along the middle of the road, so a message was sent to Chelsea, informing them that there was an incident on their boundary.

Dealing with a suspected terrorist incident in central London will always present a whole range of problems. It is vital to create a safe area with a wide perimeter around anything we think might be a bomb. It may be stating the obvious, but we need to make sure that there is nobody inside the perimeter. However, my experience is that this is often easier said than done, especially when there may not be many officers there in those first few crucial minutes.

The incident at Chelsea Barracks was quite different from other terrorist incidents that I had been to in several ways. No location in central London could ever be described as a 'good' place to have a suspected terrorist bomb. However, it could be said that this one was better than most.

The first positive factor was that this was a military base and, as expected, the army had reacted quickly. Their contingency plans were now being activated, and this gave me a chance to think about everything else outside the barracks. It was night, so there were very few people on the streets. This also meant that any extra police we needed could reach the scene quickly.

Another important factor was that there were no buildings on the other side of the road. Ranelagh Gardens is a large area of open land where the Chelsea Flower Show is held every year, and at night it was in total darkness. The only place that caused me some concern was a block of flats just south of the barracks, not far from Chelsea Bridge. I took up position in Ebury Bridge Road, close to the flats. We had to assume that the box was a bomb, and the blast from an explosion would certainly hit those buildings. One of the sergeants from Gerald Road arrived, and I asked him to evacuate the people who lived in the flats. He went straight over to the buildings, taking four or five PCs with him.

I was pleased to think that we had sealed off the immediate area so quickly. Maybe things had gone too smoothly, I then thought. Something told me not to be too complacent. What if the army was not the intended target? Should we be thinking about a second device? This made me think about the Tite Street bombing some years before. Tite Street was only a short distance away from where we were standing, and in that attack, there had been a second bomb timed to go off a few minutes after the first one.

Bombs kill in random fashion. The police officers and others who were injured at Tite Street had been very lucky to survive without serious injuries. Tragically, the three Chelsea officers and three civilians killed in the Harrods bombing had not had luck on their side that day. All of this started going through my mind. If I were a terrorist, where would I put a secondary device? My first thoughts suggested a car bomb close to the place where the suspected device had been left. Then, of course, there was Ranelagh Gardens on the other side of the road – now starting to look dark and sinister.

While I was thinking about this, the explosives officer arrived. He was based in central London, and it had only taken him five or six minutes to reach the scene. We stood in the street together, and I briefed him. While we talked, he was looking all around him at the surrounding area. Then he mentioned that he was thinking about a second device, and he asked me if I had thought about it. 'Yes,' I told him, but I pointed out that we were still doing all the basic stuff at the scene.

However, by that time the situation was improving as more officers arrived. The explosives officer pointed at the parkland on the other side of the road and told me that this would be an ideal place to put a secondary device. Naturally, I did not want him to think that this was something that I had not considered. I had planned to carry out a search as soon as we had enough people to do it.

The explosives officer picked up a bag of equipment, and we walked along the street together. We reached the spot where the suspected bomb was, and I pointed it out to him. He nodded and then suggested that I move back down the street to the spot where we had met a couple of minutes before.

'There is no point in both of us getting killed, is there?' he said quietly.

I walked back towards the road junction just south of the barracks to a spot where I felt reasonably safe but where it was possible to see the explosives officer. I called one of my sergeants and asked him to find some PCs to search Ranelagh Gardens. Then I looked back down the street at the explosives officer. He was kneeling down in front of whatever the object might turn out to be.

He was not there for long. It might have been two or three minutes or longer. Then he walked back to where I was standing. He told me that it was an IRA bomb and he was going to defuse it. He turned and walked back to the bomb. It seemed strange to me that he could remain so cool headed and professional going into this type of situation.

At this time, we had reached a stage when IRA bombs had become more sophisticated than they had ever been before. We knew that they were often fitted with as many as two or more anti-handling devices. If you lifted them, they might detonate. If you touched certain parts of bombs, they might go off. Some had been designed to be sensitive to light, and therefore it was not a good idea to shine a torch on them. It might be the last thing you did on earth. I had seen explosives officers at work before, and their calmness always amazed me.

Since the IRA terrorist campaign had started, two explosives officers working for the Met had been killed. We had lost Roger Goad in 1975 and Kenneth Howorth in 1981. Both had been killed trying to defuse terrorist bombs. It was rumoured that at least one explosives officer had been retired on medical grounds after suffering a serious mental breakdown. We all hear people talking about being stressed, but my opinion is that stress, like everything else, comes in different levels.

It is a strange experience watching someone carrying out a task whereby they can be blown to pieces at any moment. It seemed that time had slowed down, and the seconds were ticking by that bit slower than usual.

Meanwhile, the evacuation of the flats was going on. Most of the residents were elderly, and it appeared to be quite a slow business. But the officers there were gradually moving them into a yard at the rear of the flats, where they would be safe. I could also see torches shining in the darkness of Ranelagh Gardens, where the search for a second device was being carried out.

Then I saw the explosives officer walking back towards me. He told me that he had defused the bomb, and we stood on the pavement discussing it. We needed to wait until the search for any second device was finished. We stood there for a few more minutes, until the sergeant who had been in charge of the search reported that nothing suspicious had been found.

My last job at the Barracks was to call Rochester Row and update them on the situation. What we had now was a crime scene, and a message was sent to the Anti-Terrorist Branch, who would have the job of investigating it. Two officers were given the job of guarding the scene pending the arrival of the investigation team, and the residents of the flats were returned to their beds. After that, I drove back to Rochester Row – known as Roch by all the officers who worked there.

A serious incident like this always made me take stock afterwards and made me think about what I had done over the past two decades. On the streets, an operational police officer needs to be confident. Dealing with people and a wide range of incidents had given me knowledge and confidence. All the same, it seemed strange that I would now be regarded as a veteran. It was 1986 and later that year the commissioner would be presenting me with my Police Long Service and Good Conduct Medal.

In 1964 I had been a new probationer. My thoughts sometimes went back to my first few months in the job, when my uniform was brand new and my enthusiasm usually ran a couple of miles ahead of my experience.

2

Sandgate, 1964

'Borrowdale, Eastbourne, sir.'
        'Smith, Kent, sir.'
    'Ramsay, Hampshire and Isle of Wight, sir.'

A ripple of sound rolled along the three lines of uniformed men. One by one, each officer called out his name and the name of his police force. There were gaps in the pine trees ahead of us, showing tantalising views of the English Channel with the surface of the water shimmering in the sunshine. As I stood there that morning, my eyes took it all in, and it seemed that everything was going well.

Then I had the feeling that there was something wrong, and my head moved a fraction to my right. Will Squires, the drill sergeant, was coming in my direction, his swagger stick jammed hard under his arm, as usual. 'It does not mean that he is going to say anything to me,' I thought hopefully, but the fact that he stopped in front of me, with an angry look on his face, seemed to suggest otherwise.

Will Squires waited until the roll call ended, and then he touched my right leg with his swagger stick. The stick moved downwards until it reached the bottom of my right trouser leg, after which it lifted my trousers by 4 or 5 centimetres. Then he exploded.

'Ramsay, Hampshire and Isle of Wight! What do you think you are? Red socks! You are wearing red socks. I have never seen anything like it. You Hampshire hog. Red socks! I have seen everything now. Thank God that we've got a navy. You really are a count.'

I stood rooted to the ground, standing to attention, not saying anything but hoping that a large hole might appear next to me so that I could conveniently drop into it and disappear from sight. Will Squires went on to say a few more words. He gave everybody his views about Hampshire policemen generally and me in particular. Then he just looked at me for a moment, shuddered, and walked away.

There was a simple reason for what had happened, and that was that I had run out of blue socks. I never ran out of them after that. It was the same dealing with criminals, in a manner of speaking. You learned from your mistakes, and if someone made a fool of you, it was important to make sure that it did not happen a second time.

As time went on, it became clear that Will Squires was a bit of an actor. He liked being a drill sergeant and could appear to be a martinet, but there was no real malice in the man. He enjoyed catching out recruits, and he would explode from time to time, but there was always an undertone of humour. He was from the Kent Police, and for some reason or other, policemen from Hampshire tended to be the butt of his jokes. Will had some choice comments, such as, 'What are you doing, you Hampshire hog?'

Every morning on the parade ground there was an inspection of the blue-uniformed ranks standing there, the police recruits of Course 200 at the No. 6 District Police Training Centre. The district covered most of the police forces in South East England, and its training school was at Sandgate in Kent, a couple of miles from Folkestone.

The main building was large and impressive, having been built by a wealthy aristocrat who wanted to live close to the sea. Many years later, after the First World War, it became a Star and Garter Home for wounded soldiers. The classrooms were less impressive, prefabricated huts tucked away at the sides of the main building.

There were lessons on self-defence and some military-style drill at Sandgate, but the recruits spent most of their time in class doing their best to get to grips with English criminal law and police procedure. The course was divided into five or six classes, and each morning we made our way to our classrooms. We had each been given a book to use for our studies, called *Moriarty's Police Law*. Moriarty had been a senior officer in the Royal Irish Constabulary, many years before, who thought that a standard textbook was needed to give police recruits a good basic knowledge of the law.

The instructor for Class B2 was Sergeant Cole, a very experienced officer from the West Sussex Police. Sergeant Cole gave each of us a book that came from the Home Office, entitled *Student Lesson Notes*; it covered most of the subject matter on the course.

If there was one word that seemed to dominate our lives at Sandgate, it was 'definition'. Soldiers are trained to look after their rifles, learning to take them apart and put them together in the dark. It seemed that learning definitions was the police equivalent of what soldiers did with their rifles. A great deal of our study consisted of learning definitions of criminal offences. Sometimes the instructors would put us on the spot in the classroom to test our knowledge.

'Ramsay. Give me the definition of larceny.'

'Spencer. Give me the definition of indecent exposure.'

'Lyons. Hearsay evidence! When can it be given in evidence? There are four exceptions to the general rule. What are they?'

There is a legal definition for every offence, and policemen on the streets need to be able to identify them quickly. What was the crime? Could it be false pretences, theft, burglary, robbery?

We had to learn all of those definitions by heart, and equally important was to know whether the offence had a power of arrest attached to it.

Some of them were what our instructors described as our 'bread-and-butter offences', those that we were going to come up against time and time again. We would be dealing with thefts and burglaries regularly, for example, not to mention assaults and drunkenness. It was important to know that there was no power of arrest for those people who were simply drunk, but only when aggravated by other factors, such as when they became disorderly or were unfit to look after themselves.

Anyone who visited Sandgate in the 1960s would have seen men in uniform walking up and down and mumbling to themselves as they did their best to commit definitions to memory. We each owned a small book of definitions, published by an insurance company that specialised in providing cover for police officers, and this proved to be very useful.

English law comes from two sources: common law and statute law. At that time, common law was divided into two categories of offences, felonies and misdemeanours whereas statute law consisted of three types, felonies, misdemeanours and summary offences. Common law felonies included many serious crimes, such as murder and kidnapping. An important piece of legislation under statute law was the Larceny Act 1916 that defined theft, burglary, and most other offences against property. As part of our training, the instructors narrated situations and stories to us that included various offences, all aimed at making us adept at identifying them quickly.

It was always important for us to know which crimes were felonies, because there was a straightforward, wide power of arrest for all felonies. Interestingly, members of the public had virtually the same powers to arrest felons as the police did, and this was due to the relatively short history of policing in the UK. The Metropolitan Police was founded in 1829, and before that there was very little that could be described as an organised policing structure. For several years after 1829 there was virtually no police system outside London and its suburbs.

When it came to misdemeanours, the situation was more confusing for us. In many cases, there was no power of arrest, and when there was one, it was often conditional on other factors, such as when the offence was witnessed by a police officer. Generally speaking, misdemeanours were less serious than felonies, but they included offences such as indecent assault, false pretences (now criminal deception) and incest.

It struck me fairly quickly that much of the law did not appear to be based on logical ideas, and it certainly appeared as though it needed to be brought up to date. I thought about powers of arrest, for example. Why was there a power of arrest for the offence of indecent assault on a man but not for indecent assault on a woman?

We were told about the offence of assaulting a constable in the execution of his/her duty and then warned of the problem areas that came along with it. This should have been a fairly straightforward matter, but not everything in law is the way it might appear to be. Parliament had enacted legislation to give police officers extra protection from assaults. It is an example of how laws can sometimes end up doing the opposite of what was intended. As they say, the devil is in the detail.

The problems arise from six words in the definition: 'in the execution of his duty'. Defence lawyers can have a field day when they cut their way into those six words. In simple terms, English courts take the view that there are circumstances where it is lawful for a person to assault a police officer in order to gain their liberty.

A police officer is not deemed as being in the execution of his/her duty in a number of situations that are fairly common. This includes an officer making an arrest that is technically unlawful (this would have included an indecent assault on a woman, at that time) or removing a trespasser from private property without a court order.

We recruits also needed to have a good knowledge of liquor licensing and the various laws that applied to public houses. The law stated that a licensee had the right to refuse to serve anyone that he/she did not wish to serve. 'What happens if the customer is a black man, and the licensee does not wish to serve black people?' asked one of my fellow probationers.

It was a good question and represented an obvious problem for the police, because the Licensing Act gave publicans an unconditional right to refuse anyone that they did not wish to serve. Sergeant Cole explained that under the Licensing Act police would have a duty to help the licensee to eject any customer, black or white, from the premises if the licensee objected to his presence.

This was a time in the UK when there was a considerable amount of discrimination against black people. In Bristol, the local bus company would not employ any non-white person as a driver or conductor. Many licensees took the view that if one or more black men came into a pub and asked to be served that they were there in order to cause trouble. This was not a hypothetical situation; it was something that occurred quite often during the early sixties.

Class B2 was made up of twenty-three police recruits from Hampshire, Reading, Kent, and Jersey. On our first day, Sergeant Cole told us that he wanted us to elect a class captain, and one of our classmates nominated Gordon Trench, who was in the Reading Borough Police.

Trench had some important qualifications for the job of class captain. One of them was the fact that, as far as I was aware, he was the only one of us who had any police experience. He was a few years older than most of us, had worked as a PC in the British Transport Police, and was an amateur boxing champion.

Trench was a tough, confident-looking man, and he was quickly voted in as class captain. When we talked about his previous work as a railway policeman, he spoke in a matter-of-fact way about dealing with thieves, robbers, rapists, and flashers. Most of the older men in the class had served in the armed forces. Compared with many of them, I started to realise, my life had been quite sheltered.

In terms of age, background, education, and experience, we were a very diverse group of men. There were seven Hampshire policemen in the class, and we were all in our early twenties, except for two of our number who were ex-cadets and had joined the regular police as soon as they were nineteen.

Young people could serve as police cadets from the age of sixteen until they were nineteen. Being a police cadet provided an interesting introduction to the police service, and to a certain extent it was like a sixth-form college. Cadets were encouraged to improve their education by taking O levels and A levels. They were often assigned to work schemes or social projects, in this country and abroad, to widen their general life experience.

As a 19-year-old ex-cadet, Peter Spencer would have been one of the youngest officers on the course. At the other end of the range of ages was the Hampshire officer who had been a chief petty officer in the Royal Navy. He was in a different classroom to us, so we did not see much of him, but as he was so old – 31 – we all treated him with the sort of respect you would normally reserve for older people in your family circle.

There were two policemen from the Reading Borough Police in the class: Gordon Trench and a younger man called Brian Kenton. I would describe Kenton as a very intelligent man and probably very ambitious. He always put a great deal of work into his studies and achieved high marks in all the written tests. Kenton's career in the police service was destined to be a short one.

The five policemen from the Jersey States Police stood out as being that bit different from the others. Their arrival at Sandgate had made history in its own way, because it was the first time that officers from Jersey had been sent to the mainland for their initial training. The Jerseymen told us that, technically, the States Police only had jurisdiction in the Parish of St

Helier and not in the rest of the island. It seemed strange to me that they were sent to Sandgate, as Jersey has its own criminal code, much of it based on the French legal system.

After spending thirteen weeks struggling with definitions and powers of arrest, these Jersey officers would return to St Helier, where they would be told to forget most of what they had been taught. However, in some ways, this problem applied to everyone else on the course. The fact that there is no national police force in the UK means that each one has its own system of crime reports, accident report books, and everything else.

Policies relating to enforcement and administration varied in some degree from force to force. After leaving Sandgate, all the Hampshire officers were due to complete the Local Procedure Course at Winchester in order to cover these issues. An example of this in Hampshire would be the offence of indecent exposure, which was recorded in the Occurrence Book (OB) at police stations and not as a crime. In a similar way, those assaults classified as common assaults were not treated as crimes but also recorded in the OB. In hindsight, it now seems obvious that victims of domestic assaults were not receiving a great deal of help from the police.

1964 saw the introduction of important new procedures that were to be followed by all police officers in England and Wales; this was the updated Judges' Rules. An important English legal principle is that people who are suspected of having committed a criminal offence have the right to remain silent. This is the case when they are questioned by law-enforcement officers or by prosecutors at court. The Rules covered aspects relating to the questioning of suspects and provided advice to police, so that statements made by suspects would be admissible as evidence.

It was necessary for police to use a form of caution when they had evidence that someone had committed a criminal offence. It was always something that caused problems for probationers like me, because the defining word was 'evidence', as distinct from 'suspicion'. The words used for the caution were these: 'You are not obliged to say anything unless you wish to do so, but what you say may be put in writing and given in evidence.'

Where there was sufficient evidence to carry out the formal charging procedure at a police station, the wording of the charge had to be followed by another caution, and the actual words spoken at that time by the suspect had to be recorded. We were given training on how to take a written statement from a witness and how to record those made by suspects. It would take me some time before I started to feel confident understanding all of the technical bits and pieces that came with the Judges' Rules.

The instructors often mentioned that when we eventually arrived at our police stations we would spend quite a lot of time investigating reported crime. Later, it seemed strange to us that we were given virtually no training on how to go about it.

We were all left amused or bemused when we were shown a film aimed at making us think about what clues we should look for at the scene of a crime. The film was a silent one that had been made in about 1928 by the West Riding Police. We saw a villainous-looking burglar break into a large country house. Within a couple of minutes, he was confronted by the butler, so he picked up a poker, hit the butler over the head with it, and killed him. After this, he ran away across open country, clutching a bag of stolen silverware.

At first, we were not sure whether Sergeant Cole was having some kind of joke at our expense. It turned out that this was the official film used by the training school for this element of training, and we wondered how long it had been in the storeroom. It was like being taken back in time – the film might have been useful as a kind of historical document.

When the characters opened their mouths, we could hear nothing and could only guess what was being said. The people moved about in that strange, stilted manner that was typical of the early days of cinema. The uniforms worn by the police in West Riding might as well have been something from France in the eighteenth century. None of us had ever seen policemen dressed like that.

There were a few suppressed giggles and groans from my classmates as they tried to make some sense of it. After the film ended, everyone was busy cracking jokes about how lucky we were to have all this modern equipment for our training needs.

Sergeant Cole showed us some typical crime reports and then told us how they were to be completed. They had to be typed in triplicate, and therefore you needed a typewriter and two sheets of carbon paper – which left me wondering how many of us were good at typing. I knew that I was not one of them. The sergeant explained that this was a sample of the new national crime report and that every force in England and Wales would be using it within the next couple of years.

After leaving Sandgate, we never came across crime reports that looked remotely like the ones that we had been shown that day. Hampshire had just introduced a new system that had five categories of crime report, depending on what the offence was. They were multi-form documents, designed to be handwritten and easy to complete.

The senior police officer at the Sandgate Training School had the title of commandant and held the rank of a chief superintendent in the St Helens force in Lancashire. We were still in the era of city and borough police forces, and many of them, such as St Helens, were very small.

Later that year, there was a change of government, and when Roy Jenkins became home secretary, the writing was on the wall for many forces. Jenkins's view was that having a large number of small forces was not efficient, and within a few years there would be a major reorganisation of the national policing structure. Small forces, such as Tynemouth and Eastbourne, would cease to exist, taken over by their larger neighbours, and a number of chief constables would be left high and dry.

Overall, there was a fairly relaxed regime at Sandgate. However, there was a certain amount of military-style discipline at the training school, and we were all subject to a curfew that came into effect at 9.30 p.m. Naturally, there were a few recruits who saw this as a challenge rather than a restriction.

The notorious 'broken-window incident' occurred as a direct result of the curfew. One night, four recruits returned to the training school after the curfew. After some banging and tapping on windows, they were able to convey their situation to their comrades inside, and eventually a window was opened. All four climbed through, one at a time. The last of the four curfew-breakers to enter was Peter Spencer. Peter decided that he should close the window after him. He pushed down the bottom part of the window frame. It seemed that much of the wood was wafer thin, and the glass in the bottom pane broke, cutting one of his fingers.

Peter stood for a few moments with the thought that his police career was probably as broken as the bits of glass on the floor in front of him.

Childhood memories came flooding back. He recalled using his catapult and somehow managing to break the window of a boathouse on the River Hamble. He had been caught by someone who'd come rushing out of the boathouse, and he'd faced the wrath of the village constable who'd confiscated his catapult – the incident was made that bit worse because the policeman was his own father! In fairness, Peter always maintained that both incidents were accidents and stressed that it was important that we should all believe him.

After that, all four curfew-breakers fled to their respective dormitories. Peter Spencer hopped into his bed fully clothed, pulled up the blankets, and did his best to pretend that he was asleep. We all knew that one of the senior officers at Sandgate carried out a patrol of the buildings every night. This included visiting all the dormitories. Peter has always suspected that one of his co-conspirators decided to turn 'grass' at this point.

One of the senior police officers at Sandgate was a grim-faced chief inspector from the north of England who was doing his tour of inspection that night. The chief inspector entered the dorm that Peter was in and switched on the light. Then he walked over to Peter's bed and stood there looking at him.

'Have you got something to tell me, Spencer?' he asked.

Peter has never really managed to forget these words, because Mike Lyons was in the next bed, and he heard them. For the next fifty years or so, Mike, also known as Mick, took great delight in greeting Peter with those words whenever he saw him. There was some controversy as to what was actually said that night in the dormitory. Mick's memory was that Peter did his best to try and talk his way out of it.

However, Peter Spencer maintains that he made a quick decision to confess his part in the window-breaking incident and was told to report to the commandant's office the following morning. Peter and the other three recruits stood for some time in the corridor, waiting to see the commandant. The chief inspector made a brief appearance and told Peter that what he had done was very serious. He concluded by telling Peter that this would be the end of his career in the police.

The four of them were left to stand outside the Commandant's office for some time, sweating profusely. However, Peter was destined to live to fight another day. The Commandant looked suitably grim faced when he spoke to them, but at some point he actually smiled. They were ordered to pay to have the window repaired. Split four ways, it was not going to be too expensive. Peter paid his fair share: one pound, three shillings, and sixpence. Since then, Peter Spencer has never been known to breach a curfew.

At the training school, the Hampshire men tended to socialise together, as did the probationers from the other forces. Mick Lyons and I would sometimes take a walk around the centre of Folkestone. In those days, Folkestone was a ferry port, like Dover, and quite busy during the day, but it did not take us long to realise that its night life was nothing to become too excited about.

When it came to questions in the classroom, most of us had problems remembering some of the definitions. When tested in class, Mick made a couple of mistakes and was ordered by Sergeant Cole to report to his flat at 5 a.m. Mick had to present a cup of tea to him and repeat the two definitions that he had struggled with in the classroom. This idea did not work, because Mick got one of them wrong – not surprisingly at that time in the morning.

It seemed strange at first to be sharing a dormitory with seven or eight other men. Gerry Marsh, another of the Hampshire officers, was in the bed next to me. He was a big man with a build that made me wonder whether he had been a professional wrestler in a previous life. The problem was that he liked to wrestle, and from time to time he would throw out a challenge to me to take part in a no-rules bout.

At the tender age of twenty-two, I was a tall and slender youth who would probably be described as puny compared with many of my fellow recruits. In terms of bulk, there was very little of me when compared to Gerry, but it would probably have been seen as a bit cowardly not to accept a challenge from time to time.

There are always useful lessons to learn as you progress through life. One good rule is not to wrestle with men who are a lot bigger than you are unless you have some experience and skill and know what you are doing. Another thing you learn is that breathing becomes painful when you have bruised ribs.

Some months after leaving Sandgate, my reporting sergeant in Hampshire showed me what had been written about me at the training school. It made me sound like some sort of muscular, action man who had missed his real calling, like the Army, probably serving with Special Forces. It made me wonder whether they had confused me with someone else or whether Sergeant Cole was just a man with a twisted sense of humour.

I had always been a strong swimmer, and was part of a group to be told that we would be trained as life-savers. If we passed the course and did not manage to drown anybody, we would be awarded bronze life-saving medals. We were taken by bus each week to a Royal Marines base near Dover where there was a large swimming pool. Diving into the pool delivered a nasty shock to the system, as the water was very cold!

On the first day of our training, we splashed around for ten minutes or so while we waited for the instructor to arrive, and this helped to keep us from feeling too cold. One of my fellow life-savers shouted out that this was part of the training and that if we did not die in the first fifteen minutes of being in the water, we were in line for another medal. Coping with the cold water could have been part of the training. If we were called upon to rescue someone from the sea, a river, or a lake it was unlikely that the water would be a pleasant, warm temperature for us.

In the comfort of our classroom, Sergeant Cole told us that our first duty as policemen would always be the protection of life. He used the example of one of us chasing a burglar along the seafront at Folkestone and then seeing that there was a person drowning in the sea.

'Forget the burglar. Your duty is to rescue the person in the sea,' he told us.

The police service was not happy with the idea that in the future one of us might be watching someone drown and explaining to members of the public that we could not do anything to help because we could not swim. Those recruits at Sandgate who could not swim or were weak swimmers were given swimming lessons.

Splashing around in the cold water, I was reminded of the famous British Army saying: 'Never volunteer for anything.' Our life-saving group would be trained to carry out four different life-saving techniques. Each of us was teamed up with a classmate, and we took it in turns to play the part of the rescuer and the drowning man. The instructor would call out the number of the rescue technique, and then the life-saver would swim towards the drowning man and carry it out.

Procedure Number Four involved shouting out the words 'Don't panic, I'm a life-saver' as you swam towards the drowning citizen. During the thirteen weeks that we were at Sandgate, these words proved to be a source of great hilarity. Soon we were shouting it out in many situations that had nothing to do with saving drowning people. Eventually, all of us in the life-saving group passed the course and were awarded our bronze medals.

There were written tests on our knowledge of police duties and the law. Several of my fellow recruits were exceptionally diligent and had learned many definitions by heart. I did a lot of reading but was never particularly good at learning definitions. Brian Kenton and Peter Spencer always did well in the written tests, and when it came to results, they were usually at the top of the class.

I felt that I knew most of the important legal points and that much operational police work would revolve around logic or common sense. This was a little arrogant on my part, but as a general rule it proved to be true. In terms of the marks I received in my written tests, my position was usually about halfway down the list, probably between the two groups of recruits. There were those who studied very hard or had good memories, and there were those who found studying quite difficult. In hindsight, I probably should have pushed myself a bit harder.

When I chatted to Gordon Trench about everything that we had to study, he was quick to reassure me about the outside world. 'There's no need to worry about all this stuff. You need to know the basics, but when you get to your station, what counts most is common sense. That's the real world. It's not the same as here.'

Towards the end of the course, the Hampshire officers were told what divisions that we were going to. Three of us – Mick Lyons, Gerry Marsh and I – were to be posted to the Winchester division. Mick came from the Isle of Wight, but he seemed pleased to be going there. I knew Winchester and liked the idea of living there. However, the division was divided into three subdivisions: Winchester City, Winchester Rural, and Andover. It turned out that I had made a wrong assumption. My posting was to Andover, while my two classmates would be in Winchester City. The Winchester Rural subdivision did not take probationers.

There were the usual discussions about the merits of the different places we were going to. Peter Spencer was posted to the Fareham Division and was obviously pleased about it. The Fareham Division was on the coast, taking in Fareham and Gosport, and was considered to be the busiest one in Hampshire.

All of us would have to successfully complete a period of probation lasting two years. We were told that we would be expected to study regularly and go to training classes one day each month. This also included a monthly written test on law and police procedure.

We would all have a reporting sergeant. This sergeant would ensure that each one of us was given the opportunity to carry out a variety of tasks and would keep a watchful eye on our progress. Under Police Regulations, we could be dismissed during these first two years if our supervisors reported that we did not have the right qualities to become efficient police officers.

When we left the training school, we were all given leave for one week. My first job was to find accommodation in Andover. It was a pleasant feeling to go out into what Trench called 'the real world'. I filled two large grip bags with my uniform and equipment and headed for Andover.

3

In 1964, the north of Hampshire was mainly rural. However, this would soon start to change, because two towns, Andover and Basingstoke, had been chosen by the Government for major development as 'London Overspill'. During the early sixties, both were fairly small market towns, but new housing estates were being built, and large numbers of Londoners were moving into them.

The old, wide High Street in Andover, with its historic coaching inns, had remained the same for many years. Although the High Street would not change much, the rest of the town was destined to expand and change at a rapid rate, far beyond the imagination of its residents.

Andover police station was a modern-looking building a short distance from the High Street. On my arrival, I introduced myself to the PC at the front counter. He waved me inside and passed me on to one of his colleagues. The man gave me a ten-minute tour of the station and then took me to the sergeants' office. One of the sergeants gave me some information about Andover and the type of work that might come my way. After that, he showed me my uniform locker and handed me a key for it.

The sergeant gave me the names and addresses of two women who were both landladies, approved by the police, who provided lodgings for officers who were single. The first one was a Mrs Morgan, living in Vigo Road, Andover.

In the parade room there was a large map of the town, which showed me that this address was not far from the station. A walk of ten minutes or so brought me to Vigo Road, where I introduced myself to the Morgans.

They seemed to be a friendly couple, and three days later I moved into a room in their house.

The Hampshire contingent from Sandgate all met again the following week at police headquarters in Winchester, the county town of Hampshire. We met Sergeant Fielder, who was in charge of probationer training, and he explained how the training system worked. After that, he took us through the basic reporting systems, such as using our notebooks and making entries in accident report books, process books, and crime reports.

He also told us that we needed to have a good knowledge of the police as an organisation and understand how it operated. During our first twelve months, each one of us would be posted to a country beat so that we understood the work carried out by officers who worked on their own in rural areas. We would also have attachments to the two main specialist departments within the police service, the CID and Traffic Division.

We had all been to an ancient-looking building in West Hill to collect our uniforms and equipment. This was the old headquarters that stood next to Winchester Prison, and its history went back a hundred years or so. By the sixties, this Victorian red-brick edifice seemed to be mainly used for storage, and a new building in North Walls, another part of Winchester, was being used as the county police headquarters.

A short distance from the prison in West Hill, a plot of land had been bought as the site for a new headquarters. When the construction work was finished, everyone would move from North Walls into the new HQ in West Hill, and North Walls would become the police station for Winchester. At that time, the operational station was inside the Winchester Guildhall, situated in Broadway, a few steps from the famous statue of King Alfred.

At headquarters, our first visit was to Information Room. This is the central communications hub for any British police force, where emergency calls come in from people using the 999 service. In all urgent cases, radio calls go out to mobile units, but the backbone of the system was a network of teleprinter machines that linked headquarters with all divisional and subdivisional stations. As well as dealing with 999 calls, the Information Room, or IR, was used as a command and control centre for any major incident, such as a large public-order event or a serious transport accident.

Every vehicle reported stolen was recorded on a card, and all the cards were filed in numerical order inside steel drums. The procedure had been designed to be quick and efficient, and we saw officers working at IR who would reach out for the drums and spin them around at speed until they located the card that they wanted.

An experienced officer could complete a stolen vehicle check in two or three minutes. However, finding names and addresses of registered owners was a long, slow process. It was before the computer age and before the Driver Vehicle and Licensing Agency (DVLA) was set up. There was no centralised database, and police would have to telephone the individual city or county where the vehicle was registered.

Sergeant Fielder gave us a list of dates for probationer training. We would have to go to the training unit one day each month and were expected to achieve marks of at least 60 per cent in the written tests. There was, added the sergeant, the danger that an officer who failed to achieve good results each month would be required to resign.

After all of this, Sergeant Fielder gave us details of the chief constable's official car. 'Remember the number of the Chief's car: XNT 789.' We all wrote the number in our notebooks.

We were introduced to someone from the Police Federation, and we all signed up for membership. Although not a trade union, the Federation was our staff association. It negotiated with the Government on police pay and provided legal support if we were to face criminal or discipline charges relating to our work. The monthly deduction from my pay would be one shilling, the equivalent of five pence in decimal currency.

We all visited SOUCRO (the Southern Criminal Records Office), which kept the records of all people who are convicted of criminal offences in Hampshire, Dorset, and the Channel Islands. The identification of criminals is based on fingerprints, which are always taken when someone is charged with a 'recordable' offence. In plain language, 'recordable' relates to those matters that are regarded as crimes and excludes minor matters such as traffic offences and drunkenness.

We also had a visit to the Crime Intelligence Unit, probably the most interesting part of the course. The unit had a nominal index of all professional or active criminals in Hampshire and the rest of the

SOUCRO area. In the days before computers were an everyday tool, all of this information was on card systems.

We met officers who had specialist roles, such as Special Branch, Traffic Patrol, dog handling, and working in Information Room. They all gave us some basic information about the work that they did.

At the end of the course, we all sat down to hear an address by the deputy chief constable. Some high-ranking police officers are very good public speakers, but the deputy chief was not one of them. He spoke about police work in general terms and the high standards that he expected from us. What he said was probably very good, but it was lengthy, and there was no drama, humour, or anything else that might have brought it to life. It was quite a warm day, and the room felt airless.

After a while, my head started to droop and my eyes closed. In order to stop myself from falling asleep, I jabbed the fingernails of my right hand into the knuckles of my left hand. This seemed to be working well for about five minutes or so, but then I became aware that my eyes were starting to close again. Some more fingernail torture was necessary to keep me looking at least half interested in what was being said.

However, it seems that all of this was in vain. My head dropped forward bit by bit, and my body started to tilt over towards the man sitting next to me. At some point, my head found itself a comfortable position on my colleague's shoulder, and shortly after this, the deputy chief constable's speech was interrupted by a couple of loud snores. It did not take me long to guess that something was wrong. My return from the Land of Nod was assisted by my colleague shaking me and my awareness that the deputy chief's voice had suddenly risen by a few decibels. It seemed that whatever he was saying had something to do with me.

'Am I boring you? I thought that you might have the good manners to stay awake while I was talking.' The deputy chief was looking directly at me, and he did not seem very happy. I mumbled some sort of apology, and he carried on. It suddenly became very important for me to stay awake until he had finished. Afterwards, one of my colleagues pointed out that the deputy chief constable was the person who had overall responsibility for all disciplinary matters in the force.

'You'd better not get yourself in any trouble,' he said, laughing. 'He's bound to remember you now.'

Each one of us was looking forward to our first day 'doing the job'. In Hampshire, the policy was that we would all work with experienced officers for twelve weeks. Often known as a tutor constable, mentor, or buddy, he would do everything during the first six weeks and the probationer's job was to watch and learn. Following that, there would be a second period of six weeks during which the rookie would do everything, but his buddy would be there to give advice and guidance.

My first day of duty was listed for a Sunday, starting at 8 a.m. On Saturday evening I went for a walk around the centre of the town. One of the Andover policemen recognised me and stopped to chat for a few minutes. He told me that a PC McLaughlin had been chosen to be my buddy. He said that 'Mac' was an experienced officer who was highly respected by everyone at the station, but he added that he was on holiday for a few days. I strolled back to my lodgings at Vigo Road and was watching television when there was a knock at the front door. One of the Andover officers was standing there with a message for me to report to the station at six the following morning.

'We are sending people down to Hayling Island,' he explained. 'There's been some trouble there.'

This did not mean much to me, and I wondered what it was all about. At Sandgate, we had all talked about the hours that we would have to work as policemen, and everyone had agreed that we would need a flexible attitude to cope with it. Looking back, this seemed to have been an understatement. My hours had been changed before I had even arrived at the station for my first day of duty.

Early next morning, I cycled through an almost-deserted town centre on my way to the station. By quarter to six, I had changed into my uniform. While brushing it, I glanced at my shoulder number – HC 868 – this was now my identity as far as the world was concerned. 'So, this is it,' I thought. This is the real world. Then I made my way to the parade room and sat down. It seemed strange that there was nobody else there. After a few minutes, a PC walked in and told me that everyone was upstairs, in the canteen. It was more of a kitchenette rather than a canteen. There were three or four tables, and it felt crowded with eight or nine men gathered there. The place was noisy with conversation and full of smoke from pipes and cigarettes. Someone handed me a cup of tea, and I sat down and listened to the general chatter and banter around me.

At the training school there had been some talk about our status as probationers at police stations. Trench had said that the best thing for a 'probie' – or rookie – was to do a lot of listening and say as little as possible. We were told that there were some stations where the 'old sweats' would not even speak to us. It might be a serious breach of station etiquette for me to sit down at a table used by older men in the canteen without a specific invitation. There was a chair that seemed to be on its own and not too close to any of the tables, and this seemed like a good place for me to sit.

Whatever else happened, new probationers tended to be the butt of jokes, and the canteen was a good place for it to happen. Everyone seemed to ignore me except Paul Boswell, a PC who appeared to be a few years older than me. He said a few words and handed me a battered-looking piece of paper that had come from the teleprinter room. It helped to explain why I was sitting in the station canteen at six o'clock that Sunday morning.

My arrival at Andover had coincided with a weekend when the simmering tensions between two groups of young people had finally exploded into violence across the south coast of England. In the early sixties, two youth cults had emerged, and tens of thousands of teenagers had joined the ranks of either the Mods or the Rockers. From time to time they would fight each other, but now this rivalry seemed to have developed into a full-scale war.

Traditionally, at this time of year Londoners headed for the seaside resorts of the south coast, and the May Day bank holiday of 1964 was following the same pattern. At first, there was nothing that would indicate a serious public-order situation when thousands of Mods arrived in the south coast resorts such as Margate, Bournemouth, and Brighton. However, the police soon realised that they could be faced with a major problem when information started to come in suggesting that thousands of Rockers had made the same holiday plans.

As soon as the two groups came into contact, fighting started, and large-scale battles were taking place all over the south coast. Brighton was the scene of the most serious of these disturbances; well over a thousand young people were involved in pitched battles on the beach and in the town. Reinforcements were flown in on chartered aircraft from other forces.

There was some trouble on the Hampshire coast, although there had been no large-scale incidents. However, there had been a number of clashes on Hayling Island, where Mods and Rockers had set up campsites close to the beach. A large number of police had been sent to the island, and orders went out to all divisions to supply personnel to take over from them on the Sunday morning.

Between the end of World War II and 1962, when the British press started taking an interest in Mods and Rockers, Britain had been through a period of great change. The Empire had come to an end, National Service in the armed forces had been abolished, and the economy had started to boom. It was the beginning of what would be called the 'consumer society' and a time when young people found that they could earn enough to purchase many of the goods that were now available in the shops.

Credit was becoming more and more available, giving everyone increased spending power at a much faster rate than ever before in the UK. In 1964, a twenty-pound down payment meant that a teenager could drive away on his or her own brand-new motor scooter.

The 'Mods' were very fashion conscious. Their wardrobes would always include turned-up Levis, often shrunk to size by being worn in the bath, plus Fred Perry shirts and desert boots. If Mods took drugs, it would be limited to amphetamines, and they were usually fans of ska music and The Who. For special occasions, they wore designer suits covered by parka jackets. They rode around on motor scooters that were lovingly adorned with large wing mirrors, numerous headlights, crash bars, whip aerials, whitewall tyres, and high-backed seats.

Rockers rode motorbikes, often at high speed and without crash helmets. They wore leather gear and listened to the songs of Gene Vincent and Elvis Presley. The two groups tended to come from different social backgrounds. Mods were usually city dwellers, many with well-paid jobs, while many Rockers came from rural areas, often earning a living as manual workers. The Mods would probably describe Rockers as greasy and uncouth, while Rockers would see the Mods as effeminate and full of themselves.

There were four or five police cars parked in the yard at the rear of the station. The Hillman Husky was the standard patrolling vehicle used by Hampshire Police at that time. The cars were nearly all metallic grey in colour and referred to as section cars. The design of the Husky was practical because it was half car and half van. If officers were dealing with a traffic accident, they could open the back door and pull out various bits of equipment, such as warning signs and flashing lights.

Paul Boswell was about thirty but looked younger with his baby face and mischievous grin. There were two men who were much older sitting near him, both country-beat officers. One of them had a considerable array of medal ribbons on his tunic and must have been a World War II veteran. This officer sat smoking a pipe and gave the impression of being in charge. Boswell dropped some car keys onto the table where the three of them were sitting; it appeared that he had been nominated as our driver. He called out to me, his face in a broad grin.

'Richard, did you bring your stick? You are going to need it today.'

I ran my fingers down my right trouser leg and onto my truncheon pocket, tapping the hard piece of wood that was concealed there as if to convince myself that it was probably going to save my life in the next few dangerous hours. The country-beat policeman with the pipe and the campaign ribbons glanced in my direction.

'A new probationer,' he said with a dismissive grunt. The tone of his voice and his expression might have meant anything but probably conveyed something that fell between contempt and amusement. Or maybe it was just a bit of concern that he was stuck with a 'bloody probie' who was likely to be more trouble than he was worth.

'I suppose that we had better look after him,' he said to the others. 'If anything happens to him, we'll probably spend the rest of the year writing reports about it.'

'Don't worry,' said Boswell, looking in my direction. 'We shall try and bring you back in one piece.'

'We need to get going,' said the veteran, looking at Boswell. A few minutes later, we headed south from Andover, with Boswell driving and the pipe-smoking veteran in the front passenger seat. I sat in the back with the other country-beat officer. Hayling Island is in the south-east corner of Hampshire, the opposite end to Andover, so this involved a long drive across the county.

The island is joined to the mainland by a bridge, which was being defended like an international frontier in time of war. Four or five policemen were there to guard the frontier and were checking all vehicles going onto the island.

As we drove towards the seafront, we saw a large array of police vehicles, mainly grey Huskys and dark-blue vans, covering the main road junctions and areas close to the beach. Our pipe-smoking war veteran used the radio to call Information Room with our location, and we were told to report to an inspector at a control centre close to the beach. When we arrived, the inspector did not tell us much, but he gave us a map of Hayling Island and told us to patrol an area that he had marked in red ink.

We drove along a road parallel with the beach, where we saw dozens of motor scooters parked next to tents that had been set up on open land close to the sea. It was a cool, cloudy, misty morning, and there was no obvious sign of human life. Up ahead, we saw another Hillman Husky parked close to the beach with three or four policemen inside, and Boswell pulled in next to them. They seemed to know much more about what had been happening the previous day.

When the trouble started, Chief Constable Sir Douglas Osmond had come to Hayling Island and taken personal charge of police operations. He had directed officers to carry out searches of all the tents for weapons or drugs and had searched a number of people himself. Several people had been arrested and many others had left the island.

The sun never emerged from the clouds that day; it remained dark, sullen, and damp. We noticed three or four youths walking along the beach, all of them looking quiet and dejected. After that, we saw a few more. It must be said that they appeared to be the least warlike group of young people in the country. It would have provided a bit of excitement for me if something had happened, but nothing did.

This was my first real day as a police officer. It was strange to think that it was also my first experience of a public-order operation. The newspapers ran riot with frightening stories of large-scale battles being fought all along the south coast. Readers were probably left with the impression that many towns had been razed to the ground and the dead and wounded were numbered in thousands.

Writing in the *Sunday Telegraph*, Donald McLachlan tried to introduce some common sense to everything that was being said about the Mods and Rockers. He reported that the amount of damage caused to property was not as extensive as people might think. He also pointed out that violence was regrettable but nothing new. Nor was such behaviour confined to people who could be described as underprivileged. McLachlan mentioned the occasion about one hundred years earlier when Eton schoolboys had gone to Winchester for their annual cricket match against Winchester College. On the return journey, 200 Etonians had run riot and smashed up the train that they were travelling on.

Journalists would probably not agree with me, but there are occasions when accurate reporting can ruin a really good story. The facts were that there had been no loss of life, few serious injuries, and damage to property had been relatively minor. To put all of this into some proper perspective, accidents caused by motorists during the holiday weekend killed ninety people and caused financial loss that came to a total of more than £100,000 – in 1964 costs!

4

In 2014, the population of the Hampshire Police area was approaching two million. To put that into context, the province of Northern Ireland, with its six counties, has a smaller population than Hampshire. A great deal of the county remains rural and agricultural, but by the 1960s, much of the coast had already developed into a large urban sprawl. This area includes Southampton, the largest city in the South East of England outside London. Anyone travelling east from Southampton will remain in urban areas as they approach Portsmouth, the UK's only island city. This coastal region consists of two cities and several large towns all close to one another. During the 1960s, there were suggestions from town-planners that this conurbation could be made into one large city. A name was even suggested: Solent City. There was another built-up area in the north east corner of the county that included the two Surrey towns of Camberley and Farnham and the Hampshire towns of Aldershot, Farnborough, and Fleet. At the opposite end of the county was the conurbation that included Poole, Bournemouth, and Christchurch.

Historically, Bournemouth and Christchurch had always been part of Hampshire, but they were cut off from the rest of the county by the New Forest. The logical situation would be to have this urban area on the borders of Hampshire and Dorset covered by one police force. However, Poole was policed by Dorset and Christchurch by Hampshire. Bournemouth had its own independent county-borough force, and this resulted in three different police forces covering parts of what was a fairly small conurbation in terms of population. A few years later, this problem was solved by the

Boundary Commission when the decision was made that Bournemouth and Christchurch would become part of Dorset.

Geography dictated that police work within the Isle of Wight division would be somewhat different from the mainland. Generally speaking, the pace of life was that bit slower and there was less crime. However, during the summer its seaside resorts became quite busy and extra policemen were needed. This was done by drafting in single officers from the mainland divisions for the holiday season.

In 1964, the Hampshire and Isle of Wight Constabulary had ten divisions, including Traffic Division. Each one had a divisional commander who would be a superintendent or chief superintendent, depending on the population and the work level of the division. Divisions were usually divided into two or more subdivisions with an inspector or chief inspector in charge.

The Andover subdivision consisted of the town and a large area surrounding it, bordering on Berkshire to the north and Wiltshire to the west. The army had a strong presence in the area, and there were military bases all over the subdivision. There was a section station at Tidworth, on the boundary with Wiltshire. A typical section station would have a sergeant with four or five PCs plus three or four country beats. Tidworth was a small military town in what seemed to me to be a fairly remote location, halfway between Salisbury and Andover.

Before officers had personal radios, communications were poor. Many country-beat officers patrolled on Velocette motorcycles that were equipped with radios, but it was only possible to contact them when they were on their Velocettes.

In towns or cities, officers patrolling a beat used a traditional system where they made a scheduled point every fifty minutes at a police box or public telephone kiosk. The PC had to wait at the point for ten minutes, and this was the only time when he could be contacted by the station. In order to vary the officer's movements, there were seven or eight schedules for the point system and they were changed each week.

A basic element of supervision was sergeants meeting their officers when they made points. This would nearly always be an unannounced visit, and the PC would make a record of the meeting in his notebook that would look like this: '10.6.64. 3.50 p.m. Nelson Street TK. Met by PS 25 King.'

The notebook entry would be signed later that day. In most cases, the sergeant would arrive by car, open the window, and raise a hand. The hand would twist to the left and then to the right, and then the car would disappear into the distance. An onlooker might start to wonder about the meaning of this bizarre secret signal. It was simple enough: 'Put the meeting in your notebook, and I shall sign it later.'

In Hampshire, the official notebook was used like a diary. On each day of duty we had to write the day and date, followed by the tour of duty, i.e. 2 p.m. to 10 p.m. The entry had to include the actual time when we took our forty-five-minute refreshment break. When we made an arrest, our original notes were made in our notebooks, and in other incidents we had to write a brief log entry.

We were told that it was important that notebooks be kept up to date and that sergeants would check them from time to time. Sometimes my notes were two or three days in arrears, and this resulted in me being ticked off when this came to light. On at least two occasions, red ink entries appeared on the offending pages, with comments such as 'Ensure that this notebook is kept up to date at all times.'

At Andover, the traditional patrolling system with its point system existed in name only. A shift team would normally consist of a sergeant and four or five constables and they would have to be ready to respond to any incident within the town or anywhere else in the subdivision. Two PCs would patrol in a car, and often they would be the only people available to deal with incidents. Occasionally, when manpower allowed, an officer would patrol the centre of the town on foot.

The day after going to Hayling Island was my first proper day at the station. I met the chief inspector in charge of the subdivision and, a couple of days after that, the inspector who was his deputy. PC McLaughlin was still on leave, and the sergeant on duty needed to find someone to work with me. He decided to put me with Ken Price, the Andover dog handler. Ken Price was a slim, dark-haired, smart-looking man in his thirties who was enthusiastic and hard-working. He took me into the station yard and introduced me to his dog, Rebel.

Ken drove the dog van to the centre of a village a few miles from Andover, where we parked and he explained to me how the radio system worked. It was all basic stuff but important. Ken told me what the call sign was for the dog van and showed me the correct way to answer if we were called. Hampshire operated what was known as a stand-by system. It was possible to hear everything that was said by officers at IR, but when a mobile unit was sending a message, it was only possible to hear an annoying 'bleep, bleep' sound.

For a few minutes, we sat listening to calls going out to units on other divisions. Ken explained that he was looking for an army deserter who was believed to be living in a village a few miles from Andover. Ken gave me a brief description of the man, and then we made our way to the village and pulled up outside a neat, red-brick semi-detached house. Ken told me to stay in the dog van and listen to the radio. After reminding me what our call sign was, he walked to the front door of the house. I saw him talking to a woman there for about five minutes, and then he walked back to the dog van.

'He's not here,' he said as he dropped back into the driver's seat. We drove away from the village, and after a few minutes we came to a large area of forest. Ken wanted to give his dog some exercise, so he asked me to listen to the radio while he let Rebel loose. He disappeared into the woods with Rebel, while I sat in the dog van and listened to the radio. A number of messages went out over the air but nothing that involved our area. It would have been good to hear what the officers in the cars were saying, but all that I could hear was the frustrating 'bleep, bleep' sound when they spoke.

After about twenty minutes, Ken and Rebel returned to the dog van, and we drove for a while. Then suddenly, there was a radio message for us; it took me by surprise. I was a bit slow, reaching for the handset with some obvious hesitation. It did not go down well with my colleague. Ken grabbed it from me and answered it, with an impatient glance in my direction. He was probably thinking, 'Why am I stuck with this idiot probationer?' or something like that.

It appeared that the call was about the army deserter, and we headed back to the village where we had been earlier. As we drove into the village, I noticed a public phone box up ahead of us. Ken had not given me any background information about this, so the whole business was a bit of a mystery to me. There was a man in his twenties standing inside the telephone kiosk, making a call. Ken jumped out of the dog van very quickly, followed by me. He opened the door to the phone box and I could see that the man inside fitted the general description of the deserter that Ken had given me earlier.

Ken Price asked the man some questions, and he admitted that he was a deserter from the army. When told that he was going to be arrested, he shrugged his shoulders and said nothing. We walked back to the van with him. 'Where are we going to put him?' I thought. There were only two seats in the dog van, but Ken did not spend a great deal of time worrying about that particular problem. He opened the door at the back and put the arrested man in with Rebel.

'Don't worry – he won't bite you,' he said. 'Well, he might – but only if you try to escape,' he added with a grin.

'We have arrested someone,' I thought. It seemed like a bit of an anticlimax. Ken Price was shown as the arresting officer, but the paperwork showed me as a witness. Not many probationers were sent to Andover around this time, and for the next few days I was partnered with different PCs, all of whom were very experienced.

One of my first memories of Andover was of collecting meals for people detained at the police station. Defendants or suspects held at stations were always referred to as 'prisoners'. The police had a contract with a local café to supply cooked meals. When we collected the food, I would be in charge of a set of metal plates and containers. While my colleague drove, I would have everything balanced precariously on my knees.

We heard the news about the sentencing of the train robbers, the men involved in what is referred to as the Great Train Robbery in 1963. There was quite a lot of discussion about it in the station. It seemed that many of the officers at Andover thought that the gaol terms of thirty years imprisonment were excessive.

'Mac' McLaughlin returned from holiday, and we went out on patrol together in one of the section cars. It was soon obvious that Mac was a thoughtful and conscientious policeman. While we drove around the subdivision, he asked me a few questions about the law and police procedures to see whether I had learned anything at Sandgate.

My knowledge of the police as an organisation was very limited, but Mac explained how everything fitted together. Essentially, a British police force is divided into three main parts: Uniform, CID, and Traffic Patrol. The Uniform Branch is always the largest, and in Hampshire its official name was Uniform Patrol. However, within the service, it is normally referred to as one word: Uniform.

Uniform is responsible for patrolling, with the objectives of preventing and detecting crime. In military terms, Uniform could be referred to as the infantry, as it holds the ground; an important part of its patrolling function is to deal with emergency calls from the public and investigate all initial reports of crime.

A major responsibility for Uniform officers will always be public order on the streets and dealing with disorder when it occurs. There are specialist units within Uniform, such as dog handlers, public-order units, mounted police, marine-support units, and vice squads.

At this point, some readers might complain that I have made no mention of women within the police service and the work that they do. However, there is a reason for this. During the sixties, the Women Police operated as a separate unit within the Uniform Branch and had their own rank structure. A woman police constable was always known as a WPC, in the same way that a PC who became a detective was always referred to as a DC (detective constable).

Women officers had their own offices in police stations and were responsible for carrying out specific duties, such as enquiries regarding missing persons. Another important part of their work was helping CID officers in cases where sexual offences had been committed against women or children.

Under Police Regulations, women had a different contract of employment, by which they were paid less but only had to work a shift of seven and a half hours as opposed to the eight hours worked by male officers. Nowadays, this would rightly be seen as a device to prevent them from receiving the same rate of pay as men.

Every police force in the UK has its own Special Branch, often referred to as SB. This branch works closely with MI5, Britain's security service.

Its main function is to investigate offences against the State, including the threat posed by terrorists. An important role for its officers at the ports is to prevent terrorists coming in and to identify wanted people who are trying to enter or leave the UK.

Mac informed me that there were people within the force who had specialist knowledge of every policing issue that could be imagined. If you needed expert advice, it was just a matter of finding the right person, he said. However, during my first few months, much of the policing world seemed quite bewildering to me. It was as though someone had given me a large jigsaw with three or four pieces slotted together and left me to work out where all the other pieces fitted.

Mac had seen about nine years' service. Before becoming a policeman in Hampshire, he had done his National Service and served in the RAF Police. He gave me some useful guidance about how to survive as a probationer, and it was similar to what I had heard before. 'Do a lot of listening, and don't say too much.'

Mac gave me advice as to how officers should deal with members of the public. Everybody should be treated with courtesy, but Mac followed that up with several tips about carrying out stops. He pointed out that, when it came to stops, we always had to think about our safety. In most cases, we would not know the background or personality of people that we came across. They might be wanted by the police, they might be violent, or they might be carrying weapons. So the bottom line was that we needed to treat everybody with care.

One important issue is that British police officers nearly all patrol without firearms. The only weapon we carried was a truncheon to defend ourselves in the event of a violent attack. During training, we were told that we should not hit anybody on the head and that a blow from a truncheon should be aimed at the arms or legs. Mac made the point that we should only use our sticks if it was really necessary. He also pointed out that the piece of wood in my truncheon pocket was not going to provide a good defence against violent people armed with knives, iron bars or firearms.

He told me the best angle to stand at when carrying out a stop in order to protect myself from a sudden attack, and this proved to be very good advice, which I used for the next thirty years. Two years later, his words returned to haunt me one night when the person I was stopping suddenly threw his bicycle at me and sprinted away into some nearby woods.

The truth of the matter was that it was about four in the morning, and sometimes I was not at my best on night duty when things were quiet. When we eventually caught him, it turned out that he had broken into a shop in Southampton, and the bag he was carrying was full of stolen cigarettes. The burglar must have decided that he was going to 'leg it' before we found the loot. Spending the first few vital seconds falling over the bike must have helped to wake me up. The officer that I was working with took off like a greyhound after a rabbit, leaving me in third place.

It would have been useful if we'd had torches, but events had moved a little faster than we'd expected. For a few minutes it appeared that the darkened forest had swallowed all three of us, and it seemed like a good idea to stop and listen. So, for two or three minutes I stood perfectly still and concentrated, hoping to hear some sound of movement. Everything was silent. There were three men in the forest, each listening for someone else to make a move.

There was a small gully just in front of me that was invisible in the dark but proof of its existence soon became clear when I took a few steps forward and found myself falling into it. While I was climbing out, I heard other noises, and they sounded quite close. There were some smaller crashing noises followed by a louder crash.

The incident came to an end when my colleague collided with the suspect, and the two of them wrestled for a few seconds until they both fell into the gully that I had just climbed out of. There were some shouts and a lot of noise as the wrestling match carried on. The shouting, crashing, and banging made them easy to find, and the suspect decided that he would give up. He later made a written statement admitting the burglary in Southampton.

I had great respect for Mac and took his advice seriously, so that type of incident just reinforced everything that he had told me. However, by its very nature, a great deal of police work has to be learned the hard way. Even experienced officers have lost their lives or have been seriously injured because of mistakes they've made. Sometimes something bad can happen, and it's nobody's mistake. There might be a day when you could be unlucky, when your luck just runs out.

On one of our first days together, we were sitting in our car and listening as message after message came over the radio in quick succession. There had been a wages robbery at a business in the New Forest, and it appeared that someone inside the building had managed to dial 999. Two PCs had reached the scene within a few minutes, where they had been attacked by the robbers and both been seriously injured.

Within a few minutes, roadblocks and checkpoints had been set up all over the county, and a description of the car that the robbers had used was circulated. We were told to take up a position on a main road a few miles outside Andover. There was no point in worrying too much about this type of thing, but it made me think about the job I was doing. This was the real world, and the police world could often be a violent one. We would all have to go in harm's way, but as Mac pointed out, all you can do is to be careful and reduce the risk where you can.

He gave me some tips about obtaining the correct details from people that we stopped, identifying them and checking them with CRO. Mac gave me a practical example when we stopped a man one night and identified him as someone wanted in Reading for theft. It made me realise that there are always large numbers of wanted people on the move.

Dealing with reported crime was going to be one of my bread-and-butter tasks. My first visit to a crime scene was a walk-in burglary at a house in a village near Andover. The side door to the bungalow, which gave access to the kitchen, had been left open, and the burglar had simply walked in and stolen a radio.

We spoke to the couple at the house and asked them whether they had seen anything or had any information as to suspects. After that, we spoke to their neighbours, but nobody had any useful information. There were no marks or anything that justified a forensic examination.

I began to understand some of the realities of crime. First of all, it seems that real policemen are not as clever as the ones in police dramas on television. The aces on TV can crack any case wide open in about thirty minutes. Someone who commits a murder, an armed robbery, or anything else will find themselves sitting in a cell by the end of the programme, if not sooner.

Secondly, most offences relate to property, and often the goods stolen are of low value. When it comes to detecting crime, many cases fall into what might be called a black hole – there are no suspects, there are no witnesses, and there is no forensic evidence. Another factor is time. The officer who investigates a crime may only have forty-five minutes or so in which to solve it.

At this burglary, we carried out some basic enquiries, and then Mac showed me how to complete the crime report.

Every station in Hampshire had a book called a crime complaint book. Entries were in duplicate, and the name and address of the person who reported the crime and the name and address of the victim were written down. The exact words used were recorded, such as 'My house has been broken into' or 'Someone tried to rape my daughter.' The front page was passed to the officer investigating the offence and attached to the crime report. This was obvious duplication, although it might have some practical value when it came to offences such as sexual assaults. Within a couple of years of my arrival at Andover, the crime complaint form was discontinued.

The normal shift system in Hampshire was based on three shifts. Early turn started at 6 a.m. and finished at 2 p.m. Late turn was from 2 p.m. until 10 p.m., and night duty started at 10 p.m. and finished at 6 a.m. We were expected to report to the parade room a quarter of an hour before the official starting time of our shift, where the sergeant would brief us before we went on patrol.

The Parade Book was a rough-and-ready means of providing general information and street-level crime intelligence to PCs when they reported for duty. All officers were encouraged to make entries in it about local criminals, stolen property, or anything else that they thought might be useful. Teleprinter messages giving details of serious crimes in surrounding areas would be pasted into the book. Officially, officers 'paraded' for duty, but in Hampshire the general rule was that we all sat down at a long table and were briefed by the sergeant.

Apart from Uniform and CID, there was a Traffic Division unit based at Andover, consisting of a sergeant and six or seven constables. The patrol cars that they used were large, powerful Wolseys and Austin Westminsters. Traffic Division had the only cars that were fast enough to do the job if there was a high-speed chase, and TD officers were all specially trained drivers. Andover was surrounded by some of the fastest roads in the country and the dangers of this were soon very much apparent. Shortly after my arrival there, a head-on crash resulted in three people being killed and two others seriously injured. The cars involved were brought to the station so that TD officers could examine them. Looking at the two mangled vehicles, we could easily see how little protection the average car provided in the event of a high-speed accident.

In many police forces, area cars were used for patrolling, usually forming the spearhead of the police team. An area car would usually be a more powerful vehicle than a section car and would have a crew of two: a driver and a radio operator.

At that time, Hampshire did not have area cars, and on night duty, Traffic Patrol took on that role. On day duty, they were mainly involved in traffic matters, but at night their officers carried out stops on vehicles and dealt with a wide range of emergency calls.

The busiest period of time for emergency calls in Hampshire was usually between 5 p.m. and 1 a.m. Because of this, subdivisions operated a system of crime cars with a crew of two, often starting at 5 or 6 p.m. Within a few weeks of my arrival in Andover, Mac and I were posted to the crime car for a week.

Our car was a Hillman Husky, equipped with a magnetic blue flashing light that could be fitted to its roof whenever we needed it. One of my first memories was of travelling along roads close to the River Test on hot summer nights, where we would drive through huge clouds of insects. There must have been millions and millions of them.

While we were on patrol we did a lot of talking, with me trying to remember to do most of the listening. Mac explained how the subdivision worked and what our local policing problems were. Andover was fairly small, but it had its own contingent of troublemakers, known to us as 'the yobs'. It was a small number of people, but they made their presence felt. Soldiers came into the town from the military bases nearby and from time to time there would be fights between them and some of our local troublemakers.

One evening, when we were a few miles to the south of Andover, we received a 999 call about a disturbance involving people on the north side of the town. This meant that Mac had to drive back to Andover and then cut across the town to the location given.

The two men concerned were neighbours. Neither of them had garages for their cars, and they parked in the street. On this day, for some reason, it turned out that one of them had parked outside his neighbour's house instead of in his usual spot in front of his own house. This had escalated into a shouting match, with the men squaring up to each other in the street. The wife of one of the two warring neighbours had become concerned and dialled 999.

As we spoke to the two men, I noticed that Mac was angry. This was the only occasion on which I saw him this way. He told them that this was not a matter that should have involved the police and that we had driven some distance in order to reach them. He told them that they needed to sort out their dispute themselves – and quickly!

After that, he explained that if there were to be a second call from their street, he intended to arrest both of them for breach of the peace. The two of them stood there, looking sheepish, and started mumbling apologies. Mac and I walked back to the police car and drove away into the sunset.

There were a lot of things on my mind in 1964. Apart from training to be a policeman, I was planning to be married that year. I had first met Maureen about five years before when we worked together in a bank in central London. One day in June, she came to Andover to visit me and see the town. She had just had her twenty-first birthday party, but now the main topic of conversation was our wedding, planned for September. We had a walk around the town centre, with its Georgian-style High Street. Maureen seemed to like the look of Andover.

There were two railway stations in the town. Andover Town was on the main line to London, and Andover Junction was the link if you wanted to travel south to the coast. The River Anton ran through the centre of the town from north to south, and the A303 Road ran through the town from west to east. Over the years, the A303 developed its own sort of mystique, the British equivalent of the legendary Route 66 in the United States. Books have been written about it, and there have been television programmes that praise the wonders of this famous British highway to the west.

However, it seems unlikely that this rosy view was held by many of the drivers who used the road during the sixties. There were always long queues of traffic trying to get through Andover, and in the summer it became even worse. There was no bypass, and the traffic on the A303 had to inch its way through the town centre. The traffic lights at the junction with the High Street always caused a big build-up of traffic, and there was another one when drivers reached the level crossing near Andover Junction station. At busy times it was quite normal for drivers to spend an hour just getting through the town.

All of this traffic would pass an old, established butcher's shop owned by Herbert Noyce a short distance from the police station. Herbert was a man in his sixties who had decided to retire and sell his business. He had a son who owned a farm a few miles from Andover and another son in Australia. Herbert and his wife, Connie, planned to take a six-month holiday in Australia.

They owned a large, comfortable house in Junction Road, Andover, and they thought that they should take in tenants while they were in Australia. Under police regulations at that time, an officer who wanted to be married had to ask permission from his/her chief constable to do so. Nobody seemed to know what the reasons were for this regulation, and there were rumours that discreet enquiries were made about the future spouse. I put in a written report to my superintendent detailing my plans for a September wedding.

'Herbie' Noyce was an amusing character and very much a typical Hampshire man of his generation who had been born and bred in the Andover area. At some point he was in conversation with one of the sergeants and mentioned the trip to Australia. My name cropped up during this conversation, and the police officer told Herbie that I was looking for accommodation.

Another section of the regulations stated that the chief officer of police was responsible for providing officers with suitable accommodation or giving them a housing allowance. There were no police houses on the subdivision that were likely to become available, so I arranged to meet Herbie Noyce. He told me that he would be happy to have me as a tenant for the six months when they would be in Australia. About a week later, I introduced Maureen to the Noyces, and we all got on well together.

Herbie Noyce introduced me to two or three of his friends. One of them was a member of a shooting club, and I told him I had an interest in rifle shooting. I had not fired a shot since my schooldays, but Herbie's friend took me to his club, deep in a forest just east of the town. The club members let me use their rifles, and I went shooting there three or four times.

I continued living at my lodgings in Vigo Road. Mrs Morgan was a good landlady and did everything she could to make me comfortable.

During my first six weeks at Andover, the amount of responsibility that fell on my shoulders was very limited, but after that, things changed. I was expected to make decisions and take whatever action was necessary. When we came across traffic offences, Mac would always indicate whether the person should be reported for process or whether a verbal warning would suffice.

I normally carried my notebook, three or four process books and three accident report books. Process books were used to record evidence in cases where summonses would be issued, and these would be mainly for traffic offences. My first process book was written when we stopped two 15-year-olds on the same bicycle, commonly referred to as 'two on a bike.' Anyone then who was under seventeen was classified under the law as a juvenile, and his or her case went to the local juvenile court.

A juvenile cannot be questioned about an offence unless a parent or guardian is present. In a traffic case such as two on a bike, the procedure was that we would go to see the parents afterwards and inform them about the action we had taken. The parents' names would be noted in the process book. Mac told me that they would probably not be taken to court, but he wanted to see how I dealt with people and whether my knowledge was up to scratch.

A major problem in small towns is that everyone seems to be related or known to everyone else. A couple of days later, Mrs Morgan told me that her 15-year-old nephew had been reported by a policeman for the heinous crime of two on a bike. She probably guessed that I was the PC involved, but I just maintained a poker face. If her nephew had never come to the notice of police before, he was likely to receive a written warning, and this is what eventually happened.

In a small town such as Andover, the problems of the outside world seemed much further away than would have been the case in London. It was only a few months after President Kennedy had been assassinated. In the United States, what was to be known as the Freedom Summer was underway, when black people were challenging the laws that enforced segregation in some of the southern states.

In Rhodesia, Britain's last African colony, the white minority was hanging onto power and was soon in confrontation with the British Government, who warned them that the time had come to give full voting rights to their African citizens who made up the bulk of the population. In response to this, Ian Smith, the prime minister of Rhodesia, threatened that he would break away from the British Commonwealth.

It seemed that Rhodesia was moving down the same path as its neighbour, South Africa, a country that had developed a social system of racial segregation known as apartheid. In South Africa that year, a black lawyer and political activist by the name of Nelson Mandela was convicted of treason and sentenced to life imprisonment.

It is against the law for anyone to camp on a public highway. There were a number of gypsies living in the area near Andover, and some of them broke the law by doing this. Mac and I would come across illegally parked caravans from time to time, and he showed me how we should deal with these cases.

We would speak to the man or woman who was living there and give them a warning that they were breaking the law. We would make a second visit to the spot seven days later to see whether they were still there. In most cases, they would have moved by the time of our second visit. If not, the person concerned would be reported, and a process book would be submitted with an attachment saying 'gypsy case'.

As their name suggests, Travellers do not always stay in the same place in order to make it easy for police to serve summonses on them. In these cases, a summons would be issued by the court within twenty-four hours, and the police officer would serve it personally on the defendant. The court date would be scheduled for the following week, when they would usually be fined two pounds.

My first arrest was reported in a local newspaper under the headline 'Had Been in the River'. It was a warm summer night when Godfrey White, a 53-year-old man, had a few drinks too many and then jumped or fell into the River Anton. Mac and I were in the crime car together when we received a call telling us that someone was in the river a short distance from the police station.

We found White leaning against a wall, dripping wet from head to toe, and although he was very drunk, it seemed that he had managed to crawl out of the water. Or had a local resident rescued him from drowning? We felt a bit sorry for him, but drunks are not the easiest people to deal with, and there is always a limit to how many times you can ask someone who they are and where they live. Despite our best efforts, White gave us no information that made any sense.

A short time later, White found himself sitting in the charge room at Andover police station. The sergeant who dealt with the charge found a large towel, and we helped White to remove all his clothes. I helped him to dry himself, and after that he stood in the charge room looking a bit sheepish with nothing but a towel wrapped around him. The sergeant spent some time patiently trying to find out his name and address until, eventually, he managed to get some common sense out of him. It turned out that he lived in Abbots Ann, a village that was a short distance from Andover.

One of my colleagues went to White's home, picked up his wife, and brought her back to the station. He was charged with being drunk in a public place, and then the sergeant released him on bail. The unfortunate man was handed over to the custody of his wife.

At Andover Magistrates' Court, White pleaded guilty and was fined two pounds. He was a married man with five children. 'It is the first offence of my life,' he told the court.

The presiding magistrate commented quickly, 'And I hope it will be your last. We cannot have you running about the street drunk or swimming in the town river. You must pull yourself together.'

Many officers at Andover thought of a posting to the crime car as something to be avoided. The hours – 5 p.m. to 1 a.m. – were certainly unsocial, but it was always a busy time for police work. The bottom line was that it was great experience for a probationer, so I let it be known that I was happy to do it.

One week, Ken Price and I found ourselves assigned to the crime car together, and we patrolled in the dog van instead of one of the section cars. It amused me when we drove past groups of local youths who were known to us as troublemakers, because Rebel always seemed to recognise them and would start growling.

5

Ken Price and Mac were both very good police officers for a new probationer to work with. But there were a few days when I found myself working with an officer who did not show as much interest in the job that he was doing. One evening we received a call to go to a house where there had been a burglary. There was no sign of a forced entry, and when we talked to the people at the house, we soon had the name of a suspect. A man called Macklin had previously been a tenant there, and one of the neighbours had seen him near the house around the time when the break-in had occurred.

I was a probationer, keen to make an arrest for housebreaking, and the officer with me seemed happy to leave it to me. A few years down the line, I would have seen the problem quite clearly. My colleague must have been aware of my lack of experience and should have made sure that I was given the right advice. After taking witness statements from the people at the house, I was sure that Macklin was the burglar. In the following few days, I made some enquiries to find him, but it seemed that he had disappeared from Andover.

My next move was to have Macklin circulated as wanted, and his case appeared in police gazettes a few days later. *The Police Gazette* was an official publication that was published by Scotland Yard twice weekly and then circulated to police stations all over the UK. This publication disappeared when the police service moved into the Age of the Computer. It seemed quite clear to me that Macklin was the person responsible for the burglary, but in police terms he was technically a suspect rather than a wanted person.

In my first few months in the job, it was not always easy for me to appreciate the wide gap that exists between suspicion and evidence. When someone is shown as wanted, it indicates that there is some credible evidence and that the person can be charged when arrested. Many of those on the wanted list are defendants who have 'jumped bail' before court proceedings have been completed.

As luck would have it, Macklin was arrested a few days later. A CID officer in Birmingham had been investigating a case of theft and had questioned Macklin about it. The officer decided that Macklin was probably not involved in the theft but decided to do a CRO check on him. This showed that he was wanted by the police, so the DC arrested him and a message was sent to Andover.

It might seem that this was really good news for me, the investigating officer. Two PCs from Andover went to Birmingham and brought him back. However, when Macklin arrived at Andover, the sergeant on duty was not very happy with the situation. There was no direct evidence against Macklin that would justify charging him with housebreaking. It did not help that the suspect protested his innocence and complained about having spent the last twenty-four hours or so in police custody. The sergeant tried to contact me but with no success. Andover's ace investigator was taking a few days of annual leave and was in Wimbledon visiting family and fiancée.

My short holiday came to an end the day after Macklin arrived at Andover. A message had been left with Mrs Morgan for me to report to the station on my return to Andover. The sergeant on duty did not appear to be a happy man. He waved a finger at me as he pointed out a few things. The main point was that he was holding someone in the cells, a man who had been in police custody for more than forty-eight hours and had not been charged. He added that there did not appear to be any evidence to charge him with anything in the first place. The sergeant told me to report to Detective Sergeant Jacob, the officer in charge of the CID at Andover.

My concerns grew during my short walk to Sergeant Jacob's office. When I spoke to him, the DS was clearly not happy about Macklin being circulated as wanted, but he started to explain the situation to me patiently without showing any sign of annoyance. He made the point that the arrest was lawful, as housebreaking was a felony, and there was some suspicion that Macklin had committed the offence. At the same time he told me, with a straight face, that it was always useful to have some evidence before we charged someone with a criminal offence.

What Roland Jacob was actually thinking is not known, but he had a probationer standing in his office, obviously out of his depth, a suspected housebreaker sitting in a cell, and no evidence that would support a charge. He must have known that the only way forward was to obtain a confession from Macklin. Although I could claim to be the 'officer in the case', it was generous of the DS to allow me to remain involved with it.

Very shortly I would have a lesson on interrogation by someone who was an expert. The two of us went to the cells, took Macklin to an interview room, and then we sat down together and DS Jacob started talking. It seemed strange to me, because the DS did not appear to have any interest in the burglary. It just seemed to be a friendly chat, with Roland Jacob asking Macklin about where he came from and his family life.

Within a few minutes, Macklin was talking about his childhood in Birmingham and the way that he had been treated as a young boy by his parents. He had been brought up in a household where both parents were heavy drinkers, and he had a father who had often been violent towards him.

Jacob never raised his voice, and his approach was gentle and sympathetic. Macklin's life story emerged bit by bit. He was someone who had run away from home as a teenager, and his life had been constantly marked by trouble and tragedy.

The suspect did nearly all of the talking, and it went on for thirty minutes or so. Macklin told us that four years previously his fiancée had been killed in a car crash. He spoke openly about the trouble that he had been in and the fact that he had several previous convictions for burglary and theft.

'You have done some silly things in your life, haven't you?' said DS Jacob quietly, and Macklin readily agreed.

'And this housebreaking was one of them, wasn't it?'

'Yes,' said Macklin. 'I'm afraid it was.'

The DS turned sideways towards me with a face that was totally devoid of any expression.

'Maybe you should take a written statement from him, Richard,' he said.

The detective sergeant watched as the ace detective he was working with started to fumble around in the stationery cabinet looking for the correct form for recording written confessions. He said nothing but was probably quietly amused when I pulled out a copy of the Government white paper on the Judges' Rules from my jacket pocket. While trying to appear cool and professional, my eyes went straight to the part that mentioned confessions.

The DS leaned forward and pointed at the relevant paragraph. The first part of the statement consisted of the caution, which I wrote and then read out to Macklin. The second part related to the burglary, which I recorded in his own words, and the third part was a certificate in which he stated that he had told the truth and had been given the right to correct, alter, or add anything that he wished. I read everything out to him, and Macklin signed all three parts of it.

It was an important day for me. My first written confession was in my hands, and the station sergeant completed the charge sheet for the court and carried out the formal charging procedure. It was also a day which made me realise how little I knew.

An even more important day was approaching for me. It had been a hot summer, with day after day of sunny weather, which left us wondering whether it would last until our wedding in September.

It turned out that Mac and four or five others at Andover had planned a stag party for me about a week before the big day. Our evening started at an old country pub in a village a few miles from Andover and ended in a Chinese restaurant in Winchester. As anticipated, I did have too much to drink, but my colleagues delivered me safely to my lodgings in Vigo Road. Luckily, the following day was my rest day, and this gave me a chance to have a long sleep.

'The Day' finally came, the fifth of September, and the weather remained hot and sunny. Our wedding at the Sacred Heart church in Wimbledon was a large family event and was followed by a reception at

Southfields, about 2 miles away. The tradition was that newly-weds would disappear fairly quickly after the wedding breakfast, but we stayed until about ten that night. Then we said our goodbyes to everyone and were driven to the Ariel Hotel at Heathrow.

The hotel was a new circular building, and in the sixties it appeared to be the last word in modern architecture. For some reason we had booked a flight to Jersey at about seven on Sunday morning, and this resulted in a last-minute rush to catch our plane.

We arrived at our hotel in St Helier at the same time as another couple of newly-weds, and the four of us spent some time together chatting. The other couple had hired a car, and they invited us to go with them to other parts of the island. One evening, as I was walking with Maureen along the seafront at St Helier, we came across one of the Jersey policemen who had been at Sandgate with me. We spent some time talking about police work and life in Jersey.

Honeymoons, like everything else in life, do not last forever, and the following week we returned to the real world at Andover. We moved into the house at Junction Road, and my diary was soon filling up with the various training courses and attachments that I would have to complete.

Probationers in Hampshire had to complete two CID attachments. The first one would be at the Andover CID office and the second one at the divisional CID office at Winchester. I would also have to work on a country beat and carry out an attachment to Traffic Division.

Three days after our return from Jersey, I reported to the Andover CID office in plain clothes. The office consisted of DS Jacob, three or four DCs, and a Scenes of Crime Officer, usually referred to as a SOCO. Sergeant Jacob arranged for me to work with Bill Scorey, one of the DCs. Bill Scorey had about nine years' service and had been in the CID for about a year.

Bill gave me some general information about the Criminal Investigation Department and the type of work that its officers were involved with. Although policies relating to crime investigation vary from force to force, the general rule is that CID officers investigate offences that are serious and are likely to involve lengthy enquiries. Many forces have specialist CID units dealing with specific crimes, such as murder, company fraud, or rape.

A PC who applies to join the CID will be assigned to a CID office or a plain-clothes squad to gain experience. These might be division-based crime squads or drugs squads. Those who are selected to join the CID go on a detective-training course at one of several detective-training schools in the UK. Once they have successfully completed this course, they are given the title of detective. Although this is not a rank, a PC who joins the CID is always referred to as a DC – a detective constable.

I went with Bill Scorey to a number of crime scenes, mainly burglaries. The terminology was different back in 1964, and the offences would have had names such as larceny dwelling, housebreaking, shop-breaking, etc. To add a little further colour and confusion to all of this, it must be mentioned that one of the CID officers at Andover was investigating an offence of 'sacrilege' – a historic term which meant the crime of breaking into a church and stealing property.

The definitions of breaking and entering had provided lawyers with a treasure trove of opportunities to argue hundreds of technical points of law. Supposing Fred Smith had inserted his hand through a hole in a shop window and pulled out a silver pepper mill. Was this 'breaking'? By the 1960s, legal arguments on the word 'breaking' had resulted in a mass of case law.

To complicate matters further, the word 'entering' had also received the same attention from the legal profession. Had Fred Smith 'entered' when he inserted his hand? The Law Lords at the House of Lords were kept busy for many years handing down decisions, and the case law on this grew and grew. Although this may now seem very strange, it was very important because these legal decisions would decide what a particular action could be defined as. Could it be a burglary, or a theft, or possibly not a crime at all?

In 1968, when the new offence of burglary was introduced, it replaced all the breaking and entering offences and simplified the working life of the police. At one stroke, so much legal argument disappeared into the dustbin of history. Whether the legal profession was happy about it has never been recorded.

When I arrived at the CID office one morning, I learned that we had someone in custody for burglary. An offence classified as burglary at this time was actually quite rare, because the definition specified breaking and entering a dwelling-house during the night with intent to commit a felony.

The felony in question was most often a theft, but of course it could relate to any other felony, such as rape.

In this case, the house was in a fairly remote location some miles from Andover. A 999 call had been made at about three in the morning, and the Andover Traffic Division car had taken the call. The two TD officers had arrested a suspect at the scene, who had been overpowered by a male householder. Initially there was a problem, as the suspect was refusing to answer questions, and we needed to establish his motive for breaking into the house. A young woman had been in the house at the time of the burglary, and the arresting officer suggested that the intended felony might be rape.

A CRO check showed that our suspect had previous convictions, but there was nothing that related to violence or sexual offences. Sergeant Jacob questioned him, and he was able to get him talking about the burglary. The DS was soon satisfied that the man was not a rapist. The real story appeared to be one of a vagrant who was hungry and looking for food to steal. He was charged with burglary. As this involved a house and night-time, people convicted of burglary were often treated fairly severely by the courts.

On my first day in the CID office, Sergeant Jacob said that he would find some crimes for me to investigate. On my third day, when I walked in, he waved to me, pointed at the binders that contained our crime reports, and said, 'Bikes.'

Over a period of several weeks, a large number of bicycles had been stolen in Andover. Generally, the detection rate for crime on the subdivision was very good, but it appeared that nobody had been arrested for stealing a bike for a long time. DS Jacob would have been aware that our lack of success in clearing up bicycle crime was having an adverse effect on the detection rate. My first move was to read all the crime reports relating to bicycles and then make notes of anything of interest. None of the reports had any names or descriptions of suspects. There was a section on every crime report headed Method, which I read, but this did not give me any pointers. There was another section that was headed Details of Investigation, but there was little to help me there, either. If anything, reading the reports on stolen cycles made the whole thing look more and more difficult to solve.

Many bicycles reported as stolen were later found abandoned near military bases. Public transport at night was virtually non-existent, and soldiers did not want to face a charge of being absent without leave. So it seemed that some bicycles had been unlawfully 'borrowed'. It was easy enough to see a pattern emerging in relation to bikes being taken by soldiers. As a general rule, there would be no evidence of intent to permanently deprive the owners, and these reported thefts would often end up being classified as 'no crime'. All crime reports that were classified as 'no crime' were not counted when it came to calculating the detection rate.

My hope was that some amazing clue was going to jump out of the pages at me, as happened to detectives in fiction. However, there was nothing like that. Although I spent a long time thinking about it all and making plenty of notes, the investigation did not move forward in any meaningful way.

There were other angles to consider. A thief had to be able to sell stolen property somewhere, and this me made me start to think about who might buy second-hand bikes. This was soon narrowed down to four shops in the town. My next plan was to visit the shopkeepers, tell them about the stolen-bicycle crime wave, and promise to give them a list of stolen bikes.

It took me some time to do, but eventually I completed a typed list of about thirty bicycles that had been reported stolen. My list went back over about three months, and there was a description of each bike, with identification features such as frame numbers and badges. The four shopkeepers were all given a copy of this list and a note asking them to contact the station if they had any useful information. It seemed to me this was all I could do at that point.

Bill Scorey asked me a few questions about my stolen-bike investigation, so I told him what I had been doing, and he gave me a nod that seemed to indicate some sort of approval. He invited me to join him in the canteen for a coffee, and there he told me about a new case that he was dealing with.

Bill had been a PC at Andover for several years but was fairly new to the CID, having completed his Detective Training Course only a few months before my arrival at Andover.

He was an extrovert and someone who had become famous – or maybe notorious – for some incidents that he had been involved in. He had a good sense of humour and always managed to throw some wicked one-liners into a conversation. There were a number of stories about him floating around the police station.

One of the best known of these went back a few years, when Bill Scorey had been on night duty and patrolling the centre of Andover on foot. The sergeant in charge of the night duty had decided to take a walk at about 4 a.m. and meet Bill at his next point. When the sergeant was a few yards away from the River Anton, he saw the shadowy silhouette of a man on his knees, brandishing a weapon of some sort in his right hand. Then the man swung the weapon downwards, accompanied by the famous words, 'Die, you bastard, die!'

I can imagine that it must have stopped the sergeant dead in his tracks – until he recognised who it was and guessed what was happening. Bill Scorey had been lying on his stomach next to the river for some time, tickling a trout. He had obviously not been aware of the sergeant approaching when he'd suddenly flipped it out of the water and used his truncheon to deliver the fatal blow.

While we drank our coffee, Bill told me about the case of 'the international petrol thief', as he called him. The facts of the case were straightforward. Someone had driven a Mini into a petrol station near Andover on the A303, and after filling the tank with fuel, driven off without paying. There had been a 999 call, and the officers in the Andover Traffic patrol car had spotted the Mini on the A303 a short time later. The driver was now in custody at Andover.

Bill told me that frauds were something that the CID would normally deal with. The theft of fuel from a petrol station would not usually be a matter for a detective, but Bill had been given a cheque fraud in Andover to deal with, and he believed that both the offences were linked.

The man we had in custody was Edward Hampden, a smartly dressed and well-spoken 28-year-old man from London. I carried out a CRO check on him, and this showed him as 'no trace, not wanted'. I made a quick note: N/T, N/W. In police shorthand this meant that he did not have any previous convictions and was not currently wanted for anything in the UK.

Bill told me that he thought that the 'international petrol thief' might be a fraudsman. After a short conversation with him, I found that Bill was fairly confident he was dealing with someone who had been arrested before. He suspected that the name and date of birth that we had been given were bogus. When someone is arrested, police carry out what is known as a bail enquiry, which involves establishing whether the person in custody is actually living at the address provided. In this case, the result was inconclusive, because there was nobody at the address given, and the neighbours did not know anything about the person or persons who were living there.

We sat down with Hampden, and after Bill questioned him about the fraud and the theft of petrol, he admitted to both. He was formally charged with the two offences, and then I helped Bill with the paperwork.

Whenever a person is charged with a criminal offence, there are two separate pieces of paperwork that have to be done. First, the prosecution case papers have to be completed; these would include details of the charges, a summary of the evidence, and witness statements. The second job is to complete the information needed for police records. The standard procedure then, was that a 'descriptive form' would be completed and forwarded to Scotland Yard.

Once the descriptive form was typed, the defendant would be fingerprinted and photographed. The basic ingredients of a file at the Criminal Records Office would always be the descriptive forms and sets of fingerprints. In Hampshire, all of this was done in duplicate, with one set going to Scotland Yard and the other one going to SOUCRO at Winchester.

Fingerprint Officers checked all incoming sets of fingerprints in order to identify criminals correctly. Anyone who had been convicted in the past would have a unique identification number, known as a CRO number; in police circles, criminals with previous convictions were often referred to as CRO men. When court cases were completed, the results were forwarded to the Criminal Records Offices so that records could be updated.

Andover Borough Magistrates' Court was due to sit the next day. Hampden indicated that he intended to plead guilty, and we made sure that we had completed all of the paperwork that evening. When we arrived at court, we found that one of the sergeants at Andover was acting as prosecutor, and there was a solicitor present to represent Hampden. We anticipated that Hampden would plead guilty and the case would be adjourned for pre-sentence reports.

Bill Scorey told Hampden's solicitor that it appeared Hampden had no previous convictions and it was unlikely that there would be objections to bail. Bill told me that he would recommend that bail be set at twenty pounds. Before we could go ahead with the case, we needed verification from Fingerprint Branch that Hampden had no previous convictions, but that morning there was some delay. Our only tactic was to play for time, and Bill went to see the court sergeant and asked him whether the case could be put to the end of the list.

Hampden's solicitor soon realised that something was going on, and he started to press the sergeant about it. The sergeant then had a whispered conversation with the Clerk of the Court and asked whether the case could be put back until after lunch. We had a problem on our hands when Hampden's solicitor addressed the court on the question of bail. He made the point that his client should not have to suffer because of police administrative failings.

The court sergeant was doing his best to counter these arguments, and while all this was happening, an urgent phone call came through to the court from the station. Hampden had been identified by fingerprints. His real name was Roger Ringshaw-Roper, a man with ten previous convictions for theft and fraud. He was also a disqualified driver and this would mean that he faced a further charge at court.

The court sergeant called Bill Scorey to make an application to the court that the 'international petrol thief' should be remanded in custody. While Bill did this, Ringshaw-Roper's solicitor was looking angry and glaring at his client. No application was made for bail, and the defendant was remanded in custody for a week.

On my arrival at the police station the following day, one of my colleagues handed me a copy of a phone call that had been received at the police station about an hour before. One of the shopkeepers that I had spoken to had some information for me. A teenager had come to his shop trying to sell a bicycle. The shopkeeper had taken the opportunity to examine it carefully and believed that it was one of the bikes on the list that I had given him. He had not purchased the bicycle but had told the youth that he was interested in buying other bikes from him and had managed to obtain a name and address.

The following day, I set off on my bicycle to the address of the suspected cycle thief, on the outskirts of Andover. It was an attractive-looking house in one of the best parts of the town. In answer to my knocking on the front door, a woman appeared and informed me that the person I was looking for was her 15-year-old son. When I spoke to the boy, he seemed totally shaken by my appearance. His father arrived home shortly after I got there, and both parents were shocked when they realised that their son had been involved in stealing bikes.

The four of us sat down together at the dining room table, and the youth admitted that he had stolen several bikes; he mentioned the name of one of his friends who was involved. My suspicion was that he had not told me everything, but I obtained as much information as possible from him and soon had a written statement under caution, in which he admitted six bicycle thefts. I told him and his parents that a report would be submitted regarding the thefts and that a summons would be applied for.

On my return to the station, I explained to Sergeant Jacob what had happened. He must have guessed that this was likely to turn into what is known as a 'snowball case'. Bill Scorey was called in to give me a hand, and the first thing we did the next day was drive to the address of the second youth. The house was totally different from the one I had been to the day before. We saw a very run-down building, which had the shell of a very old, rusting car in centre-stage position in the front garden.

A couple of knocks on the door revealed Suspect Number Two, a tall, scruffy-looking 16-year-old, together with his mother. The lad looked very frightened and readily admitted that he had been involved in the theft of a large number of bicycles. We went with him to the area at the back of the house, which looked more like a scrap-metal yard than the garden that it had once been. We could see several bicycles and a large number of items that had come from bikes. Apart from the bikes, Bill and I spotted something that immediately caught our attention.

It was a petrol-powered machine of some sort, and we both stood looking at it and searching our memories. The sight of it started to ring some bells.

'Where did you get this from?' asked Bill

'The railway station,' the boy answered, looking even more worried than he had a couple of minutes earlier.

Then it clicked. 'The railway station,' I thought. What we were looking at was a very valuable piece of equipment that had been used at Andover Junction railway station for lifting and loading goods onto trains. It had been reported stolen about three weeks earlier. The four of us sat down together in the house, with Bill doing most of the talking, and we soon realised that the first youth who I had interviewed appeared to have been economical with the truth. We were soon hearing about other offences and the fact that a third teenager was involved.

One of our colleagues brought the station van to the house, and we loaded it with a large amount of items from the garden. Once we had transported all the stolen property to the police station, Bill showed me how each item had to be listed. It took us a long time to record everything. Once that was done, we went looking for Suspect Number Three, a 15-year-old youth. At his home, we found a bicycle that he had stolen, and he readily admitted being involved in other thefts with one or both of his accomplices.

After this, Bill Scorey and I discussed what our next step was. The three youths had made written statements admitting a large number of thefts. However, we would need to try and identify all the stolen property that we had recovered, although we soon realised that many items would never be identified. It was necessary to interview Suspect Number One again. When we sat down with the teenager and his parents, he admitted a number of other thefts that he had not told me about the first time. We discovered the reason they had stolen the loading equipment from the railway station. The three boys had a plan to build a boat, and they'd thought that they could adapt it and use it like an outboard motor.

Bill Scorey and I sat down in the CID office and reviewed all the evidence that we had gathered. At this point, I started to realise how time consuming crime enquiries are, bearing in mind that this case was fairly straightforward and the youths involved were admitting everything. It was easy to see how CID officers found themselves regularly working long hours investigating crime.

The case was listed for Andover Juvenile Court, and we needed to complete the paperwork. Bill asked me to complete a witness statement, and this is where my inexperience showed. My statement was written in the style of a police report and must have looked very strange to Bill.

'Who wrote this?' he asked with a grin. 'Enid Blyton gave you a hand with it, did she?'

He laughed and then read through my statement, taking out all the hearsay and other bits and pieces that were not needed. Eventually I managed to complete a statement that looked quite professional. Bill showed me how to put the prosecution file together with details of the offences and an application for summonses. He also told me about the procedure at juvenile court.

At Andover Juvenile Court, the three teenagers pleaded guilty to the theft of the equipment at the railway station and guilty to stealing a large number of bicycles. They were all fined. At the end of the proceedings, I was taken aback when the sergeant on duty addressed the bench, stating that I was a probationer who had showed great initiative and diligence in investigating these offences and he wished to bring this to the attention of the court.

The chairman of the bench then told me that the court wished to give me a commendation for my work on the case. Unknown to me, DS Jacob sent a report to the chief constable with details of the case and highlighted the fact that the court had given me a commendation. A week later, Bill Scorey handed me the file with a big grin on his face. By this time it had a minute attached to it signed by the chief constable, asking that his congratulations be passed on to me.

6

In October 1964, there was a general election that resulted in a narrow victory for the Labour Party and its leader, Harold Wilson. The following year, Edward Heath would become leader of the Conservative Party and he and Wilson were destined to dominate the political life of the country for the next decade or so.

That same month, Ringshaw-Roper appeared at Andover Magistrates' Court and was sentenced for theft, fraud and driving whilst disqualified. He received a probation order for the first two charges and was fined one pound for driving whilst disqualified. Bill Scorey came up with a good one-liner when he commented on the result, but it was not suitable for print.

Following my time with the CID, I started my attachment with the Traffic Division unit at Andover. All traffic officers were trained as advanced drivers. Their patrol cars were large and powerful, and it felt quite luxurious sitting in the front passenger seats. Of course we were called to a number of traffic accidents, and I dealt with some of them.

Traffic Division, often referred to by its initials 'TD' has the role of enforcing road traffic law, dealing with accidents, and ensuring the free movement of traffic on the roads. It has its own specialist units, such as traffic accident investigators, specialist vehicle examiners and motorway patrol officers. At that time, the official policy regarding the reporting of traffic accidents in Hampshire was simple and straightforward; it was based around the idea that if there was a traffic accident it followed that someone was at fault. The officer dealing with the accident was expected to investigate it and submit a file for dangerous or careless driving. What we referred to as a 'without due care', or WDC, involved less paperwork than a crime case, but the same principles applied in terms of finding out what happened, obtaining witness statements, and putting a prosecution file together.

If there were two or more officers at the scene, they needed to come to a quick agreement as to who was actually dealing with an accident. One officer would take responsibility for the investigation and deal with the paperwork. In accident cases, the first task was completing the accident report-books which included several pages of accident statistics. After that, a diagram of the accident scene had to be completed, witness statements obtained, and a file submitted.

We tend to think about motorists being prosecuted for traffic offences, but we don't always think of cyclists. The law also holds cyclists responsible for their actions on the roads. One day we received a call to an accident on the A343 outside the Army Air Corps centre at Middle Wallop. One of the army sergeants stationed there had gone on a cycling holiday for a few days, and as he was returning to the base, he turned right across the path of a car coming in the other direction. The driver of the car slammed on his brakes, skidded, hit the grass bank at the side of the road, and turned over. Luckily, nobody was seriously injured.

The veteran TD officer with me was quick to 'volunteer' me to deal with this one. It was the only case of riding a bicycle without due care and attention that I dealt with in all my time as a police officer. The sergeant went to court and was fined.

There were two occasions on night duty when we rode 'shotgun' on mail trains moving across the county. The Post Office operated mobile sorting offices on mail trains that criss-crossed the UK, in what appeared a highly efficient system. While the train was on the move, Post Office staff would be busy sorting out the mail. However, these trains also carried large amounts of cash across the country, and the weakness of the system became blindingly obvious in 1963 when the Great Train Robbery took place in Buckinghamshire.

The money stolen totalled about £2.5 million, which in 1963 was a huge sum. There had never been a robbery on that scale in this country, and it seemed strange that nobody in authority had had enough foresight or imagination to think that mail trains might become targets for criminals. As far as I am aware, these trains had no guards, armed or otherwise, no alarm systems, and no radio communications.

Operation Primrose was set up to counter any future attacks on mail trains. Following the robbery, mail trains were equipped with radios that were linked into police communications systems across the UK. Primrose involved two or more patrol cars driving at very high speed across the county on roads that ran parallel with the railways used by the mail trains. In 1964, Traffic Division had the only cars in Hampshire fast enough to keep pace with these trains, and they would have to provide the initial response to any potential attack.

Articles about the Great Train Robbery in the British press came with all sorts of theories and were sometimes tinged with an element of snobbery. The general tone was this: 'The people involved are working-class criminals from London. They would not have the brains to plan it, so therefore there must have been a criminal mastermind, maybe an ex-army officer, behind it.'

They soon came up with a name for this criminal mastermind: Otto Skorzeny, a German who had been a colonel in the SS. During the Second World War, a coup in Italy had overthrown the Italian Fascist leader Benito Mussolini. He had been placed under arrest by the Italian provisional government and taken to a remote hotel in the mountains, guarded by a small contingent of police.

Hitler wanted to help his old ally, and Otto Skorzeny was put in charge of a rescue mission. The SS commando unit used light aircraft to make a daring landing in the mountains, and they rescued Mussolini. At the end of the war, Skorzeny fled to Spain, and it appeared that he was living there quietly during the sixties. As far as I know, there was absolutely no evidence to support these 'mastermind' stories – but they probably helped to sell more newspapers.

After my time with Traffic Division, I started my country-beat attachment at Middle Wallop with Con Harper, the PC who had that beat. I was expected to live and work on the beat, and Con found accommodation for me in a bungalow on a smallholding near his police house. I knew that

Maureen would be lonely if she were on her own in Andover, so I asked the people at the bungalow if she could stay there with me. They had no problem with this, although Maureen and I soon found that there are disadvantages to sharing a single bed.

The family where we stayed consisted of a farmer, his wife, and her mother, who was French. The Frenchwoman told me her sad memories of the First World War. She was one of eight children, but she was the only girl, and all of her seven brothers were killed serving in the French Army. We all knew there had been terrible loss of life in that war, but hearing a personal account like that made it even more tragic.

Con Harper's beat stretched over a large chunk of countryside along the county boundary with Wiltshire and took in several small villages and hamlets. It covered what were called 'The Wallops', the three villages of Nether Wallop, Over Wallop, and Middle Wallop. I worked with Con for six weeks, and we travelled all over his beat on our bikes. He explained the various enquiries that he was doing and introduced me to many of his 'parishioners', as he called them.

Con Harper's most important 'village' in terms of population would have been the Army Air Corps at Middle Wallop. Enquiries would take us there at least once a week. Country-beat officers need to be confident and experienced, as they work on their own with surprisingly little supervision or assistance. We investigated crimes that occurred on the beat and made all sorts of routine enquiries such as taking witness statements or applications for firearms certificates.

In rural areas, many people hold certificates for firearms or shotguns. A few years before my arrival at Middle Wallop, it had been very easy to obtain a shotgun certificate; you just walked into a post office and bought one over the counter. However, new legislation had tightened everything up, and Con sat down with me and explained how the firearms and shotgun licensing systems worked.

Maureen found work at a village shop in Nether Wallop and was soon busy helping the shopkeeper sorting out orders for Christmas.

There was a large turkey farm on Con Harper's patch. Shortly before Christmas the previous year, the farm buildings had been broken into and a large number of turkeys had been stolen. Con told me that this had also occurred the year before that, and he wanted to prevent it happening a third time. At about eight o'clock one night, we cycled to the turkey farm and hid our bikes nearby.

It was an isolated place, and Con found a spot where we could see anyone approaching. I soon realised how cold it was; this was good experience in itself. As they say in Canada, there is no such thing as bad weather, just bad clothing.

We carried out the observation until midnight, when we went home. It did not take long for me to understand the problems of preventing crime in rural areas. The most obvious factor was the lack of a police presence, especially at night. Country-beat men did not normally work later than midnight, and the only night-duty cover on the subdivision would be the three or four PCs at Andover. Naturally, our local criminals took full advantage of this. The bad news was that the turkey thieves struck again that Christmas, stealing many birds.

One day Con Harper received a call to a burglary at a house in Middle Wallop. We found a witness who had seen someone near the house around the time we were interested in. Even better, the witness said that he had recognised the man and gave us a name.

It gave me the opportunity of notching up another burglary arrest, so I asked Con to let me deal with it. He agreed but said that he intended to keep a close watch on everything and make sure that the suspect did not slip through our fingers. Next day, we found out that he was living in Winchester, so we went there and arrested him.

When the arrested man arrived at Andover, DS Jacob asked Bill Scorey to keep an eye on everything. Bill was very good. He acted as an advisor and did not try to take over the case. Luckily, it was all fairly straightforward. Bill and I interviewed the suspect, who admitted that he had committed the burglary. Soon there was another signed confession in my hands, and he was charged with the offence.

Then Bill Scorey pointed out that our magistrates' court was not due to sit for another two days, and the defendant was not suitable for bail. One of the local JPs owned a shop in the centre of Andover that sold beds, and Bill phoned him to say that we had charged someone with housebreaking and we would like to apply for a remand in custody. It all seemed quite strange. We walked to the shop with the defendant and presented him to the magistrate. The four of us stood in a group, surrounded by beds, where

Bill made a formal application that the defendant be remanded in custody until the next sitting of the court. The application was granted, and we walked back to the police station with the prisoner.

When I'd completed my time at Middle Wallop, Maureen and I returned to the house in Junction Road. Maureen had always been a little nervous in the house when she was there on her own, and her parents gave us their dog, Shandy, who quickly proved to be an efficient guard dog. She was an intelligent, friendly animal; her mother had been a well-known show-business dog. We later found out that Shandy had been mistreated as a puppy by members of the family she was with before my in-laws got her.

Events that occurred during our time in Junction Road made Maureen feel even more nervous living there. Once when I was working on late turn at Andover, Maureen received an obscene phone call. This was upsetting enough, but within a few days there was a second incident that was more dramatic.

We were sitting together in the lounge one evening when I heard Shandy suddenly start barking, so I decided to find out what was happening. A corridor ran from the lounge to the kitchen and breakfast room, and on the right was a door to the dining room, which Shandy was trying to get through, barking frantically.

After I opened the door, it was obvious that the French windows leading to the garden had been forced open. I took a quick look at the dining room and garden to see if there was any sign of anybody, but it appeared that the suspect or suspects had fled. After that, I picked up the phone quickly and rang the station.

Five minutes later, Ken Price and Rebel arrived at the house. The dog picked up a scent straight away, and Ken and Rebel disappeared into the darkness. Ken returned to the house about fifteen minutes later and told me that they had followed the scent for about 200 metres and then the trail had suddenly gone cold. His theory was that the intruder must have had a vehicle parked there.

It was a worrying experience. Maureen had never enjoyed living in Andover and, not surprisingly, was feeling increasingly nervous in the house. I spoke to Mac about the situation, and he said that the best thing that I could do was to move. He helped me to draft a report.

At that time, probationers were usually transferred to another division or station after their first twelve months, so it was quite likely that I would be moved anyway. My report requested a transfer to another station and included an application for police accommodation.

My request was dealt with sympathetically and quickly. It turned out that a police flat in Winchester was due to become available in a couple of weeks' time so we went to look at it. The officer living there was Peter Churchward, who was about the same age as me and was about to be transferred from Winchester to Alresford, a section station a few miles from Winchester.

What we found was a pleasant, modern flat in a fairly new block of flats owned by Winchester City Council. It consisted of a large lounge/dining room, a small kitchen, two bedrooms, and a bathroom. It was well decorated, and there was a balcony from the lounge that gave a panoramic view, looking downhill over the centre of Winchester.

We both knew and liked Winchester. Until about four years before, my grandparents had been living in the nearby village of Headbourne Worthy. My father-in-law wanted to help us move, and he hired a van to transport our furniture that was in storage. The Churchwards moved out of the flat, and a couple of days later we moved in.

7

In January 1965, the death of Sir Winston Churchill was announced. He was the outstanding British leader and statesman of the 20th century and his state funeral was a large public event. Churchill's passing was seen by many as the end of an era.

What sort of country was Britain in 1965? There was a great deal of truth in the famous quote by an American secretary of state, Dean Acheson: 'Britain has lost an empire but has not yet found a role.'

Many British politicians felt that the future of the country lay with Europe. However, most people did not see themselves as Europeans, and the French had vetoed our application to join the Common Market. Britain had close cultural and trading links with Commonwealth countries such as Canada, Australia, and New Zealand. It was natural that the loyalties of British people would be with the people of those countries, who were seen as kith and kin. Over a period of about ten years, there had been a steady improvement in the standard of living, and the early sixties were quite different in many ways from the early fifties. There were the first signs of what would be called the Consumer Society, and one obvious difference was the huge increase in traffic on the roads. In 1950 there were only about 2.3 million cars and vans in Britain, but by the early sixties there were over three times that number, and by 1970 there were 12 million. At the same time, life in Britain in the early sixties would have been seen by most people as a little grey. What would become known as the swinging sixties had not arrived.

Anyone able to peer back into the early sixties would have seen a very orderly and deferential society. British people were inclined to regard the social class in which they were born as being the class in which they should remain, and there was a tendency to show deference to those who came from a higher echelon of society. During this time, approximately 95 per cent of people over the age of 40 were married, and the divorce rate was fairly low.

As a general rule, British society was quite good at policing itself, and the crime rate was low. The riots involving the Mods and Rockers in 1964 were mild by the standards of later years. An important factor was that few of the youths involved would have been carrying lethal weapons. People convicted of murder faced the death penalty, and this provided a strong deterrent to violence and carrying weapons. This was a time when Home Office figures put the annual total of murders in England and Wales at about sixty.

Although I was never a supporter of capital punishment, it now seems that the death penalty had a deterrent effect. Very few criminals carried firearms, knives, or other lethal weapons. The last executions occurred in August 1964, and after that the death penalty was suspended for a period of five years. At the end of this period, the death penalty for murder was abolished. In 1998 the death penalty was abolished for the two remaining capital offences, piracy with violence and treason.

Major social changes were coming, but the big problem facing the country was the economy. British people congratulated themselves on what they had done in the war and the important role that Britain had played in the defeat of Nazi Germany. By 1945, most of Germany's cities and factories had been destroyed by British and American bombing, and the Germans were forced to start again from nothing. Faced with a total collapse of their society, they planned a new democratic political system and started rebuilding their industries.

The situation in Britain was quite different from that in Germany. Many of our political leaders seemed to believe that we were still an important world power, and large sums were spent on the armed forces. While other countries, such as Germany and Japan, were starting afresh and investing their money in their industries, this was not the case in the UK. British people returned from the war and went back to their factories, often old-fashioned ones, assuming that there would always be people around the world who would continue to buy our goods.

By the sixties it was clear that many British manufacturers were facing increasing difficulties and struggling to compete effectively with foreign competitors. The Germans and Japanese were proving to be highly organised and were soon producing high-quality goods. Britain could no longer guarantee that countries that had been part of our old Empire would continue to supply us with cheap raw materials and buy the goods that we made in our factories.

Winchester is famous for its cathedral, which even had a pop song written about it during the 1960s. Another famous landmark is the statue of King Alfred the Great, which stands a short distance from the Guildhall. The history of Winchester is closely linked to the story of this famous Anglo-Saxon king, once described by Winston Churchill as the most important Englishman in England's history.

Born in AD 849, Alfred became the outstanding figure of the Anglo Saxon era. As king of the West Saxons, he defended his country against Viking attempts at conquest. Alfred was reputed to be an educated and merciful ruler who encouraged education, improved the quality of his people's lives, and built up a strong army and navy capable of defending his country against foreign aggression.

The Vikings had been raiding the Anglo Saxon kingdoms for many years, but in AD 865 they launched a full-scale invasion, and the young prince Alfred soon found himself on the run in his own country. Later, as the newly crowned King of Wessex, this 21-year-old must have wondered whether it would ever be possible to defeat the Vikings. But he soon organised an army of 27,000 men as 'a rapid reaction force'. At the same time, he embarked on an ambitious building programme, setting up a network of well-defended settlements across the south of England.

The settlements were called 'burhs'; in later years they would be called 'boroughs'. The largest and most heavily defended burh was Winchester, Alfred's capital. Each burh was no more than about 19 miles from another burh. This meant that if one of them came under attack, the Anglo Saxon forces could reach it within one day.

Eventually Alfred defeated the Vikings, and by the time of his death he had become the dominant ruler in England. He was the first king to use the title 'King of the Anglo-Saxons' and the only one to be referred to as 'the Great'.

Apart from everything else that he did, Alfred was a great lawmaker. His royal palace at Winchester would have been a court, using the legal meaning of the word. He reviewed all the existing judgments that had been passed down from previous rulers and decided which ones he approved of and which ones he did not. He then produced a written law code called a 'domboc', consisting of 120 chapters. This was the first time that there had been a large definitive body of Anglo-Saxon law.

King Alfred insisted on acting as a court of appeal, reviewing the legal decisions made by his nobles and judges, and he would make rulings as to whether these judgments had been just or unjust. He also decreed that his judges had to be able to read and write, and failure to comply with this rule about literacy would lead to loss of office.

Alfred's influence on the development of a legal system in England was far reaching. The process would take hundreds of years, but it would eventually be called English Law. This system was destined to travel across the world and become the foundation stone for the laws of many countries, including the United States and the nations of the British Commonwealth.

Some years before my arrival there, the City of Winchester had its own police force. The first fully constituted police force in Hampshire was the Winchester City Police, founded in 1832. Seven years' later, the Hampshire County Constabulary was established. One reminder of the old Winchester force was the sight of the traditional 'Tardis' police boxes that could be seen all over the city.

Winchester is the county town of Hampshire and the home of the county council. The High Street is the central point for business and shopping, extending from the Broadway uphill to the Westgate, which is one of the few remnants of the old city walls.

There were three operational shift teams within the Winchester City subdivision, and I was assigned to one of them. We worked in what was called the Broadway police station, on the ground floor of the Guildhall. There were two sergeants and seven or eight constables to each team. In addition to the sergeants on the teams, there were several long serving sergeants who were referred to as station sergeants. They had responsibility for everything that happened in the police stations, and their most important job was to deal with charges. When an arrest was made, the station officer had to decide whether the evidence was strong enough to support a charge.

Many years later, the Police and Criminal Evidence Act created a specific job title with legal responsibilities attached to it, and after that these sergeants would be called custody officers. As this title did not exist before that time, I have referred to these sergeants as station sergeants or station officers. The station sergeant was often assisted by a PC who dealt with members of the public at the front counter.

One of the officers on my shift was Gil French, who was a probationer like me. Gil and his wife were neighbours of ours in the next block of flats. The two of us would often be seen cycling to work or coming back on our bikes together to Winnall at the end of a tour of duty. It turned out that Gerry Marsh, my old wrestling adversary at Sandgate, worked in the same team as Gil and me, but Mick Lyons worked on another team.

The standard shift system was based on a simple three-week rota consisting of one week of night duty, followed by late turn, followed by early turn. Layered on the top of this, each PC on the team had an individual weekly leave roster that included a long weekend every four weeks. When we were posted to a foot beat, we operated the time-honoured system of making a point every fifty minutes.

Andover officers were used to patrolling in vehicles, because the subdivision was so large. Winchester police station was the base for two subdivisions: the city subdivision and the rural subdivision. In the city subdivision the traditional foot beat was very much part of a policeman's life, especially for probationers like me. We had the historic problems of communication, but we knew that some police forces were experimenting with radios being issued to officers on foot patrol, and we learned that a pilot scheme for radios was being planned for Winchester.

The centre of Winchester was divided into two beats, with the High Street in the middle acting as a dividing line. These two beats contained all the important commercial properties, and when it came to postings they were given priority over the outer beats. There was also a High Street patrol that was covered between 8 a.m. and midnight. As always, manpower was the crucial issue, and often we only had enough officers to cover the two central beats. The outer beats were usually doubled up, which involved a

PC covering two beats by bicycle – so we all needed bikes. My purchase of a bike for patrolling entitled me to a monthly cycle allowance.

The two sergeants who supervised our team were John Snelgrove and Geoff King, both of whom had spent time in the armed forces. John Snelgrove had a fairly relaxed style, but Sergeant King imposed a strict military-style discipline on all the PCs that he supervised. He had served in Army Special Forces during the Second World War and he looked like a tough character. We all soon learned that it was not a good idea to do anything that was not 100 per cent correct when he was on duty. A frequent question asked by sergeants was, 'Have you checked your properties?' When people went away on holiday, they would notify the station and an entry would be made in the Unoccupied Property Book. Each beat always had a list of houses that were unoccupied, and we had to check them during our patrols.

On night duty, the officers on the two central beats were expected to check all the shops and any other commercial premises to make sure that they were secure. In the 1960s this was more important than now, because many shops and businesses did not have burglar alarm systems. Those winter night beats could be chilly! Even with a pullover, a scarf, and a heavy woollen overcoat, known as a 'British warm', you could still feel the cold.

Because Winchester was the administrative centre of Hampshire, it was a very busy place during the daytime, but after about six in the evening it was usually fairly quiet. There were a large number of pubs, but they closed at 10.30 p.m. However, as everywhere else, we spent a great deal of our time with drink-related offences for the first couple of hours of night duty.

There were a number of military bases around Winchester and barracks close to the centre of the city, the home of the Royal Green Jackets Regiment. Fights did occur between soldiers and some of the locals, but this was a rare occurrence. Overall there was little violence, and Winchester was a pleasant place to live and work in.

In January 1965, I spent three days on a Diseases of Animals Course, and this was followed by my probationer attachment to the Divisional CID office at Winchester. It turned out to be an interesting time for me, as there was a murder investigation going on. A taxi driver had been murdered near Eastleigh, a town between Southampton and Winchester. A murder squad had been set up, and most of the CID officers at Winchester were assigned to it.

The most experienced PC on our shift was Jimmy James, who had been a petty officer in the Royal Navy. As the CID office was short of staff, Jimmy had been brought in to help provide cover for a few weeks. He seemed to be a natural detective, being very shrewd and streetwise; he was someone who always gave me good advice. It turned out that we worked together most of the time.

A man who was well known in the Southampton underworld fell under suspicion for the Eastleigh murder, and he was arrested and brought to Winchester. He was a smartly dressed man in his late twenties. I was present when he was being questioned about his movements over the past few days.

He protested his innocence and looked very worried. The taxi driver had been killed for his money, and this was therefore a capital crime. In plain language, a person convicted of this murder would be hanged. The thought that he might end up facing the hangman's noose must have helped him focus his mind. He provided an alibi, which was checked and found to be true.

Jimmy James explained to me how quite a few unrelated crimes were always solved during a large murder investigation such as the Eastleigh enquiry. Criminals being questioned about a homicide would often confess to offences that they had committed elsewhere in order to distance themselves from the scene of the murder.

It would take several years for the Eastleigh murder to be solved, and this happened when a fingerprint was identified following the arrest of a man for burglary in another part of Hampshire.

One evening in February, I was on a foot beat and returned to the police station at about eight o'clock to complete some paperwork. Fred, the switchboard operator, always worked late turn, and there was some friendly banter between the assistant station officer, Fred, and me. Nobody knew how old Fred was, but I would have guessed that he was about one hundred and twenty or thereabouts. From my age, he just looked ancient. He had a garrulous sense of humour, and he enjoyed a joke especially if it was at the expense of probationers like me. We talked a bit about what had happened the previous day.

At 6 a.m. the night duty PCs would gather at the station, waiting to be booked off by their sergeant. That morning, there was a problem. One of them was missing. This was something that was always taken seriously and even more so if it was the night-duty team. Anything could have happened to the missing officer. He could have been taken ill and collapsed. He could have been attacked by a burglar and be lying somewhere seriously injured.

The sergeant in charge of the night duty organised a search. This would need to take in the missing PC's beat, adjoining areas, and all the streets between his beat and the station. Every available officer from the night duty and early turn became involved. The people of Winchester had probably never seen so many police on the streets before.

All of us had felt tired on night duty at some time or another. I know it had taken me quite a long time to become used to working at night. There were several times when I'd felt 'shattered' and struggled to keep going. It was much worse if things were quiet. There would be a great temptation to sit down somewhere, and this could lead to trouble. It was a question of the spirit being willing but the body being decidedly weak. So, when an officer was missing, it was fairly safe to give odds of 100 to 1 that it was a 'falling asleep job'. These were sensible odds, but no good skipper would ever make that assumption.

Within twenty minutes or so of the search getting underway, the missing PC walked into the station, looking sheepish. What a surprise! His fellow PCs probably felt some sympathy for him, knowing that he would have to face his sergeant, an ex-military man who would be furious about what had happened. There was some talk that the officer had come up with quite a good story to try and cover his tracks. That may have been, but we guessed that the other PCs on the shift would not allow him to forget about it very quickly.

The conversation about the missing PC eventually petered out. Having completed my paperwork, I told the other two that I would be returning to my beat, but Fred was quick to jump in.

'Well, you won't catch many burglars loafing around the police station,' he said.

'Don't worry,' I replied boldly. 'I shall nip out and arrest one for you, if you want.'

'That will be the day,' said Fred, shaking his head and looking up at the ceiling.

Four or five minutes' walking brought me to St Georges Road, a road that ran parallel with the High Street. I stood for a few moments looking at the old Georgian building that housed our local newspaper office, and then I walked into the car park at the back.

One corner of the car park gave access to an alleyway that ran along the back of a parade of shops. I had to work my way through a jumble of rubbish bins and discarded cardboard boxes of all shapes and sizes. My plan was not to use my torch as I moved forward, so as not to give advance notice of my approach. At the same time, it was the sort of place that a health-and-safety officer would have had nightmares about. It was not really possible to see where I was going, and it was only a matter of time before I fell over something or into something. However, I did my best to move forward quietly.

There was a slight sound somewhere ahead of me, and it made me stop suddenly. At night, there are all sorts of things that make you jump. Darkness can conjure up all sorts of strange sights, and innocent shapes and shadows can appear to be sinister and threatening. I took a few steps forward, and my torch picked up the face of a man in the darkness. He was hiding in an alcove, 2 or 3 metres from me, partially covered by a large cardboard box. It was not easy to see him. The man was dressed in dark-coloured clothes, black or dark blue. He was holding a torch in his right hand and using his left hand to try and cover his face. The beam of my torch picked up the glint of a knife lying on the top of a cardboard box next to him.

Suddenly the man stood up, and my right hand went down onto my truncheon. There are situations in boxing when both fighters spend a lot of time on defensive moves, ducking and diving, weaving and bobbing, but not managing to land any punches. This was a bit similar, as the two of us did some sort of strange dance around each other. My first thought was that he was going to attack me, but it appeared that he had the same concerns about me.

'Don't hit me,' he said in a frightened voice.

'What are you doing here?' I asked.

He said nothing, and the two of us circled one another like gladiators for a few more seconds. Something told me that this might be a good time to grab the knife, so I moved forward quickly, picked it up, and dropped it into my raincoat pocket. It went through my mind that this suspect might not be alone. The beam from my torch revealed a hole in the door at the back of the shop, but there was no sign of anyone else. I took a firm grip on his left arm and told him that he was under arrest. Something made me think about the Judges' Rules, and at that point I babbled out a caution, but he said, 'There is no need to grab hold of me. I won't give you no trouble.'

It took me a few minutes to walk him back to the station, and as we made our way there, I asked him for his name and address. He told me that his name was William Edwards and he lived in Eastleigh. My main concern at that point was that he might suddenly break loose and run for it, but he made no attempt to escape. At the station I spoke to Sergeant Hunter, the station sergeant, showed him the knife, and gave him a brief account of the arrest. The sergeant told me to search Edwards and put him in a cell.

At this point, it seemed to me that if we could not prove a burglary, we could charge him with Possession of Housebreaking Implements by Night. The offence, then known as HBI by Night for short, was a useful piece of preventative legislation and unusual under English Law, because the legal onus was on defendants to prove that they were in possession of the implements for a lawful purpose.

Sergeant Hunter quickly wrote up the custody record for Edwards and told me that he wanted to take a look at the shop. As we walked there, I realised that I did not even know the name of the business. We checked the front of the shop, Peter Swift, Shoe Repairs, and observed that it had not been touched. We then went around to the back and used our torches to see what the situation was there. Sergeant Hunter took a look at the hole in the back door.

There was a window near the door, and this gave access to a toilet inside the shop. Looking closely, we could see a large number of putty fragments scattered all around, and we realised that Edwards had been using the knife to scrape away the putty from the window pane. It seemed that his intention had been to remove the window pane intact. If this had been successful, he would have avoided smashing the glass and making a noise.

We returned to the station, and Edwards agreed to make a written statement. He told me that he wanted to confess to a break-in at another business in Winchester. By this time, I had become quite good at recording written confessions. In his statement, Edwards told me what he had done and why he had done it. He said that he had run out of money and could not support his wife and two children.

Edwards went to court and pleaded guilty to the two charges. He was sent to prison for six months. As for Fred the switchboard operator, all I can say is that he continually made comments about probationers, but I noticed that he generally left me alone after that.

Although burglary was always treated as a serious offence by the courts, there were different cultural attitudes to some other offences, such as causing death by dangerous driving and driving whilst unfit. However, some fundamental changes were on their way. The Road Safety Act, 1967 was the law that would soon introduce the breathalyser to the motoring public. Before 1967, the concept of driving when you had too much to drink did not exist in law, and it was necessary to prove that a driver was unfit to drive through drink or drugs. The defendant had the right to elect trial by jury, and juries tended to feel sympathy for the defendants in these cases. A high proportion of drink-and-drive prosecutions resulted in verdicts of not guilty.

Many people regarded this situation as a good thing. They would probably have said that the civil liberties of individuals (the motorists) were being protected by the law against the tyrannical state (the police). But the other side of the coin was that other road users were being killed and seriously injured in great numbers, and therefore their civil rights and those of their families were being violated much more dramatically than those of drinking drivers.

One of my colleagues at Winchester arrested a man for driving whilst unfit in what was a fairly typical case of its time. The arrested driver was a retired army officer who had been to a regimental reunion in Jersey for the weekend. He openly admitted that he had been drinking all day on the Saturday, and then on Sunday morning he flew to Southampton airport, where he picked up his car. He later told the arresting officer that he had been drinking again on Sunday and had nothing to eat all day. He then started driving back to his home in London.

Somewhere to the north of Winchester he decided to stop at a petrol station. When he paid for his petrol, he was unsteady on his feet and his speech was slurred. The person at the petrol station was so concerned that he dialled 999 and gave police details of the man's car. Two of the officers on my team spotted his car and followed him for about 3 miles along the main road towards London. The car was veering from side to side, and at one point it went off the road and onto the grass verge. The same thing happened again two or three minutes later, shortly before they managed to arrest him.

I watched the procedure at the police station. A doctor was called. He carried out his tests and stated that the arrested man was unfit to drive a motor vehicle. I noticed that the man's speech was slurred and he was unsteady on his feet to such an extent that he had difficulty standing without assistance. He later pleaded not guilty and elected to go for trial at the crown court. The jury deliberated for about fifteen minutes before returning a verdict of not guilty. It seemed to me that if it was not possible to obtain a conviction in a case like that, there needed to be changes to the system.

8

As mentioned earlier, at the time of my posting to Andover, Mick Lyons, my classmate at Sandgate, went to Winchester. In August 1964, on the first day that he was allowed to patrol on his own, he had no idea that he was about to face the most terrifying episode in his life. The High Street in Winchester runs uphill at a steep angle. A lorry driver had stopped his heavily laden vehicle in the upper part of the High Street outside a shop that he wanted to visit.

The brakes had not been set properly, and as soon as the driver left the cab, the lorry started moving downhill. As Mick Lyons started up the High Street, he saw the lorry coming in his direction and spotted a panic-stricken driver running in pursuit of it. All the time, the lorry was gathering speed as it continued downhill towards oncoming traffic. Mick saw what was happening and the obvious danger that this posed to all and sundry.

Mick ran alongside the lorry and then jumped, managing to hang on to the side of the vehicle. He struggled for a few seconds, desperately trying to hold on and get inside the cab of the lorry. He could see other vehicles coming towards him, swerving in all directions to avoid being hit. The lorry struck a wall, cannoned off it, and then hit a car coming up the High Street. This slowed the speed of the lorry enough that Mick was able to climb into the cab and pull on the handbrake. To his horror, he found that the handbrake was not working, and the only thing that he could do was to try and steer the lorry onto the pavement. However, there was also the problem of pedestrians, and Mick was desperate to avoid hitting any of them. He grabbed the steering wheel, but before he could gain full control of the lorry there was a tremendous crash as it ploughed into the front of a tobacconist's shop.

It was not a good day for the tobacconist, the lorry coming to a stop with its cab embedded in his shop. Mick found that he was shaking like a leaf, but everyone else was impressed by the determination and courage that he had shown. Sergeant Snelgrove realised that Mick was suffering from shock and placed him on the sick list for three days. Stella, Mick's girlfriend, worked in the police station, and the sergeant suggested that she should contact his parents on the Isle of Wight and arrange for him to go there for a few days.

Mick later received a Meritorious Service Award diploma from the Royal Society for the Prevention of Accidents and a commendation from the chief constable.

Our shift was on night duty when Gerry Marsh disturbed a burglar at a shop that sold electrical goods. At about three in the morning, Gerry was on foot patrol in the centre of Winchester, on the footway opposite the shop in Jewry Street. There was an alleyway next to the shop, and Gerry noticed that there was a car parked there. He also thought that he had noticed some movement, and he stepped into a doorway to keep an eye on the shop. He heard a slight noise and could see someone moving around behind the car. It had all the signs of a break-in, but Gerry was not sure how many people might be involved. He decided that the best course of action was to put in a call for assistance. There was a police phone close by, at the junction of Jewry Street and the High Street. It was inside a steel box on the wall of a building with a direct line to the switchboard at the police station.

Gerry ran to the police phone, made the call, and within two or three minutes we were all there. We could see that there had been a burglary and noticed a pile of electrical goods next to the car. However, there was no sign of any suspects. The other interesting thing was the pair of men's shoes lying on the ground close to the car. We knew that the suspect or suspects had made off on foot and that they could not be too far away. Somewhere there was a burglar running through the streets of Winchester without shoes on his feet.

We were fairly confident that we would catch the person or persons responsible. Three police cars were soon busy criss-crossing the centre of Winchester. We knew that there would be very few people about at that time of night, and we were looking for someone running barefoot. I thought that it was just a matter of time. We checked every likely hiding place, but it seemed that the person or persons had vanished into thin air. One of our colleagues suggested that he must be a local man, living in the centre of Winchester, or that he had another vehicle parked close by.

It would be two or three weeks before we knew what had happened. The case was assigned to one of the DCs at Winchester, and the car was taken into police custody for forensic examination. It had not been stolen; the previous owner had sold it for cash some weeks earlier. It did not come as a great surprise that the name and address provided by the young man who had bought it were totally fictitious. The SOCO examined the vehicle for fingerprints or other marks, but this revealed nothing.

The DC searched the car and found a few pieces of paper and bits of rubbish, the sorts of things that would probably be lying on the floor in most cars and vans. There was only one thing that was of interest, and that was a receipt for goods which had the name and address of a shop in Romsey.

The CID officer went to the shop in Romsey and took the receipt with him. The shopkeeper was helpful in having some sort of description of the man who had been in his shop. The DC had a stroke of luck when the shopkeeper explained that the receipt was a down payment on goods that the customer had ordered. It seemed that there was a reasonable chance that the person concerned might return to the shop at some point to pick up the goods that he had ordered.

It was agreed that the shopkeeper would phone Romsey police station if that particular customer came back to the shop to collect his goods. A few days later the call came, and this resulted in a man being detained. Police brought him to Winchester and questioned him about the burglary at the shop in Winchester. He admitted the offence and stated that he had removed his shoes so as to make less noise. He told the DC that he had spotted Gerry Marsh and made off. The Wessex Hotel, next door to the cathedral, was then a new hotel. He had sprinted straight to the hotel, walked into reception, and booked a room for the night.

The burglar had a couple of previous convictions and was sent to prison. He had an unusual background for a burglar, as he came from a very wealthy family and had been a pupil at one of the most expensive public schools in the country. One of my colleagues remarked that this proved that Winchester was a very good class of town, where even our burglars had been provided with the best education that money could buy.

One week on night duty we had almost the whole shift available, and the sergeant posted me to cover two of our outside beats. It was important to read the schedule of points and details of unoccupied houses that needed to be checked. After doing that, you could work out how much time you had to do all of this. Turning up a couple of minutes late at a point was not a good idea and really bad news if Sergeant King was there to meet you.

There was a petrol station on one of my beats that stayed open all night. This was quite unusual at that time, and I wondered whether I should call in there and speak to the man who worked there alone. On my second night, I cycled onto the forecourt and had a chat with him and he appeared to be reassured by seeing me. Maybe I would drop by the following night, I thought, but the system of making points did not always allow for such things. While I was making a point at a public phone box, the phone rang. It was a call from the police station, asking me to make an enquiry at an address on one of my beats. Once that was done, I looked at my watch and saw that my next point was in five minutes' time and it would take me at least five minutes to cycle there.

I whizzed off to my next point on my bike, passing the petrol station on my way. After making the point, I had time to check a couple of unoccupied houses nearby. Fifty minutes later, I was making yet another point.

While I was standing there, the phone rang. There had been a robbery on my beat. I asked where it had happened.

'The petrol station, the one that is open all night.'

This could not have been called the crime of the century. However, this was during an era when there were few robberies, especially in Winchester, and two of our CID officers were given the case. Two men had approached the attendant at the petrol station, and one of them had threatened him with a knife. The robbers had spotted me on the main road on my bicycle, and they'd dragged the attendant around to the back of the building, where they could not be seen from the road. They had held a knife close to the victim's face and told him that if he made a noise his throat would be cut.

What happened that night was something that made me think. If I had not been running late, I would probably have cycled into the middle of a robbery. Would they have run away? Would they have attacked me? Whatever happened, it was likely that I might have been taken by surprise. In my view, the weakness of the patrolling system was the business of continually having to move from point to point. However, it might have been the fickle hand of fate or even the system itself that had saved me from death or injury that night.

There was a little gang of six or seven men who formed an alliance of vagrants or semi-vagrants in Winchester. Two of them were arrested for the robbery at the petrol station, and it turned out that the man armed with the knife had been deported from the United States a few years before after serving a sentence for armed robbery.

On early turn, I had to get used to getting washed and dressed at speed and heading down into the centre of Winchester on my bike. I usually shaved the night before. Getting dressed would involve putting on a police shirt and a collar. The reader may ask the question, and I shall answer it. No, the collar was not attached. I would usually wear the shirt for two days and change the collar every day. A police tie is always one that clips on. This is a safety issue, because there have been attempts to strangle officers with their ties.

Gil French must have operated at the same level of speed as I was, because we usually found ourselves cycling down the hill from Winnall together. One morning, as we arrived at the station, one of the PCs from the night-duty shift was coming out. We could see that he was upset about something, as his voice quivered lightly.

'We've got a policeman in the cells,' he said, shaking his head. 'It's one of ours.'

The people on the shift arriving for duty at quarter to six were not normally full of the joys of spring, but on this particular morning there was a distinct shortage of friendly banter. An air of gloom and despondency hung over the station. Harry Fenton was a PC on another shift at Winchester. I did not know him very well, but someone told me that he had transferred to Hampshire from a police force in the north of England two or three years before. The story emerged over the next few days. Fenton had been in debt, and he had broken into a shop not far from the railway station where he had stolen £300 in cash.

Fenton's arrest seemed to hang like a black cloud over the station for some time. A few days later, I spoke to one of the DCs who had been given the job of taking Fenton's fingerprints and completing some of the paperwork that related to the case.

'I hope that I never have to do that again,' he said sadly.

Fenton had been arrested by two CID officers at Winchester, but nobody seemed to know why he had fallen under suspicion. I heard that he had paid off all his debts within twenty-four hours of the burglary; this would have been suspicious to anyone who heard about it. I have no idea what led him to do what he did, but one of my colleagues suggested that he had a gambling problem. I would not describe any of us as being well paid at that time, but I had seen Fenton when he was off duty in Winchester, and he'd always looked like a man who was hard up.

Fenton pleaded guilty and was sent to prison for six months. Two police officers escorted him to police headquarters, where he appeared before the chief constable. As he had been convicted of a criminal offence, he was automatically in breach of the police discipline code.

Sir Douglas Osmond told him that he was a disgrace to the force and that he was being dismissed from the service. He was then driven the short distance to Winchester Prison.

Later that year, Winchester police station became one of the first in Hampshire to be equipped with personal radios. In terms of police communications, this was a crucial new development. PCs on the streets could now be contacted by their stations when necessary. Equally important was the fact that they could make contact and call for assistance where necessary. The traditional system with officers on beats making points had suddenly become history.

The first personal radios were quite heavy and cumbersome. A battery was attached to the base of the radio, it was clipped onto the officer's belt, and the mouthpiece was attached to the tunic. It was important that the batteries were put on charge at the end of each shift and tested to ensure that they had enough power to last for at least eight hours.

Within a few days of receiving the radios, we had an incident on night duty that showed how useful they were. One of my colleagues, patrolling the centre of Winchester, heard the sound of breaking glass, and it turned out that one of our local yobs had smashed a shop window.

The PC saw someone running off and gave chase, but the young man was moving fast, changing direction with left turns and right turns, and running that bit faster than his pursuer. The PC chasing on foot gave a very good running commentary for some distance, but then he lost the suspect. However, within a matter of seconds, the chase was taken up by another officer on foot, and we eventually caught him. Later, when he was questioned, the suspect laughingly complained that whenever he turned a corner and thought that he had shaken us off he would spot a police car or a policeman in front of him.

Most of the older policemen had military experience, some of them from the Second World War. There were other men who had served in paramilitary police forces in various parts of the world, dealing with rebellions, unrest, and everything else that had afflicted the Empire in its last years. As a general rule, those officers had a hard-nosed attitude to dealing with people who caused problems on the streets. People who I would describe as the hooligan element tended to treat that generation of older PCs with a fair amount of respect, because they knew that they might live to regret it if they did not. In any town or city the size of Winchester, the policeman was likely to come across them again.

The attitude of police was that it was of great importance to control the streets. Winchester City Magistrates' Court did not tolerate bad behaviour, and many people who caused problems on the streets received prison sentences or heavy fines. Some people were sent to prison for doing things that most people might think fairly minor. For example, it was not a good thing to shout abuse or insult a police officer in Winchester.

One of my colleagues was on duty in the High Street one night when he saw a young man walking towards him eating fish and chips from a newspaper. As he passed the policeman, he finished eating and dropped the greasy pile of remains almost on top of the PC's boots. The litter lout must have received a nasty shock when the greasy paper was picked up and pushed into his face and a second nasty shock when he was sent to prison for three months for assaulting the officer.

One night I was posted to one of the outside beats that covered a dance hall. There was a note in the parade book about a dance taking place there, organised by some university students. Sergeant King asked me to make a couple of visits. When I reached the dance hall, I parked my bike and peered through one of the windows. A large number of people were there, but everything seemed to be going well. We learned later that a number of young men from the town had gone to the dance with the intention of causing trouble, but at this point all was peaceful.

On my second visit about twenty minutes later it, it had gone 'pear shaped.' I could see that the dance floor was now the scene of a full-scale battle. Men were fighting other men with their fists. Chairs and other projectiles were flying through the air, and women were screaming. I had never seen a disturbance of that size, and for the first couple of seconds I probably stood rooted to the ground, before I used my PR.

'Control from 868. Dance Hall, serious disturbance – large number of people fighting.'

A thought went through my head that it was my job to go in there and sort it out. As I did so, someone I recognised suddenly emerged from the building. He had been a police cadet in Hampshire and was now a PC in the British Transport Police.

'Don't go in there,' he said and then repeated it. There were times when my actions had been impetuous, but even I had worked out that a solo intervention right now might not be a good idea.

Within about five minutes, Sergeant King and five or six PCs had arrived at the scene. If the fight had started again, we would have had some difficulty in controlling the situation. Sergeant King took me with him into the dance hall. The place looked as though a bomb had hit it, but the fighting had stopped. Sergeant King told the organisers that the dance was over and that he wanted everyone to go home. There was no argument from anyone, and they all started to leave. There were several people with injuries, but nobody made any complaint about being assaulted.

We knew that there were not many of us, so we stood together in a line, keeping a close watch on everyone as they walked or limped out.

Some of the people leaving shouted and traded insults with each other as they walked away, but it seemed to me that everyone just wanted to go home. All the students left the area fairly quickly, and the only potential for trouble was a group of about ten young men hanging around outside the dance hall.

They were all from the town, and it looked as if they did not plan on going away. We guessed that these were the people who had started the trouble in the first place. I saw our local traffic division car arrive; that meant we had another couple of officers on the scene. Sergeant King spoke to the youths, who were still showing no sign of wanting to go. 'I suggest that you get yourselves off home,' he said.

Some of them drifted away, and before long there were only four of them left standing in front of us, looking defiant. It could well be that they thought that we were going to turn around and walk away.

'I suggest that you get yourselves off home,' said Sergeant King again.

None of the four seemed to be taking much notice of this advice. Standing next to the sergeant was John Holt, an older officer who had spent time in one of the colonial police forces that had been dotted over the British Empire. He was not a big man, but he had a reputation for being tough. The four remaining troublemakers were whispering among themselves and laughing. As usual, drink had made them bold. I recognised one of the youths, called Norton, the son of a local fireman. Norton said something to one of the others and whatever it was seemed to have been aimed at Holt. They all laughed, and I had the feeling that the incident was not destined to end peacefully.

I noticed that Norton had some paper in his hands, and I watched as he played around with it and rolled it into a small paper ball. Then he threw it at Holt. The paper ball hit Holt on the chest, bounced off, and landed on the ground. I took a deep breath, and my lungs took in the taste of frosty air. Something told me that this situation was not going to end well.

John Holt took a couple of steps forward, and when he moved, the speed of it took everyone by surprise. Norton fell to the ground heavily, and Holt stepped back a couple of paces and looked directly at Norton's friends, who were suddenly not looking as confident as they had been a couple of minutes before. Norton was soon on his feet, and he took a couple of steps towards Holt, both fists in front of him in the stance of a boxer. 'I'll get you for that,' he said.

'Something has to be done about this,' I thought. Moving quickly, I grabbed Norton from behind. He was a powerfully built man, but I was able to prevent him swinging his fists.

'What the bloody hell are you doing?' asked Sergeant King, glaring at me.

Various thoughts were going through my head. First of all, I wanted to prevent Norton from hitting Holt and so bring the incident to a close. Having gone in behind enemy lines to fight the Germans in the Second World War, Sergeant King had probably been in situations that were a bit worse than this.

'Let him go. It's a private matter, nothing to do with you,' said the sergeant with a dismissive shake of his head.

After I released my grip on him, Norton moved forward towards Holt with both fists clenched. John Holt was a man in his forties who looked much smaller than Norton. Norton took a swing at him, but Holt sidestepped and the blow only hit the cold night air.

Norton took another swing, but Holt moved too quickly for him. It all happened very fast. Norton was hit by three or four punches and he collapsed to the ground. There was a lot of blood, and his face looked as though it had disintegrated. Everything went quiet, and nobody spoke for a few seconds. Then Sergeant King said a few words to Norton's friends.

'Your friend has had a lot to drink. As you can see, he has fallen over. He probably needs a trip to casualty. You had better take him with you.'

Norton's three friends lifted him off the ground, and the four disappeared into the night. The incident at the dance hall was over. It had ended with a form of Wild West justice being meted out. This had been the way that police sorted out things like that in the 1930s, but the style of policing had changed quite a lot since then. For several days after that, my concern was that there was probably a serious complaint winging its way to Winchester police station, one that would involve me. But nothing more was heard from anyone involved in the fight, and nobody reported any injuries. The paperwork consisted of a brief entry in the Occurrence Book which mentioned a disturbance at the dance hall.

Norton seemed to be unlucky. Some weeks later, when I was on night duty again, a call was received about a disturbance at the entrance to Peninsula Barracks in Winchester. Norton and his friends had all been drinking heavily and were standing in a group a short distance from the guard house. The corporal in charge of the guard heard screams and could see Norton and another youth apparently attacking another man who was lying on the ground. He was the one doing the screaming. It was just horseplay, but the corporal did not know that, and he ordered his men into action. The soldiers sallied forth clutching their pickaxe handles, and Norton and his friend found themselves lying on the ground after receiving blows from those pickaxe handles.

It happened on my beat. The actual injuries were minor, but Norton made a complaint against the soldiers. After I spoke to the corporal and the soldiers involved, I put it down as a common assault. My opinion was that the corporal had genuinely believed that a serious assault was taking place and had used his powers under Common Law to protect life and prevent a breach of the peace.

In cases of common assault, police did not normally take any action apart from reporting it. The people involved would be advised to apply for a summons at the local magistrates' court.

There were different methods of reporting incidents. First of all, there was the Occurrence Book, normally referred to as the OB. A brief entry was made when certain matters came to the attention of police: sudden deaths, landlord/tenant disputes, domestic disputes, common assaults, industrial accidents, and various other incidents. It seemed odd to me that complaints of indecent exposure were also recorded there. There was no power of arrest for these except with a warrant, and officers dealing with these cases would obtain a description of the man concerned and apply for a descriptive warrant.

The Police Act 1964 contained legislation relating to complaints against police officers. Every complaint would have to be investigated by a senior officer, and the Act laid down the required procedures. However, there was no definition of 'complaint' in the Act, and this led to a few strange events. One complaint about a PC in Hampshire came from one of his neighbours – who alleged that the officer's garden was untidy. This was serious stuff!

This was before the days of 'political correctness.' At that time, a complaint made against a police officer by someone from the local hooligan element would probably never see the light of day. One evening, a short time before 5th November, I noticed a group of teenagers who were throwing fireworks at each other in the street. One of them appeared to be the ringleader, but as I walked towards him he ran away. I had a chat to the others and gave them some suitable advice about fireworks.

The teenager who had run away from me turned up at the police station about twenty minutes later. He told the sergeant on duty that he wished to make a complaint about me and gave the sergeant my number, 868. The sergeant asked him what he wanted to complain about, and he alleged that I had cornered him against a wall and kicked him in the shin.

This was dealt with quickly, without any paperwork. The sergeant, another grizzled war veteran, asked the youth which leg had been kicked, and the complainant pointed at his right leg. The sergeant then gave him a quick kick to his left shin and provided him with advice that included connotations of sex and travel.

When one of our local criminals came into the station to make a complaint about a colleague of mine, he must have been pleased when he found himself speaking to an inspector. However, the complaint investigation did not last long. As I was walking in, the complainant was being thrown out by the inspector – thrown out bodily into the street.

The reader may feel that I am painting a negative picture of policemen during the 1960s. It was certainly a different era, in many ways. There were some policemen who could only be described as tough guys. However, it was a time of change for the police, and even then, the traditions of Wild West justice were going out of fashion.

What happened at the dance hall was that a hooligan was given a beating by a policeman for overstepping the mark, and most of my colleagues would probably have said that he deserved it. In terms of balance, it is important that I add a brief statement. In my thirty years as a police officer, this was the only time that I was a witness to this type of Wild West justice. I am not saying that officers did not dish out the occasional slap or kick, but the times were changing, and in many ways they were changing for the good.

9

In May 1965 the white voters in Rhodesia gave their prime minister, Ian Smith, an election victory. His party was in favour of independence from Britain, and Rhodesia had started along a path that would eventually take her out of the Commonwealth. During the year there were various attempts made by the British Government to try and resolve the crisis, but they were not successful.

Apart from the Rhodesian problem, Harold Wilson's Government was facing major problems with the economy. The Government was having difficulty paying its debts, and Wilson asked the United States for financial assistance. The problem was that President Johnson wanted Britain to send troops to assist the Americans in Vietnam, but Wilson was strongly opposed to British involvement there. No money was forthcoming from the United States, and the economic struggles continued. The United States had its own problems to contend with. The civil-rights campaign for African Americans had led to unrest and violence, and riots were breaking out in the black areas of some American cities. At the same time, opposition to the war in Vietnam was increasing day by day, and this issue would polarize American society for many years.

In Winchester, all of this seemed quite remote. People might grumble that they did not have enough money, but generally there was not a great deal of interest in events outside the UK. As far as work was concerned, my confidence and knowledge was increasing day by day, and it was possible to see much more of the dark-blue jigsaw. Manpower was always a problem, and there were times on night duty when I would be the only PC on foot patrol covering the centre of Winchester.

A lot of my time was taken up seeing victims of crime. In most cases, the officer who took a report of a crime would be responsible for investigating it. In Hampshire, most crime was investigated by the Uniform Branch, except for those offences that were obviously CID matters. Traffic accidents involved me in a lot of paperwork. In most 'due care' cases (driving without due care and attention) it was necessary to send reports to other police forces with requests for witness statements to be taken, and this added to the time that it took to complete the prosecution file.

It was necessary to ask permission to return to the station to complete paperwork and sergeants did not always authorise this. Sergeant King hated to see any of his PCs in the station. His favourite expression was, 'Get on your way; get up the street.' Another gem was 'A good policeman never gets wet.' I never quite understood that one.

That summer, I found myself dealing with my first fatal traffic accident. A lorry had been travelling south on the A33 from the London area to the Ford vehicle factory in Southampton, with a load of steel sheets weighing several tons. The evidence suggested that the driver had been going too fast. He'd lost control of the lorry, which had travelled to the wrong side of the road, colliding with a bus and a motor scooter coming the other way.

The scene of the accident looked like a battle zone, and we could see straight away that there were casualties. We were going to need a lot more people there. My colleague contacted IR to request further assistance. Within a few minutes, there were several other units at the scene, including two traffic division cars.

A large section of bodywork on the offside of the bus had been ripped open as if someone had used a giant tin opener on it. We checked for casualties, and there were nine of them, the rider of the motor scooter and eight people who had been passengers in the bus. Two ambulances arrived at the scene very quickly, and several others were on their way. Priority was given to a seriously injured man in his sixties. He was barely conscious when he was lifted into an ambulance, and we could see that his stomach had been torn open.

The first priority at any accident is always the casualties. All police officers are given first-aid training, but we were quietly grateful that the

Ambulance Service had arrived at the same time as we had. We helped the ambulance men to ensure that all the injured people were removed from the scene and taken to hospital.

After the impact, the bus had ended up sideways, totally blocking the road, and the lorry had come to a halt 24 metres south of the bus. The steel sheets from the lorry had been thrown forward and lay across the road surface, covering a distance of about 20 metres. The motor scooter was damaged and had been left at the side of the road on the grass verge.

Sergeant Thornton reached the scene of the accident about ten minutes after my arrival. He was one of the oldest and most experienced sergeants at Winchester. He had been a sergeant major in tanks during the war, and he looked the part with his silver hair and his military-style moustache. We had a quick discussion about the accident, and I volunteered to deal with it.

The thought went through my mind that the sergeant might not agree to a probationer like me dealing with this kind of accident. There were already signs that this one could end up as a 'fatal', but Sergeant Thornton nodded and told me that he would keep an eye on everything.

Fatal traffic accidents have different aspects to them. Firstly, all cases have to go before a coroner's court, and the police have a duty to the coroner to ensure that the matter is properly investigated. Secondly, a fatal accident may result in a prosecution for causing death by dangerous driving, which is a homicide, at that time punishable by a prison sentence of up to five years. Because of this, the scene of the accident needs to be treated in the same way as any other crime scene.

It was the policy in some forces for a CID officer to take over the investigation if there was some evidence suggesting a case of death by dangerous driving, but in Hampshire the Uniform Branch always dealt with these cases. Officially, a sergeant would have responsibility for supervising the investigation, but as a rule, most of the work would normally be done by the PC who dealt with the accident. It seemed that Sergeant Thornton had decided to keep a close eye on everything.

Nowadays most police forces have specialist officers who are trained as accident investigators. They make notes of all the marks on the road surface and use mathematical formulae to determine the speed of vehicles immediately before the accident. They are treated by the courts as expert witnesses, and their evidence is often crucial in obtaining convictions. This was not the case in 1965, and this type of investigation could easily fall on the shoulders of someone like me.

My first task was to draw a diagram of the scene. Sergeant Thornton called headquarters and asked for a police photographer to come to the location. Once the casualties were on their way to hospital, we had to think about the traffic situation. The A33 was the only direct main route that linked Southampton with Basingstoke and London, and it was always busy. The accident had totally blocked it in both directions, and Sergeant Thornton contacted IR to arrange for traffic diversions to be set up.

After that, the two of us started taking measurements of the marks at the scene, working our way from north to south. The accident scene covered a large area. There were tyre burn marks from the lorry extending south for 34 metres prior to the point of impact. South of the point of impact, there was a deep scar in the road surface made by the lorry for a distance of 6 metres. One of my first thoughts was how lucky the lorry driver had been, because his load had shifted and been thrown forward, smashing through the cabin of the lorry. This meant that a large number of steel sheets had flown forward at considerable force, which could have sliced him in half. When we took the measurements, we saw that there were steel sheets covering the road surface for 24 metres.

From north to south, the accident scene covered a length of about 76 metres. The marks indicated a fast speed by the lorry prior to the accident. It showed that after hitting the bus and scooter it had continued for about 24 metres before stopping in the centre of the road. A police photographer arrived and did his work. Sergeant Thornton told me that we needed to go to the hospital as soon as possible and obtain details of all the injured people.

Once we had completed our investigation at the scene, the road could be opened up to traffic. Before that could happen, someone would have to remove the damaged vehicles and the steel sheets. Sergeant Thornton directed several officers to deal with this while the two of us went to the Royal Hampshire County Hospital in Winchester.

At the hospital, we were told that the badly injured man that we had seen earlier had died a few minutes before our arrival there. We were also told that his wife had been informed that her husband had been injured and that she was on her way to the hospital. She arrived a few minutes later, and Sergeant Thornton took on the sad task of telling her that her husband was dead.

After that, we needed to see what the situation was with the other injured people. None of the other casualties had serious injuries and they were all discharged from hospital within 24 hours or so. Before doing anything else, we checked that messages had been sent to inform their families.

The next task was to have the deceased man identified by a relative, and his wife asked to do it. In such cases, it is crucial to have continuity of evidence relating to identification. After his wife had identified him to me, I attached a tag to the dead body with his name on it. The chain of continuity went from his widow to me and then from me to the pathologist.

The next day, I was present when the pathologist carried out a post-mortem. In Hampshire, going to autopsies was seen as an important part of the training for probationers and was normal for all cases of sudden death. In any homicide, the prosecution had to prove that the victim's death was caused by the defendant's actions and not from some other cause.

The driver of the lorry, William York, had been slightly injured, and Sergeant Thornton and I spoke to him briefly at the hospital. He was informed that one of the injured people had died and that the accident was being investigated.

Sergeant Thornton went with me to the opening of the inquest. It was important to make an application for the inquest to be adjourned, as the death was being investigated by police. The application was granted, and during the next three or four weeks I was busy gathering statements from witnesses.

Eventually the case file was complete. Once Sergeant Thornton had read it, he made a recommendation that proceedings be taken against York for causing death by dangerous driving. The file went to our solicitors' branch and came back to me with the decision that proceedings should be taken.

A summons was served on York to appear at Winchester County Magistrates' Court, where he was committed for trial at the Hampshire Assize Court. York entered a plea of not guilty, and the trial was listed to start at the end of November.

After giving evidence, defence counsel cross-examined me and suggested that I must have become confused at the scene of the accident. He suggested that the accident had been the fault of the bus driver and produced some photographs that showed damage to the lorry and the bus.

At that time, when it came to court cases, I was not battle hardened. A defence barrister would probably see a young probationer such as me in the witness box as an easy target. In this case, if my credibility as a witness were to be badly damaged, the prosecution case could be in serious trouble.

This business with the photographs had taken me by surprise, and for a few seconds I just stood looking at them. They had come from a local firm of solicitors in Hampshire who were representing the defendant. The defence barrister was now looking very relaxed and confident. He probably smelled blood, and he stood there with a smile on his face. He was ready to finish me off.

I did not say anything, which must have pleased the defence counsel. Time seemed to have slowed down; I felt as though the whole world were waiting for me to say something. About a minute had gone by with me just standing there, looking at the photographs. There was something about them that just did not look right, and then suddenly I knew what it was. The photographs had been made back to front, so that something that was on the left would appear to be on the right and something on the right would appear to be on the left.

I pointed this out to the judge, who directed a serious judge-like frown at the defence counsel. That man seemed to lose his air of confidence and started to look worried. Photographs used in evidence have to be 'proved', as with any other type of exhibit. You cannot just produce photographs in court without knowing who took them. A photographer has to make a witness statement and identify them as exhibits. This had not happened, and the photographs had been suddenly produced like a rabbit out of a hat. Blame, like many other things, tends to travel downhill. There was a quick conference between the defence counsel and the defendant's solicitor, who was now the one who looked worried.

The judge decided that there should be a brief adjournment. There was then a meeting which involved the prosecuting barrister, defence barrister, defence solicitor, and me. It was the first time that I had come across anything like that at a court. Now it was the defendant's solicitor who was in the firing line. He did his best by blustering and being evasive, but he eventually admitted that he was unsure who had taken the photograph.

The defence counsel looked embarrassed and glared at the solicitor. A few minutes later, the defendant changed his plea to guilty. He was fined fifty pounds and disqualified from driving for five years.

A couple of weeks after my case at the Assize Court it was announced that there would be a competition for the title of Best Probationer of 1965. It appears that every divisional commander in Hampshire had been asked to nominate one of their probationers, and my superintendent had nominated me. Peter Spencer was the nominee from Fareham Division. Nine of us went before a board of senior officers at headquarters for interview.

The board seemed to be impressed that I had already dealt with a case of death by dangerous driving, and this was mentioned by the officer who chaired the board. Going in front of boards in this type of interview situation was never one of my strong points, and I did not feel that I shone. Naturally, I was pleased to have been nominated. Although he did not win, Peter Spencer did well, coming in as the official runner-up. Neither of us can now recall who the winner was.

It was about this time that I found myself investigating an indecent assault. About midnight, the sound of a woman screaming brought me to a halt. A woman screaming at that time of night might mean she was drunk, but something told me that there was something seriously wrong. I stood and listened, trying to pinpoint where the screams were coming from. It seemed to be fairly close, so I headed in the direction of the sounds.

The screams stopped then, but I carried on my search of the surrounding streets. Another five minutes brought me to the theatre in Jewry Street, but there was no sign of anyone or anything that looked wrong. Was I wasting my time? As I walked along a side street, a man stopped me and told me that a woman neighbour had been attacked a few minutes before. I called Sergeant King and he told me that he would be with me shortly.

Sergeant King was at the scene within two or three minutes of hearing my call. He told me that the important thing at that point was to find out how serious the attack was. Was it a rape? Was it an indecent assault? We spoke to the victim of the attack, Mary Wilson, a 27-year-old married woman. Mrs Wilson had been out for a drink with a woman friend. The two women had returned to Mary Wilson's house, where they'd spent about an hour chatting, and then the friend had decided to go home.

Mrs Wilson had decided to take her dog for a walk and accompany her friend home. As Mary Wilson was returning home with her dog, she had been approached by a man who tried to strike up a conversation with her. She'd asked him to go away, but he'd walked alongside her for some time. They were passing the car park of a car dealership, which was normally deserted at that time of night. There were some bushes near the entrance to the car park, and the man grabbed her and pulled her towards the bushes.

This is when she had started to scream. The man had then put one hand around her throat and was holding her arm with his other hand. She was wearing a low-necked dress, and the man put his hand down the front of her dress. He tried to kiss her, and she bit his lip hard. This made him release his grip. Whilst all this was happening, the dog was jumping up and snapping at him. Mary Wilson broke free and ran to her home nearby. She told her husband, and then the two of them had gone out looking for the assailant. At that point, we did not know all of this. What we needed was a brief summary of the incident, so that we knew what offence had been committed. Even more important at that point was a description of the man who had attacked her. I immediately sent out a message on my PR with the man's description.

Sergeant King told me that a written statement would have to be taken from the victim and that this job would be given to a woman officer. One of the CID officers at Winchester was a woman, and she contacted me to find out what had happened. Next day, she interviewed the victim and took a detailed statement from her.

As this was an indecent assault, I thought that it would be assigned to a CID officer. To my surprise, a decision was made to leave the enquiry in my hands.

Two weeks later, I submitted an application to our magistrates' court for an arrest warrant based on the man's description. For three or four weeks I did my best to identify the suspect but without any success. As far as I know, this offence still remains unsolved.

After his marriage to Stella in 1965, Mick Lyons left Winchester and was posted to Leigh Park, a subdivision of the Havant division. An important thing to know about Leigh Park is that it is the largest council estate in the UK and the second largest in Europe. Portsmouth was badly bombed during World War II, and this had resulted in a large number of homeless people. The answer to this problem was to build a very large council estate at Leigh Park.

At first there were plans to build it as a new town, with a population of 40,000. Leigh Park's population grew fast, but it never exceeded 28,000. It had a range of problems of the kind often associated with large council estates. The number of unemployed people and single-parent families tended to be high. Mick Lyons and the other police officers who worked there were always kept busy.

In later years, there were social changes when many residents bought their council houses through the-right-to buy scheme. By the beginning of the twenty-first century, 45 per cent of the houses would be privately owned. Mick Lyons was destined to stay on the Havant division for the next twenty-eight years.

A car was essential for travelling around Hampshire, and towards the end of the year I took my driving test and passed it. We owned an old Morris Minor, which did not look very sporty but was always reliable and not expensive to use. Probationers were not allowed to drive police vehicles, but my probation was due to end in January 1966. Apart from being able to drive our own car, I would have a wider choice of duties as a police driver.

Although Sergeant King was a tough character and a martinet when it came to discipline, he could be quite different when he was not on duty. One evening when we had a day off, I joined a couple of my colleagues for a drink in one of the local pubs, where we bumped into him, and he immediately insisted on buying us drinks. He was drinking with another man who was one of our local ambulance drivers.

There was something about the ambulance man. For someone in his late forties he seemed very fit and had the look of a man who was much tougher than he appeared at first glance. Sergeant King did not say anything that evening, but a couple of weeks later he told me that they had served together in Special Forces during the Second World War.

The ambulance man had been part of a small unit dropped by parachute into occupied France to assist a French Resistance group. Unfortunately for him, he had been captured by the Germans and held prisoner for several weeks, but his captors must have underestimated their prisoner. He had been severely beaten and tortured, but he had not told them anything, and after surviving a great deal of mistreatment, he'd managed to escape.

As Christmas approached, one of the older PCs pointed out that we were scheduled to be working early turn on Christmas Day and that our sergeant would be Geoff King. This news came as a nasty shock. The idea that we would arrive for work at quarter to six in the morning at Christmas and be out on the streets in the cold fifteen minutes later was not very appealing.

When Christmas Day came, we went through the usual routine. Sergeant King told us what beats we were on and read a few entries from the parade book. I do not believe that anyone said Merry Christmas or anything like that. Then, at about one minute past six, he just sat looking at us. 'This is like torture,' I thought, standing up and moving towards the door.

That is when our sergeant spoke. 'Right, who is making the tea?' he asked. Then he produced a bottle of brandy and held it up high.

'Merry Christmas!'

10

The year 1966, will always be remembered for England's victory over Germany in the World Cup. It was a great result, and for a brief moment it was possible to forget all the problems facing the country. The economy continued to remain stagnant, and the Government decided to bring in austerity measures. Most people found that their spending power was being hit by rising inflation, a poor economy, and calls from the Government for pay restraint.

When the new police headquarters was completed at West Hill, we moved to our new station in North Walls. Leaving the old building at the Broadway was like making a move from the nineteenth into the twentieth century.

North Walls was modern, and the working facilities were much better, but the pattern of work rolled along as usual. On day duty I would spend a lot of my time dealing with victims of crime, writing crime reports, and investigating accidents, disputes, and common assaults. The first couple of hours of night duty would usually involve drink-related problems and arresting drunks.

Carrying out stops has been a traditional method of crime prevention and detection used by British police. There were always two main reasons for carrying out stops: a person's movements or property that they were carrying. As the years went by, there would be a steady increase in other reasons for stops, such as drugs, weapons, or terrorism. Sometimes a stop would result in an arrest, but in most cases it did not and the reason for it would be recorded. The legal powers relating to carrying out searches of people or their vehicles was very much a grey area. In practice, much was left to the common sense of the police officer carrying out the search.

Basically, a stop is carried out to prevent crime. A stop may result in an arrest, but the amount of valuable crime intelligence that is gathered when known criminals are stopped is equally important. For example, details of people that they are associating with or a vehicle that they are using may be important.

Inexperienced PCs will always make quite a few unnecessary stops. Those officers who have more experience tend to make fewer stops but better ones. As a general rule, if large numbers of people who are not criminals are being stopped, it indicates that something is wrong.

I was pleased to spend a week working night duty with Morrey Annetts, a very experienced TD officer who had developed his own simple method for deciding when to stop a car. It did not work at night, as he needed to see the face of the person he was looking at, and the person needed to be able to see him. It was simple but effective. As they drove past, some drivers would touch their face in a nervous manner when they saw him.

Morrey said that touching the face was a gesture that indicated concern of some kind, and he would always stop anyone who did it. It proved surprisingly effective, and he made a large number of arrests by using this method. There were people driving stolen vehicles, some carrying stolen property, disqualified drivers, and people who were on the wanted list.

At about two o'clock one morning we were on the A30 near Basingstoke. On a lonely stretch of road, we spotted a white van parked in a layby, and it looked as though there might be someone inside. Morrey decided to turn around and take a closer look, and we saw that there were two men in the van, smoking and talking.

Both of them were surly and obviously not happy that we had decided to speak to them. First of all we checked out the vehicle with Information Room, and then we ran checks on them. Between the two of them, they had about twenty previous convictions that included illegal possession of explosives, firearms, burglary, and armed robbery. They had both come from the London area originally but now lived in Basingstoke.

A few metres from the van there was a gate and a footpath leading to an attractive looking thatched cottage. Using my torch, I worked my way around the outside of the cottage while Morrey kept an eye on the two suspects. It appeared to be unoccupied, but it was full of property. There was no sign that any attempt had been made to break in, but we decided to search them and their van. We both hoped that we could find something, such as HBIs, but they had nothing that would have justified any charge.

They were both experienced criminals and must have known that there was no point in carrying break-in tools if you did not need them. All sorts of items can be picked up in a garden and used to smash a window. There was nothing that we could arrest them for, but we both believed that we had prevented a crime.

The information about the stop went to headquarters as crime intelligence, and we later received some feedback on it. Apparently, it was already known that the two men were associates and involved in crime together. Another piece of news that came back to us was that one of them had told some of his friends that his ambition was to murder a policeman. I am pleased to say that he was arrested for burglary two months later and never achieved his ambition to murder a police officer.

There were things happening in my life apart from police work – the World Cup, for example. Everyone at Winchester police station wanted to see England play, and our names went into a raffle. Maureen and I never saw our national team in action, but we did go with a group of police officers and their families by coach to Wembley, where we saw Mexico play Uruguay. Using all my police expertise, it was easy to identify the Mexican supporters. They were the ones wearing sombreros.

Around this time, there was a hair-raising car chase along the Winchester bypass. It resulted in the arrest of two young men who later turned out to be innocent. Initially, there was an incident at about 3 a.m. in Southampton. A policeman on foot patrol spotted a car that had been reported stolen, and he signalled it to stop. The car was driven at him, but luckily he managed to jump out of the way. Three or four minutes later, two officers in a vehicle tried to stop the car, but it swerved around them and went off at a fast speed.

The stolen car reached the Winchester Bypass with two or three police cars in pursuit. At this point, the driver deliberately drove north along the southbound carriageway. The two carriageways were divided by a hedge so that the pursuing police cars were going north on the north-bound carriageway, trying to keep up with the bandit car on the other side of the hedge. It was a horrific situation, but luckily there were no other vehicles on the southbound carriageway for two or three vital minutes. Officers from Winchester – including me – were on our way to the bypass, listening intently to the messages coming over the air. We could hear that two men had jumped out of the car and run into some woods nearby. A few minutes later, we reached the bypass and saw two men in their early twenties standing at the side of the road, who were being questioned by officers.

The two suspects were from Jersey. Their story was that they had walked from Winchester railway station to that spot because it was a good place to find a lift to hitch-hike to Southampton. An officer involved in the chase said that he recognised one of them as having been the driver of the car in Southampton. However, both of them denied any involvement in the matter.

They were arrested and taken to Winchester police station. A short time later, a policeman from Southampton came to the station, looked at the two men in custody, and identified the second man as having been the passenger in the car. The two of them now faced a number of charges that included TDA (taking and driving away of a vehicle) and dangerous driving. After the charges were read out to them, they both strongly denied any involvement. The station sergeant did not think that they were suitable for bail, and they were held in custody at the station, awaiting their appearance at court.

The following day whilst on station duty, I received a phone call from a clergyman in Jersey. He said that he was a friend of the parents of one of the young men and was enquiring about his welfare. He went on to say that he knew them both quite well and thought it highly out of character that they would be involved in a criminal offence.

There was a lot of discussion at the station about what had happened, and it soon became obvious that some of our officers had concerns about the case. Brian Constable was an experienced PC who had been involved in the search for the suspects. He made the point that the two men involved had run into an area where there was quite high grass that was wet. This would result in their shoes and the bottoms of their trousers becoming wet. However, he had noticed that the clothes and the shoes worn by the two men from Jersey were dry.

These concerns were raised with the chief inspector in charge of the division while the superintendent was on holiday. The chief inspector spoke to the detective inspector and asked that a CID officer be assigned to the case to make further enquiries. The two men from Jersey had both said that they had been at Winchester railway station for some time and that they had spoken to a member of the railway staff. They continued to insist that they had walked from the railway station to the place on the bypass where they had been arrested.

One of the DCs went to the railway station and spoke to a member of the railway staff who had been on duty at the relevant time. The railwayman stated that he had seen two men there and that they had spoken to him. The CID officer then asked him for descriptions of the two men, and they closely matched those of the defendants.

A decision was made by the chief inspector that the charges should be withdrawn. The two men were given an apology, released from custody, and told that there was no need for them to attend court. There have always been cases where wrong identifications have led to innocent people being convicted, and this was a good lesson for everyone involved in this case.

Witnesses, including police officers, can sometimes make serious mistakes when it comes to identifying people. One of my enquiries involved identification and was destined to take the opposite path from the case involving the two men from Jersey. One afternoon, a call on my PR took me to an office in the centre of Winchester where there had been a theft. All visitors to the company would enter a reception area and be faced by a receptionist sitting at her desk. The two women who worked in the reception area told me what had happened.

Two men had walked into the company's reception area and stated that they were looking for work. At this point, there had been only one woman there, and she'd walked into another office to look for her manager. She returned after about one minute and had a brief conversation with the two men. After that, both men left the building.

A few minutes later, the receptionist noticed that something had been moved on her desk. She kept a small cash box with a float for administrative expenses in one of the drawers. When she looked inside the box, she saw that all the banknotes were missing. The receptionist had seen both men, and her colleague said that she had seen one of them. They were both described as white men in their twenties. One had very blonde hair and his companion had very dark hair and was described as looking like Elvis Presley.

That day, by chance, I came across some information that had been sent by teleprinter to Winchester and several other places by an officer based at the Regional Crime Squad office in Southampton. There are two ways of investigating offences committed by professional criminals. There is the usual system, in which a crime is reported and the police investigate it. However, the RCS took the opposite route: rather than investigate reported crimes, they investigated criminals to see what they were up to.

Two men had been due for release from Winchester Prison that day, and the RCS officer believed that they would commit crime as soon as they walked out through the prison gates. Reading through it, I could see that the descriptions of the two men and my two suspects matched each other.

A quick phone call to the prison revealed that the two men had been released about one hour before the theft had occurred. 'Case solved,' I thought – but I wondered whether this was all too easy. I sought the advice of one of the sergeants, who suggested a photographic identification. I would need eight or nine photographs of similar-looking dark-haired men and eight or nine of fair-haired men.

After that, I met with the witnesses to carry out the photographic identification process with them. A photograph of the dark-haired suspect was placed on a table with those of similar appearance who were not suspects. After that, I carried out the same procedure with the photo of the fair-haired one.

It was a disappointing result for me. One suspect was positively identified by both women. However, the second man, 'Elvis', had only been seen by one woman, and she identified someone who was not a suspect, adding that he was definitely the one. Four or five weeks went by, and then the two of them were arrested for a theft in Reading that had a very similar MO to my case in Winchester. I contacted the officer dealing with the case and told him about my theft case. It ended with the two of them admitting a large number of offences, and this included the one at Winchester.

Shortly after completing my probation, authorisation came through for me to drive police vehicles. This gave me the opportunity to reach incidents quickly and increased my chances of making arrests. It also gave my feet a rest.

A month or so later, I was sitting in a section car in a side street in Winchester, listening to the messages coming over the radio. Suddenly there was a whole flurry of messages that caught my attention – a prison break!

A coach containing a number of prisoners guarded by prison officers had been travelling along a country road a few miles south of Winchester. Suddenly, some of the prisoners attacked the officers, overpowered them, and made off. One of those who escaped was John McVicar, who was serving a sentence of twenty-three years for armed robberies. McVicar was a man with a very high profile, and Scotland Yard had tagged him as Public Enemy No 1. One of the largest police operations in Hampshire was about to start.

By the time I reached the scene, there was a huge array of police vehicles. It turned out that some of the prisoners had not taken part in the escape and had stayed in the coach waiting for the police to arrive. Within a short time, roadblocks were in place, and a perimeter had been set up, several miles in diameter. The obvious problem was that it was a rural area. It is easy to seal off a road, but it is a different situation with fields and woodland.

As soon as the news was reported on television and radio, we started to receive hundreds of calls from the public with reported sightings. Units were sent to check out each call, and some of the fugitives were captured. After many hours, a decision was made to stand down everyone, but McVicar and several others had not been found.

McVicar had escaped from custody on several occasions. In 1970, he was arrested by police and was sentenced to twenty-six years in prison. He subsequently took an Open University degree in Sociology and was awarded a BSc first class. After being paroled in 1978, he studied for a postgraduate degree at the University of Leicester and wrote his autobiography, *McVicar by Himself.* He also scripted the film, *McVicar* which starred *The Who's* lead singer, Roger Daltrey, in the title role. John McVicar became an author and journalist and never went back to crime.

This was an era when homosexuality was very much in the news. Sexual relations between men, whether or not they were consensual, were always illegal, and a conviction for the offence of buggery would always result in a prison sentence. Any other sexual acts involving men could result in a prosecution for gross indecency, and this usually resulted in a fine.

Some members of parliament favoured changes to the law, and there was a proposal that sexual acts between men should be decriminalised in certain circumstances. The idea favoured by many MPs was to legalise sex involving men where both parties consented, were twenty-one years of age or more, and were in a private place.

In relation to women, there had never been any equivalent legislation. Many of the laws relating to morality had been introduced during the Victorian era, and there was a story that when lesbianism was mentioned to Queen Victoria she said that there was no such thing.

Public opinion was split on the issue; overall, the general public was probably less tolerant than their representatives at Westminster. There was a lot of disagreement among police officers when it came to discussing these proposed changes in the law. It seemed to me that some people were born with a different sexual identity and bringing in laws to penalise them was a form of persecution.

During the 1950s, at least one home secretary had criticised chiefs of police for what was seen as a lack of zeal by their officers in arresting and charging people for this type of offence. These new proposals would not alter the policing situation very much, as police officers were not in the habit of patrolling the bedrooms of the nation.

One of the PCs at Winchester arrested several men for the offence of gross indecency. This involved close attention to public toilets and other likely meeting places on his beat. Many of the men he arrested were well known within the local community, and their details appeared in the local press. One of them was a well-known local solicitor, but whatever their social status, the convictions and subsequent publicity had the potential to ruin their lives. There were many police officers who were not sympathetic to homosexuals, but on the other hand, there were very few who went out of their way to arrest them.

Dealing with people who have had too much to drink has always taken up a huge amount of police time. One night I found myself struggling with a man who was drunk and disorderly and did not want to be arrested. He was not particularly aggressive but he kept on struggling, and we rolled around on the pavement in the High Street for a couple of minutes. All police officers had been trained in methods for restraining violent people, but we soon discovered that it all worked better at Sandgate than it did in the real world.

I saw one of the older officers appear on the scene from a side street. 'I don't think much of your restraint techniques,' he said whilst he looked on with a big grin on his face.

It was never a good thing when people tried to strangle me. Apart from anything else, it always made me angry. When the drunk put both hands around my throat and started squeezing it, I gave him a jab in the stomach and then used both hands to take his hands off my windpipe.

My colleague who had been watching with the smile on his face decided that it was time to help me. We each took one of the drunk's arms and managed to get him to his feet. He started to calm down, and my colleague put up a call on his PR for the van.

It is quite common for officers to be assaulted by drunks, but in this case I decided to go for a charge of drunk and disorderly. There can be a fine line when deciding whether or not to bring a charge of assaulting a police officer. If we charged every person who was guilty of a minor assault on an officer it would tend to devalue the offence.

Heavy drinking always results in heavy costs to society. This includes the policing costs, the value of damaged property, and the costs to the National Health Service. There are assaults on many people who are just doing their jobs, such as railway workers, hospital staff, ambulance personnel, and police. There is a close link between drunken behaviour and the high casualty rate in the British police service. And this is only part of the story. If an officer injures his/her back arresting a struggling drunk, he/she can sometimes end up on the sick list for several months at great cost to the taxpayers. If you pick out any day, at any time of the year, there are always hundreds of police officers on the sick list in the UK as a result of injuries arising from incidents involving people who have been drinking.

Although Winchester had always been one of my favourite places, I decided that it might be a good idea to ask for a transfer to a busier division. During the summer of 1966 I put in an application for the Aldershot division. The transfer was to come through within a few weeks. One day, as Maureen and I were in our flat in Winchester, she was watching television in the lounge and I was making a cup of coffee in the kitchen. Suddenly, Maureen shouted out to me, and I walked through to the lounge to see what was concerning her.

A story was breaking on television which was going to dominate the news for some time: the murder of three Metropolitan police officers in Shepherd's Bush. The first we learned about it was that the three murdered men had been the crew of a 'Q' car. It was reported that they had stopped a car with three men in it, and all three officers had subsequently been shot dead.

A Q car has no police markings and is manned by three officers in plain clothes. The first TV pictures showed a green Triumph saloon and the body of at least one policeman covered with a blanket. We saw an angry-looking sergeant, who appeared to take a swing at a press photographer who was getting too close to the bodies. That particular piece was edited out of the subsequent broadcasts.

The murders caused a general feeling of revulsion throughout the country. Many people linked the murders at Shepherd's Bush to the suspension of the death penalty, and this did a great deal to reignite all the arguments about capital punishment.

Government ministers moved quickly to deal with the concerns of the public, and there were announcements that people convicted of murder would spend the rest of their lives in prison. Within a few days, officers investigating the Shepherd's Bush murders had identified the three men involved, and details of all three were circulated as wanted for murder. This was the beginning of one of the largest manhunts of the twentieth century.

Two or three weeks went by, and my transfer to Aldershot Division was confirmed. It surprised me to find out that my posting was actually going to be to Hartley Wintney, a police station in a rural part of the division. Maureen and I drove there to look at the police house that we would be moving to, and we liked it straight away. We both hoped that we could have children, and we felt that this was a good location for us.

11

Hartley Wintney was what is known as a section station, with a sergeant in charge. Our police house was in Phoenix Green, about a mile west of Hartley Wintney. It was a warm, sunny day in September when we arrived. A group of three or four women had gathered in a garden across the road and watched us as we moved in. We viewed this with a mixture of amusement and annoyance. Seeing the new policeman and his wife arriving might have been their idea of excitement, especially if there was nothing very much on television that afternoon.

We were both pleased about the house. It was semi-detached, with three bedrooms and a pleasant garden at the front and back. There was an almond tree next to the front gate, and the rear garden looked over open country. In the background, we could hear the lowing of cattle.

However, in common with most houses at that time, there was no central heating, and when the winter arrived, we found that the house was difficult to keep warm. On my second day, while we were still sorting out the house, a man knocked on the front door and told me that he wanted to report a traffic accident. This is where definitions came in handy! After hearing my definition of a police station and my definition of a house, he went on his way.

Hartley Wintney had a different shift system to what I had become used to, and I was surprised to learn that we did not do night duty. Early turn started at eight or nine, and late turn normally finished at 2 a.m. Occasionally, if there was a serious incident on the section, someone at

Aldershot or IR would ring straight through to call out the early turn officer and probably the sergeant as well.

Generally during the night, when there was nobody on duty at Hartley Wintney, incidents could be dealt with by officers from Fleet or anyone else who was available on the division. When the late-turn officer came off duty, the public phone line was put through to the extension of the officer posted early turn. If a member of the public dialled the number, the whole household could be woken up. Our house at Phoenix Green had no telephone and therefore we could not be contacted.

The A30 was the most important route linking London with the South West of England, and the police station was located there. The M3 motorway had not yet been built, and the traffic on the A30 was heavy most of the time.

The police college at Bramshill was on our patch, and I drove through the grounds to look at it. The main building was an impressive looking Elizabethan mansion, and it looked the way I expected it to look. Historically, many senior military men had been appointed to ACPO rank with little or no police experience. The college had been founded to ensure that senior officers were given training to develop their leadership and management skills. All chief constables would eventually be promoted from within the service rather than being parachuted in as political appointees.

On my first day, I met the sergeant, Don Hanson, and Martin Dickens, the PC who would be working with me. Not surprisingly, Martin had been given the nickname Charlie. He was the same age as me, was newly married, and had just been transferred from Aldershot police station. The other two PCs were older and more experienced, and it seemed strange that Martin and I would be working together. Apart from anything else, neither of us knew our way around.

Hartley Wintney police station was a large red-brick building that probably dated from the end of the nineteenth century. What could be called the west wing of the building was the sergeant's house. The police station consisted of the rest of the building, except for the flat on the first floor where Martin Dickens and his wife lived. There was a front office, a sergeant's office, and two cells.

One of the cells was being used for storing stolen property and a variety of other items that had come into our possession. The other cell was rarely used, because arrested people were normally taken to Fleet or Aldershot. The section consisted of five beats. There was the HW beat; that consisted of Hartley Wintney village and the surrounding area. There were four country beats on the section, with the officers working from their own police houses at Mattingley, Eversley, Yateley, and Blackwater.

During the sixties, Yateley was going through a period of rapid growth. New houses were being completed at a fast rate, and the population was increasing day by day. Because of this, two PCs had been posted to Yateley. Sergeant Hanson was in charge of the section, and the senior officer for the subdivision was Inspector Morris, at Fleet.

Working in rural areas was quite different from policing towns and cities. On early turn, the station had to be open to the public between 9 a.m. and 1 p.m. It was also open for four hours each evening. When we were patrolling and there was nobody on duty at the station, all incoming phone calls were diverted to Fleet.

If there was only one officer on duty, the time available for patrolling was very limited, and there were some obvious problems of communications. Firstly, the phone system on the subdivision was quite confusing to the public. Secondly, none of the officers on the section had personal radios, and thirdly, our station provided no cover after 2 a.m. A fourth problem was that the section car was linked to IR by a main-set radio, but HW officers could not be contacted if they were away from their vehicles.

HW was like a miniature police force, with Uniform, CID, and Traffic Division. We had our own DC, Peter Faulkner, who had a desk in the sergeant's office, and Bob Middleton, a TD motorcyclist. Bob was an ex Royal Marine who had his own motorcycle beat that covered several miles of the A30.

The Fleet subdivision was divided into three sections: Fleet, Odiham, and HW. Odiham was another section station, with the usual complement of a sergeant, four PCs, plus two or three country beats. There was one building at Odiham, which housed both the police station and the local magistrates' court. Standing in front of the court there was a set of stocks. I wondered when they had last been used.

As a section, HW had gained an unwelcome reputation for the large numbers of serious traffic accidents that its officers dealt with, mainly on the A30. My colleagues at Winchester did their best to cheer me up by telling me that I would spend most of my time at inquests, as there would be at least one fatal accident every month for me to deal with. It did not take long to find out that this was an exaggeration, but a great deal of my time was, in fact, taken up dealing with traffic accidents.

Hampshire had a strategy for dealing with fatal and serious accidents. All major highways in the county were divided into beats, and a TD motorcyclist was given responsibility for a specific beat that covered several miles. If a serious accident occurred on his beat the officer would be called to it and would be responsible for dealing with it. The instructions were that if an accident occurred when the traffic officer was off duty, he should be called out to deal with it, but as they were not paid any allowance or overtime for this extra responsibility, they were not easy to find when they were off duty.

The investigation into the murder of the three police officers in Shepherd's Bush was still going on. Of the three men who had been involved in the murder, two had been arrested fairly quickly. The third man, now the most wanted man in Britain, was called Harry Roberts. He had served as a soldier in the British Army. The investigating officers believed that Roberts was using his military skills by hiding in the forests and living off the land. Because of this, all the officers at HW received calls to sightings of people camping in various places, and one afternoon a Harry Roberts call came over the radio to me. Bearing in mind that he was involved in the murder of three police officers, I reckoned that he had little to lose by killing another one. It seemed highly unlikely that this would be Harry Roberts, but my strategy was to sneak up on the camp rather than make a full frontal assault. The two Canadian students camping there were surprised to see me appear in their forest glade. When I explained and said 'Harry Roberts', it was obvious that they knew nothing about him.

Harry Roberts was captured shortly after this. He had indeed been camping in a forest, and the police used a professional tracker to help them find him. Roberts later received a sentence of life imprisonment, and the judge who sentenced him recommended that he serve at least thirty years. He was destined to remain in prison for many years longer than that and was finally released on life licence in 2014.

Physically, I felt better for not doing night duty. At Winchester, I would have finished at 6 a.m., gone home, and slept until about 2 or 3 p.m. As a general rule, sleeping during the day would leave me feeling a little bit out of kilter. Thus the hours of work at HW seemed quite civilised.

One day, when I was on station duty, a local resident came in and told me that he wanted to make a complaint of dangerous driving. Nearly all of these cases were the result of traffic accidents, but this one related to a near miss.

He explained that he had been driving his small Austin saloon along a country road near Hartley Wintney. It was a typical stretch of country road, narrow and flanked by hedgerows. As he approached a bend in the road, he had noticed a Morris saloon coming towards him. Then, to his horror, he saw that there was a Jaguar saloon overtaking the Morris on the bend, coming straight at him at speed.

Luckily for everyone concerned, the driver of the Austin saw an opening to a field on his left and did the only thing that he could do. He managed to swerve his car onto a small patch of grass in front of a farm gate. The complainant had been a fighter pilot in the RAF during the Second World War, and he certainly appeared to have quick reactions. We sat down together, and I started writing his witness statement. He had written the registration number of the Jaguar on a piece of paper, which I took from him as an exhibit. It turned out that his wife had been in the car with him, so I took a statement from her next day.

All police enquiries follow a certain path. Whether the offence is theft, dangerous driving, or the investigation of a serial killer, the basic steps are always the same. First of all, you need to examine the scene and look for clues, find witnesses, interview them, and take written statements. The next step is to interview the suspect, when you have one. Finally, you must do the paperwork and sum up the strength of the evidence. When that is all done, you send the file to the prosecutor.

Next day, I had a look at the scene of the incident. I took some measurements and drew a plan of that stretch of road, with the bend shown in the centre. After making a few enquiries in the area, I traced the driver of the Morris car that had been overtaken on the bend. A third witness statement was soon in my hands. One of the older officers at HW told me about the man who owned the Jaguar. He was a very wealthy man in his thirties, who had inherited a considerable fortune from his father three or four years previously. He lived in a large house a couple of miles from HW.

The next stage in the enquiry was to interview the owner of the Jaguar. He admitted that he had been driving it at the time of the incident, and I informed him that he would be reported for the offence of dangerous driving. He told me that he did not wish to make a verbal or written statement. After that, it was just a matter of putting together the prosecution file. It went to Sergeant Hanson, who recommended that action should be taken against the Jaguar driver for dangerous driving.

There seemed little doubt that this was going to result in a serious battle at court. At that time, anyone facing a charge of dangerous driving had the right to elect trial by jury. In this case, the defendant requested a full committal hearing, and the magistrates would need to make a decision whether the evidence justified the case being committed to the crown court. The defence would make a submission to the court that there was no case to answer.

The committal hearing took place at Odiham Magistrates' Court. It was not called a trial, but it might as well have been, because a full committal was very similar to a grand jury hearing used in some American states. The procedure gave the defence the advantage of seeing what the prosecution witnesses were like under pressure so that they could assess their strengths or weaknesses.

When I gave my evidence, it was the first time that I had come under a ferocious and sustained attack by a defence solicitor in a courtroom. There were several questions relating to police procedures and the diagram I had made of the scene of the incident. A major part of the defence case was that I had deliberately drawn my diagram to make the bend appear to be much worse than it was, and the solicitor suggested that it was possible for drivers to see around the bend when approaching it.

Seeing a young-looking policeman standing in the witness box, the defendant's solicitor had probably hoped that he (I) would prove to be a soft target. It would help their case if this young policeman could be hammered down or maybe made to look like a total fool. The questions came in thick and fast. There were a couple of questions about Judges' Rules, and there seemed to be dozens about the bend in the road.

This is where court cases can go off the rails. The basic facts were simple. Nobody in their right mind would overtake another vehicle on a bend. However, the Jaguar driver would come to a spot where he could see the road straighten up ahead as he started to come out of the bend. Many questions thrown at me were aimed at trying to make me say that the bend was not particularly severe. They all appeared to be simple, straightforward questions. However, it seemed that the long series of questions had been prepared in advance, all aimed at receiving a yes or no in reply. It brought to mind the famous courtroom classic: 'Officer, do you beat your wife often? Just answer *yes* or *no*.'

After being asked question after question about the bend, I started to get annoyed. Eventually, I told the defence solicitor that there was no point in continually asking me the same question time after time. I maintained that I had seen the bend, it was quite a sharp bend, and no driver approaching it could see what was coming in the other direction until they started to emerge from the bend.

The solicitor who was cross-examining me was clearly not pleased that she had failed to trip me up. My comments seemed to fire her up, and she opened up on me with a salvo of three or four questions, one after the other, at high speed. The defence case ended when she made a submission that there was no case to answer. This was rejected by the court, and the defendant was committed for trial at the crown court. In police jargon, he went 'up the road'.

A few months later, the trial went ahead at Winchester. Stepping into the witness box to face defence counsel to be cross-examined, I was prepared for the battle that would surely come. He asked me about the caution that I had given in accordance with the Judges' Rules when I had interviewed the defendant. 'What words did you use, Officer?' I replied word for word. Then I waited for the second question.

'Thank you, Officer,' said the barrister.

The committal hearing had prepared me for the worst, so I did not move. Defence counsel was looking at me and wondering why I was still standing there. Surely my cross-examination could not be over? I stepped out of the witness box, thinking that things must have gone better than I thought at the committal hearing. The prosecution was in the hands of a very good barrister by the name of John Bull. His cross-examination of the defendant was quiet, steady, but extremely professional. The defendant's answers did nothing to help him. In front of a jury, he came over as a thoughtless and selfish personality.

When the judge addressed the jury, I tried to prevent myself from smiling too much. His summing up was amusing but to the point. As I recall, it went something like this. 'Do not worry about the law. I can tell you all about the law if you need to know anything. Just use your common sense to think about this case. If you had been that unfortunate man driving along in your motor car, and you had seen that Jaguar hurtling towards you, you might have said, "Oh dear. That is a little bit careless." If you think that, you must acquit this defendant. However, you might have said "Ooooooh! That was dangerous! Dangerous!" If you believe that his driving was dangerous, you must convict him of this charge.'

The word 'dangerous' was loud and heavily stressed, and the judge took in a deep breath and slapped a hand on his desk as he said the word. There seemed little doubt which way the case was moving, and the jury was out for about ten minutes before returning with a verdict of guilty. The defendant received a heavy fine and was disqualified for eighteen months. If the disqualification had been one month longer, the defendant would have had the right to appeal against the length of it. It seemed that he had not made a good impression on the judge.

One October evening, Martin and I were patrolling on the A30 when we received a 999 call directing us to a house at Star Hill, about a mile east of HW. The call was made by a man called John Wainwright, who lived in a side turning at Star Hill. He was reporting that his car had been stolen.

He had been doing some work on his Riley car in the driveway of his house, a short distance off the A30. At about eleven o'clock that evening, he'd gone into the house to wash and left his car keys in the ignition. A couple of minutes later, he'd heard the sound of his car being started up, so he'd run outside, just in time to see his car heading towards the A30. He chased it for a short distance, but when the car turned onto the A30, he'd run to a nearby phone box and dialled 999. The details of the stolen car went out to Hampshire, Berkshire, and Surrey.

We were with Wainwright within about two minutes of receiving the call. He sat in the police car with us while we listened to the police radio, wondering if the car had been spotted. We talked about where his car might be and wondered if it was still on the A30. If so, that would not have been a good move on the part of the thief, we decided.

I picked up a statement form and attached it to my clipboard. It seemed like a good time to take a witness statement from Wainwright. After I had only written a few words, I was interrupted by a flurry of radio messages. The stolen Riley had been spotted by Surrey police near Camberley, and a couple of police units were in hot pursuit.

It was looking as though Wainwright's car was going to be recovered, so we took him with us and headed east along the A30 at some speed. Information Room had opened radio links with Surrey, and it seemed that there were a number of Hampshire and Surrey units involved in the chase.

The two men involved in the TDA were a couple of 19-year-olds, Anthony Penney and Patrick Gregson. Penney was the driver, and he was doing his best to outrun the pursuing police vehicles. The chase continued along the A30 towards London, where it came to a sudden end at Sunningdale.

There is a railway level crossing at Sunningdale, and the barrier gates were closed. This always causes a build-up of traffic, but Penney may not have realised what was ahead of them and started to overtake the stationary traffic. He and Gregson must have realised that there was a problem when they saw the crossing gates looming up in front of them. Penney braked, and they both jumped out of the car while it was still moving. The Riley struck another car, knocking it into the barrier gates. Both men ran for it but they were chased by Surrey officers and arrested within two or three minutes.

We arrived at Sunningdale a few minutes later. The Surrey people had done all the real police work and in traditional police jargon had 'nicked the bodies.' However, Martin and I were there to grab the 'bodies' from them and sort everything else out. The two of us had a quick discussion to decide which of us would deal with it. It was going to be my case, and Martin said he would help me with the paperwork.

Penney and Gregson had been taken to Egham police station. The three of us from Hartley Wintney arrived there shortly before midnight, and we saw that the blue Riley was parked in the police station yard. Naturally, the owner was worried about what had happened to his car, but luckily the damage to it was not very serious. I sat down with him and completed the witness statement that I had started writing earlier. We gave Wainwright his car back, he said thank you, and he drove it back to HW.

We spoke to the two TDA men in the cells at Egham. At night, people under arrest were taken to our divisional station. When we arrived at Aldershot, we gave the station sergeant a verbal report on everything that had happened. We then spent a couple of hours completing all the basic paperwork. The sergeant agreed that there was enough evidence to detain the two young men, and we drove back to HW.

The following afternoon, I returned to Aldershot to interview Penney and Gregson, and the two men made written statements under caution. They both stated that they had been hitch-hiking from Bournemouth to London and had spent about three hours on the A30 near Star Hill, where they'd hoped to hitch a ride. This had not been successful, and they'd decided to look for a car that they could take. Penney also admitted that he was a disqualified driver.

They shared a flat in North London, but it turned out that they had received notice from the owner to leave. The sergeant who was station officer at Aldershot decided that he was not prepared to release them on bail. I prepared an apprehension report for the prosecutor at Aldershot Magistrates' Court. They appeared at court on 10th October 1966 and were remanded in custody for three days.

In 1966, there was very little paperwork, compared with the present-day situation where prosecutions are the responsibility of the Crown Prosecution Service. The prosecutor at magistrates' courts was often a solicitor employed by the Hampshire Police. Sometimes inspectors or sergeants prosecuted. If it was a plea of guilty, the matter was quickly dealt with, and if a defendant pleaded not guilty, a date would be arranged for a trial.

Both men were sentenced to six months in prison. In addition, Penney received three months for driving whilst disqualified and three months for driving without insurance cover.

Bits and pieces of information and gossip came over the police grapevine about the men who had been at Sandgate with me, the class of '64. Only one of the Hampshire recruits had resigned, and the others were spread all over the county. Peter Spencer was earning a name for himself, having made a large number of crime arrests.

Then there was some interesting news about someone else from Sandgate, Brian Kenton. Not long after my arrival at HW, I spotted his name in a local newspaper. Kenton had been called to a fatal traffic accident near Reading. On the face of it, it had just been an accident, but Kenton had started to suspect that something was wrong. He became convinced that the incident was a murder that had been set up carefully to look like a traffic accident. His suspicions had led to an arrest and a conviction for murder.

Kenton had always been a clever man, I thought. I imagined that next time there was some news about him it would be of him receiving a medal or being promoted. This was not destined to be the case. A few months later, I picked up a newspaper and saw his name again – but this time the news was of a different sort. Kenton had been convicted of theft. I read the article and then read it again, as it was difficult to believe. It came as a shock to everyone who knew him. Kenton had stolen five pounds in cash that had been handed to him as found property. He had been sent to prison for six months.

12

During the sixties, the standard of living of most people in the UK had risen, and the increase in car ownership was an important indicator. Overall the economy was struggling, but by 1967 one person in five owned a car. The Government talked about wage restraint, but inflation was rising fast and pay rises for public service workers, including the police, were being held down.

Maureen started work as a cashier at the Westminster Bank in HW, a small branch in the High Street with a staff of six. Having two salaries and no children to support, we felt quite well off.

Many years later, I read that 1967 was a year marked by one interesting but obscure fact. From the time that World War II ended until the end of the twentieth century, it was the only year in which a British soldier was not killed in action. This gives us an idea of what was happening during that period, when countries inside the Commonwealth were gaining their independence one by one.

In some countries it happened peacefully. However, there were other places, including Kenya, Palestine, Aden, and Cyprus, where there was violence and bloodshed. In 1967, we did not realise that the next flashpoint would be much nearer home.

We received requests from all over the UK to obtain witness statements from people living on the section. One afternoon, I drove to a house near HW to see a local resident and take a written statement from him. Before parking the section car, I turned the radio off and then switched it back on after taking the statement. A few key words started coming over the air:

'house … burglary … suspect disturbed.' The call signs of the cars involved were all from our subdivision. Whatever was going on involved Yateley. Several units had been sent to the scene, and there was a series of radio messages going car to car. I recognised a couple of voices, one of which belonged to Peter Faulkner, the DC at Hartley Wintney. After finding out where it was, a house close to Yateley Common, I was on my way.

There were six or seven officers at the scene. One of them was Roy Green, one of the Yateley officers. Just after my arrival at the location, a call came over the radio about a traffic accident about 3 miles away. The officer who had that beat was also with us at Yateley Common, and he asked me if he could use the section car to go to the accident. I handed him the keys and then did my best to find out what was happening.

It seemed that a local resident had returned home and disturbed a burglar, who had run away. The first officers to arrive at the house spoke to the householder, who told them that all he had seen was a fleeting glimpse of a man running away. He had not seen the man's face and did not think that he would be able to recognise him if he saw him again.

One of the officers had spotted a Mini saloon parked on some open land three or four minutes' walk from the house where the burglary had occurred. Shortly before my arrival, a man called O'Toole had been seen walking towards the car. He was a short, stocky man in his thirties.

Peter Faulkner had asked him a few questions about the car and what he was doing in Yateley. He'd said that he was the owner of the car and had been driving from Woking to Reading to visit his mother. He had given a credible reason for being where he was. He did not look like a man who had been running, and he showed no particular signs of concern.

As it was a residential burglary, our CID officer would be in charge of the investigation. Peter Faulkner whispered to me that we would probably have to let O'Toole go, as there was no evidence that linked him to the break-in. At the same time, Peter thought that he should have a quick word with the householder to see if there was any further evidence that might help us. By this time some of the officers had left the scene, but there were still three or four of us there.

The house was about two minutes' walk from O'Toole's car. Peter asked me to keep an eye on O'Toole while he went back to the house to speak to the householder. He said that he would be back in a few minutes.

The other officers walked back to the house, and I stayed with O'Toole and his car.

O'Toole told me that he was concerned that he was being treated as a suspect. He had promised his mother that he would meet her at a particular time and he was already late. The best thing I could do was to keep him relaxed for a few minutes until the return of my colleagues. So, after giving him an apology for any inconvenience we were causing him, I did my best to engage him in conversation.

There is bound to be a limit to goodwill in these sorts of situations, and after we had been standing in the same place for about fifteen minutes, it was obvious that O'Toole was becoming less friendly. He told me that his mother suffered from a particular illness and tended to become agitated easily. I told him that my colleagues would be back in the next couple of minutes and that he would probably be on his way to Reading very soon.

'Where on earth are they?' I wondered. In my mind's eye I started to imagine them sitting down with the householder drinking tea. Another three or four minutes ticked by and I started to become concerned about the situation. With the exception of Martin Dickens and me, all the others on the section were experienced officers, so I did my best to reassure myself that they must know what they were doing.

However, the more I thought about it, the more bizarre it seemed. O'Toole had not been arrested, so we had no power to force him to remain where he was. If he called my bluff and insisted on leaving the scene, it would be decision time for me. He was technically a suspect but only in the widest sense of the word. So, legally, there were only two things that I could do: let him go or arrest him. If he was a suspect, it seemed strange that my colleagues had left me on my own with him and out of radio contact. This left me with a few worrying thoughts. Had they searched him? Had they taken his car keys away from him? Could he have a weapon on him?

At that point, my colleagues at the house might well have some evidence that linked O'Toole to the burglary, but we could not contact each other. None of us had PRs, and there was no access to the force radio system, as the HW section car was elsewhere. The only way they could make contact was by walking back to the car to explain what was happening.

Meanwhile, O'Toole's attitude was becoming more and more hostile, and he started to pace up and down alongside his parked Mini. I stayed with him within grabbing distance. Hindsight is always an excellent mode of thinking because it tends to have a good measure of logic thrown in. Maybe I should have marched him back to the car and made him sit in the passenger seat. This would have given me better control of the situation. At the same time I needed to bear in mind that he was not under arrest.

I thought it might be better to play for time. I did my best to defuse the situation by chatting to him, but I could soon tell that this was not doing much to help. He continued walking up and down and complaining that his mother would be very worried about him. Then he walked a few metres away from his car and confronted me in a more aggressive manner than before, saying that we had no right to detain him.

I positioned myself in front of him, and we stood for a few seconds staring at one another. 'It looks as though I shall have to arrest him,' I thought. Suddenly he lunged forward, with his right fist aimed at my stomach, and for a split second it went through my head that he had a knife. I stepped back instinctively, tripping over the large protruding root of a tree. O'Toole did not have a weapon and did not actually strike me. It was more like a boxer's feint, and afterwards I realised that he had managed to position me where he wanted me. As I was falling, O'Toole sprinted back towards the Mini. It had all happened very fast.

I picked myself up and went after him as fast as my legs would carry me. In what seemed to be no more than a couple of seconds, O'Toole had jumped into the driver's seat of his car and started the engine. As I reached the driver's door, the car started to move. As I came alongside it, my left hand came down on the roof of the car for maybe half a second. There was a bit of wheel spin and a cloud of dust as O'Toole hit the accelerator, and the Mini shot forward.

I found myself on the ground again. As I stood up, I threw my truncheon. It was an act of frustration as much as anything else, because the Mini was out of range. I was left standing in open country without a vehicle or any means of communication. I ran to the nearest house, spoke to the occupant, and used his phone to call IR.

About an hour later, the Mini was found abandoned about 5 miles away. Peter Faulkner made contact with RCS officers to help in identifying

O'Toole, and within a few days we knew who he was. O'Toole was one of several aliases used by the man, a professional burglar who had escaped from Parkhurst prison a few weeks before. In fact, when I read *Police Gazettes* it became obvious that he was one of the most active burglars in the country, and this made the whole sorry saga even more frustrating for me. He was arrested a few months later in another part of the country. Many years later, I heard more about O'Toole when he was arrested in London by Met officers. During police interviews, he admitted to more than 2,000 burglaries.

Of course Sergeant Hanson asked me what had happened at Yateley, and I did my best to give an account of it as diplomatically as possible. In my opinion, the episode was a terrible mess. It had left me with mixed feelings about what had happened; I was feeling a bit guilty but angry about the situation that my colleagues had put me in. Charlie Dickens told me a couple of weeks later that the sergeant had blamed the other officers at the scene for what went wrong. However, it was a useful lesson for me.

A few weeks later, Sergeant Hanson asked me to take some urgently needed official reports to headquarters. I drove to Winchester, delivered the correspondence as requested, and then made my way down West Hill into the centre of the city. As I did so, calls started coming over the radio about an armed robbery. Two cars were on their way to the scene, and other units were being sent to cover main roads surrounding the city.

Traffic in the centre of Winchester was heavy and moving slowly, and I was doing my best to remember the location of the street where the robbery had taken place. I saw a police car coming in the opposite direction, and as we drew opposite one another, I waved at the officer driving it. 'Where is it?' I shouted.

I recognised the driver, who was an inspector based in Winchester, and he just looked at me with a totally blank expression. 'He has not got his radio switched on,' I thought. He certainly looked as if he had no idea what was going on.

Then my memory started to click back into action. It was just around the corner, I remembered, and I pulled my section car up outside the address before any of the Winchester officers arrived. The buildings here looked like ordinary houses, but then I recalled that this place was a hostel for men who had recently been released from prison. The manager of the hostel was standing at the front door and waving at me. I asked him a few questions about what had happened. About fifteen minutes earlier, two men had entered the hostel armed with handguns. They had gone to the manager's office, threatened him with their guns, and forced him to hand over all the cash from his safe. They had then made off in a car with about £300 in cash.

First I had to obtain details of the car that they were using. Luckily, one of the residents had seen the car and written a description, including the registration number. This was crucial information, especially as the robbers had only made off about four or five minutes before my arrival.

When the Winchester officers reached the scene, they saw me using the radio and were obviously puzzled about how I had managed to get there before them. While we discussed what had happened, the radio went quiet for a while. Then the air waves suddenly became very busy.

A Traffic Division PC in his patrol car on his own had spotted the suspects' car on the main road between Winchester and Petersfield and started to follow it. The driver of the getaway car had slammed the brakes on coming to a sudden stop, and a man had jumped out, brandishing a handgun. As the officer retreated to the back of his patrol car, the gunman had fired a volley of shots into the police car, hitting the radio, radiator, and tyres. The bandit car had then driven off at speed.

There was a call directing me to go to headquarters as quickly as possible. On my arrival at West Hill, I was given a box containing firearms and ammunition and instructed to take it to a rendezvous point close to where the shooting incident had occurred.

A sergeant and about ten PCs were waiting for me at the RVP. The sergeant then handed out handguns and ammunition to everyone, including me. We all received a revolver and ten rounds of ammunition. My firearms training did not take long.

'Do you know how to use a gun?' he asked everyone.

'I'm okay with a rifle, but I've never used a pistol,' I said.

'Look here. If you want to shoot someone, point it like this, and pull the trigger. Aim at his chest.'

The sergeant showed me how to load the revolver and then placed it inside a holster.

'Put it in your pocket. If you use it, don't shoot yourself or any of us.'

By this time a large number of roadblocks had been set up, and the armed officers were divided into pairs as search teams. The sergeant put me with an experienced older PC, and the two of us drove to a place where the suspects had last been seen. From there, we were sent to a village a couple of miles away, where there had been a report of an abandoned car.

We found the car, but it had been there for at least six hours and had no links with the robbery. The roadblocks and search teams were kept busy for several hours, but the trail was starting to become cold. It appeared that the robbers had managed to get clear of the surrounding area, and eventually the search was called off.

It was the first incident that I had been called to involving criminals using firearms, and it was the only time I carried a firearm as a police officer. The fact that shots had been fired was serious, but it appeared that the objective of the robbers had been to damage the police car rather than the policeman in it.

At that time, training officers to use firearms was not given a high priority in the police service. There were very few incidents in which criminals used guns, but another aspect was that nearly all of the older men had completed military service, often as National Servicemen. Some had served in the Second World War or in Korea.

However, during the sixties there was a new generation of young men and women coming into the police service who had not served in the armed forces, and many had probably never seen a firearm. By this time, the Hampshire Police was carrying out proper firearms-training courses that lasted four days. I was among the officers selected for training. Many of the weapons that the force owned dated back to the Second World War, but by 1967 these were being replaced by Browning semi-automatic pistols.

The arrival of immigrants in large numbers to the UK was becoming a major political issue. There had always been immigration into this country, but in previous centuries immigrants had arrived in fairly small numbers and easily integrated into our society. One of the basic ideas of the British Commonwealth was that its citizens could move freely from one Commonwealth country to another.

From 1948 until 1962 there had been what could be described as an open-door policy, and this had resulted in large numbers of immigrants arriving from the West Indies and the Indian subcontinent. The fact that these immigrants were not Europeans meant that race would always tend to be an underlying issue. Immigration added another dimension to police work in many parts of the UK, as officers found themselves dealing with people from a variety of cultures. Not surprisingly, many immigrants had attitudes and beliefs that were different from the Anglo-Saxon majority.

European citizens and people from countries outside the Commonwealth were classified as 'aliens' and subject to restrictions under the Aliens Act. Police had to keep records of all aliens living in their area, and at HW there was a card-index system holding the details of about twenty foreigners who lived on our section. By law, every alien had to register with the police upon arrival in the UK and had to inform police of any change of address. We had forms in the front office at HW to complete whenever one of them called at the station to give us the details required.

Apart from the issues relating to immigration and race, there was the question of Britain's relationship with Europe. The president of France, Charles de Gaulle, had blocked Britain's attempt to join the European Common Market a few years before, and many British people were anti-European. Most people living in the British Isles saw themselves as quite different from the people living on the European mainland, and our history ensured that we had closer ties with the countries in the Commonwealth.

There were changes at this time in the laws relating to divorce and this made it easier for married people to obtain a divorce. Since the early sixties, an oral contraceptive pill had been available for women. In 1970, Family Planning Association clinics started prescribing 'the Pill' to unmarried women. Although abortion remained a crime, the law was amended, and it became fairly easy for a woman to have an abortion legally. This all happened over a fairly short period of time, and in later years these changes were referred to as part of a 'sexual revolution'.

From time to time I would pick up information on the grapevine about some of the 'old boys' from Sandgate. I knew that Peter Spencer was always keen to become a detective and during 1967 he had been appointed to the CID as a DC. With only three years under his belt, this was very good going, and Peter must have overtaken several other officers with quite a bit more service than he had.

One afternoon, while on patrol, I received a short radio message: 'Alpha 72. Call from a woman at a house called Sunnyville, A30, Phoenix Green. Theft. Suspects disturbed. One person detained by informant's husband.'

Finding places in a hurry was always a problem in country areas, but I knew exactly where this house was on a stretch of gravel road alongside the A30. A man living in the house had disturbed two men stealing petrol from his car, which was parked outside his house. He had overpowered one of the men, and the second man had run off. As I was some distance away, it took me at least five minutes to reach the house.

The man who had been detained was a 25-year-old called John Conway. When I questioned him, he admitted straight away that he had been stealing fuel. When I asked about the other man, he said that he did not know who he was. Conway's story was that he had been travelling from Cornwall to London in his jeep and had given a lift to someone he had met the previous day. I knew there were two things I had to do. Firstly I had to make sure that Conway could not escape, and secondly I had to find the other man.

After putting Conway in the Hillman Husky, I used the radio to call for some assistance at the scene. It took about fifteen minutes before the promised reinforcements arrived, in the shape of one officer, a TD motorcyclist. This was frustrating, because it did not move the situation forward any further.

We had to wait for another ten minutes before a police car with two Fleet officers reached the scene, and during that time I had the chance to take a look at Conway's vehicle, which appeared to be an American-made jeep. I looked closely at the vehicle excise licence on the windscreen. One of the things that I had learned in the last three years was how valuable a VEL could be in providing useful information in all sorts of cases.

One of my colleagues told me that Ford made jeeps, and the VEL confirmed that the make was a Ford. I asked the two PCs from Fleet to look after Conway, and they put him into their car. With the motorcyclist, there were four of us, and we decided to carry out a search of the immediate area. The man we were looking for had run off in the general direction of Winchfield, where our local railway station was, and so we decided that would be the first place to visit.

There were three or four people standing on the London-bound side waiting for a train, but none of them fitted the description of the suspect. We checked the rest of the station buildings, including the toilets, but it later became clear that our search had not been as thorough as it should have, because our suspect was at the station. It turned out that he could see us but we did not see him.

Using both cars, we searched the surrounding area, but there was no sign of the man we were looking for. At Fleet, I asked Conway a few questions about the jeep that he had been driving. I had a strong feeling that there was something wrong. Eventually I told Conway that I intended to check the chassis number and frame number on the jeep.

Conway then told me that he wanted to confess to stealing the jeep and that he had given me a false name and address. After completing a second CRO check, I felt that I now had the proper identity. The check showed that he had two or three previous convictions for theft.

It turned out that the jeep was not a Ford. Conway had been living in north London. He told me that he could not afford to buy a car, and one day he had noticed a grey Willys jeep parked in a street about half a mile from where he lived. He had decided to steal it, and his MO had been simple but effective. Conway had spotted a blue Ford saloon parked in a side street, so he had broken into it one night and stolen the vehicle licence from the windscreen.

The following day, he had vehicle number plates made with the same number that appeared on the stolen VEL and managed to find a vehicle key that could start the jeep. He then drove the jeep away and parked it in the street where he lived. Next day, he repainted the jeep with blue paint and put on the new number plates. After that, he put the stolen VEL on the windscreen, which meant that the number on the tax disc matched the number plates.

The enquiry had moved a couple of notches higher up the ladder of criminality. The sergeant at Fleet decided that Conway would be detained for the time being while enquiries were completed. The Metropolitan Police was contacted to obtain a statement from the owner of the jeep. There was nothing further that I could do for the time being, and so I decided to go home. By now the section car had been taken back to HW for Jim Cotton, the PC on late turn.

Fleet is about 4 miles from Hartley Wintney, and Jim Cotton came over to Fleet to pick me up. When we were about halfway back, we drove past a man standing at the side of the road, and it struck me that he fitted the description of the second man we had been looking for. We drove back, and I spoke to him. He seemed nervous. I asked him some questions about the theft of petrol, and he looked quite dispirited. Then he admitted that he had been involved. Five minutes later we were back at Fleet.

'That was quick work,' said the sergeant, looking impressed.

The name of the second man was Eric Seddon, and I asked him where he had been hiding while we were looking for him. He grinned and told me that he had been in the toilets at Winchfield railway station. He had seen us coming and climbed upwards onto a rafter above the door. He had been looking down at us when we looked into the toilets. I wanted to kick myself – that had been careless! It was another useful lesson. 'If you are going to carry out a search, don't forget to look up as well,' I thought.

Seddon had not been involved in the theft of the jeep. He went to court and was fined for the theft of petrol. Conway was sent to prison for six months.

At HW crime arrests were few and far between, because so much time was spent dealing with traffic accidents. At any one time, I would be working on at least two or three careless driving cases. All completed files went to Sergeant Hanson, who would decide whether or not to recommend proceedings. The file would go to Fleet, and from there it would go to the Process Office at Aldershot, and an application would be made for a summons.

Our crime cases went to Aldershot Magistrates' Court, and our traffic cases went to the court at Odiham. Most people pleaded guilty, and I was not often called to give evidence. Most of the prosecutions were dealt with by one of the sergeants from the subdivision. In the event of a contested case, the prosecution would normally be placed in the hands of a solicitor working for the Hampshire Police.

In the summer of 1967, Maureen and I went on holiday to Ireland with her parents. My father-in-law, Charles McDonald, worked for Gallaher's, the tobacco company. The company had close links to Northern Ireland and had begun as a family-owned tobacco manufacturer in Belfast. It had expanded, and by 1967 it was one of the largest British tobacco companies, owning several other tobacco producers including Senior Service.

We thought that it would be a good idea to split the holiday into two parts. We would visit Northern Ireland for the first week and the Irish Republic for the second week. My father-in-law had come originally from a small village in County Carlow, and there were relatives that we could visit in that area. He had lived in London since he was in his twenties and had served in the British Army in the Second World War. He had always been very pro-British, although like most Irishmen of his generation, he was not happy that Ireland had been partitioned. As a young boy in Ireland, he had lived through the years known as the Troubles. These problems did not end in 1922 when the Irish Free State was set up. Within a short time, those who were against partition were in rebellion, and this would plunge the new state into a bitter civil war.

The anti-treaty paramilitaries who had opposed the Irish Free State Government in 1923 were destined to remain at war on and off for the next few decades. They would be known as the Irish Republican Army, and the last few decades of the twentieth century would be marked by a new period of the Troubles.

The managing director of Gallaher's, Stewart Moore, owned a holiday home on the coast of Northern Ireland, near the village of Port Ballintrae. At some point, the fact that we were planning a holiday in Northern Ireland must have come up in conversation. Stewart Moore told my father-in-law that we were welcome to stay in his house at Port Ballintrae for our first week. We had an invitation to stay on a farm in County Kildare with one of Maureen's cousins the following week.

In 1967 there were signs that all was not well in Northern Ireland. Its society was divided into two distinct social and political groups, nationalists and loyalists. Linked to this was a sectarian divide because, as a general rule, nationalists were Catholics and loyalists were Protestants. There was also an ethnic dimension, as nationalists mainly came from a background that was native Irish, whilst loyalists were descended from people who had arrived from England or Scotland. Loyalists usually voted for the Unionist Party, and nationalists voted for nationalist or republican parties, such as Sinn Fein.

Northern Ireland had a devolved Unionist government with its own prime minister. Loyalists outnumbered nationalists, and the Unionists had managed to devise a system of constituency and ward boundaries so they could maximise their political power. This system, known as 'gerrymandering' was bitterly resented by nationalists. There was a considerable amount of discrimination against nationalists when it came to housing and employment. The situation was further confused because two of the six counties of Northern Ireland had nationalist majorities.

During 1967, there was a rise in tension when Nationalists started a civil-rights campaign. Terence O'Neill, the Unionist prime minister of Northern Ireland, was seen as a moderate, and Harold Wilson told O'Neill that there had to be reform when it came to housing and local government boundaries. There was an election in Northern Ireland, the Unionist party split, and O'Neill found himself out of office.

At that time I knew very little about Northern Ireland. We had gone there for a holiday, but we soon became aware of some of the tensions there as we travelled around. Sir Robin Kinehan, one of the directors of Gallaher, lived in a large country house a few miles from Belfast. We were surprised to receive an invitation to call in for tea from the Kinehans. They were charming people and probably typical of those who would be considered the landed gentry of Northern Ireland.

They asked me what I did for a living, and when I told them, Sir Robin said that he had a friend who was a policeman. When I asked him who that was, it turned out that he was talking about Colonel St Johnston, the chief constable of Lancashire.

Colonel St Johnston was regarded as one of most progressive chief constables in the UK and had been one of the pioneers in the development of personal radios. I explained to Sir Robin that PCs such as me were not usually on first-name terms with chief constables. Sir Robin had been lord mayor of Belfast and had concerns about the sectarian divide and employment in the city.

Gallaher's did not employ Catholics in their Belfast factories. Sir Robin said that he would like to end that type of discrimination, but the loyalist workforce was bitterly opposed to the idea that Catholics be employed there, and the company feared a violent backlash if they tried to change things.

Sir Robin's house had extensive grounds, and we were shown an interesting reminder of eighteenth-century Irish history. In 1798 there had been a large uprising in Ireland against British rule. Although the rebels had eventually been defeated, Protestants and Catholics had united to fight the British, which had come as a serious shock to the government of the day. Sir Robin showed us a cemetery on his land where Protestants who had been killed in the uprising were buried.

Northern Ireland is a very beautiful place, but many people think about its recent history and are concerned about going there for a holiday. We enjoyed our visit there and then headed south for the second week. Eventually, we arrived at Des Connolly's farm in the countryside of County Kildare.

When we arrived, Des was having a meeting with a representative of the Erin Food Company. Des had just sold two or three fields of peas to Erin and had opened a bottle of Irish whiskey to celebrate. My father-in-law and I joined the two of them in the lounge. Whiskey was handed around in large glasses, and it did not take long for a second bottle to be opened.

My father-in-law and I were not heavy drinkers and certainly not able to drink whiskey at the speed that it was being downed. As we tackled the third bottle, I was aware that the room was starting to move from side to side. I stood up and found that walking was not going to be as easy as usual.

'Sure, you need something inside you,' said Des.

He then handed me a large glass of Guinness. I started to drink it but did not believe that it was quite the right cure that Des believed it to be. Shortly after that, I headed for bed. I did not think that Ireland had problems with earthquakes but there was no doubt in my mind that there was something like that going on. The farmhouse was moving around like a ship at sea.

The next day, the house seemed to have settled down, but I did not feel very well. 'There must be earthquakes in Ireland,' I thought. 'Maybe the Irish Tourist Board just does not want to mention them.'

13

One afternoon, a radio call took me to a spot on the A30 about 2 miles west of HW. A woman had seen a man she suspected of being a poacher on some farmland.

After finding a place to park, I had a muddy walk to a clump of trees on the other side of the field in front of me. After reaching the trees, I looked in all directions. There was no sign of anyone, so I moved forward, crossing a second field.

At the other side there were some woods, and I went on for a few metres. I observed a man ahead of me, some distance away and I moved forward quietly. Then I saw the man kneel down and take aim with a shotgun. He stayed in a kneeling position for two or three minutes but did not fire at anything. Then he stood up.

By this time, I was very close to him. Something told me that it would not be such a great idea to sneak up on him and take him by surprise. There were quite a large number of accidents involving shotguns, and there was always the danger that he might hear a noise, wheel round, and open fire. Maybe Plan B would be better. I called out to him, and he turned around and stood facing me.

He was a man in his mid forties. He was wearing blue jeans, a sweater, and what I would describe as a leather hunting jacket. It was all slightly unreal. If I had been in the cinema watching a western, this would be the point at which a caption would appear on the screen, saying something like 'New Mexico Territory, 1872.'

The man was carrying a modern-looking shotgun and wearing a bandolier over his shoulder, Mexican-bandit style, with enough ammo for a military campaign. There was a huge Bowie knife in a sheath attached to his belt. In order to ensure that he stayed abreast of hunter-style fashion, he was wearing what appeared to be a leather Austrian-style hat with a feather in it.

I approached the man and asked him to unload his shotgun. After he had done that, it was time for a few questions.

Did he have a shotgun certificate? He produced a certificate from a pocket and admitted that he was looking to bag a rabbit – or whatever he could find.

Did he have permission to be on that land? He said that a friend had recommended this area as being 'safe' to go shooting in. He was carrying a hunter's bag, but it was empty. His clothing suggested that he was a fearless hunter, but he had not managed to shoot anything.

I took his details, gave him a warning, and sent him on his way.

During 1967, there were major changes to the structure of policing in the UK. Home Secretary Roy Jenkins was determined to push through his plans for amalgamating police forces and this would mark the end of all the small city and county borough forces that had existed for many years. It would also mean the end of some of the smaller county forces.

Planning started on the proposed Hampshire amalgamation during 1966, and the following year, the chief constable, Sir Douglas Osmond, announced that the three local forces, Hampshire and Isle of Wight, the Portsmouth City Police, and the Southampton City Police were to be amalgamated. There would be one force, the Hampshire Constabulary that would be divided into eleven divisions, with its headquarters at Winchester.

We all knew that many issues would need to be addressed. There was some amusement when police officers were told that everyone would be divided into two categories: 'frozen' and 'unfrozen'. Police Regulations had given all police officers a number of safeguards when it came to the question of transfers. This meant that officers who had joined a particular force that later became part of a larger force could not be transferred out of their original force area unless they agreed to move. If they wanted to stay in the force that they had joined they could do so and would be classified as 'frozen'. If they were happy to move to another part of the new, larger force, they would be designated 'unfrozen'.

Rest days would quickly become a divisive issue. In Hampshire, the official policy was that we worked a forty-hour week, with leave days spread across a four-week period. However, we had always had a manpower problem. For example, in 1965 Hampshire had an establishment of 1346 officers but an actual strength of 1137. This meant that during the four-week schedule we worked two rest days, for which we were paid. These rest days were known as Additional Rest Days, referred to as ARDs.

Our colleagues in the two city forces had never been expected to work ARDs, and it seemed that most of them did not wish to do so. The regulations stated that officers were not allowed to take any other form of paid employment without the authority of the chief officer of police. However, rumour had it that some of those in Portsmouth and Southampton were moonlighting. There was a strong feeling by many officers in the county force that this was the main reason that our city colleagues did not wish to work ARDs.

The amalgamation process seemed to go very smoothly in Hampshire, although this was not the case in many other parts of the country. There were some people in the two city forces who did not like the idea of amalgamation. This was especially true of officers in Southampton, who continued to show their displeasure for several years when they had to work with their county colleagues.

Every officer had an overtime card on which all hours of overtime worked was recorded. It was useful when you needed time off. For example, if you wanted a whole day off, you could take eight hours 'time-off'. My understanding of the regulations was that any overtime that was three months old and had not been taken as time off could in theory be submitted for paid overtime. However, supervisors kept a close watch on the overtime cards, and when any overtime was nearly three months old, we would be told to take some time off.

The result of this was that every day there were a large number of officers in Hampshire shown as 'time-off'. Naturally, this made the manpower situation that bit worse. The overtime budget in Hampshire was small and normally only paid when there were large-scale incidents or public-order operations. The authority of the chief constable was usually needed before paid overtime was approved. During my service in Hampshire, I was only aware of two occasions when paid overtime was approved.

About this time, a natural gas pipeline was being constructed across Hampshire. The pay was very good, and there were many stories doing the rounds about police officers who had taken jobs on the pipeline. They took other jobs, as well. On a couple of occasions I spotted policemen working as barmen in pubs, usually ones that were off the beaten track.

Dealing with sudden-death enquiries is one of the most important jobs that police have to deal with. Most deaths are from natural causes, and in the vast majority of cases, doctors are happy to issue death certificates, and then family members can go ahead and organise a funeral. However, there is general rule that all sudden or unexpected deaths where a doctor has not attended within the previous two weeks must be reported to police.

The coroner has a legal duty to enquire into certain types of sudden deaths, and this includes homicides, industrial accidents, road traffic accidents, and cases where people die in police custody or in prison. In every case, police have a duty to the coroner to ensure that all sudden deaths are properly investigated and must do all that is possible to check whether foul play could be involved.

A typical sudden death is when someone collapses and dies unexpectedly. Unless there are some unusual circumstances, police enquiries will be limited at this stage. The officer dealing with the matter needs to ask a few basic questions and ensure that there is nothing that appears suspicious. The officer should then complete a brief report for the coroner. A CID officer is always informed but will not usually become involved unless there are some unusual circumstances.

'Mac' McLaughlin had explained to me that a sudden-death enquiry was a very important task that put a lot of responsibility on the shoulders of a PC who was dealing with it. What might appear to be an accident or a suicide could actually be a murder, as has happened on many occasions. Over the years there have been quite a few murder cases in which officers have missed clues that they should have spotted. However, all is not lost at this point, because the next line of defence against a murderer walking free is the pathologist.

The post mortem examination is the next stage of the investigation. This is when the pathologist should spot that something is wrong. There have been cases in which police officers have stated that there is nothing suspicious but then the pathologist has found something that points to foul play. It can be embarrassing when the pathologist rings a senior CID officer and points out that the dead person has been stabbed or shot. A murder enquiry can get off to a bad start if the crime scene has not been kept intact and useful evidence is lost.

One summer afternoon we were called to a house where a 52-year-old woman had committed suicide. The woman's daughter had become concerned when she'd gone to visit her and not been able to gain entry to the house. Finding the doors locked and all the windows closed, she'd contacted her husband, who had come to the house and managed to force one of the windows open.

After he had gained entry to the house, he found his mother-in-law lying on the floor in her bedroom and seen straight away that she had injuries. He'd then made a phone call to the family GP, who went straight to the house. After seeing the body, the doctor phoned the police station.

On my arrival at the house I could see that the dead woman had a deep cut to her left wrist, a small cut to her right arm, and bruises to both legs. I was later told that the deceased had been under psychiatric care for much of her life and had been suffering from serious depression since the death of her husband six months earlier. I found a letter, consisting of three sheets of paper, lying on a cabinet next to the woman's bed. This was written in the woman's handwriting and told of her intention to take her own life.

On the floor near the bed there were three kitchen knives, a knife sharpener, a small bottle of acid marked 'poison', and some tablets. I removed all of these items from the house and placed them inside a plastic bag. As it was a suicide, DC Faulkner and the sergeant came to the house to make sure that everything was being done correctly.

There was nothing that pointed at anything except suicide. At the station, I completed a report for the coroner, and a few days later an inquest was held at Aldershot police station. The cause of death was a haemorrhage from the left radial artery, and the inquest verdict was suicide.

The following month, we received a call to a fatal traffic accident on a road that ran alongside Blackbushe Airport. I was the first officer on the scene and dealt with it. We soon discovered that this was an incident that could only be described as tragic, in every meaning of the word.

A van driver had been delivering items to factories and offices in Hampshire. He'd brought his wife and two young children with him in the van. It seemed that he'd wanted them to have a trip with him while he delivered his goods to the various locations on his list. The driver had stopped a short distance from the factory that he was going to, near the airport, and his wife and children got out of the van.

They stood in a group at the side of the road near the van, and the wife told me later that she'd planned to take the two children for a walk while her husband carried out his delivery. As the husband started to drive away, one of his children, a 2-year-old boy, suddenly ran into the road directly into the path of the van. It all happened in what we might describe as a split second. The child suffered severe head injuries and died within a few minutes.

As I reached the scene, the ambulance went past on its way to the nearest casualty unit with the mortally injured child and his family. John Snook, one of the sergeants at Fleet, arrived at the scene of the accident a few minutes after I did. While I was drawing a diagram of the accident scene, John Snook sat in the driver's seat of the van to ascertain what could be seen by the driver. Sergeant Snook reported that if a small child were standing close to the vehicle by the front near side, the driver would not be able to see him.

Next day, I drove to see the parents of the dead child at their home in Guildford, in order to take witness statements from them. My work as a police officer took me into some very sad situations from time to time, but this case was the most tragic of them all. I wrote their statements for them at their dictation and then returned to HW. There would be an inquest, and I would have to complete a report for the coroner.

In police work, experience is very important, and the only way to gain experience is to do the job. Looking back on those early years, it seemed as though I was trying to assemble a giant jigsaw with the name Police Work on the box. Those first years, from 1964 to 1967, gave me a chance to sort out a large piece of the jigsaw, and my self-confidence increased bit by bit as I did so.

Becoming a policeman had been a major change in my life. In 1963 I had been working for an American bank in London when I made the decision to apply to join the Hampshire Police. It seemed to come as a shock and a surprise to many of my friends and family. No member of my family had ever been a police officer.

That was not quite true, I discovered later. There had been one policeman on my father's side of the family in Northumberland, England's most northerly county. This was John Knipe, who had been a PC in the Northumberland Constabulary. His link to the family was that he was married to one of my father's aunts.

He was an Irishman from County Armagh who had become a police constable in 1884. He worked at twelve different stations in Northumberland and spent his last six years at Wallsend. When he retired in 1912, the article in one of the local newspapers had this headline: 'King's Medallist – Local Constable's Meritorious Conduct'.

The history of Northumberland and the border country in general has been marked by considerable violence and lawlessness in the past. It has been fought over in the wars between the English and Scots, and for many years after that the border area remained quite ungovernable. The border clans spent much of their time either feuding with other clans or carrying out raids to steal their cattle; they had no particular loyalty to the kings of England or Scotland. It seems that some of this lawlessness carried on into more recent times.

The newspaper article mentioned some of the arrests that PC Knipe had carried out during his service. One of these was the arrest of a man called George Fair, who had been wanted by police in Roxburgh, Scotland for a criminal assault on a man described in the newspaper as an imbecile. The newspaper referred to George Fair as a 'notorious border character' well known for being violent. PC Knipe found Fair asleep in a barn in a remote part of the countryside at four o'clock one morning.

Nowadays, an arresting officer would use his/her PR to call for transport, but it was not quite the same in those days. The newspaper article referred to Fair as a desperate character, a violent criminal who had terrorised the Borders countryside for some time. Fair had been arrested several times but had never been taken single-handedly. PC Knipe was patrolling by himself and had no means of calling for assistance, but he managed to walk his prisoner for 7 miles until he reached Wooler police station.

After that, he took Fair across the border to Kelso and handed him over to the Roxburgh police. PC Knipe was awarded the Badge of Merit for making this arrest, and Fair was sentenced to eighteen months' hard labour in Calton Prison, Edinburgh.

I learned that, while working at Stannington, a country beat, PC Knipe had been attacked by a gang of poachers. He had been badly beaten and left for dead. When he failed to return to the police house, his wife had contacted his colleagues, and a search had been carried out by the police and local people. He was found but with serious injuries – he was off duty for four months.

The year before he retired, Knipe was awarded the King's Silver Coronation Medal for long meritorious and good conduct in the police service. The article mentions that he was forty-nine years of age and that he was the only constable to be awarded the medal that year.

I am unsure how many children were in the family, but I understand that there was at least one son and a daughter. Apparently, a son had emmigrated to the United States and lived in Boston. After retiring from the police, John Knipe had gone to live in Boston, and his wife and a daughter had gone with him. His son had joined the United States Army in World War I and been awarded a number of decorations for bravery. This included the Croix de Guerre, awarded by the French.

My link with this branch of the family was my American cousin, John Love, the grandson of John Knipe. Our first meeting must have been about 1951, when I was a young boy living in Northumberland and John Love came to visit us. My cousin was very fond of his British and Irish connections and always kept in touch with me. Many years later he provided me with much of the information about his grandfather.

Much like family heirlooms, there are stories in families that are passed down a few generations, and so I heard another story about John Knipe. It paints an interesting picture of the man and the times in which he lived. This was an era when Jews were being persecuted in Russia, and many of them left the Russian Empire and made their way to England. This story is about a Jewish man who was travelling around the north of England selling jewellery.

He might have been described as a pedlar or travelling salesman. It would not make any sense for a salesman to carry all his stock with him. The travelling jeweller stopped at a small country inn for a couple of nights while he travelled around the surrounding area selling his goods. At the inn, he handed a bag containing the bulk of his jewellery to the innkeeper for safekeeping.

When it was time to leave the inn, he paid his bill and asked for the bag that contained his jewellery. The innkeeper's reply was 'What bag?' He denied ever having received the bag.

Shortly after that, a distressed jewellery salesman knocked on the door of the local police house, where he met my father's aunt. She told him that her husband was on patrol and asked the man to wait for him at the house. Sometime later, John Knipe returned home to have his evening meal, where he met the jeweller. They had a cup of tea together, and then John Knipe went to see the innkeeper.

I would have liked to have been a fly on the wall at the inn that day. The innkeeper told PC Knipe that he had never seen any bag containing property. This did not go down well with John Knipe. I can only imagine what he might have said, in his Armagh accent, and the look of contempt on his face.

'I want that bag back.'

The innkeeper's memory must have received a strong surge of energy at this point. He suddenly remembered that he *had* been given a bag to look after, and he went and found it. PC Knipe was able to hand it back to its rightful owner. Back at the police house, the travelling jeweller was invited to have supper with the family.

The jewellery salesman was overjoyed to have his property returned to him and offered John Knipe some money for what he had done, but this was politely refused. At some point, the jeweller went on his way, but there was an interesting end to the story. The following day, Mrs Knipe found a valuable piece of jewellery lying on a mantelpiece in the house.

At the time I left school, my maternal grandparents were living in Headbourne Worthy, a village just outside Winchester, and I would often go there to visit them. On one occasion in 1963, I saw a police recruiting trailer parked near King Alfred's statue in the centre of Winchester. At that time I was starting to lose interest in banking and was wondering whether it would be a good idea to do something different.

Inside the trailer there was a display of photographs showing police officers doing all sorts of things. Some were driving fast-looking patrol cars, and there were dog handlers working their way through forests, tracking down criminals. A couple of detectives were shown examining the scene of a murder, and there were shots of policemen abseiling down the sides of high buildings. I did not know what on earth they were doing, but it looked exciting!

An inspector and a sergeant were standing outside the trailer, answering questions from the public. I had a bit of a chat with the inspector. He must have realised that I was interested, so he handed me a card with the address of the police headquarters. My life was destined to change course after that. We may all try to control our destinies, but every so often chance plays a part in our lives.

It is a fact that in John Knipe's time policemen would sometimes mete out summary justice to people who broke the law or caused them problems. As I have mentioned, by the 1960s the old 'Wild West' style of doing things was rapidly going out of fashion.

The relationship between the police and public in Hampshire was usually very good, and generally it was that bit better in the rural areas. However, there was always a hooligan element, even in the countryside. In small towns and villages, most troublemakers knew better than to upset their local policeman. There was a certain line, and those who crossed it risked some kind of retribution.

When Sergeant Hanson went on leave for two weeks, an experienced PC by the name of John Hilton was brought in from another part of the division to take over as acting sergeant. It happened that a dance had been organised for a Saturday night at a community hall in Yateley. That night, a 999 call was received advising that a fight had broken out involving a number of youths, and the acting sergeant went there with one of the officers from HW.

A group of youths who lived in and around Fleet had arrived at the dance and had clashed with another group, who lived in Yateley. It did not appear that there was much of a fight, but when the police arrived, a large number of young people were milling about outside the hall. John Hilton recognised some of them, including an 18-year-old who had a reputation as a troublemaker and the leader of a local gang of youths in Fleet.

Nobody was arrested, but the two officers spent some time there to ensure that there was no further trouble. The section car had been parked in the car park at the hall. Upon returning to the car, they found that they could not drive it away, as two of the tyres had been slashed.

John Hilton noticed three or four members of the Fleet gang standing not far away, and it seemed that they found the situation amusing. This included the 18-year-old gang leader. The amusement was not shared by the two officers, and Hilton let it be known that he intended to find out who was responsible.

One evening about two weeks later, the 18-year-old gang leader was walking home past a parade of shops. He was grabbed from behind and dragged into the entrance of one of the shops, where he was punched two or three times. He arrived home later with his clothes covered in blood and told his parents what had happened.

Within a couple of hours, an official complaint had been made against John Hilton, alleging assault, and the DCI was given the job of investigating the matter. However, the PC had an alibi. John Hilton said that he had been nowhere near the parade of shops when the assault took place and that he had been playing cards with some local men in Fleet. All the card players were well-respected local residents, and they told the investigating officer that John Hilton had been with them at the time the assault took place. The allegation against Hilton soon became a dead duck.

The Road Safety Act of 1967 was to change people's driving habits forever. Barbara Castle was one of the Government's most dynamic personalities. When she was first appointed Minister of Transport, about 8,000 people were dying in accidents each year on Britain's roads. She was so determined to do something about it that she brought in a totally new set of laws. The Road Safety Act introduced the offence of driving with excess alcohol and the concept of a legal limit of alcohol for drivers.

Police could now carry out breath tests on drivers. The first breathalyser kits were fairly crude, but they indicated that a driver had consumed more alcohol than the legal limit and provided a power of arrest.

When a driver was arrested, the sergeant at the station would carry out a procedure in accordance with the Act, and a police surgeon would be called to the station to take a blood sample from the detained person. The sample would be sent to a forensic science laboratory for analysis to see whether the level of alcohol in the blood was higher than the legal limit. If it was above, a summons would be issued. Another important factor was that defendants lost their right to elect trial by jury at the crown court.

Any major change like this was bound to be controversial. The new legislation was described as undemocratic by many people, including some politicians and journalists. There was an outbreak of anger and complaints by all sorts of people who should have known better.

During the first twelve months the breathalyser was in use, the death toll on the roads fell by 1200. By the dawn of the twenty-first century, the annual death rate would have fallen to about half of what it had been in the early 1960s. It is not easy to calculate how many lives have been saved by this legislation, but my own calculations suggest that between 1967 and the year 2000 it was probably about 90,000. The National Health Service has saved billions of pounds, and the roads are considerably safer.

With one fell swoop, the problems of enforcement that had bedevilled the police for many years were swept away. There were also a few stories doing the rounds that one or two of my colleagues had managed to settle a few old scores. One related to a businessman from Basingstoke who had been arrested for drunk driving on three different occasions. He had been found not guilty at crown court three times. Adding insult to injury, he had assaulted the arresting officer on one occasion.

A new law came into force during the night, when the hands on a clock moved gently past midnight, and shortly afterwards the businessman from Basingstoke was stopped for speeding. He was probably not very happy about being breathalysed and arrested within fifteen minutes of the new legislation coming into force. However, it seemed that his luck had finally run out.

The earliest point at which a PC was allowed to sit the promotion examination for sergeant was after completing three years' service. However, all candidates had to pass three educational exams before they could sit the sergeants' exam.

I passed the educational exams during my probation, and early in 1967 I started studying for the promotion examination, which was held in November. A few weeks later, the results were published, and I received a phone call from Sergeant Hanson telling me that I had passed.

14

1968 was destined to be remembered as a year of violence and revolution throughout the world. In the United States, Martin Luther King and Robert Kennedy were murdered. Nigeria had a civil war that resulted in mass starvation and the deaths of thousands of its people. In China, the population was being terrorised by the Red Guards of the Cultural Revolution, while in France large-scale rioting by students would result in the fall of de Gaulle. There was a peaceful revolution in Czechoslovakia, and it seemed that democracy had finally come to that country. This became known as 'The Prague Spring' – and only lasted a few weeks until the Russians invaded, using their tanks and massive firepower to crush all resistance.

Compared to these dramatic events in the outside world, life in a rural area in Hampshire could have been seen as a little unreal. One day, my knowledge of policing was expanded in a different direction when we learned of an animal suffering from a deadly disease. Even though I had been on a course to deal with such matters I could not claim to be an expert on this subject.

Sergeant Hanson told me that we had a case of a pig suffering from anthrax and that a veterinary surgeon had gone to the farm to put it down. The sergeant then told me that that my responsibility was to supervise the burning of the pig's body.

In a field some distance from the farmhouse, two farm workers were building a large funeral pyre of logs. The body of the pig was placed on it and then more timber was piled on top. After that, petrol was poured over it and ignited, and soon there was a huge bonfire. Although anthrax is not highly contagious like foot-and-mouth disease, it is very dangerous. Someone handling a pig suffering from anthrax runs a considerable risk of becoming infected, especially if that person has an open cut on a hand. It is likely to be fatal; an infected person will start to bleed from all the natural orifices in the body. The more I knew about anthrax, the less I liked the sound of it.

The burning went on for some time. The idea was to ensure that there was tremendous heat and that the burning continued until all that could be seen was a pile of ashes. I stood and watched the fire until everything seemed to have disappeared. There were no bones left, just ash. The pig was no longer a danger to anyone.

Shortly after the incident with the anthrax pig, I spent a week on the crime car, working with an older PC from Odiham. The hours were from 8 p.m until 4 a.m. Our first two nights were quiet, and the third night seemed to be following the same pattern – until 2 a.m. That's when we received a call that took us to the home of a robbery victim, deep in the countryside, 2 or 3 miles from Odiham. Luckily, the officer I was partnered with knew exactly where the house was.

When we arrived we found a man and woman who had been victims of what can only be described as an old-style highway robbery. They had been driving along a country road, about 5 miles from their home, when they'd seen a man standing in the middle of the road, waving a torch at them and signalling them to stop.

The driver had stopped the car, and that's when a second man had appeared, pointing a shotgun at them. The two people had been forced to hand over their wallets and other items of value. The two robbers had then jumped into their own car and raced off. The victims had driven back to their home and the man had dialled 999. They were able to give us good descriptions of the people involved and the car that they had been using. I made a quick note of everything and contacted IR by radio.

Nowadays, victims of armed robberies are usually offered counselling, and this is done by Victim Support, a charity set up to help victims of crime. To be threatened with a firearm is always likely to be traumatic, but in the sixties that sort of support did not exist.

We sat down and chatted with the two victims for a short while. After this, we made arrangements for CID officers to interview them later that day, and we continued our patrol. Then our radio burst into life, with message after message coming over the air about an armed robbery near Alton, only a few miles away. It had to be the same people, we decided.

Mobile units were being directed to cover every stretch of road around Alton. For ten minutes or so it seemed that the robbers had gone to ground. Sitting in the crime car, we tried to guess what the robbers might do. We decided that the most sensible thing for them to do would be to hide their firearms, dump the car, split up, and find somewhere to hide until daylight. Driving along main roads would get them caught. However, our two robbers were young and they obviously saw themselves as modern-day highwaymen.

We heard a call from a Surrey area car, saying that the car involved in the robbery was on the A31. The land between Farnham and Guildford is dominated by a high ridge called the Hog's Back, and the A31 runs along the top of it. When signalled to pull in, the driver of the bandit car put his foot down on the accelerator and raced off. The driver of the Surrey car accelerated and managed to draw level with the suspects' car.

When this happened, the passenger in the bandit car levelled a shotgun at the two policemen. The shotgun blast shattered the front windscreen of the police car, and both officers were showered with fragments of broken glass. The police driver lost control of his car, which swerved, hit the grass verge, and turned over. Luckily, neither officer was seriously injured. Shortly after this the robbers turned off the main road, abandoned their car, and tried to escape across open country. The Surrey Police soon found the car and started a large-scale search for the suspects, using dogs. Both men were arrested within a couple of hours.

If you use a shotgun to fire at a target, you will notice that the shot hits a wide area. It is a very dangerous weapon in the hands of criminals. During firearms training I had to take part in a simulation film sequence, and at one point I was confronted by three armed men. One was waving an automatic pistol, one had a sub-machine gun, and one had a shotgun. The question was, if you were armed and facing these three criminals, which one would you shoot first? The firearms instructor was quite clear about it.

'Shoot the man with the shotgun first.'

As mentioned, a shotgun is a very dangerous weapon, but in the sixties it was easy to obtain a shotgun certificate if you wanted one. Most farmers owned shotguns, and there were no legal conditions in relation to the security of the guns. They were easy to steal, and during my time at HW I dealt with two thefts in which shotguns were reported stolen from farms.

A firearm certificate is different and covers the holder for a specific weapon, such as an Enfield L42 rifle, serial number 13489. There are strict conditions for storage and security. For example, a firearm would have to be kept in a locked steel container that was bolted to the floor within the owner's home.

There were obvious problems relating to shotguns. It was not unusual for police to notice shotguns lying on the back seats of unlocked cars. The weapons would be seized, and a report would go to headquarters. The person concerned would receive a letter of warning about the dangers of shotguns being stolen. However, with shotguns being left lying on kitchen tables, in barns, and in farmyards, it was not surprising that so many fell into the hands of criminals.

Police have a legal power to refuse to issue a firearm or shotgun certificate, but the applicant has the right to appeal to the crown court. When there is an appeal, the decision is taken by a crown court judge, who can decide to allow the appeal. If that happens, police have to issue the applicant with a certificate.

In June 1968, there was a very important event in our household: our daughter, Amanda, was born. Some weeks before the big day, I started work on the third bedroom of our house, turning it into a nursery for the new arrival. Nobody would describe me as a great DIY expert, and it took me longer than it should have done to fit a new linoleum floor with its nursery design. A few more touches and the room started to look much more attractive. Everything was completed about four weeks before the planned arrival date.

It had been arranged that Maureen would go to the hospital in Alton to have our baby. However, it was the weekend, and there was some concern about staffing levels at the hospital. A decision was made to move Maureen to the Royal Hampshire County Hospital in Winchester. We had a long wait, but eventually Amanda was born. Maureen and Amanda were kept in hospital for ten days and then I drove to Winchester to collect them. We put Amanda in a carrycot placed on the back seat of our car. By twenty-first century standards, this would not be regarded as a safe method of transporting children. Although I was excited about bringing them home my memory is that I drove slowly and carefully on the return journey to HW.

Fred Tanner, one of our country-beat officers, was having trouble with one of the people living on his patch, a man called Phillips who had some previous for theft and poaching. There were very few people on Fred's beat that could be described as criminals, but Phillips was one of them.

For several months, there had been a number of incidents involving Mr and Mrs Phillips. Put simply, Mrs Phillips was the victim of domestic violence, which took place when her husband had been drinking, and he did quite a lot of drinking. It was frustrating for Fred Tanner, who had gone to the house many times to keep the peace. I went there myself on one occasion with him, when we confronted Phillips, a tall, slim man with a thin, mean-looking face. There was little that we could do, as Mrs Phillips was always unwilling to give evidence against her husband.

Even the Church of England became involved when Mrs Phillips went to see her local vicar and asked for his help. On one occasion when her husband threatened her, she phoned the vicar instead of the police. This member of the clergy was a strongly built Welshman who probably played rugby in his spare time, judging by his appearance. Arriving at the house in the middle of a domestic disturbance, he placed himself between the two parties and gave some suitable advice to Phillips.

This did not go down well with Phillips, who took a swing at the clergyman. The vicar sidestepped the blow and went in with both fists. Phillips found himself lying on his back on the floor wondering what had hit him. The vicar then threw him out of the house and told him to come back when he was sober. Things went quiet at the Phillips' household for a while after that.

The South African rugby team, the Springboks, had planned a series of fixtures in England. One of the games, against United Services, was scheduled to take place in Aldershot, and Hampshire Police realised that this was likely to be a political hot potato. An anti-apartheid group calling itself Stop the Tour had announced that they would do their best to prevent the games taking place. The chief constable anticipated trouble, and a large number of officers, including me, were sent on public-order training courses. The leader of the Stop the Tour group was Peter Hain, who later went on to become an MP and the secretary of state for Wales.

For large public-order events, police are divided into units, usually referred to as serials or squads. As a general rule, a serial will consist of an inspector, two sergeants, and twenty PCs. The demonstrators said that they planned to march through the town, and two or three serials, including mine, were to be held on reserve at Aldershot police station.

'Ho, Ho! Ho Chi Minh! … Ho, Ho! Ho Chi Minh!' As we sat around in the police station, we could hear the marchers chanting.

'Ho, Ho! Ho Chi Minh! … Ho, Ho! Ho Chi Minh!'

Ho Chi Minh, the communist leader of North Vietnam, seemed to be one of the most beloved political leaders for many left-wing groups at that time. When the marchers eventually passed the station, it was a bit of an anticlimax. The noise suggested thousands of marchers, but there were only about 200 of them. There were a couple of arrests at the rugby match, but the day passed without any real trouble.

To get back to the gypsy issue, the county council had built a site for gypsies at Star Hill, close to the A30, about a mile east of HW. It looked as though the council did not want the site to be too visible, as their first job had been to dig out what I would describe as a small valley. After that was done, the bottom of the valley was levelled and hard standing was put in for twenty caravans. Next to each caravan there was a tap with running water and a toilet.

Enquiries of different kinds kept taking me to the site, and I soon got to know most of the families there. Although it was normal to refer to them as gypsies, it was soon obvious to me that there were distinct groups of people within the travelling community. At Star Hill there were three or four families of genuine Romany people, and their caravans were beautifully decorated in traditional Romany style. The others were Irish tinkers or Hampshire travelling people, often referred to as 'didicoys'. The Romany people tended to be very honest, but this was not the case with some of the others.

In Yateley, the council had built what was known as a rehabilitation centre. There was a policy to encourage travellers to move away from their traditional nomadic life in caravans and encourage them to live in houses. The first stage in this plan was that those who wanted a more settled existence would be moved into the rehabilitation centre, which consisted of a row of battered-looking red-brick houses. It has to be borne in mind that the housing was for people who were not used to living in houses or staying in one place. After some time living at the rehabilitation centre, they would be assessed as to their progress, and if deemed suitable, they would be moved into social housing.

There were a couple of problem families at the centre, and one day there was a call to a disturbance there. Roy Ramsier, one of the Yateley officers, joined me at the scene. One of the men involved in the disturbance looked familiar to me. He was known to have a very low IQ, and I was concerned when we first arrived, as he was shouting like a madman and waving a scythe that came close to my face on a couple of occasions. In such situations, it is always good to have someone at the scene who knows the people involved. Roy Ramsier knew them all, and they listened to him when he told them to start behaving themselves. After a little while they all quietened down, and we went on our way.

Police officers will always be faced with different types of dangerous situations. We were aware that dealing with traffic accidents on the A30 always had the potential for danger. We carried signs and flashing lights in the back of our Hillman Husky. When we dealt with traffic accidents, we used all those things to warn drivers that they were approaching an accident. Most of them would slow down, but there were others who did not.

Time and time again when dealing with accidents on the A30, we would have cars whizzing past us at 70 or 80 miles an hour. On some occasions there were only two officers, including me, to deal with these accidents. Examining the scene of an accident means that your mind is concentrating on what you are doing, and there is always the danger that you might just take a step backwards at exactly the wrong moment.

In order to give ourselves a bit more safety, we usually stopped all the traffic in both directions. This gave us an element of control over the situation, and we could then signal vehicles to proceed when it was safe.

Apart from the A30, there were several other fast roads running through our subdivision. One night I was called to a fatal traffic accident on the A33 Road just north of Hartley Wintney. Two men had been travelling from Reading towards Basingstoke, and the driver had been drinking. His driving was unsteady, and his passenger became more and more concerned. He begged him to stop driving, but the driver refused to listen. It was a country road that was unlighted and had no footpath.

A man and woman were walking along this stretch of road, and the man was carrying a baby aged about eight months. They were at the side of the road when the car ploughed into them. The man was fatally injured, and the baby flew through the air, landing in a bush. The woman was not injured, but the baby had a broken arm. An ambulance had reached the scene before my arrival, and the ambulance men were carrying out emergency first aid. I had a whispered conversation with one of the ambulance men, and he told me that the injured man was likely to die.

One quick look at the driver was enough to know that he had been drinking. A breathalyser test was positive, so I arrested him and took him to Fleet police station, while two or three of my colleagues dealt with the accident scene. When analysed, the blood samples revealed an alcohol content that was more than double the legal limit.

A witness statement was taken by the passenger in the car. He stated quite clearly that he knew that the driver had been drinking heavily, that his driving had been badly impaired, and that he had begged him to stop driving on at least three occasions. One of my colleagues contacted the hospital in Reading and was told that the injured man had died. It was the third fatal traffic accident I had dealt with, but it was the most serious. This case was going to be a death by dangerous driving, aggravated by the drink-driving element.

I told the driver, who was under arrest, that the man he had run down was now dead, but he showed very little sign of any remorse. He made a few comments about the dead man, such as 'He was just a long-haired hippy.'

There were two counts on the indictment when the defendant appeared at the crown court in Winchester: causing death by dangerous driving and driving with excess alcohol. A plea of not guilty was entered, and the trial started. A legal submission was made by the defence regarding the charge of excess alcohol. It was a technical matter relating to the taking of the blood samples. There had been a previous case where the same defence had been put forward. The problem we were facing at court was that the previous case had reached the House of Lords, the final court of appeal, but the law lords had not reached any decision.

I had a meeting with the prosecuting barrister, who told me that the defence had offered us a plea-bargaining deal. If we accepted, the prosecution would offer no evidence on the excess alcohol, and the defendant would plead guilty to the death by dangerous driving. I thought of the victim and his family and said that I was against such a deal.

The prosecutor, who was quite a young barrister, said that he felt the same and decided to seek advice from one of his more senior colleagues who was at court that day. The advice he received was that we had little choice as the judge would not allow the drink-drive charge to go before the jury.

The defendant was fined fifty pounds for causing death by dangerous driving and disqualified for five years. I was quite shocked at the sentence, but this was the normal type of penalty for this offence at that time. The judge had decided to disregard all the evidence relating to drinking and driving. Even so, the defendant could have received a prison sentence up to five years for the offence that he pleaded guilty to.

It seems strange to me how cultural attitudes to different offences change over the years. There was a pervading attitude then of 'It's just an accident.' It seemed strange to me how many people convicted of TDA were sent to prison, but if you drove recklessly and killed someone with a car you were likely to be fined.

Police officers who are lazy and do not pull their weight are referred to as 'uniform carriers'. At large police stations, uniform carriers can cruise along without drawing too much attention on themselves, but it is not so easy at smaller places. As we did not have personal radios when we were on patrol in the GP car we could only be contacted on the radio from IR. If a PC at HW wished to avoid dealing with incidents, one way would be not to hear radio messages.

It provided an easy defence for someone who was lazy. Once you walked away from the section car, it was not possible to hear the police radio, and in fairness, we would all be away from the car at some time or other. At HW, there was usually only one PC on duty patrolling the section. If he could not be contacted, another unit would have to be assigned from another part of the division. It soon became obvious to me that we had an officer who was not pulling his weight. His name was John Cotton.

The matter came to a head one evening when a call came through on the police internal line about a serious traffic accident on our patch. Cotton was the only officer on late turn, and he was on station duty. He would have known that he needed to close the station and deal with it. Cotton phoned one of our country-beat officers and asked him to help him at the scene of the accident. He explained that he was dealing with something at the station and could not go to the accident straight away but said that he would be on his way within five minutes or so.

The accident had occurred at a crossroads on a fast stretch of road. The country-beat man went by motorcycle and arrived at the accident to find a scene of carnage. Three people were dead and three seriously injured. He received assistance from other units within the division, but there was no sign of John Cotton, who only arrived on the scene when most of the work at the accident had been done. The PC from the country beat found that he had become the officer in the case – and he was not happy about it.

One of the sergeants from Fleet arrived at the scene and took overall responsibility for supervising the enquiry. The sergeant would expect that the PC from the country beat who had been the first to arrive would be dealing with the accident investigation, inquest and everything else that had to be done.

Soon after, I heard rumours that an enquiry had been started to look into the action (or lack thereof) taken by Cotton. The relationship between Sergeant Hanson and Cotton had never been particularly good, but this pushed it into open warfare. It seemed likely that Cotton could find himself facing a discipline board, but we all knew that, whatever happened to him, his time at HW was coming to an end.

John Cotton had been at HW for several years, and I was not aware of him ever making an arrest. Apart from that, he never seemed to be available when calls came in about accidents or other incidents.

Cotton's wife approached me on a couple of occasions and did her best to influence me against Sergeant Hanson, but my opinion was that the sergeant was a fair-minded supervisor, and I did not intend to turn against him. It did not help Cotton that his colleagues saw him for what he was. As expected, Cotton was transferred to another division. The whole saga had been a stressful experience for Sergeant Hanson, who was off sick for several weeks after that.

15

During 1969 there was mounting concern about the situation in Northern Ireland, where there was increasing conflict between nationalists and loyalists. In a different part of the world, the British armed forces and police were involved in a peacekeeping operation in the small Caribbean island of Anguilla. What happened in Anguilla is now just a historical footnote, but the invasion of the island was to keep the press busy and their readers entertained for several weeks.

The Foreign and Commonwealth Office had decided to create a federation in that part of the West Indies, linking the islands of St Kitts, Nevis, and Anguilla. It was natural that the power base of the federation would be St Kitts, as it was the largest island. The Anguillans were concerned about this because they did not want political control from St Kitts, and they made it known that they wished to remain a British colony. However, nobody in Whitehall showed much interest in the wishes of the people in what they must have seen as a remote and insignificant corner of the Commonwealth.

The press started running stories about what was alleged to be happening in Anguilla. One rumour was that American organised crime had plans to take it over, and there were stories of members of the Mafia being seen on the island. There were also rumours that Anguillans were arming themselves, and talking about resisting any outside political control.

A junior British Government official was sent to Anguilla to try and persuade them to accept the federation plan. Within a short time of his arrival, he reported that he was under siege and that shots had been fired at the house where he was staying.

The British Government decided that law and order had broken down on the island and planned a military response. It was decided that the Parachute Regiment was to spearhead an invasion of Anguilla, and a contingent of 120 volunteers from the Metropolitan Police would go with them. The troops made a beach landing at dawn and were ready for any eventuality, but things then started to move into a comic-opera situation.

The naval personnel on the ships saw flashes in and around the beach as the troops went in. Was it gunfire? No, apparently not. It was journalists on the beach using cameras with flash attachments. No shots were fired, and the troops were met by friendly local people who saw the soldiers as their saviours.

In 1969, Anguilla was a poor, undeveloped island with a population of about 6,000. It had great tourist potential because the island had beautiful golden beaches, but with the exception of two ramshackle beach hotels, there was no tourist infrastructure. The Royal Engineers started to work on a number of projects to improve the life of the local people. This included building a new school and constructing a deep-water jetty. The Metropolitan Police set up three police stations and organised a policing system for the island.

The police soon found that crime here did not involve the Mafia, murder, or drug running. It was more likely to involve someone stealing five or six sweet potatoes or a bunch of bananas. Where the evidence merited it, the police imposed their own sanctions on people who had broken the law. Typical penalties were usually a small fine or two days' imprisonment.

The climate in Anguilla was picture-postcard lovely, and cartoons appeared in newspapers showing that the police appeared to be having a wonderful time on the island, sunbathing and swimming. However, life in the UK for police officers was not so sunny. In company with other public-sector workers, we were receiving small pay rises while facing rapidly rising inflation.

There were reports in the press about police officers being hard up and looking for other employment. One well-publicised story in the newspapers that year was about a Hampshire policeman with three years' service who left to drive a council rubbish lorry in order to earn more money. For my part, I soon realised that our family had less money available to spend.

Work was progressing on the new M3 motorway, which was being hacked, bit by bit, through our part of Hampshire. Several of our local country roads were blocked off, and when we were out on patrol we needed to remember which roads were still open in order to travel from A to B. When the motorway was completed, some roads continued over newly built bridges but there were others that just came to a sudden end.

One of the interesting features of police work is that suddenly things happen when you least expect them to. I was on late turn with a colleague once at about one in the morning when we arrested a team of burglars.

Driving along a quiet road between Blackwater and Farnborough, we found ourselves following an old-looking van. It is tempting to say that I had spotted something suspicious about the van that made me stop it and question the occupants. If so, I could have claimed that this was a really good piece of police work on my part. However, sometimes things just happen. Without warning, the driver of the van slammed his brakes on, a door flew open, and the man ran off like an Olympic sprinter doing the 100-metre dash. My right foot went down hard on the brake, and my colleague jumped out and raced off down the road in pursuit. Stopping the car and removing the key from the ignition was enough to cause me a few seconds' delay.

As I started to run, something brought me to a sudden halt. I had just noticed three men sitting in the van. They needed to be contained inside the vehicle, so I waved my stick at them and told them to stay where they were. None of them tried to make a move, and it seemed that they had decided to sit tight. Later, when I found out something about them, I counted myself lucky that they had. The oldest member of the group was a burly 43-year-old local man who had been of great interest to police for many years. Despite several arrests, he had never been convicted of any criminal offence. However, it turned out that he was on bail, awaiting trial on a charge of armed robbery.

The second man was a 32-year-old ex-professional boxer from Southampton, with previous convictions for robbery and burglary. Later, when I ran a CRO check, I found a warrant for him for maintenance arrears of £5,000. The youngest of the trio was a 22-year-old from Aldershot who had previous for burglary and theft.

My only plan was to try and keep them inside the van. I did not have a PR and the section car with its radio was only a few steps away, but it was not worth the risk. If I'd moved away from the van, something would have happened, and if they had come out of the van, the odds would not have been in my favour. We later discovered that the van had been stolen. They must have decided to sit tight and sort out a quick, whispered defence between them.

My colleague returned about ten minutes later, looking crestfallen after losing the man that he had been chasing. I told him not to worry too much and pointed at the three men sitting in the van. He made a call on the radio, and a several police cars arrived very quickly. The three suspects were taken to Farnborough police station.

It did not come as a great surprise when all three of them came up with the same story. They had come out of a pub in Camberley, when another man had offered them a lift to Aldershot. Naturally, they did not know his name. The van had not been reported stolen, and when local officers went to find the owner, he'd had no idea that his van was not where he had parked it. The back of the van was full of building tools, so I asked him to confirm that all the property in it belonged to him.

'Yes, it's all my stuff,' he said, pointing inside. 'Except for that jemmy and those four pairs of rubber gloves.'

'Good,' I thought. 'We can charge them with something.' If all else failed, there was the policeman's old friend, the charge of possessing housebreaking implements by night.

The enquiry was taken over by one of the Farnborough CID officers. None of the three suspects would admit to anything, and they were all charged with possession of HBIs by night. The two older men received suspended prison sentences, but the youngest of the three went straight to prison, as he had been on a suspended sentence at the time of his arrest.

We knew that we had prevented a crime but wondered what it might have been. Two months later, the van driver who had escaped from us was arrested for a burglary, He decided to admit to a large number of offences that he had committed over a period of several months. He told a CID officer that the four of them had been on their way to carry out a burglary at an RAF station. He had panicked when our police car had suddenly appeared behind the van. He was sent to prison for three years. The older man who had managed to live a charmed life for so long was later convicted of the armed robbery that he was on bail for and went to prison for several years.

Large-scale building development in Yateley had resulted in a shift in population to that part of our section. By the mid sixties it seemed more logical to have a police station at Yateley or Blackwater than at Hartley Wintney. It was no surprise when a decision was made to establish a new section station in Yateley with a sergeant in charge, covering Blackwater and Yateley. Two more officers were transferred in later so that the new section would have a total of five PCs.

Our section was reduced in size; it now contained just Hartley Wintney with Mattingley and Eversley, our two country beats. However, HW officers would still receive calls to the new section from time to time. One afternoon, there was a 999 call to a robbery at a petrol station on the A30 near Blackwater. The man making the call was John Downs, who was in charge of the station and had been working there alone. He told me that a man had entered the office, threatened him with a baseball bat, and forced him to hand over the money in the cash register.

As it was an allegation of robbery, it would have to be investigated by a CID officer, but I asked a few questions and made notes on my clipboard. After circulating a description of the suspect over the radio, I sat in the police car thinking about the robbery. It is quite difficult to explain what was bothering me except to say that there was something wrong.

Basically, I felt that Downs had not told me the truth. The more I thought about it, the more suspicious I felt, but at the same time it was not possible to put my finger on any one thing that was obviously wrong. On the face of it, the petrol station had been robbed, and there was no evidence to suggest otherwise. With any police investigation, you follow the evidence, but police work has all sorts of other ingredients thrown in, such as suspicions, feelings, hunches, and even elements of ESP – extra sensory perception – from time to time.

As I was sitting in the section car on the forecourt of the petrol station, one of my colleagues from Yateley drove up, and we sat down together and talked it through. He listened to what I had to say about everything and told me what he thought about it. His opinion was that there was no evidence against Downs and the evidence pointed towards a robbery. Although I could only agree with this, my suspicion seemed to be increasing by the minute, and something was telling me to arrest Downs. There was no evidence, I agreed. But I was still suspicious.

It was time to take the bull by the horns, so I walked back to the petrol station and told Downs that he was under arrest on suspicion of theft. We watched as he locked everything up. My thoughts were that he should have been angry or indignant at being arrested. After all, he was the victim of the robbery, wasn't he? He denied being involved in any theft but at the same time showed little sign of surprise or resentment.

We took him to Fleet police station, where the sergeant on duty was given a brief summary of the arrest. After that, my next job was to find a CID officer. The only one available was Tony Vincent, an experienced DC who had been at Fleet for several years. We sat down together, and I explained everything to him. Tony looked as if he had been working his way through a busy day and was looking forward to going home, but he asked me some questions and then looked slightly doubtful. However, he nodded and I could see that he was keen to find out what had happened.

In the interview room, my questions did not open up any holes in Downs's story. Then Tony Vincent started asking questions, and bit by bit he added a little psychological pressure. With the suspect listening, Tony told me that Downs must have had an accomplice. We would find the other person involved and then charge both of them with conspiracy.

Downs became a little flustered but stuck with his original story, making me start to wonder whether my action had been too quick off the mark. He probably did not like the sound of the word 'conspiracy', an ancient Common Law offence, one that came with no maximum term of imprisonment laid down in law. I looked at Tony and could see that he was thinking the same thing as I was. There was something wrong, but it did not look as though we were ever going to prove it

Then Tony pointed at Downs. 'Take off your shoes,' he said.

Downs took off his shoes, and I picked them up and shook them. There was nothing inside.

'Take off your socks,' said Tony.

Downs removed his socks, and a five-pound note fell to the floor. I felt inside his socks and found two more five-pound notes. Downs suddenly started to look forlorn, as if all his confidence had just drained away. He then admitted that he had discussed the idea of stealing money from the garage with a friend by the name of James Bonham. He'd arranged for Bonham to come to the petrol station and then handed most of the money over to him. They'd planned to meet a few hours later and divide the cash between them. After hearing this admission, I next had to take a written statement from Downs – in which he confessed the whole thing.

One of the Yateley officers went with me to look for Bonham. We arrested him at his home in Camberley, recovered the stolen cash, and took him to Fleet. I questioned him and took down his written statement, which implicated Downs and himself in the offence. Both men were charged with theft and later received suspended prison sentences. Crime enquiries tend to be very time consuming. They always resulted in a large number of hours on my overtime card.

After passing the promotion exam, I was given a temporary promotion to acting sergeant and took charge of the section when the sergeant was on leave. It was my job to send out enquiries to officers and check all incoming reports. Because we dealt with so many accidents, a large amount of my time was spent in checking 'due care' files, assessing the evidence and deciding what cases to recommend for court proceedings.

One aspect of my temporary promotion was that nearly all the officers on the section had more experience than I did. Generally speaking, their paperwork was of a good standard, and it was rare to have to send anything back to them. Whenever possible, I went out on patrol with one of the PCs. It was important for me to keep an eye on everything that was going on and involve myself with everything that a sergeant would, such as reported crime, sudden deaths, and serious accidents. Before long, I could even spell the word 'recommend' without too much difficulty.

During August 1969, Northern Ireland went 'pear shaped' (in police parlance). The worst rioting took place in Belfast, when loyalists, many armed with machine guns and other firearms, attacked nationalist areas in the city. Street after street of terraced houses were set on fire. Eight people were killed and at least 800 injured. About 100 of the injured people had gunshot wounds.

There was considerable criticism of the Royal Ulster Constabulary (the RUC) who seemed to have lost control of the situation. Hundreds of people fled their homes. The Irish Government set up refugee camps and military medical centres close to the border. The British Government decided to send in the Army to bring the situation under control.

Whilst all this was happening, my thoughts were on my own career and where I was heading. The chief inspector had suggested that at some point I should transfer to a police station in an urban area to widen my experience and give me the opportunity to be an acting sergeant in a place that had a wider range of challenges. The training system in Hampshire was very good, and about 500 constables had passed the promotion examination. There were about fifty promotions to sergeant each year, and I knew that there were some very good candidates who had waited many years before being promoted.

This made me start to think about transferring to the Metropolitan Police. One attraction was the fact that the 'Met' had a competitive examination system and this made for a faster promotion system. Money was another important consideration, as there was virtually no paid overtime in Hampshire.

From a policing point of view, it did not make much sense. We were usually fairly thin on the ground and each time we took eight hours' time off it meant one less PC on the streets that day. Officers going on leave were often told to take an extra 30 hours or so in time off in order to reduce the amount shown on the overtime cards.

Attitudes in Hampshire towards the Met varied considerably. To officers in county forces, it appeared that the Metropolitan Police had huge coffers of cash available for overtime, and Hampshire officers were impressed when they heard about this. Scotland Yard, the headquarters of the Met, had become world famous for its expertise in handling public order and for its specialised detective squads. At the same time, there were quite a few worrying stories doing the rounds about police corruption in London.

For about twelve months, I had wondered what the best course of action might be. One option would be to ask for a transfer to another station within Hampshire rather than wait to be moved on at some point in the future. Another consideration was buying a house. Maureen and I decided that it was important to climb onto the property ladder before too many years went by.

In September 1969 I wrote to Scotland Yard, stating that I should like to transfer to the Metropolitan Police. The following month a letter arrived inviting me to an interview at the Recruiting Centre in Southwark. The interview went well, and on 7 November I received a letter from Scotland Yard informing me that my application was still being considered and asking me to send them a certificate that I had been vaccinated for smallpox.

In November, a letter arrived from the Met telling me that they had accepted my application to transfer, with an instruction for me to report to the Recruiting Centre on Monday, 5 January 1970.

We were informed that a police flat would be provided for Maureen and me in Chelsea. Wray House was a large, old-fashioned block of police flats opposite the police station, with an entrance in Elystan Street. We were on the third floor. There were no lifts, and the building on the outside looked quite old and bleak. However, although it was old fashioned, our flat was quite spacious and had three bedrooms. It was a two-minute walk from both Fulham Road and King's Road. We decided that it was a good location for us.

During the next three or four weeks, I said my goodbyes to everyone that I had worked with on the subdivision and the friends that we had made within the community. A drink was arranged at a pub in Yateley and there were six or seven of my colleagues there to say goodbye.

On 2 January 1970 we moved to Chelsea. We watched as all our goods were loaded onto a furniture lorry and then watched later as everything was carried up three flights of stairs at Wray House. We did our best to sort out our furniture on that first day. We put Amanda to bed in her new bedroom, and soon she was fast asleep.

That evening, Maureen and I sat talking. For more than three years we had been living in a rural area that could only be described as a pleasant place to live. We thought about our house at Phoenix Green, how we would walk in and out of the front gate, framed by the almond tree. We were now in a flat in central London, and we both felt quite unsettled. I started to wonder if this move had been a mistake.

16

In 1970 the Met was divided into twenty-three operational districts, each one being identified by a letter of the alphabet. Every station had a map of what was called the MPD, the Metropolitan Police District. 'A' District covered the southern end of the City of Westminster and included Whitehall, Victoria, Pimlico, and Belgravia. 'B' District covered the Royal Borough of Kensington and Chelsea, and 'C' District took in the central part of Westminster, the West End, and Soho. It would take me a little longer to get to grips with the rest of the alphabet.

A commander was the officer in charge of a district, and each district would usually have two or three divisions in it. The Met had a publication called Police Orders. This had been in existence since 1829, when the force was founded, and it provided news about deaths, commendations, promotions, transfers, and disciplinary punishments. There were also details of major events, changes in the law, and new police procedures.

My first three weeks was spent on what was called a transfer course, at Hendon. There was a group of twelve, including me. It consisted of officers who were transferring in to the Met from other forces or those who were returning to the Met after having done something else.

At Hendon, we all kept a close watch on the binder in our classroom that held Police Orders. An entry appeared stating that PC 161040 Ramsay was to report to 'A' District HQ at 9 a.m. on 25 January 1970. Every Met officer was issued with an individual warrant number; this system had started shortly after the formation of the force in 1829. Once you knew someone's warrant number, you knew how much service he or she had.

However, in my case, as a transfer from another force, the number would be misleading, as I had nearly six years' service by then.

I was pleased that some consideration had been given to the fact that our flat was in Chelsea, and in policing terms, 'A' District was right next door. We all discussed the advantages and disadvantages of the various places that we might find ourselves posted to. Cannon Row division had only a handful of streets that could be described as residential but was full of important buildings, including the Palace of Westminster, St James Palace, Buckingham Palace, and Downing Street, the residence of the prime minister.

There are many Government ministries and agencies around Whitehall which need police protection. One of my colleagues referred to the police at Cannon Row as 'monument watchers'. There was general agreement that a posting there was probably not a good thing – and it looked as if that was where I might be going.

Cannon Row police station was a short distance from Parliament Square and shared a large gated yard with the famous Norman Shaw Scotland Yard building. The headquarters of the Met has always been known as Scotland Yard, NSY, or the Yard, but is usually referred to by its officers as CO, short for Commissioner's Office. Three years before, CO had moved to a new location in Broadway, just off Victoria Street, which would now be described as a typical sixties building.

At Cannon Row I was welcomed to 'A' District by the Commander, Victor Coventry. He asked me a few questions about my previous experience and told me that he had decided to post me to Rochester Row. After that, I went to see the duties sergeant, who found a district number for me. By the time I walked out of Cannon Row, I had become PC 799 'A'.

It took me about twenty minutes to walk to Rochester Row where I met a PC called Ray Heath in the divisional administration office on the second floor. Ray Heath was known as the chief superintendent's clerk; he had been doing the job for many years. He was a man who was quiet and dependable, someone who knew everything that was going on and where everything was.

Ray told me that the chief superintendent was not available, so he took me down to the inspectors' office on the ground floor and introduced me to Inspector Holness, who had the title of Unit Commander. Rochester

Row division was using a system of policing called Unit Beat Policing, and I was informed that Inspector Holness had special responsibility for the system within the division.

Inspector Holness gave me the name of the inspector in charge of my relief and told me to report for night duty the following day. That evening, in our Chelsea flat, I spent some time putting my district number onto my tunics, raincoats, and cape. On the underside of each numeral there was a small screw, and each one had to be screwed into a small circular plate on the other side of the epaulette.

I made a point of arriving early and was sitting in the parade room at Rochester Row by 9.40 p.m. The police team that now included me was called a relief. There were another nine or ten PCs with me. I had never seen such a large number of policemen in a parade room before. Although I was not a probationer, I was new to the Met and to the division, and one of the more experienced PCs, Phil Doyle was assigned to patrol with me for my first two weeks.

Divisions in county forces normally covered very large areas, but Rochester Row was a typical central London division of its era, with one station covering a fairly small inner-city area that had a large residential and business population. From the station, it was possible to walk to the boundaries of the division within about twenty-five minutes or less. Looking at the divisional map, I could see that Vauxhall Bridge Road acted as an unofficial boundary that divided the division into two distinct halves. Pimlico was the western half, and the eastern segment covered the rest, usually being referred to as Victoria or Westminster.

There were three reliefs at Rochester Row, the basic system within the Met. Each relief had an inspector in charge who would be the duty officer, responsible for the operational policing of the division. The inspector's deputy would be a station sergeant, and at Rochester Row each relief had three or four sergeants and about twenty-five PCs.

Unit Beat Policing was a policing system that had been developed throughout the UK in the sixties, and the structure at Rochester Row was very similar to what existed elsewhere. My memory was that the Pimlico part of the division had six foot beats and four home beats, supported by a panda car, with the same establishment east of Vauxhall Bridge Road.

In addition, there was a divisional area car with a crew of three, the spearhead of our response to incidents. A PC would be posted as van driver, and there would usually be someone posted to the GP (general purpose) car. On night duty it was usual to double up, with two officers in the GP car. Rochester Row, like most inner London divisions, had a PC who patrolled on a lightweight motorcycle known as a 'Noddy bike'. Rochester Row was known to everyone as Roch for short, or Alfa Romeo, based on its radio identification, using the NATO phonetic alphabet.

After I had completed my first three or four weeks at Rochester Row, I spent five days with one of the home-beat officers in Pimlico. There were echoes of the country-beat system in Hampshire, as these PCs were not part of a relief and were assigned to a home beat for several years, whereas officers on reliefs were usually posted to a different beat every four weeks. The most obvious difference from the country-beat system was that none of the home beat PCs lived on their beats or had offices there. Most of them lived miles away in the suburbs.

The PC on the home beat showed me around his patch and introduced me to people who lived or worked on it. He also took me to three or four of his 'tea holes'. These are places where the occupier provides cups of tea or coffee in return for a chat. It was noticeable how small the home beat was and how much time we spent in tea holes. Home-beat officers were in a very good position to pick up information about local criminals, and it seemed that some home-beat officers were particularly good at this.

The Met had its own policing style, and my first impressions were of a well-structured organisation. However, one of the aspects that surprised me was that for a big-city force it did not appear to be very crime-minded. Public order, the protection of the royal family, Government ministers, and diplomats were given priority over everything else. During the seventies, this was very noticeable in a force that was always short of manpower and continually struggling to keep up with its responsibilities.

Many police stations in London were antiquated and badly designed and this made the job more difficult when it came to processing arrests and completing paperwork. Also, it seemed that the system of crime intelligence was not as effective as it should have been. One reason was that communications between CID and Uniform officers were not always good.

At that time, the shift system used by the Uniform Branch in the Met was based on a cycle of nine weeks. It seemed quite daunting to find out that night duty lasted for three weeks, but my body seemed to adjust to this quite well, and night shifts were followed by six weeks of day duty. Each PC was a member of a leave party, and days off were taken during night duty and daytime shifts.

At that time, there were a number of police posts on the division, and they supplied the same service to the public and the police as the more traditional police boxes had done. There was a telephone for people to pick up which went directly to the switchboard at the police station.

However, unlike police boxes, they did not provide a warm place of shelter for us when it was freezing cold in the middle of the night. In 1970, all patrolling officers had PRs and rarely made use of posts, but the fact that they were still there played a part in my first arrest at Alfa Romeo.

It happened during my first few weeks at Rochester Row. I was on foot in Victoria Street at 3 a.m. when I noticed a man who was walking towards me. He approached me to say that he had seen a couple of men smash a shop window at the other end of Victoria Street about five minutes earlier. 'Where might they be now?' I asked. He pointed at two men who were walking along the other side of the street, heading in our direction.

He told me that he was willing to provide a written statement about what he had seen. As the two men started to get closer, I could see that they were both large, strong-looking individuals, and the manner in which they were talking told me that they had been drinking. It would be sensible to have some assistance before stopping them.

'Alfa Romeo from 799, over.'

The only response was silence, not even a crackle to suggest that there was any spark of life. After I'd tried at least three calls and received no reply, it was obvious to me that the battery on my radio was dead. Further along Victoria Street there was a police post, and I asked my witness to go there, pick the phone up, and ask them to send me some assistance. Off he went, leaving me to hope that the phone line was still in working order. By then, the two men had crossed Victoria Street and were heading towards Strutton Ground, a street that was just across the road from the Scotland Yard building in Broadway.

During the day, Strutton Ground was always a busy spot, with its shops and its well-known street market, but at that time of night it was a quiet, dark spot. I moved close in behind the two men as they turned into Strutton Ground and called out to them. They turned to face me, and I told them that I was arresting both of them for criminal damage. One of them swore at me, and neither of them seemed happy about the idea of being arrested. They pushed past me and headed towards a nearby side street.

I made a grab for one of them and managed to get a grip on him from behind. He shouted, 'Let me go!' but while he screamed abuse at me, my hands went under his armpits and closed behind his neck. His friend came at me like an enraged bull, and I pulled my prisoner backwards until my back was lodged firmly against a brick wall. My plan was to use the man that I was holding as a sort of shield and make sure that the second man could not get behind me. I made a point of swivelling from side to side to make it difficult for him to land a blow on me or get a grip on me. It was tiring work, and I knew that there was a limit to how long I could hang on.

The second man threw a punch at me, but I moved at the right moment and his fist smacked into the brick wall. After that, he tried to get a grip on one of my arms and pulled at it. I was starting to wonder where the cavalry was – in those situations it always seemed to take a long time! Then, to my left, the reflections of a blue flashing light appeared on a couple of shop windows. Two GP cars and a van arrived at the same time, and suddenly the street appeared to be full of policemen. The man who had been attacking me made the mistake of throwing a punch at one of the approaching officers. There was a short struggle in the street before two or three of them picked him up and threw him into the back of the van.

A couple of PCs grabbed the man I was holding and put him in the back of a police car. One of the older men on the relief asked me if I was all right. The struggle had left me out of breath, but I was all in one piece, apart from a couple of small scratches on my hands. At the station, my first job was to give a summary of the arrest to the station officer. Later, I noticed that both my prisoners had injuries that they had not received during their encounter with me. The sergeant commented on the injuries, but after that there was no further mention of it. I took my witness, a schoolteacher, to the canteen on the first floor, made him a cup of coffee, and took a written statement from him.

There was clear evidence against one man, but at the time the window was smashed his friend had been standing some distance away and had played no part in what had happened. I explained this to the station officer, and he read the witness statement and my notes. He signed my notes and then formally charged one of the men with criminal damage. The station officer decided that the defendant would stay in custody and appear at Bow Street Court that morning.

After that, the sergeant released the other man and wrote a report in the Detained Persons Register about the arrest. At that time, the Met would refer to a case like that as a 'refused charge' and the sergeant recorded the whole story, commenting that the arrest of both men had been justified.

I did the paperwork and fingerprinted my prisoner. As he was going straight to court, there was no need for me to complete a prosecution file on the case. After fingerprinting him, I guessed that my next job would be to take his photograph, but there was no sign of any camera, so I asked the sergeant where we took photographs. He looked at me as though I had just arrived from another planet.

'Photographs! What are you talking about? This is the Metropolitan Police. We don't take photographs of people we charge. We're far too busy to do things like that.'

This came as a surprise, because it had been my understanding that it was standard procedure in all British police forces to photograph people who were charged with criminal offences when they were fingerprinted. The other issue that surprised me was that I was now the prosecutor for my criminal damage case, a role that I had never taken on in Hampshire. Although my shift finished at 6 a.m., there was little point in returning home to Chelsea. I had to see the manager of the shop and obtain a witness statement, together with an estimate of the cost of repairing the window. After that, I needed to be at Bow Street Magistrates' Court by 10 a.m. to prosecute my case.

I had a quick discussion with my colleague, Phil Doyle, about my role as a prosecutor.

'Not much to it,' he said. 'When you get to the court, give CRO a ring and see if "chummy" has any form. They should have checked his prints by then. Tell the court usher that you are off night duty, and they might move you up the list. When they call your case, jump up and tell the beak that you are asking for summary trial. If your body goes guilty, give the brief facts and his previous. If he has lots of form, give them the last three. Don't speak for too long, or the stipe will probably tell you to shut up.'

It seemed strange to me at first, but the system of police officers acting as prosecutors appeared to work quite well. There was usually very little paperwork, but officers had to submit reports applying for legal representation in certain categories of offences. These reports were referred to as 'legal aid reports' and would mean that a file on the case would be prepared and sent to the Met Police Solicitors' Department.

At about nine thirty that morning, I walked through Covent Garden Market in order to get to Bow Street. By 1970 the famous vegetable and fruit market had completely outgrown its historic site. If you wanted to use the words 'organised chaos', this was the place for it. It was an amazing sight. Dozens of lorries and vans were trying to force their way through the narrow streets. Drivers were desperately looking for parking spots and would park anywhere they could. Many vehicles were double-parked and appeared to have been abandoned. A policeman from Bow Street was standing in the middle of the road and doing his best to sort out the chaos around him.

He was standing with his back to me, and when he turned in my direction I had something of a surprise – he was black. I took a second look. Yes, he was black. I had never seen a non-white police officer before. 'Norwell Roberts' I said to myself when I realised who it was. He was the first black officer in the country, and I could remember reading about him in newspapers.

For several years, articles had appeared in newspapers on the subject of people from ethnic minorities joining the police service. Officers appearing on promotion boards or applying for specialist roles in Hampshire were sometimes asked their views on the recruitment of blacks and Asians. The response from many of them was that the public would not accept police officers who were not white.

Having seen a black policeman on the streets of London, I wondered what other wonders were going to come my way. There were a couple of excellent JPs at Aldershot, but as a general rule, the speed at which cases were dealt with in Hampshire was very slow and deliberate. I had no experience of dealing with stipendiary magistrates, and this would prove to be a culture shock.

In terms of criminal justice, Bow Street was probably in a class of its own. My case had been listed for Courtroom No 1, and the chief magistrate was presiding that day. Before he dealt with the list of charges, there were three or four bail applications. Solicitors representing the defendants made their applications, and police officers appeared to give their objections to bail. The defendants were all 'banged up', and then the magistrate started working his way through the list of charges. It would be better to use the verb 'charge', as he went through the list at a fast gallop.

It seemed that the magistrate wanted to clear all the less-serious charges out of his way first. There was a long list of typical central London cases, including drunks and highway obstruction. Checking my watch, I realised that he had dealt with about thirty cases in around thirty-five minutes. This included two men who had entered a plea of not guilty to highway obstruction.

'So you were sitting on the pavement with your backs against the front of the shop and your legs across the pavement, were you?' asked the chief magistrate.

'Yes, sir. I suppose we were.'

'And the policeman asked you to move on, and you did not move on. Is that right?'

'I suppose so.'

'Case proved. Both of you are fined twenty pounds. Next case, please.'

It was like a very busy cattle market. A policeman attached to the court was busy shouting out suitable dates for cases that were being adjourned for one reason or another. The clerk of the court was writing future dates and results on charge sheets at high speed. It looked like a madhouse, but somehow it seemed to work. Then my case was called, and I asked for summary trial. My window-breaker pleaded guilty, and I gave the brief facts of the case and followed this with the information that he had no previous convictions.

'This is a man of previous good character,' I said.

'Yes, but he isn't now,' said the magistrate. 'Conditional discharge for twelve months. Compensation of thirty-two pounds. Next case.'

The clerk of the court thrust the charge sheet into my hand, and I took my defendant through to the gaoler's office. The gaoler sergeant handed my window-breaker some court papers relating to the compensation that he had to pay and released him. Then the sergeant asked me for my court card, worked out the hours completed, and added on an extra hour. He initialled my court card, and it was time for me to go home. It was tiring, but it cheered me up to think that my bank account would be in better shape.

The Met had its own prisoner-transport system. Every day, hundreds of people in custody were moved between police stations, courts, and prisons, and each prison van had its own regular route. There had to be a central point that worked like a bus station, wherein prisoners could be moved to the right van to take them to the correct destination. In 1970, this central bus station was based at Rochester Row, and it took a lot of manpower to deal with it.

At eight in the morning on weekdays, we needed nearly all the relief to guard prisoners when they were being moved from one van to another. Before that could happen, we had to make sure that the station yard was clear of all vehicles. Then, each prison van would manoeuvre slowly into position in the yard. At first, I did not see how we could fit them all in, but we always managed to do it with a few centimetres to spare.

There was a wooden gate at the front of the police station, in Rochester Row, and one at the back, on Vincent Square. As soon as the gates were closed, we started moving prisoners. As far as I know, we never lost any of them, and hopefully they all arrived at their correct destinations. Some of the younger prisoners would look out of their van windows and shout insults at the policemen standing in the yard. It must have come as a bit of a shock when the realisation came that they were about to be escorted across the yard by the people that they had been shouting at a few minutes before. Some received the odd punch or kick on their short walk between prison vans.

There were steps leading down to the men's toilets in one corner of the yard. One morning, I noticed a scuffle and two PCs dragging a prisoner down the steps. There was a lot of shouting that carried on until the man's head was forced down into one of the toilets. One of the sergeants was on duty in the yard, and I saw him run downstairs into the toilet block at some speed as the flushing process was going on.

I heard shouts of 'Stop that! That's enough of that. Just put him in the van.'

Most of the policemen at Rochester Row were young and did not have much service under their belts. They seemed very keen to do the job but had limited experience. As a general rule, PCs in county forces tended to be given more responsibility. However, several of my new colleagues had the idea that policemen in county forces spent their time cycling around quiet country lanes, looking for poachers or lost dogs.

The inspector in charge of the relief recommended me to be authorised as a standard driver which would cover me to drive GP cars. In Hampshire, I had been authorised to drive GP cars and then area cars when it was decided to establish an area car system. In the Met, PCs had to pass an advanced driver's course before they could drive area cars, and this was obviously a good thing. In Hampshire, I had received my authorisation to drive area cars after completing a short test that involved driving a sergeant around the division for about thirty minutes.

I was sent on what was called a 'standard' driving course for two weeks, at the driving school based at Hendon. Part of the course was known as the nuts-and-bolts module; it dealt with the technical aspects of a car and how its internal combustion system worked. However, on most days we had the opportunity to drive all over the south of England with an instructor keeping an eye on us. One day we drove along the A30 through Hartley Wintney, and it seemed strange being on my old patch but in a different police force.

At the driving school, they kept a couple of battered Jaguars that had been area cars and were kept exclusively for use on the skid pan. We all took it in turns to see what it was like trying to control a car when it went into a skid. The instructor said that we would feel it in our stomachs, and we soon discovered how true this was.

After the course, I was often posted to a GP or panda car, and this gave me the opportunity to reach calls before the foot patrols. At that time, most GP cars in the Met were Hillman Hunters. They were nearly all automatics and ideal for the driving conditions of central London.

One Sunday afternoon, I was patrolling a foot beat in 'the Jungle'. When I heard my colleagues refer to the Jungle, my first thought was that this must be a dangerous area to patrol alone. In fact, the reason for its name was that once you were in the Jungle, it all looked the same. The Jungle consisted of a gridiron pattern of streets in Pimlico, between Lupus Street and Warwick Way. Once you became familiar with the Jungle, you noticed that its streets, such as Cambridge Street and Winchester Street, had a few landmarks to identify them. There were several one-way streets and a limited number of places where you could enter or exit the Jungle that were useful to know. Andy Barrett, one of the senior PCs on the relief, was an acting sergeant that day. He was patrolling the division in one of the GP cars, a Hillman Hunter. He asked me to jump in, and we drove slowly through the streets of Pimlico together. Although the GP had no police markings, we all knew that our local criminals would have no difficulty in spotting us. After about fifteen minutes, we went back into the Jungle again and spotted a motorcycle ahead of us with two youths on it.

'It's worth giving them a pull,' I said. 'They look quite young.'

As we followed the motorcycle, it suddenly turned right, and we did the same. It turned left, and we turned left. It turned right, and we followed again. It was obvious that Andy was thinking the same as I was, and he accelerated until we were level with the motorcycle. I signalled the rider to pull in, but the motorcycle suddenly hurtled forward and swerved right across our path. Andy slammed the car into reverse and then gunned the car forward and turned right. We saw the motorcycle gather speed and do a quick turn to its left, followed by a right-hand turn. The Jungle was living up to its name. It was not easy to know where you were and by the time you worked it out you were somewhere else.

'Alfa Romeo from Alfa Romeo Three. In the Jungle, trying to stop a motorcycle. Two up, not stopping for police.'

My call was answered by a cacophony of voices over the PR, as all the mobile units on the division and some foot patrols called to say they were on their way to the Jungle. We knew that if they stayed there we would catch them fairly quickly. The motorcycle continued doing lefts and rights, and then suddenly we came out of the Jungle.

'All units – Lupus Street, Lupus Street,' I shouted into the radio.

The motorcycle turned into a side street off Lupus Street, and our first thoughts were that this was good, because the road ended abruptly with a high brick wall at the other end. What I did not know was that there was an alley on the right, and that was where the rider of the motorcycle planned to go. Andy Barrett slammed the brakes on, and we squealed to a stop by the entrance to the alley.

There was no possibility of driving any further. At the same time, the driver of the motorcycle was having his own problems, as he came face to face with a large iron bollard in the middle of the alley. He went in too fast, avoided hitting the bollard, but clipped the brick wall a few metres from the entrance. Both youths left the motorcycle and ran off along the alleyway that led into the Churchill Gardens estate. I jumped out of the GP car and went after them.

My knowledge of Pimlico streets was very limited, but I did my best to carry on a running commentary on my PR. Glancing back, I could see that Andy had abandoned the GP car and was following me. The main Met radio channel was patched into the Alfa Romeo PR, and calls started to come in from all sorts of units. After running through the Churchill Gardens estate, the two youths split up. Andy went after one of them, so my decision was to concentrate on the other one, who by this time was sprinting across Lupus Street like an Olympic hopeful.

It seemed that the whole of the Met Police had become involved in this incident. There were a couple of units on their way from Gerald Road, our neighbouring division. Calls came in from a Flying Squad car and a couple of Traffic Patrol units that they were coming to assist. Running at my top speed made me quite breathless, and my radio messages were probably not intelligible.

It must have been confusing to all and sundry, because each time my suspect ran into a street, they could hear me shouting out the location while Andy was doing the same thing. Then we found ourselves back in the Jungle, and I did my best to note the names of the streets. The gap between the suspect and me was starting to increase, and the thought went through my mind that he might escape, but I managed to keep him in sight.

Everyone would have heard me say, 'Towards Warwick Square,' followed by a few pathetic gasps that suggested I could end up as the subject of the station's next sudden-death report before too long. By this time, my strength was fading quickly and I was slowing down. My suspect was now running down one side of Warwick Square, but ready to meet him at the other end were three or four police cars and several police officers.

'You're not going to get very far,' I thought. The youth stopped running and looked back at me. He must have decided that it was a good time to stop running, and he just stood there waiting for me. It turned out that Andy Barrett had caught the one he was chasing and two or three minutes later we were back at the station.

'The bad news is that they're juveniles,' said Andy. They were both fifteen years of age and from local families living in Pimlico.

The Met had a system for dealing with juveniles that was very similar to the system in Hampshire. The parents were contacted and asked to come to the police station. We then interviewed both youths, who made statements admitting the offence. One of our colleagues had found the owner of the motorcycle, who confirmed that nobody had been given permission to use it. So it was a straightforward case of TDA. Following on from that, there were offences of no insurance and no driving licence.

The station officer wrote up an entry in Book 12A, the detained persons' register. The youths were handed over to their parents to await a decision regarding court proceedings. Andy and I completed the case papers and forwarded them to the District Juvenile Bureau. The normal policy was that if juveniles had not been convicted before they would be given an Official Caution by an inspector. If proceedings were recommended, they would receive a summons to appear before a juvenile court.

Summonses were issued for both teenagers to appear at Westminster Juvenile Court. I had been to juvenile courts on several occasions in Hampshire, where the defendants had always been well behaved. This was to be my only visit to Westminster Juvenile Court, and the expression 'the animals were running the zoo' came to mind.

The defendant in one of the cases before mine was a very large 16-year-old wearing a black leather jacket. He was facing a charge of burglary. It came as quite a shock to me, as he was very aggressive and swore at the JPs on two occasions. The chairwoman of the court was acting more like a shocked aunt than a magistrate.

'Oh dear, Jimmy, please do not talk like that. Oh dear, we just want to help you.'

It was all a bit embarrassing. I looked at the PC on duty at the court, who glanced at me and raised his eyebrows towards the ceiling. The impression given was that the JPs appeared to be apologising to the defendant. In the next case, the defendant was a girl aged sixteen. She was not aggressive like the previous defendant but showed complete contempt for the court. I had never seen youths behave like this at a juvenile court, but the magistrates appeared to accept it as normal.

By comparison, my two juveniles were quiet and well-mannered when they appeared. They pleaded guilty and were each fined twenty pounds.

A couple of weeks later, I had an arrest for burglary at seven o'clock one morning. While I was driving past Westminster Cathedral, a 999 call came in from a nearby office building. That time of day was normally fairly quiet, and several officers responded to the call, but by then my panda car had pulled up at the entrance of the office block. There was a woman cleaner standing in the reception area and she told me that she had come across an intruder on the first floor.

'Do you know where he might be now?' I asked.

'I think that he is probably still there. He's asleep.'

I walked quietly across the main office on the first floor, and ahead of me I saw a man slumped across a desk, sleeping. His hands were on the desk, but my main concern was the huge Bowie knife lying a few centimetres from his right hand. I heard a movement behind me and turned to see two of my colleagues quickly coming into the office. I signalled them to stay where they were and moved forward quietly. I picked up the Bowie knife, waved it, and handed it to one of the PCs. He looked annoyed that he had not reached the scene before me. The suspect remained asleep until I started to shake him.

When I questioned him, he admitted that he had broken into the offices during the night, intending to steal anything that was worth stealing. We walked around the offices with him, and he identified a number of places that he had searched and property that he had moved. It seemed to me that there were some close similarities with another burglary that I had been called to the day before. The previous offence had been in an identical block of offices a short distance away, and the method of entry had been identical.

It seemed like a good time to question him, as he appeared to be in a frame of mind to confess, so I sat down with him and asked him about the other burglary. He admitted that he had done it, and I asked him whether he wanted to make a written statement. He then made a three-page statement, in which he admitted both burglaries. A detective sergeant took over the case as investigating officer but he was quite impressed when he discovered there was not much left for him to do apart from the paperwork.

We were right in the centre of the world of politics and government, and if anyone wanted to demonstrate, picket, or march, it seemed that they made their way to Westminster. During 1970, I was posted to marches and demonstrations on six or seven occasions. A typical route for a march was one that started at Speakers' Corner, wound its way along Park Lane, and ended in Trafalgar Square or the Embankment. It seemed that whatever the cause, they all went through 'A' District.

Most of these events passed without any problems, but the potential for a flashpoint was always there, especially when two opposing political groups were at the same location. The police use methods designed to maintain the peace, and sometimes this appears to be in conflict with the democratic principles of free speech and the right of assembly. The Met has a long history of dealing with public order, going back to 1829. Since then it has faced every type of situation, from some that were very friendly to others in which there was a high level of violence.

A great deal of planning is required to ensure that events pass smoothly and peacefully, and the expertise of the Met in this field is highly regarded throughout the world. However, despite the amount of planning, police can sometimes be taken by surprise. There will always be small, violent political groups who plan attacks on people they do not agree with. Sometimes their target will be police officers. There were events at which we had too many officers and others at which we had too few. It often seems as though the media are obsessed with violence, and a short TV news clip of an event can give a misleading idea of what actually happened.

A general election was held in June of 1970. The opinion polls predicted a win by Harold Wilson, and it came as a blow to the pollsters when Edward Heath emerged victorious. The headquarters of the Conservative Party in Smith Square was on our division, and it was soon crowded with hundreds of their celebrating supporters. Switching on the television at home, we saw Edgar Maybanks, the chief superintendent, and a number of my colleagues doing their best to control the crowds. What was not reported was that a man lunged forward and jabbed a lighted cigarette into the prime minister's neck. The assailant was quickly arrested by a Rochester Row PC, but the new PM did not want to have the man charged, and he was released a few hours later.

On my transfer to the Met I was given a ceremonial uniform in addition to my standard police uniform and equipment. Essentially, it was a Victorian police uniform that was worn for ceremonial occasions. There was no shirt or tie, and the tunic was buttoned to the collar. Instead of a raincoat, there was a rolled up cape that fitted onto my belt. Would it ever be necessary for me to wear it? Yes, summer came, and I was on duty for Trooping the Colour. This occasion, also known as The Queen's Birthday Parade, required all the Uniform officers involved to wear their ceremonial uniforms. It was a hot day, and I changed into my ceremonials with a T-shirt under my tunic.

Our chief superintendent, Edgar Maybanks, was in charge of several serials, including mine, and we were all assigned to St James Park and Horse Guards Road. The uniform became more splendid bit by bit, depending on rank, and Edgar Maybanks could only be described as dazzling, covered in silver braid and wearing a cocked hat resplendent with white plumes. It made me think of people such as the Duke of Wellington and Lord Nelson, and I wondered what the commissioner must have looked like.

A number of large marquees had been errected for the use of police and other services in St James Park. On this fine day, the surrounding area was full of people. As the event was coming to an end, I found myself dealing with a distressed mother who had lost her 9-year-old daughter. My first job was to write a description of the girl and her clothing in my notebook. I did not have a PR but a short distance away there was a Cannon Row PC who did. He called the police incident room with all the details, while I did my best to reassure the mother that all would be well.

A message came over the PR, telling us to stay where we were, and a few minutes later a woman police officer appeared, walking in our direction, hand in hand with the missing girl. The mother was overjoyed; she thanked us several times. I started to walk back towards the park, looking for my serial. On a large public-order event there could easily be thirty or forty serials involved. Their shoulder numbers told me that there were officers there from every alphabetical corner of the MPD – but there was no sign of the Letter 'A'. My serial had disappeared.

Then I recognised my chief superintendent standing near one of the marquees, still looking as if he were on his way to the Battle of Waterloo. He waved to me and said that he thought I might have become lost, so I started to tell him what had happened.

'You look as if you need a drink,' he said. 'Didn't they tell you about the beer tent?'

He signalled me to follow him, and he led me into a large marquee. The place was full of policemen, with their tunics open, drinking pints of beer. My serial was there. A pint of beer was thrust into my hand, and it seemed to me that this was time for a reality check. 'Beer tent,' I said to myself. Beer tent? On this hot day my glass was empty within two or three minutes. I must have had a second pint but cannot recall if I had a third.

17

'A' District supplied officers for security duty at Buckingham Palace and the Palace of Westminster on temporary attachments. A posting to Buckingham Palace was for twelve months, and a posting to POW, as it was known, was for eighteen. Rumours started to circulate that there were plans to transfer a number of PCs to these places in October.

These duties were not suitable for probationers and the postings usually went to officers with two or three years' service. As a general rule, this was not popular with the younger men, who preferred being on the streets and did not like the idea of static duty covering security posts.

One of the sergeants told me that my name appeared on the list to go to POW. A few weeks earlier I had been posted to Buckingham Palace for a day, and my memories were not happy ones. The police officers there all seemed to have at least twenty years' service, been unfriendly, and had little time for outsiders. I'd felt as though they resented me even being in their canteen.

In September it became official. My transfer to POW was going to take place the following month. By this time, my knowledge of AR division had reached the point when I knew many of our local residents and, more importantly, several of our local criminals. Maybe this was some sort of administrative error. I saw myself as a valuable member of the team and decided to see my divisional commander and explain all of this to him.

The chief superintendent had made a point of chatting to me on a couple of occasions and saying 'well done' for one of my arrests. However, it has to be said that my meeting with him on this occasion did not last very long. Mr Maybanks told me that he regarded the security of POW as very important and did not intend to make any changes to the list that he had approved.

In October 1970, I arrived at what was known as the Crossings section at the Palace of Westminster, where I had a brief meeting with Inspector Simms, the senior police officer at POW. There were three sergeants stationed there, and one of them was Sergeant Spearman, who was in charge of the Crossings officers.

The Palace of Westminster had its own regular contingent of police, and they seemed to be a more welcoming bunch than the people at Buckingham Palace. All new arrivals at POW, like me, were posted to the Crossings section. We soon realised that we were the lowest in the pecking order and most of the time we manned the outside posts. The main ones were the carriage gates and a nearby foot gate that gave access to New Palace Yard.

There was also a patrol that covered Bridge Street. Occasionally we had to man the two traffic points in Parliament Square known as the Fountain and the Scissors.

The buildings that make up what is called the Palace of Westminster cover a large area. There are the famous parts, namely the House of Commons, House of Lords, and Westminster Hall, but the whole parliamentary estate is an extensive labyrinth of buildings and courtyards.

It now includes the more recent additions on the other side of Bridge Street. As well as Portcullis House, opened in 2001, there is the old Norman Shaw Scotland Yard building and what was Cannon Row police station; all are now full of modern offices and meeting rooms.

There were several security posts that were regarded as prestigious, and each one was the proud domain of one of the veteran PCs at POW. As we sat in the canteen a few weeks after my arrival, the PC that I was with indicated one of the older officers sitting at a nearby table. He told me the post that the PC held at the House of Commons with a touch of reverence in his voice.

Sometimes on late turn, when the division bell rang, a couple of us would rush out and stop the traffic in Bridge Street. About a dozen MPs would emerge from St Stephen's Tavern and dart across Bridge Street and through the foot gate into New Palace Yard on their way to vote. It was always useful to have a pub with a division bell in that part of London.

Bridge Street runs from Parliament Square to Westminster Bridge and this was my patrol for the first three or four weeks at POW. It rained continuously and I changed both my police raincoats every few hours, although they never seemed to ever get dry. In Winchester, Sergeant King had told me that a good policeman never gets wet. Based on this definition, I would have been a great disappointment to him.

A tunnel ran from Westminster tube station, under Bridge Street, and led to one of the entrances to POW below Big Ben. Every PC on Crossings had a key that opened an anonymous-looking door about halfway along the tunnel. It was here that we entered a very old building that some years later would be replaced by Portcullis House. Inside, there was a room known as the Crossings Room. We had our lockers there and our own furniture, which consisted of four or five ancient-looking House of Commons sofas.

The Palace of Westminster is a unique place in many ways, and working there as a police officer would prove to be a very unusual experience for me. The hours worked by police were very different from anywhere else. Officers assigned to the Crossings section worked alternating weeks of late turn and early turn, and there was no night duty. However, we knew that there were all-night sessions at the House of Commons and soon discovered that we were expected to do them, as well.

Early turn normally started at 8 or 9 a.m. Our late-turn shifts were referred to as 'two 'til rise'. This meant that we started at 2 p.m. and finished when the House of Commons rose. The day's business in the House would start at 2.30 p.m. and would normally finish sometime after 10 p.m. Because of this, late turn meant that we did a lot of overtime.

Sergeant Spearman gave all new arrivals a briefing about their duties at POW and explained its unique legal and constitutional status. We were told that our main responsibility was security and that we needed to forget the style of policing that we had used in the outside world. We were now working inside the hallowed walls of the Mother of Parliaments, where there was also a force of civilian custodians and where the Sergeant at Arms had overall responsibility for law and order.

When arrests were made, they would generally be for a breach of the peace, and people who caused minor disturbances could be placed in a cell at the POW police office. A person detained in these circumstances would normally be released when the House of Commons decided to rise.

It did not take long for new arrivals to come across some of the unusual aspects of policing within the parliamentary estate. Seeing policemen in uniform drinking in the bars in POW seemed strange to me. It appeared that we had arrived in some sort of parallel universe where everything was different!

The Palace of Westminster has often been called the best club in London, and Members of Parliament, peers, journalists, police officers, and everyone else seemed to be taking advantage of the low price of food and drink in the bars and restaurants of POW. Given the hours that people worked, the amount of drinking that went on was not surprising. This was very noticeable during the evenings when everyone had to be available until the Commons rose, usually about midnight or later.

One of my colleagues told me about a place called Rose's Bar, so we called in for a drink on our first late-turn week. Rose's Bar was used by all sorts of people who worked at POW, including police officers, and beer only cost ten pence a pint.

There are certain similarities between MPs and police officers. They work unsocial hours, and most of them drink but are never drunk, although at times they can become tired and emotional. A few weeks after my arrival there, two of us went in pursuit of a very tired-looking MP who was chasing a journalist across New Palace Yard. There was a scuffle near the carriage gates until we pulled them apart, and the journalist made his escape.

My transfer to the Palace of Westminster came about the same time as our move to Southfields, a suburb near Wimbledon. It was the first house that we bought, a spacious three-bedroomed terraced house, and we paid £5,850 for it. This seemed expensive at the time, but there were indications that the price of property was set to rise during the next few years, and 1970 seemed like a good time to buy a house. Southfields tube station was only about five minutes' walk from the house, and it was a quick journey into central London.

The year 1971 started tragically with a major disaster on 2 January at a football match in Scotland. It was the famous local derby in Glasgow, when Celtic and Rangers were playing at Ibrox Stadium. Crash barriers gave way under the weight of people, leading to sixty-six deaths and many injuries. This was a wake-up call for the FA, the Government, and the police, but many more people would die before the issue of safety at football grounds was taken more seriously.

In February 1971, a British soldier was killed by an IRA gunman in Northern Ireland. He was the first soldier to lose his life in a situation that seemed to be moving from bad to worse. What had started as civil unrest was now developing into a conflict involving paramilitary groups.

In October that year, a bomb exploded on the thirty-first floor of the Post Office Tower in central London, the location of a revolving restaurant that gave its diners spectacular views of the city below. The bomb had been planted in a lavatory at the restaurant, and a group calling itself the Kilburn Battalion of the IRA claimed responsibility. Prior to the explosion, a warning had been given by phone, and a search had been carried out, but nothing suspicious had been found. I was later told that the bomb had been placed inside a fire extinguisher. Although most British people were concerned about the problems in Northern Ireland, they probably spent more time talking about decimal currency at this time. The monetary system that we were using was archaic and complicated, but British people were used to it, and many people hated the idea of any change. But the day was coming when we would change to the decimal system, and it was soon being referred to as D-Day.

Let me explain. There were twelve pence to a shilling, and twenty shillings made a pound. Each penny was divided into four farthings, and two farthings made a halfpenny – although by 1971 the farthing had been killed off by inflation. There were banknotes for five pounds, one pound, and ten shillings, accompanied by what future generations would consider to be a strange-looking array of coins. There were halfpennies, pennies, twopence coins, threepence coins, sixpence coins, shillings, two-shilling coins, and half-crowns.

Confused? It was obvious that foreign visitors were baffled by our money, and I did my best to explain to some of them how it worked. 'Now let me tell you about guineas,' I once said to a foreign tourist, but this was obviously a step too far. The guinea was a unit of money worth twenty-one shillings (£1.05 in decimal terms), which had started life as a coin used for trade in Africa. The prices of some items in the UK were traditionally quoted in guineas, such as horses or goods sold in auction houses.

The money situation was typically British. When journalists stirred the pot, they found that large numbers of people were vehemently opposed to any change in the system that they were used to. The big day finally arrived, and when we walked into the staff canteen at POW we saw some very strange-looking prices. However, within a short time it all seemed quite normal.

During the second half of the twentieth century, many European countries faced terrorism from right-wing and left-wing extremists, and British people tended to think that it could not happen here. However, England did have an anarchist group called the Angry Brigade, which launched a terrorist campaign in 1968. This group consisted of young men and women who were opposed to the capitalist system and their enemies seemed to include anyone who could be described as being part of the establishment or government. Their bombs caused damage to a number of places, including the homes of the commissioner of police, the Secretary of State for Trade and Industry, and the attorney general. Other targets included the embassies of the United States and Spain, and one bomb destroyed a BBC outside broadcast van on the eve of the Miss World contest. The public heard very little about the Angry Brigade because many of their attacks were not reported in the press. In 1971, eight people were arrested and sent for trial at the Central Criminal Court. Five of them were convicted and received long prison sentences.

You did not have to be an expert on terrorism to realise that POW was not as secure as it should have been at that time. Most police officers guessed that it was only a matter of time before the IRA launched a major campaign on the British mainland.

The security system had followed a traditional pattern of many years. There were 630 MPs and a few thousand peers who were entitled to enter parliament without let or hindrance, and there were quite a few places where they could enter or leave.

The system was quite simple and straightforward. Police guarding the entrances were expected to recognise all of the men and women who were peers or MPs and give them immediate access. High-ranking civil servants and party officials were usually given access in the same way. Many people worked at POW, and there were also journalists and others, including building contractors, based there. Day by day, the potential threat posed by a well-organised and determined terrorist group made the existing security arrangements look increasingly out of touch.

During my first three months there, I challenged a man who tried to walk past me when I was on a security post. My first impression was that he was probably a vagrant. His clothes were shabby, and there was an unpleasant smell, typical of a man who had not washed or changed his shirt for two or three weeks. He told me that he was a peer and was on his way to the House of Lords.

It is always a good idea to treat the mentally ill carefully, so I nodded and smiled in a benevolent sort of way before grabbing his arm and marching him away from the building. It came as a shock when he produced a driving licence and a letter that identified him as a peer of the realm. He just seemed amused and made no complaint about his treatment, but this sort of incident happened from time to time and underlined the security aspects there.

Parliament has never forgotten the day when King Charles the First turned up with a contingent of soldiers and a warrant for the arrest of several MPs. The door was slammed in his face, and the door-slamming tradition continues every year when the monarch arrives to open Parliament. If a police officer stops a peer or MP entering parliament, there is likely to be a major furore and probably a complaint against the officer.

Sometimes I was posted to committee rooms, and Sergeant Spearman warned me to remove my headgear when I went in. However, I know of one new PC who walked into a committee room wearing his helmet. He must have received a nasty shock when an MP shouted out, 'Point of order! There is a Queen's officer present.'

There were five or six new arrivals in the Crossings section, and we were all in our twenties. None of us had volunteered for the job, but we took the security issues seriously. When we sat together in the Crossings Room, we often joked about all the potential trouble that lay in wait for us there. One serious complaint and an officer would be sent back to his division.

We heard that the sergeant-at-arms and Inspector Simms had been meeting to discuss security and that there would soon be changes coming. The first development was that everyone who worked within the parliamentary estate, including police, would be issued with photographic identity cards. An important part of this plan was that this would include all MPs and peers. This seemed sensible to me, but many of the MPs and peers refused to carry them.

Another important change was that all visitors would only be allowed to enter by one specified entrance, namely St Stephen's. As soon as we started to enforce the new rules, there were angry scenes when we stopped people at the other points of entry.

'I am the general secretary of the Labour Party, and I always come in this way!'

'I am the treasurer of the Conservative Party, and I am meeting the prime minister in five minutes' time!'

'I am the chairman of the Liberal Party, and I am due in Committee Room Three in five minutes' time!'

One senior party official made a complaint against me, but Inspector Simms supported me and congratulated me for not backing down. It was good to see that the security system was improving bit by bit.

As far as I am aware, we had no armed police officers based there at that time, which in later years would probably seem strange. However, we were only a short distance from Cannon Row police station, where there were a large number of 'authorised shots'. Buckingham Palace, Palace of Westminster, and Windsor Castle were all part of Cannon Row division.

Standing on a security post can bring with it a certain amount of boredom, but on late turn many of the posts were worked on a system of one hour on and one hour off. This meant that we had quite a lot of free time when we could sit in the Crossings Room and talk or read or even go to Rose's Bar for a drink. For the first few months there I enjoyed the freedom of it all, but then I started to think about promotion and decided that this should be given priority.

I had a meeting with Inspector Simms to discuss my annual appraisal. Every part of the report had been marked 'very good', and the inspector's comments included a description of me as 'a useful import from Hampshire'. Although I had received a qualifying mark in Hampshire, I felt it was a good time to mention my plan to take the promotion exam as a competitor.

Inspector Simms advised me to put in an application to the district commander. A few weeks later, I received a small buff card signed by the commander of 'A' District, which was my authority to take the competitive examination. A study group had been organised by one of the station sergeants at Cannon Row, and everyone, including me, met each week at the District Training Centre. When it started there were about twenty of us, all looking keen, but as the weeks went by the group became smaller and smaller. Eventually, there was a hard core of four or five, including me.

On late-turn weeks, the hours were usually long. It was nice to know that my monthly pay was being boosted by a large amount of overtime, but it was tiring. This was a period of time when the House of Commons had a large number of all-night sessions. When this happened, those of us who had started at 2 p.m. would be on duty until six or seven in the morning. The early-turn officers would be contacted and asked to come in as soon as possible to take over our posts.

Towards the end of one all-night sitting, at about six in the morning, I found myself sitting next to an MP in one of the restaurants. We were both eating cooked breakfasts, but he was drinking red wine with his. He insisted that he needed help to finish off his bottle of wine, so we spent about thirty minutes eating, talking, and drinking red wine. As I made my way home later that morning, it made me contemplate the strange environment that I was now working in.

Everyone who wanted to sit the promotion examination had to apply for a copy of *General Orders*, always referred to as GO. I applied for a copy and found there was a cost involved, as GO had to be rented. It was a massive book, about 9 centimetres thick, and it seemed to cover every possible aspect of police duty that could be imagined.

The station sergeant in charge of our study class at Cannon Row picked up a copy of GO and held it aloft like a sacred object. He told us that every paragraph in it related to mistakes made by officers over the years since 1829 and it was an attempt by the Met to prevent the same problems happening a second time.

On late turn, there was often the opportunity to sit in the Crossings Room on my own and study. One evening, there were three or four of us sitting there and chatting. We all felt hungry and decided that someone should volunteer to go to a fish and chip shop in Bridge Street for our supper. A short time later, four portions of fish and chips arrived in the Crossings Room.

Our door was only open for a few seconds, when suddenly we had an MP in our midst. Ernest Marples told us that he had been attracted by the smell. He looked quite tired, and it appeared that he had invited himself to the party. Then he told us about a vineyard that he owned in France and explained that his contribution would be the fruits of his vines. After that, he wandered off in the direction of his nearby office, and we wondered whether he would actually return. But he reappeared carrying three bottles of wine and it proved to be a good feast.

One night at about ten o'clock, Inspector Simms stopped to talk to me in New Palace Yard and then started walking towards the police office. As he did so, Prime Minister Edward Heath appeared, and their paths appeared to cross. I could see the two of them standing and talking for a few minutes. It seemed to be a fairly light-hearted conversation, but I heard the word 'security' crop up a couple of times.

At this point I saw a very tired-looking policeman emerge from a dark corner of New Palace Yard and walk slowly past. I could see that Mr Simms had spotted him, but luckily the PC was behind the prime minister. I can imagine that the inspector was probably thinking the same thing as I was – hoping that Edward Heath did not turn around. It was a relief to see the PC open a door and disappear from sight as if he had been some sort of apparition.

There were many changes made to criminal law during the seventies. An important change was that, at long last, powers of arrest were standardised. To me, 'felonies' and 'misdemeanours' sounded solid, as if they meant something, but we now had to become familiar with something else: 'arrestable' offences. As for the poor old felonies and misdemeanours, they were dumped into the dustbin of legal history.

The rights of arrested people were very limited, and this gave police a distinct advantage in dealing with suspects. People detained at police stations had no legal right to have someone informed that they were in police custody. If a person in custody asked to see a solicitor, the station officer would decide whether or not to allow the request, and it was often refused. If a solicitor came to a police station, the same situation applied, and suspects could be held for several days before being charged. There was one case in which a man was held for twenty-one days before being charged with murder. Suspects were often said to be 'helping police' with their enquiries.

One common method of interrogation has always been the 'good cop, bad cop' technique. One police officer appears tough and aggressive while the second one adopts a gentle and sympathetic tone.

There were always a small number of officers who believed that it was necessary to break the law in order to enforce it. A few horror stories and rumours did the rounds within the police service in the early seventies about methods being used to 'help' suspects to confess.

This was certainly not typical of police behaviour, even in those days, but the system allowed officers a wide degree of latitude, and there would always be some who used dubious methods to obtain admissions. During the seventies, civil liberties became more important as an issue than it had been in the fifties and sixties. Starting in the mid seventies, more and more legislation would be passed to protect the rights of suspects.

1972 was a very good year for me for several reasons. My name appeared in police orders, in the list of those who had been successful in the competitive exam. As I was halfway down the list, it seemed likely that my promotion would occur around October or November. There was also a very important event in July, when our second daughter, Emma, was born.

It was an important year for the Metropolitan Police with the appointment of a new commissioner, Sir Robert Mark. Mark had started as a PC in 1937, in the Manchester City Police. In 1956, he'd been appointed chief constable of the Leicester City Police, and in 1967 he'd been appointed as an assistant commissioner in the Met. A year later, following the unexpected death of Commissioner Sir Joseph Simpson, he became the deputy commissioner.

In the past, the Metropolitan Police has been criticised for being quite insular in its attitude to outsiders. It appears that Mark's first five years in the Met were not happy ones. When he arrived in London, he was not given any assistance to find accommodation, and it was the City of London Police force that helped him by giving him the use of one of their flats.

However, Home Secretary Roy Jenkins was very impressed by Mark and thought that the Metropolitan Police needed to be opened up to new thinking from outside. Many of the senior officers in the Met were deeply suspicious of Mark; the person they favoured as the next commissioner was Peter Brodie, the assistant commissioner in charge of 'C' Department. This assistant commissioner was always known as ACC and had overall responsibility for the CID.

In 1969, *The Times* published an article that dealt with allegations from a south London criminal that he was being blackmailed and had to pay bribes to some Met CID officers. The journalists used listening devices in order to record what was said, and one of the officers was heard boasting that he was a member of 'a firm within a firm'. For several years after that, newspapers ran stories relating to corruption within the Met.

Irrespective of what the press reported, there was a growing perception that institutional corruption was a serious problem in the Met CID. One of the most serious episodes occurred when a newspaper reported that Commander Ken Drury, head of the Flying Squad, had gone on holiday with a Soho businessman called Jimmy Humphries, who was notorious as one of the major names in pornography.

As deputy commissioner, Mark had responsibility for discipline in the Metropolitan Police. Mark soon started an internal war at Scotland Yard when he recommended that Drury be suspended. In Mark's own words, it resulted in a final trial of strength between 'C' Department and himself, with the unfortunate commissioner caught in the middle.

The 'old guard' said that the suspension of Drury would undermine CID morale, encourage criminals and do irreparable damage to the reputation of the force. By this time, Mark was in a much stronger position, as he was now the commissioner designate, and the commissioner agreed that Drury should be suspended. Nine days later, ACC Peter Brodie went into hospital, apparently suffering from stress. He never returned to duty.

In April 1972 Mark was appointed commissioner, and he soon made major changes to the structure of the Met. For about 100 years the CID had operated like a separate force and its effective head had been ACC. At that time there were about 2300 detectives working within divisions and another 900 in branches at Scotland Yard.

CID officers working on divisions were all divisional personnel but were not responsible to the Uniform chief superintendent in charge of the division. Each division had a detective chief inspector in charge of its CID officers, and the DCI's line manager was a detective chief superintendent at the district headquarters.

Shortly after Mark became commissioner, this changed, and CID officers on divisions became responsible to their divisional chief superintendent. A Uniform assistant commissioner was appointed as ACC and therefore head of the CID. A new department, later known as Complaints Investigation Branch was formed under the command of a Uniform officer to investigate all serious complaints against police officers. The new commissioner instituted a systematic campaign to root out corrupt officers, and many were arrested and charged. Apart from those charged, many officers under suspicion started leaving 'voluntarily' at a rate of about two each week for about two or three years after Mark's appointment as commissioner.

There was strong whiff of corruption coming from the CID unit that dealt with pornography, and a major criminal investigation was launched into the activities of the porn squad, as it was known. Two separate trials resulted in several police officers who had served in the porn squad being sent to prison – including Commander Ken Drury. A new branch was set up to deal with pornography, staffed by Uniform officers. The Central Drugs Squad went the same way as the porn squad.

London, New York, and Paris are all very large cities, and organised crime has always flourished in large cities such as these. Where there are major criminals involved in organised crime, there will always be a certain amount of police corruption. The top ranks of those in organised crime will always be looking for 'friends' in the world of politics and the police. This is something that can never be totally eliminated; it will remain a challenge for law-enforcement organisations everywhere.

While there was friction at the highest levels of the Met, 1972 was also a year of continuing conflict between the Conservative Government and the trade unions. The strike by miners led to serious problems, including power cuts, and soon industry was working a three-day week. In January 1972, soldiers from the Parachute Regiment were on duty at a civil-rights march in Derry. There was public disorder, and it was alleged that shots were fired at soldiers. Some of the soldiers opened fire and shot twenty-six people, killing thirteen of them. This day would become known as Bloody Sunday. Two official enquiries were set up to find out what had actually happened. The second of these enquiries went on for many years and it was not until 2010 that the Government accepted that the action taken by the soldiers had been unjustified. In February 1972, a car bomb exploded at the headquarters of 16th Parachute Brigade in Aldershot. This bombing was the work of the Official IRA, who stated that this was in revenge for what had happened on Bloody Sunday. A military chaplain and six civilian workers were killed. Eighteen other people were injured. One of the IRA men involved in the bombing was later convicted for his part in this crime.

This was the largest attack organised by the Official IRA in Britain during what would again be referred to as The Troubles. In 1969 there had been a split in the IRA which resulted in two factions, the Officials and the Provisionals, who were often at war with each other. In May 1972 the Official IRA, nicknamed the Stickies, declared a ceasefire with the British Army, but the Provisionals were attracting more and more men and women who saw violence as a means of creating a united Ireland.

In April 1972 I returned to Rochester Row. Nothing much had changed on the division, although we had a new transport link, the recently constructed Victoria Line, so I went to look at the brand-new Pimlico tube station. I was asked to act as a mentor for probationers and was also given the rank of acting sergeant when the relief was short of sergeants.

On my first day back on the streets, I whispered to the section sergeant that he had forgotten to post any of our men to traffic points. During the rush-hour periods, many busy junctions were manned by PCs to try and prevent them from becoming blocked, and we had all been ticked off at some time or other for arriving a few minutes late on our allotted posts. This duty had never been a popular one, and there were a few officers who showed their displeasure by creating long tailbacks on some of the roads in central London. The sergeant glanced at me with a strange look on his face, but later he explained what had happened. A decision had been made at CO a few months before that we no longer had to cover traffic points.

It appeared that this duty was not as vitally important as we had been led to believe.

As an acting sergeant, I went to give advice to a young probationer who had arrested a black teenager for stealing a jacket from a department store. The youth's MO was quite simple. He had put the jacket on and walked out of the store wearing it, only to be intercepted by a store detective on the street.

He just kept saying, 'I didn't do it.' It was always useful to obtain some type of confession, but as we were dealing with a juvenile, any questioning had to be carried out in the presence of a parent or guardian. A message was sent for his parents to be informed.

The father of the detained youth was a very large, strong-looking man. He sat down with me in an interview room, and I explained what had happened. I mentioned that his son had denied stealing the jacket. The man said very little but gave the occasional smile and nod as he listened.

After that, we walked into the charge room, and father and son stood facing each other for a couple of awkward seconds. Then the father moved suddenly, and his fist smacked into the side of his son's head. The force of the blow knocked the youth backwards, and he fell back against the wall and slid to the floor. The speed of it took everyone by surprise.

'Tell the officers the truth,' said Dad.

'Yes, I stole it,' said the youth.

This was a fairly quick interrogation by anyone's standards. Father, son, and police officer sat down together, and a written statement was taken. I later wondered what might happen if he went to court and decided to plead not guilty. What would we say about it?

'Well, Your Worships, initially he denied the offence, but after being punched in the head he readily admitted everything.'

It was the first time I had been involved in the arrest of a person who was not white. This was not surprising, as there were very few black people or Asians in Hampshire, but London was a city that already contained many ethnic groups. Pimlico had its Portuguese and Italians, but there were very few black or Asian people living on the division. Some parts of London, such as Brixton, had large numbers of black people, and there were other districts with large Asian populations.

There was a certain amount of friction between whites and some immigrants as soon as the newcomers arrived, and sometimes there were problems between police and immigrants. Much of this arose from the difference in cultures, especially between the attitudes of white British people and non-white immigrants. Once, when another officer and I were posted to the area car in Hampshire, a radio call had taken us to an industrial estate, with the message 'Two suspects, acting suspiciously.'

The two male suspects were black, and we carried out a stop on them. It did not appear to us that they were doing anything wrong. We carried out the usual checks, told them that we were sorry to have bothered them, and walked back to the police car. One of them thanked us because we had treated them in a courteous manner. Our response was, 'No problem – why would we not be courteous?'

The man then went on to say that he had been stopped by police in London on three or four occasions, and they had never been courteous to him. My own experience in the Met was that the vast majority of its officers were polite and courteous but there were obviously some who were not. However, I need to add a proviso to this statement, as I never worked in areas with large ethnic minorities. One major difference between the Met and most other forces was that London had a large ethnic population which was becoming larger year by year. If there was going to be racial tension, it seemed that London would be the place where it would occur.

If people feel that they are victims of discrimination, there will always be anger and the danger of an explosion. With the benefit of hindsight, I think that British police should have learned much more from the serious riots in the sixties that swept across American cities. To cause an explosion you need a detonator, and police action can often be the spark. In one American city there was a large-scale riot in which several people lost their lives. The detonator in that case was an incident when two white policemen arrested a black man for a drink-and-drive offence.

There were officers with racist attitudes in the Met, and much of this was tolerated because many senior officers did nothing to try and improve the situation. The story of Norwell Roberts QPM gives an indication of how bad the situation could be.

Norwell Roberts joined the Metropolitan Police in 1967 and did his initial training course at Hendon. He was the first black person to become a police officer in the UK, and the press showed a continual interest in him. During his initial training course at Hendon, he was called out of the classroom on a dozen or more occasions to have his photograph taken for the international press or television programmes.

His birthplace was Anguilla in the West Indies, the island 'invaded' by the Met in 1969. In 1966 he had been working as a scientific laboratory technician in the Botany Department of Westfield College, part of London University, when he'd seen that the Met Police had advertised for people to consider a career within the police. There was no mention of black people, although the Met later carried out specific advertising aimed at people from ethnic minorities.

'I thought that I would apply for a joke,' he said many years later. 'I did not think that I would get it. I knew people who had applied before and failed, without any reason being given.'

He had made an application in 1964 and had been unsuccessful. The first thing he knew about his appointment in 1966 was a newspaper story that said, 'Coloured man on way to join police force.'

'The Met had not bothered to tell me that I had been accepted,' he added.

During the time he had worked at London University, Norwell had been treated with respect by the people he worked with, and at the training school he had been treated as just another recruit to be trained. His arrival as a new probationer at Bow Street police station was going to be a different story, and his first three years there were marked with a campaign of hatred against him by some of his fellow police officers.

In 2011 we had the opportunity to meet and discuss what had happened to him at Bow Street. Everyone knew that he had faced some difficulties, but the actual story was much worse than I had realised. Here's how he described his first memories of life as a new probationer.

'There was this older PC, an old sweat who hated black people. He seemed to use his truncheon quite a lot, and he liked using it on black people. He had his own seat in the canteen and his own place in the parade room, where nobody would dare to stand. He had a lot of influence, not just on the relief but within the station. He appeared to court the respect of sergeants and senior officers within the division. There were many young

PCs at Bow Street, and they all looked up to him. He told everyone that they should not talk to me and threatened them if they did.'

Norwell Roberts had a meeting with his reporting sergeant shortly after his arrival. The sergeant's words are etched into his memory; they must have given him some idea of the problems that lay ahead.

'Look, you nigger, I will see to it that you never pass your probation.'

Norwell was living in a section house in Beak Street, Soho. When he had finished his tour of duty, he returned to the section house and cried. However, there was little privacy there in rooms that were little better than cubicles. He did not want anyone to hear him sobbing, so he went to the bathroom and cried in the bath. The sound of running water drowned out his sobs.

Things did not improve. Norwell found that on several occasions buttons had been ripped off his uniform. There were incidents in which his private car was damaged and the tyres slashed. Matchsticks were inserted into the keyhole, making it impossible to insert his vehicle key. He later joked that it was a good thing that superglue had not been invented until some years later.

On at least three occasions, his car was moved from a place where it had been parked legally and left on a double yellow line. After that, a removal unit would arrive, and his car would be towed away to the car pound at Elephant and Castle. It would cost him ten shillings each time to retrieve it, and he remembers the smirking faces of the officers at the pound.

He told me that he still had nightmares in which his current car is towed away to a pound. He puts these thoughts down to everything in his subconscious mind that ensures that he constantly relives these experiences.

The standard procedure in the Met at that time was that if a PC dealt with an incident, he/she would write a report in an official notebook. It would be handed to a sergeant to be checked and then sent to the Admin Unit, where a report would be typed. After that, the notebook would be left in a small wooden box in the front office so that it could be picked up by the officer. On his way to the parade room one day, Norwell went to find his notebook and saw that it had been ripped in half.

At some point, the inspector in charge of the relief assigned another sergeant to be his reporting sergeant. Apart from that small ray of sunshine, his life as a policeman remained as dark and difficult as ever. He soon discovered that if he put up a call for urgent assistance, no help would be forthcoming. Not surprisingly, even though it was a long time ago, he remains bitter at the way he was treated at Bow Street.

What seems remarkable was Norwell's strength of character and his refusal to complain until one particular incident outside the Royal Opera House. It was a hot summer day, and he was standing on the pavement as hundreds of theatregoers made their way in. Norwell noticed the divisional area car drive slowly past, and the driver wound down the window and shouted at him.

'Black cunt.'

It must have been heard by several of the theatre goers. Seething with anger, Norwell went straight to the chief superintendent and told him what had happened. The reply from his divisional commander was fairly short and unhelpful.

'Well, what do you want me to do about it?'

At that point, Norwell felt at his lowest ebb. 'Bloody hell! I've lost it now,' he thought. He realised that this was the first time he had let the outside world and, more importantly, those he worked with see that he was upset by the campaign of hatred that had been unleashed against him. He suddenly felt weak and realised that he had allowed his enemies to get under his skin.

'Nothing,' he said to his chief superintendent. 'I do not want you to do anything about it.'

He then returned to the section house.

'What did I do then, Richard?' he asked me.

'You went back to your room at the section house and cried,' I said.

'That's right,' said Norwell.

Patrolling Covent Garden Market was a welcome break from the problems that Norwell encountered with his fellow officers, and he made friends with many of the people he met on his beat, such as market porters and cab drivers. He noticed that, generally speaking, members of the public seemed to respect the uniform. Black people on the streets were nearly always supportive.

'It's nice to see you, man, wearing the uniform.'

However, he was aware that some young black people were hostile to the idea of a black man in a police uniform. One morning, he was called to a café where there had been a burglary. A young black man suddenly appeared at the door, looked in at him and shouted, 'Judas!' before running away down the street.

When he had three years' service, Norwell applied to join the CID and was transferred to work in plain clothes at West End Central as a Temporary Detective Constable. After ten weeks at the Detective Training School, he went to Vine Street police station as a DC. Working within small CID units, he was treated with respect by his colleagues.

He was promoted to Uniform sergeant in 1976 and posted to West Hampstead. After a year, he went back to CID work and spent the rest of his service as a detective sergeant at a number of stations.

Norwell did a considerable amount of undercover work, and this proved crucial when he was called in to help investigate a contract killing in Acton. Enquiries took him all over the south of England and the Midlands. Within six days, five men were arrested, who were all later convicted of murder. In 1985 he received a commissioner's commendation for the work that he had carried out on the case.

In 1996 he was awarded the Queen's Police Medal for Distinguished Service, and in 1997 he retired from the police service. Since his retirement, he has raised large sums of money for different charities. Norwell was a pioneer, and pioneers often have a difficult time.

'In those days there was always the standard comment,' he says. 'If you could not take a joke, you should not have joined, and if you complained, you had a chip on your shoulder.'

He believes that things have not changed as much as they should have done, as racism still seems to rear its ugly head within the police service. He says that many senior officers do not take the problem seriously enough, and many adopt an attitude that is essentially cowardly. If they do not acknowledge its presence when it crops up, they do not have to do anything about it.

His sad comment about diversity training in the Met is that it is not fit for purpose and that most officers see it as a joke. It is seen as an encumbrance to attend it, and most question the value of the training. It is however, seen as a break from day-to-day policing and a day away from the relief. His opinion was that the way he was treated was a sign of those times, but having heard his story, I am amazed that he had the courage to hang on. Norwell Roberts is fiercely proud of his achievement.

'They will always remember the first black policeman. The second or third they are going to forget. But the first is always something special. If I had not survived in the Met, there might not have been a second or a third. Did you know that there is a Trivial Pursuit question about me now?'

18

In 1972 there were growing concerns about the IRA and what they might be planning. One afternoon, Inspector Rosser, a Welshman and one of the inspectors at Rochester Row, walked into the parade room and gave us some useful advice: 'Don't think of these people as yobs or hooligans. Don't underestimate them. They believe in what they are doing, and they are going to be very dangerous.'

It was a valuable message, but naturally everyone hoped that the terrorists would stay on the other side of the Irish Sea. However, the bombing of the Post Office Tower and the deadly attack on the army at Aldershot had indicated otherwise. In 1972, none of us realised how quickly we would find ourselves in the front line of a major terrorist campaign.

A few weeks before my promotion date, we flew to Canada to visit my mother, stepfather, and brother. Our family now consisted of four people, including Emma, who at six weeks old was about to fly the Atlantic. It was the first time we had flown for several years and our first experience of a jet aircraft. Taking off in a jet was quite a dramatic experience compared with the slow and graceful style in which a propeller-powered aeroplane lifts up from the runway. There was a feeling of tremendous thrust as the airliner pushed up into the sky, over Windsor Castle, and then towards the Atlantic.

Canada was a new experience for us all, although Emma was too young to remember it. The weather was very hot and humid. Luckily, the city of Barrie is situated on the edge of a large lake, and there was a beach that was about five minutes' walk from my mother's house. We spent several occasions swimming in the lake, and it was pleasant in the water on hot days.

We returned from holiday shortly before the start of my pre-promotion course at Hendon. My last day as a PC was spent outside the Spanish embassy in Belgrave Square. ETA, the Basque terrorist group, had begun a campaign of violence aimed at gaining independence for the land that they claimed as their homeland in the north of Spain.

One of their members had been convicted of murdering a policeman and had been sentenced to death. The method of execution in Spain was to be tied to a stake and then garrotted. The object of the demonstrators was to put pressure on General Franco and his government to commute the death penalty.

My first thoughts were that there could not be many Basques in London, but there were about 300 people gathered outside the embassy, and about half of them were wearing the traditional large Basque berets. There were also a few 'rent-a-mob' characters, those who tended to turn up at any demo, whatever the cause.

Three or four serials had been deployed on this operation, and the officer in charge decided that he would send out a half serial to guard the embassy. This would consist of a sergeant and ten PCs, including me. The others were left sitting in police buses a short distance away. Our job was to protect the embassy, and it was the standard plan. The demonstrators were asked to stand on the other side of the road, and we stood outside the embassy, facing them.

'*Franco asesino, Franco asesino.*' The shouts of the demonstrators echoed around Belgrave Square. It was noisy, but it seemed that everyone was happy to stay where they were.

This was a time when many young Americans had gone abroad to avoid military service in Vietnam, and there were three or four Americans among the demonstrators. One of them was acting as an agitator, so I decided to keep a close eye on him. He ran forward on two or three occasions, shouting, 'Come on, you guys – let's take the embassy!' When he realised that nobody was following him, he would look quite crestfallen and retreat into the crowd.

Everything remained peaceful until a television crew arrived at the embassy. The demonstrators must have decided to make everything look exciting for the television viewers, and suddenly they all surged forward. As there were only about ten of us, it was impossible to hold them back. It was only a matter of about two minutes, but the television would show hundreds of protestors rushing forward towards the embassy and overwhelming the police.

There was a very fast response from our senior officer, who appeared with reinforcements, and we quickly moved everybody back to the other side of the road. Nobody had tried to enter the embassy or cause any damage, and the American who had been of interest to me had disappeared. An hour later, all the demonstrators went home, and shortly after that we were on our way back to Alfa Romeo.

My promotion to sergeant came a few days later, and I was on my way to 'B' District, the Royal Borough of Kensington and Chelsea. One of my friends at Alfa Romeo told me that there were vacancies for sergeants at Chelsea. However, this raised some concerns in my mind, because Chelsea had been in the news for some time – for all the wrong reasons.

Everyone knew that Chelsea division had been hit by scandal. To be more specific, some of its officers had been convicted of criminal offences. The worst case concerned a PC who had become friendly with a team of burglars and had given them information about unoccupied houses. We all knew that there were several Chelsea officers who were appearing at court as defendants or would find themselves facing discipline boards at Scotland Yard.

Some months before, a newspaper article had featured a complaint from a famous football player who said that he had been beaten up in the charge room at Chelsea police station. Apart from its fair share of bad publicity in the media, the division always seemed to be in the premier league when it came to complaints made against police.

It would be fair to say that the various bits and pieces of information coming my way did not give me a very rosy picture of the division where I would be working as a sergeant. For their part, my colleagues at Rochester Row did their best to cheer me up by telling me all sorts of horror stories about Chelsea. There was much that could be described as gallows humour and many stories that were just not true or had been exaggerated. However, sadly, some of the things were true.

'Everything seems all right now,' said one of the wags, with a grin, a few days before my promotion. 'Things are settling down at Chelsea now, they only had one PC suspended last week.'

It was important to keep an open mind about the place, I thought. Whatever Chelsea was or was not, it sounded like a challenge, and Maureen was proudly sewing chevrons onto my tunics.

'B' District was divided into three divisions – Chelsea, Kensington, and Notting Hill – and all of them were busy places. Chelsea was a one-station division which housed the district headquarters on the top floor. Three new sergeants, including me, arrived on the same day, and next morning we all had to report to the district commander. This was when I first met David Fitzsimons, who would later work on the same relief as I did.

All three of us were told that we were being posted to Chelsea division. This suggested to me that some sergeants might have been moved to other places but there was no point in spending too much time thinking about what all of this might mean.

The three of us would have to report to Chief Superintendent Pickford, Chelsea's divisional commander, that afternoon. Pickford had his own style of welcoming new sergeants to the division. The best description of the meeting would be to say that we stood in front of his desk and he shouted at us, giving us his opinion of sergeants. It made me think of a couple of occasions when I had found myself in front of the headmaster's desk at school. He started by telling us that there had been a lot of problems at Chelsea, and he believed that the main reason for this had been a failure of leadership by sergeants.

From the way he spoke, he seemed to imply that we had been found guilty at this point and it was just a matter of time before we would be sentenced. Pickford carried on at a rapid pace with stories of Chelsea policemen committing criminal offences or serious breaches of the discipline code. At one point he commented angrily that his safe had been broken into.

The chief superintendent's safe had been broken into? This was a few degrees worse than bad, I thought. Pickford's speech returned to his central point, his opinion that it all came down to the poor quality of sergeants. The three of us felt quite relieved when the meeting came to an end.

In the corridor outside, I glanced quickly at David Fitzsimons. It seemed that we were both doing our best to maintain 'sudden-death' faces. The whole meeting had had a sort of black-comedy edge to it. It did not come as a complete surprise to hear that the other sergeant at our meeting had applied for a transfer to another division the next day, and he left Chelsea a couple of weeks later.

The following day, I started work with my relief and met the officer in charge, Inspector Woodhead. It was November, hardly anyone was on leave, and we had a full house of sergeants. Station Sergeant Euan Hay was the inspector's deputy, and there were four sergeants including me. My first two or three weeks at Chelsea could best be described as my honeymoon period.

A well-known passage in General Orders mentioned the importance of sergeants knowing the character of all the PCs that they were responsible for. I spent as much time as I could on patrol with them, either on foot or in a car. It became clear to me that, for a central London division, Chelsea covered a large area. It stretched west from Knightsbridge, almost as far as Chelsea football club. In the north, it covered Old Brompton Road, Exhibition Road, and part of Earls Court Road, with our southern boundary on the River Thames.

The relief had twenty-eight PCs, most of them slightly older than the men I had worked with at Rochester Row. There was a central core of seven or eight experienced officers, mostly in their early thirties, but there were quite a few probationers, and Inspector Woodhead decided that three of them would be assigned to me.

As their reporting sergeant, my role would be to evaluate their progress and help them to develop their policing skills. Part of this would mean writing progress reports on each one at specific dates within their period of probation. The crucial part would be my recommendation that a probationer was likely to make an efficient constable, or otherwise.

Chelsea was one of the few divisions that had a shift pattern based on a four-week rota: one week of night duty and three weeks of day duty. This would later become the standard shift system in the Met. Each relief had two 'spare' days during the four-week rota, when officers were available to carry out different duties, such as public-order or plain-clothes patrols. Because of the general shortage of manpower, everyone in the Met had to work two rest days each month.

There were three experienced sergeants on my relief, and all very different. Harry Fraser was a rugged-looking Scotsman in his forties, a very experienced sergeant who had been at Chelsea for several years. When it came to vice-squad work, Harry Fraser was one of the most experienced officers in the Met. He lived in a police flat in Fulham, and when we travelled to work on late turn, I would often meet up with him on the tube journey to South Kensington.

Peter Close, a quiet, thoughtful man in his forties, was as different from Harry Edwards as it was possible to be. For some reason, he tended to confide in me and tell me quite a lot about his outside interests. It turned out that he was a spiritualist and medium. Not surprisingly, this led to some interesting conversations between us.

Andrew Norman had been a sergeant for several years, and I first thought that he was probably a couple of years older than I was, but he was actually two years younger. Peter Close told me that when Andy had been promoted sergeant he had been the youngest PC in the Met to have achieved this.

Andy, as he was known, would become famous for his important role in the world of athletics rather than for his work as a police officer. It soon became obvious that his power and influence within the police service went far beyond his rank.

'You won't be seeing too much of Andy,' said Peter Close shortly after my arrival at Chelsea.

Andy Norman always seemed to have many balls in the air at any one time, and one of these was his work as an observer with the Air Support Unit. Shortly after my arrival, he spent two weeks in a helicopter before making a brief appearance on night duty. He then explained to his inspector and fellow sergeants that he would not be available after Friday night, as he had to be in Oslo, where he was organising a sports meeting for the Coca-Cola Company. My immediate reaction was that his job as a police officer would take precedence over his involvement in the world of athletics. This, apparently, was not so.

Sergeants have two main roles, as section sergeant or station officer. The section sergeant decides what beats and patrols are to be covered and then posts PCs to them. After this, the sergeant patrols the division, supervises incidents, and ensures that patrolling officers are carrying out their duties correctly.

When it came to beats or patrols, some were always given priority coverage. On night duty at Chelsea, two PCs were always posted for the first three hours to a patrol referred to as Old Brompton Road. The purpose was to maintain a police presence in the area around the Coleherne public house, then renowned for being the largest meeting place for gay men in London.

Complaints came in regularly from local residents, in writing or by phone, citing all manner of things going on in the surrounding streets, including criminal damage, importuning, assaults, and drunkenness. The objective of the patrol was to prevent these things happening, but the pub's customers resented the police presence and saw it as a form of state repression.

Every police station in the Met had a large ledger known as the duty state. There was a page for each day, and the shoulder numbers of all sergeants and PCs were recorded, together with their duties and the hours worked. Section sergeants had to ensure that all officers on the relief were accounted for and would complete the state during their tour of duty. After that, the inspector would sign it to certify that it was correct.

Station officers had a general responsibility for everything that happened inside their police stations, but their most important role would always be dealing with charges. Some years later, their status would have legal responsibilities and they would be called custody officers.

Station officers had to make key decisions on whether to accept charges or refuse them. It was important to have a good understanding of evidence and be able to sort out the wheat from the chaff. When a decision was made to charge, it was important that the correct offence was chosen and the wording on the charge sheet was accurate and legally acceptable. Station officers had to check and sign the original notes made by the arresting officers. In CID cases, if the officer in charge of the case held the rank of inspector or above, he/she would take responsibility for the charge and supporting evidence.

Much of this may sound quite straightforward, but Chelsea always seemed to be very busy. On late turn, it was quite normal to deal with eight or nine charges during the shift, and on day duty there would usually be two station sergeants. One was referred to as 'front desk' and the second one as 'back desk'.

Generally speaking, the pace at Chelsea was much faster than on 'A' District. There was still what could be described as the swinging-sixties allure of the King's Road. Wealthy Americans, Iranians, and Arabs had bought properties in the most fashionable streets, and Chelsea seemed to be busy *24/7* before this was the case in other parts of London.

On my first Saturday night at Chelsea, I went on patrol in the van with two of my PCs, and we spent two or three hours racing across the division from incident to incident. The IR channel that covered most of central London was sending out messages almost non-stop. It sounded as if there were a war going on, and in a manner of speaking, there was. There were a few moments when the radio went quiet, but this did not last more than six or seven seconds.

Our area car received a call to a disturbance at a restaurant, where a man had been injured as a result of acid being thrown in his face. There was a call from the duty officer to say that he was on his way to the scene. We received calls to disturbances, and we assisted officers by picking up people who had been arrested. There was an accident involving a driver who had been drinking and a drunk who had turned violent. Two officers were sent to a domestic dispute, and reports were coming in about criminal damage and thefts.

It sounded worse because we could hear radio calls going out to other central London divisions, and it came across as total mayhem. It was probably the busiest two or three hours I experienced in my time as a police officer, and the prisoner count probably meant four or five in the charge room. We only had one sergeant in the station on night duty, and he probably needed help. The van driver dropped me off outside the station.

'It's been busy,' I remarked as I stepped out onto the pavement.

'Yes,' said the van driver. 'Wait until the summer comes. It gets really busy in the summer.'

I had been lucky to spend so much time on the streets as a new sergeant at Chelsea, but at the same time it would be very important for me to gain experience as a station officer. However, it appeared that my inspector did not want to push me into the deep end until he had some knowledge of my swimming abilities.

It turned out that my first day as station officer was to be on a Sunday at the end of my first two weeks at Chelsea. During our pre-promotion training, much had been said about the pressure that station officers were under and all the potential mistakes and pitfalls that lay in their paths. Sundays at Chelsea tended to be fairly quiet, and for the first two or three hours everything seemed remarkably peaceful.

'Maybe things can be busy, but this actually seems quite pleasant,' I thought. For a start, it was unusual for the charge room to be empty for any period of time. Although there were two prisoners in the cells waiting to go to court, all the paperwork had been completed long before my arrival that day.

My assistant station officer was a PC called Ian Turnbull, and his main job was to deal with people at the front counter. For about twenty minutes or so we had no callers at the front counter. One of the officers in the reserve room made tea, and we sat about chatting for a few minutes. Put in military terms, we were enjoying a lull in the fighting.

The man who appeared at the front counter was a stocky man in his fifties, with an Eastern European accent. He told us that he wanted to report a crime and then started to provide us with the details.

'I was drugged by some Russian KGB agents, and they removed three of my teeth and replaced them with artificial ones. These new teeth are giving out radio signals so that the KGB always know where I am.'

Turnbull and I glanced at one another and put on our sudden-death faces. My experience dealing with people who suffered from mental-health issues suggested that it was usually best to agree with them and show some sympathy for their problems, whether real or imaginary. I picked up a pen and some paper and started making notes, and he told me that he was an Estonian with an address in Hammersmith. He had been drinking, and he started speaking faster and faster and louder and louder.

We tried to keep the man calm with a promise that one of our best detectives would be called in to take over the investigation. However, he continued talking and became more and more angry and distressed. Ten minutes or so went by, and we could see that there were two or three people standing in the waiting room. It was becoming a problem, because we were unable to deal with any callers at the front counter while we were dealing with the Estonian.

We told him that he should go home and that an investigation would soon be underway, and for a few seconds it seemed that he was happy about this. Then, suddenly, it was as though someone had pulled a switch and turned him into a madman. He started screaming and shouting and used both fists to batter the front counter with tremendous force.

Turnbull and I jumped over the front counter and grappled with him, but the man was very strong. The struggle raged on in the public waiting area for a couple of minutes, and the people standing there quickly scattered. The reserve room was close by, and one of the PCs came running out to help us. It needed three of us to overpower the man and lift him over the front counter. After that, it was a struggle to reach the charge-room doors opposite the front counter.

While this was going on, one of the PCs on a foot beat came into the front office, saw what was happening, and walked over to the front counter. In a very calm voice he called out to the people in the waiting room. 'Who is next please?' we heard him say to the frightened-looking people standing there, and I wondered what on earth they were thinking. In the charge room, we held the man over the station officer's desk and searched him. Although he was struggling violently, it was even more important in his case that he be searched properly. We removed his belt, shoelaces, and personal property and managed to put him in a cell. After that, he shouted and screamed for a couple of hours or so, and the noise echoed around the inside of the station.

Within two or three hours, our Estonian prisoner had quietened down, and I had a chat to him. He seemed fairly rational, but there was a smell of drink on him, and I wondered whether this had played a part in what had happened. I decided to charge him with disorderly behaviour in a police station.

Chelsea cases went to Marlborough Street Magistrates' Court, where there was a system called POGO, standing for Plea of Guilty Only. All less serious cases such as drunkenness would be dealt with by a police officer on the court staff, and if there was a guilty plea, the brief facts of the case would be given. If a defendant pleaded not guilty, the case would be adjourned to a future date for trial.

Shortly before my tour of duty ended, I charged him and released him on bail to appear at court. A few days later, there was a message that our defendant had failed to appear at court and a warrant had been issued for his arrest.

It seemed to me that it would be a good idea to execute the warrant the next time we were on early turn. So, a week or so later, at seven in the morning, I drove to his address in Battersea with two of my PCs. When we knocked on the front door, we found that there were some Eastern European people living at the house, and they seemed surprised to see us.

One of them was a woman who spoke good English, and she told me that the man we were looking for was dead. She handed me a letter from an officer who was attached to a coroner's court in central London. My next move was to contact the coroner's court and find out what had happened to my defendant. It seems that he had been on his way to the court and had travelled to Oxford Circus tube station, the closest one to Marlborough Street.

According to the witnesses, he had stood on the platform for a while and then jumped in front of an oncoming train. It was a tragic ending to this man's life. I wrote a brief endorsement on the warrant, explaining the circumstances, and sent it back to the court.

If you want to know how busy a police station is, the first thing to do is to find out how many people have been arrested and charged. In the seventies, when it came to charges, Chelsea was always in the top five or six in the Met, and its station officers had to learn to work at a very fast pace just to keep up with everything.

Every arrested person needs to be correctly identified. People charged with shoplifting are usually released on bail but we always need to know who they are before we release them. Fingerprints are not checked until they reach Scotland Yard, and it is never good news if a station officer at Chelsea bails a shoplifter and then finds out later that the person is wanted in Cardiff for murder.

Investigating charges is a core function, but the welfare of people in custody is equally important. For example, there have always been some basic facilities provided, such as food, drink, and medical treatment. However, it was the station officer's decision whether a detained person is given access to a solicitor, allowed to make a phone call, or have a visit from a friend or relative.

Sometimes an officer is injured making an arrest, or a prisoner is, or both of them. In such cases, the station officer must call a police surgeon to examine them. The doctor has to certify whether or not a prisoner is fit to be detained, and it always results in a lot of paperwork for the station officer.

There were days when I found myself wading through great piles of paper on my desk. It seemed that the Met had a form to cover every event that might occur in world history, and at one point I tried to find out how many different forms there actually were. Obtaining information like that proved difficult, but it appeared that there were about 5,000 of them!

After clearing a vast amount of paperwork, my satisfaction would often be dented when a more experienced colleague, such as Euan Hay, would point out that I had forgotten to submit Form XYZ with some obscure information that was needed by some branch or other at Scotland Yard.

A written report was required if an arrested person was not charged with an offence. The person would be given what the Met referred to as 'a tactful expression of regret' and some practical help would be offered, such as being given a lift home by police transport. The report would comment on whether or not the action of the arresting officer had been correct.

It did not take long to pick up a feeling that there was a morale problem at Chelsea. It manifested itself in a number of ways, and this included a lack of confidence by many of the young PCs on the streets. There was not much liaison between the CID and Uniform officers, and it seemed to me that for a division like Chelsea, there was a distinct shortage of crime intelligence.

A wealthy area like Chelsea will always attract professional criminals from other parts of London, not to mention the rest of the world. There were lots of residential burglaries, and this included a good number of 'heavy' ones. A quick look at the crime books showed that the number of arrests for burglary offences was quite low.

There were three large department stores on the division – Harrods, Harvey Nichols, and Peter Jones – with their own security officers, and this ensured a regular flow of shoplifters to the charge room. These arrests are known as 'perchers'. In plain language, they are easy arrests because there is little to be done in terms of investigation or paperwork.

Chelsea also had a good number of drugs arrests, and every drug or shoplifting charge went down as a detected crime. My thoughts were that without those charges the detection rate for crime on the division would not be very good. Because of its high crime rate, Chelsea was divided into two CID teams, one covering the western half of the division and the other the eastern part. Each team had a detective inspector in charge.

1973 was the year when Britain, Ireland, and Denmark joined the European Union. It was also a period when there was mounting concern about what the IRA was planning to do. However, my concerns were on more local matters. It seemed to me that most of the PCs on the relief patrolled their beats with a certain lack of confidence or imagination. There was also very little sign of leadership from some of the senior officers at Chelsea.

Dealing with shoplifting charges at Chelsea took up a surprisingly large amount of police time. My perception was that many officers thought that dealing with perchers was what was expected of them, rather than arresting suspects on the streets.

If they had been asked, I suspect that some of the senior officers at Chelsea might have grumbled about the quality of their PCs. In my opinion, it is important that senior officers on a division show some leadership and set a good example by their own actions, but it seemed that a laissez-faire policy was the favoured management style at this time.

There were times of the day and night that were usually quiet. These periods would include the second half of night duty and the first couple of hours of early turn. Our shift system lacked flexibility, and this often resulted in too many personnel at quiet times and not enough when we were busy.

The job of a collator is to provide crime intelligence for the division, and at that time every station had a card system with details of local criminals. I arranged a meeting with the collator in order to develop some future initiatives on the relief. During our meeting, the collator mentioned disqualified drivers, and I was surprised how many there were. A quick glance at the records showed that during 1972 there had been more than 200 of them on the division.

It could not be compared with serious crimes like rape or robbery, but my opinion was that driving whilst disqualified was still a serious offence in its own way. It was in direct contravention of a court order, and there would always be a secondary offence of driving without insurance linked in with it.

It's not surprising that research shows disqualified and uninsured drivers are involved in a large number of hit-and-run accidents. Someone else ends up paying in these cases, and it does not take long to work out who ends up out of pocket. You do. Insurance companies add on a hefty chunk to your premium to cover their losses from uninsured drivers. There will always be some disqualified drivers who will drive if they think that they are going to get away with it. When they are criminals, they are likely to do it as a matter of principle.

However, during 1972 there had been very few arrests of disqualified drivers in Chelsea. The collator said that he would send me all the information he had but pointed out that, as a general rule, we did not have photographs of them. By then the Met had started taking photographs of all people charged with criminal offences, but this did not include drink-drive charges, and these cases made up a high proportion of all disqualifications.

My idea was that carrying out a campaign against disqualified drivers was a project that could be organised without much difficulty on the relief. Its main objective was to help motivate younger PCs so that they started to see their beats as places where things happened, rather than a number of streets that they had to patrol to keep their supervisors happy.

My first job was to start a register with information going back to the beginning of the year. When we had eight entries in the first two weeks of the year, it did not take me long to realise that there were going to be quite a few of them.

My next job was to give an information sheet about each disqualified driver to the PC posted to the beat where the person lived. The officer would make a point of looking out for the person or any vehicle that they might own. Any useful information was recorded on the sheets, which were returned to me when the PC was posted to another beat. Within the first five or six days of the project starting, there was an arrest. At 1 a.m. that day, one of our officers was standing in a shop doorway a few metres from the entrance to some flats where a disqualified driver was living. The man concerned, a wealthy young Lebanese, drove along the street and parked his car directly in front of the officer. As he walked towards his front door, he was arrested.

Within the next two weeks, two more were arrested. As we started the fifth week of our project, the collator told me that one of our local criminals had been disqualified and was suspected of driving. A few days later, one of my PCs told me that he had noticed a red Vauxhall saloon parked in a street not far from our local section house. He suspected that the car might belong to the person that we were interested in.

We needed a quick and simple plan. I sent a PC to the section house in Ixworth Place, and he found a spot which gave him a clear view of the red Vauxhall. The area car went to a side street not far away, and I asked all officers in uniform to keep away from the immediate area. After about an hour, there was a call on the PR from my surveillance man, who had seen the suspect walk past the car on three occasions.

After that, there was a period of about twenty minutes when nothing happened, and then the suspect appeared in the street with another man. The two men stood near the car, talking, and then suddenly they got into the car and were on the move. A PR message from the section house told me that the disqualified driver was behind the wheel. A second message went to the area car.

'Bravo Two. Red Vauxhall on the move. Coming your way.'

About two minutes later, the area car stopped the Vauxhall in Fulham Road. The officers asked the driver to open the boot of his car and noticed that he seemed nervous. The boot was full of stolen property that had come from several burglaries in and around Chelsea.

The two men in the car eventually found themselves facing a long list of charges. They were going to prison, and we had taken them off the streets. I explained to some of the younger PCs that you cannot always divide offences into neat little boxes that were marked 'crime' or 'traffic'. There was a much bigger picture to all of this.

19

In April, I had an unexpected meeting with the chief inspector (ops). It appeared that he was very pleased about my campaign against disqualified drivers. He then went on to say that he wanted me to set up and run a plain-clothes squad for several weeks to tackle some of our crime problems. This was the last thing that I expected, especially as I had only held my rank for a few months.

The squad would consist of six officers including me, and the choice of personnel would be mine. The idea was that I take two officers from my own relief and choose one from each of the other three reliefs. My plan was to find three who could be described as young and keen and balance this with two older, experienced PCs.

Roger Lashbrook was one of the old hands on my relief; he had spent quite a lot of time working in plain clothes, including vice operations. I had noticed another experienced man, Dai Evans, who had transferred to the Met from one of the Welsh forces. Although his inspector damned him with faint praise, I decided to be guided by my own instinct. The Welshman proved to be an excellent choice.

While our local crime issues had become my priority, the planet kept on moving day and night and season by season, and it seemed as though the IRA was lurking somewhere in the shadows and ready to strike. The Met had a strategic support unit called the Special Patrol Group that was often used for public-order events and could support divisions that had serious crime problems. The SPG was given a front-line role in order to counter terrorist attacks, and it provided armed units to patrol central London.

As it turned out, the first terrorist incident that year would have nothing to do with Irish Republicans. Three Pakistani youths burst into the Indian High Commission building, one armed with a cutlass and another with an imitation firearm. Members of staff inside the building were ordered to lie on the floor, and one official received a serious wound after being slashed across the throat. A SPG unit arrived and officers entered the building, where they confronted the three young men and called on them to drop their weapons. Police fired warning shots, but two of the intruders continued to brandish their weapons. SPG officers then opened fire and killed both of them. The third youth, who did not have a weapon, was not injured, and he was arrested.

Following this incident, a large number of comments were made by members of the public and journalists, many of whom were very critical of the action taken by police. It was suggested that the three men involved in the incident were just ordinary young men and therefore could not possibly have been terrorists. Some people called for a Government enquiry into police firearms training. The police should have realised that the gun being brandished was an imitation, they said. If the suspects had been approached in a less threatening manner the outcome would be different. Etc.

In March 1973, the Provisional IRA detonated a bomb at the Central Criminal Court which killed one person and injured 174 other people. That month, two observant SPG officers who had been involved in the incident at the Indian High Commission spotted a bomb planted outside Scotland Yard, and this was successfully defused. It was one of the largest bombs ever built by the IRA. Two things went through my mind at the time. This was likely to be a long, drawn-out campaign, and the main target was always going to be London.

At Chelsea, I started planning what my squad would be doing. The chief inspector (ops) told me that he wanted us to make motor-vehicle crime a priority, but apart from that he gave me a free hand to do whatever I thought was necessary. On our first day, six of us sat down together. I gave a short briefing, and this developed into an open discussion where everyone threw their own ideas into the ring.

When the chief superintendent heard about our squad, he made a point of sending for me and telling me that he did not want us to make any drugs arrests. This surprised me, but a large amount of police time in Chelsea was tied up with drugs cases. As a divisional commander, I am sure that he must have preferred to see us making arrests for burglary and theft.

Nearly all of the drugs arrests were of users rather than dealers, and the typical seizure was a fairly small amount of cannabis. Each item had to go to the Forensic Science Laboratory for analysis, and it involved a lot of paperwork without any tangible results. At the same time, in terms of statistics, each one went down as a detected crime.

Every division in the Met seemed to have its own policy regarding drugs, and therefore it was difficult to see a clear picture of any overall strategy. All drugs offences were classified as major crime and therefore officially dealt with by the CID. However, the priority for senior CID officers was tackling pressing issues such as burglaries and robberies. Most drug arrests were made by Uniform PCs on the streets when they searched people and found them in possession of narcotics.

Some sergeants and PCs carried out their own drugs operations, gathering information and executing warrants, but there was a general lack of intelligence about local drug dealers. It was a time when drug misuse was increasing, and there was probably a strong case for each division to have its own drugs unit. In fairness to its senior officers, the Met was woefully below strength and struggling to cope with its basic workload.

All the officers on my squad were issued with PRs, but for plain clothes the radios were quite bulky. It was important that we were able to hear the messages, but at the same time we needed to keep our radios hidden and on a low volume. On our first day, my plan was to divide our team into three pairs and patrol the western end of the division on foot. It seemed to me that the wealthier eastern part that covered Brompton Road and Knightsbridge usually had more of a police presence than the western part.

It was to prove a frustrating day. Three or four hours went by quietly, and then suddenly we all heard one of our team put up a call on the PR. Two of them had spotted a man coming out of a house in Gertrude Street. The man had glanced at them, made an accurate guess as to who they might be, and was now sprinting down the street with the two policemen in hot pursuit. 'He had it away on his toes' was what we called it in police parlance. For a short while we listened to the calls coming over the radio waves, the typical sounds of a chase on foot. There was the usual mixture of panting sounds and sentences where about a third of the words seemed to disappear somewhere.

Luckily, the PC with me knew exactly where Gertrude Street was, a short distance away. I used my PR to ask for as much assistance from mobile units or anyone else that might be anywhere near. Then we started running. My hope was that the suspect might actually be running in our direction, but we soon realised that he was going the other way.

There was only one mobile unit available, but it was battling through heavy traffic in Brompton Road. My third set of officers was slightly closer to the chase than we were, and it sounded as if they might be in a position to intercept the suspect. The younger of my two PCs who were running was quite fit, but he was not able to keep up with the man he was chasing. Then there was a call from him to say that he had lost sight of the suspect.

It was important to try and stay positive and not concede defeat too quickly. 'Maybe he has not got too far,' I thought. Maybe he is hiding in an alleyway or basement area. So the six of us carried out a search of the streets where we thought he might be. However, it did not take long to realise that we had lost him and the search would need to come to an end.

The two officers who had seen the man walked back to the house in Gertrude Street, where our worst fears were quickly confirmed. The woman who lived there had just returned and discovered that her house was in a state of chaos. It was a burglary, and a quantity of jewellery and cash was missing. The officer who gave me the bad news said that they would stay at the house, write up a crime report, and arrange for the CID to visit.

It is a rare occurrence to catch a burglar walking out of someone's house, and we all had a sickening feeling to think that we had almost had him in our grasp and he had slipped through our fingers. Later, we met at a pub in the King's Road to talk about it. Our first day! The feeling of frustration was shared by everyone.

A short while before this, the detective chief inspector had set up a burglary squad, so I thought that it would be useful to see the detective sergeant who was in charge of it and talk to him about the Gertrude Street burglary. The following day, the DS came up with a suspect, a burglar who lived in Fulham. The man was arrested a couple of days later by one of our CID officers.

My two PCs both said the same thing. The arrested man was similar in appearance but they did not believe that he was the burglary suspect that they had seen in Gertrude Street. The man from Fulham denied being anywhere in the vicinity of the burglary and had an alibi. We followed up his alibi, and it all checked out. He was released within a few hours.

In the Met, all reported crime was divided into three categories, and there was a crime book for each one. All crimes recorded in the Major Crime Book were the responsibility of the CID. The normal range of offences would include fraud, drugs, robbery, and residential burglaries. In addition, all sexual offences were recorded as major crimes, including indecent exposure. Although not everyday matters, these included murder, rape, and other serious assaults. The Major Crime Book would usually be found lying on a desk in the main CID office.

The Motor Vehicle Crime Book recorded the theft of motor vehicles, TDA, thefts from vehicles, and criminal damage to vehicles. The Beat Crime Book recorded thefts and other offences that were not classified as major or as motor-vehicle crime. As a general rule, Uniform officers investigated all beat crime or motor-vehicle crime. Every division had a beat-crimes office, with a sergeant in charge who had responsibility for everything recorded as beat or motor-vehicle crime. We were still many years away from a computerised system.

Entries in the crime books were written in black ink and detections were in red ink. Supervising officers in Uniform and CID spent a considerable amount of their time checking crime reports. The information on the reports provided information, such as MO, that has always been important to investigating officers. However, they also fulfil a bureaucratic function, providing a huge array of statistics that go to Scotland Yard and the Government.

Most police officers like to think of themselves as men or women of action, and we all needed plenty of self-confidence to do the job properly. Nearly all of us would have started with a certain enthusiasm. After all, we are going to be out on the streets fighting crime, aren't we? We did not start off with any ambitions to become bureaucrats, but then we soon discovered that the war against crime is bogged down by tons and tons of paperwork.

Until 1986, prosecutions were mainly in the hands of the police, although certain serious cases were the responsibility of the director of public prosecutions. However, police have always had the job of preparing the prosecution file. As a sergeant, I realised how important this role was, but at the same time I tried not to lose sight of the importance of police officers doing the job on the streets.

During my first week in plain clothes, I read all three crime books each day, to see whether it was possible to spot any trends. Apart from noting that every part of Chelsea was plagued by crime, I saw virtually nothing that could be described as a pattern. However, there was what could be described as a cluster of motor-vehicle crimes in a couple of adjoining streets, so I decided that this area would receive our attention the second week.

Two of my PCs came across a man from Chile sitting in a car and smoking a reefer. The clouds of cannabis smoke that wafted out through the open window brought them to a sudden stop at the car, and they arrested the man. Our divisional commander had told me that he did not want us bringing in any drugs arrests, and my first thoughts were that my new job was rapidly turning into a disaster. We had been on the streets for four days, and we had managed to arrest one person, for possession of cannabis. I wondered whether the chief superintendent was going to say something about it, and straight away thoughts started going through my head about what my response might be. Dai Evans just stood looking at me with a straight face and threw in his own thoughts. 'Look, Skipper, we could classify this as motor-vehicle crime, couldn't we? He was sitting in a motor car when he was smoking his reefer.'

We stayed in the western part of the division. The following day, two of my PCs spotted a man walking along the King's Road in the area known as the World's End. They followed him into a couple of side streets and noticed that he was taking an interest in parked cars that contained items of property. It looked as though this might end up as an arrest for suspected person, otherwise known as 'sus'. However, after about fifteen minutes he had not actually done anything that justified him being arrested. The officers decided to stop him and ask him a few questions. A check with

CRO showed that there was an outstanding warrant for him in Surrey, where he had jumped bail on a theft charge.

At the end of the week, we all went for a drink together and talked about what we had done and what might be worth doing the following week. Roger Lashbrook and Dai Evans had both worked in plain clothes, and although I did not mention it, their sergeant was the new boy when it came to this type of work. Roger came up with a useful suggestion, that we should use an observation van.

'How do we get one?' I asked.

Despite my concerns about the results we had achieved, there was a noticeable drop in reported crime in the area we had been patrolling. One of the CID officers at Chelsea told me that word had spread amongst local criminals in Fulham and Chelsea that there was a major police operation in the western part of the division. We had carried out a large number of stops, and although we had not achieved a great deal in terms of arrests, there was a certain deterrent effect that was likely to last for another two or three weeks.

Roger Lashbrook went to one of the Met's transport bases and returned to Chelsea with an observation van. As it was against regulations to park it near a police station, he left it some distance away. Our 'obo' van was grey and had a slightly battered look. It could have been a builder's van and seemed to fit in well in a street full of parked cars. By the time we reached it, there was a parking ticket on the windscreen.

Over the weekend, seven cars had been broken into in the same street. Expensive cars will always have good-quality radios, and each car had been targeted for its radio. We looked around the immediate vicinity and found a nearby street with plenty of expensive cars that looked as if it might possibly be the next target for thieves.

In the evening, we drove there and found a place to park the observation van. Two of our PCs went to visit another problem street, and the rest of us sat in the van while Roger gave us his best impression of a car salesman, running through the merits of the vehicle that he had chosen for us. He pointed out the spyholes, the compartment where the radio was hidden, and some mysterious switches that duplicated the driver's controls. Then he showed us the pièce de résistance, the special toilet designed into the floor of the van. I was not planning very long periods of observation, but it was useful to know it was there.

The van was designed so that when we were in the back we had a clear view of everything in front through the windscreen. We could see two women walking towards us, and when they were quite close, Roger pulled a switch. The windscreen wipers suddenly started flicking from side to side, and one of the women looked startled. By the time she had told her friend what had happened and pointed, Roger had switched them off. She continued to look puzzled, and we hoped that she and her friend did not hear the sound of muffled laughter as the two of them walked away down the street.

Sitting inside an 'obo' van for long periods of time is never going to be a popular duty for anyone. So, I set up a rough-and-ready roster so that every pair had about two hours inside the van and then some time on the streets. A high proportion of motor-vehicle crime falls under the category of thefts from vehicles and most of these offences happen at night. So we worked late into the night for several days.

Even though we were in plain clothes, we needed to ensure that the obo van was not compromised, so it was important that officers were not continually jumping in and out of it. The officers inside used their PRs to put up calls about any potential suspects moving around outside. Several of the messages went to officers patrolling in uniform in the surrounding area. There were plenty of stops and a couple of arrests.

Breaking into a car is one of the easiest crimes to commit, and I was always surprised that people would leave valuable property visible inside their parked vehicles. Car radios will always attract thieves, but all sorts of other property are often on display.

This will include briefcases, fur coats, and wallets, but many people think that their property is safe in a parked car when it is locked. This is not so. In the 1970s, some professional criminals carried 'jigglers' with them, a bunch of skeleton keys that could open car doors. Roger told me that three or four years before, Chelsea officers had arrested two men who were breaking into cars in Knightsbridge. One of them had a set of jigglers in his pocket, and he later boasted that he could open any car in the country with them.

Another method is to use a centre punch to smash a car window. The punch is pressed against the window and the button is pushed, which results in the window being hit with high impact, shattering the glass. Of course, a less sophisticated method is just to smash one of the windows with an iron bar.

Vehicle crime has been targeted with some success by police crime-prevention campaigns, and vehicle manufacturers have done a lot of work in recent years to make life harder for the criminals. A basic piece of advice has always been that people should never leave anything inside a car that is visible to passing pedestrians. Because Chelsea is an affluent area, some of its residents can be careless with their property, and criminals are aware of this.

During our second week, two of my PCs made an arrest for the offence of 'suspected person' commonly referred to as 'sus'. Lots of people, including journalists, talk about sus, but it appeared that many of them did not know what it actually meant. It was often wrongly confused with stops carried out by police on the streets. However, being a suspected person was a specific offence under the Vagrancy Act 1824, and the object of this was the prevention of crime.

The way it worked was fairly straightforward. A person who was being watched by police and was seen to carry out a suspicious act was classified as a *Suspected Person* under the law. After that, if the suspected person then carried out a second or subsequent suspicious act, he or she was classified as 'being a suspected person, loitering with intent to commit a felony (or later, an arrestable offence)'.

A typical situation might be a man walking along a street past a row of parked cars. He tries a car door handle – a suspicious act. He tries one or two more, and he is arrested for sus. At the time it was a summary offence with a maximum fine or a term of three months. There was more and more controversy about sus and its use by the Met, but it seemed a useful tool to have in a large city like London.

People who did not like the legislation said that police arrested large numbers of suspects in dubious circumstances, especially black people. It may also have been confusing that the Met Police considered all stops in the streets that related to a person's movements were carried out under the provisions of the Vagrancy Act. As it was a summary offence defendants had no right to elect trial by jury.

A couple of days after this, Dai Evans and I were in the King's Road and made another arrest for suspected person. As we walked past a bus stop, we'd noticed two women who were both carrying shopping bags and chatting to one another. There was a man standing nearby, and he appeared to be edging closer to one of them.

Something did not look right. We kept on walking as casually as we could. It was difficult to know exactly what was going on, but we both were thinking the same thing as we walked by. We saw his hand move downwards into the woman's shopping bag. She moved suddenly, and the man jumped back. We carried on walking, and then both of us slipped into the entrance to a shop.

The man walked along the footway for a short distance, looked around, and then walked into a supermarket. We gave him a few seconds head start and then went in. He was looking at a woman shopper who was wearing a green trouser suit. She was holding a shopping basket with a handbag on top and was busy examining items on one of the display shelves. We noticed that the suspect did not have a shopping basket. We walked past slowly, doing our best to appear interested in everything that was on sale rather than him.

We split up and spent a few minutes signalling to one another, something that would have been entertaining if there had been CCTV in the store. We did our best to try and appear inconspicuous, but our heads and shoulders must have been continually bobbing up and down behind mountains of baked beans and toilet paper. At one point, I positioned myself behind a woman shopper, using her as cover, and carried out some strange movements in my efforts to try and see what was going on.

Whatever the suspect was doing, it did not appear to have anything to do with shopping. The woman with the green trouser suit was still looking at goods on the display shelves, and the man had moved in close behind her. His right hand moved forward slowly towards her shopping basket. It was frustrating, because it was not easy to see what was going on, but one of his hands dropped onto her handbag. Then the woman suddenly moved to her left, and the suspect jumped back slightly as though taken by surprise. He did not appear to have anything in his hands. Then the woman who I was using for cover started to walk away, and the suspect glanced in my direction. This made me take up a sudden interest in tomato soup or whatever was closest to me.

After a few signals between us, Dai moved in closer, and I sauntered away. Two or three minutes of sauntering brought me to a spot where I could see Dai but not the man who he was watching. It is useful to have some sort of signalling code at times like this. Now Dai could see what was going on. After a couple of minutes, we linked up for a quick conference.

We had noted the man's actions with the woman in the green trouser suit, and Dai had observed him following a second woman shopper in the supermarket. This woman had an open handbag on top of her shopping, and Dai had seen the suspect move in closer and closer to the woman. Then the man's right hand had moved slowly towards the handbag. He was fairly sure that the hand must have touched the handbag, but could not say whether anything had been stolen.

While we were talking, our suspect disappeared from view, so we had a look around and spotted him in another part of the supermarket, standing very close to a woman shopper who had a young child with her. Inside her trolley there was an open handbag on top of her shopping. The man positioned himself very close to the woman, and at this point the child turned her head and stared at him. He then started to walk away but remained inside the store.

Dai Evans and I followed him. During all the time that we watched him, he had taken no interest in any of the goods on display. It was time to 'feel his collar', so we stopped him and produced our warrant cards. I told him that we had been keeping him under observation for some time and that he was under arrest for suspected person. He made no reply, and when we searched him at the station he had no stolen property on him.

The suspect said very little. He was a 30-year-old civil servant with no previous convictions. At Marlborough Street, he pleaded guilty, and the case was adjourned for two weeks for him to be sentenced. On his second appearance, he told the stipendiary magistrate that he would like to change his plea to not guilty. He went on to say that he had a sexual fetish, and this accounted for his actions, but he had never intended to steal anything. The magistrate refused to allow him to change his plea, and he was sentenced to a conditional discharge for twelve months.

A couple of days after the arrest of the man in the supermarket, I was on patrol with another officer in a quiet street not far from the King's Road. The sound of a loud explosion from a house on the other side of the street stopped us in our tracks.

'That's a bomb!' I shouted, and the two of us sprinted towards the house.

After ringing the front doorbell, we found ourselves talking to a distressed-looking elderly man who'd appeared at the front door. He told us that the boiler in the basement had exploded, and when we went inside we saw that there was quite a lot of damage inside the house.

Then something from General Orders popped up in my memory: Police action at the scene of a boiler explosion. 'What an obscure topic,' I'd thought when I read it. 'Is there actually such a thing as a boiler explosion? How often does it happen – once every thirty years?'

An arrest for sus and a boiler explosion were both new experiences, and my introduction to the three-card trick came a few days later. What is the three-card trick? Briefly, it's a method used by the criminal element to entice the unwary into giving them a lot of money.

The game is quite simple. Three playing cards are placed on a flat surface. One of the cards is a queen, and the other two are low-value ones, such as the three of spades or four of clubs. The person who handles the cards places them face down and then moves them around at dazzling speed. When the cards stop moving, the punters are encouraged to identify the queen, with shouts of 'Find the lady!'

The three-card trick is against the law because it falls within the definition of unlawful gaming. Apart from being illegal, the three-card trick has one particular result: the punters lose lots and lots of money. Then there is another problem; the gamers have always been hard to catch. The man who deals the cards is referred to by the police as the principal, but he is just part of a team. There is often another person nearby who encourages people to try their luck as punters, and there may be three or four lookouts.

The attraction is that the people can double their money if they find the queen, but this does not happen very often. A punter is only allowed to win in order to encourage other people to try their luck. On Chelsea's patch, the punters were often foreign tourists.

'Five One from Bravo Delta. Over.'

There were two of us walking along Old Brompton Road when we heard the call.

'Bravo Delta from Five One. Go ahead. Over.'

'Five One, are you anywhere near South Ken tube station? Three-card trick in the tunnel that goes up to the museums, in progress now.'

'Bravo Delta. Received. Show Five One dealing.'

Roger Lashbrook and his partner were also a short distance away, and a few minutes later the four of us met in Exhibition Road. Roger had quite a lot of experience dealing with gamers, and he volunteered to come up with a plan. He took a walk along the tunnel, and when he returned he told me that there was no sign of anything actually going on. However, he had spotted two men in the tunnel and thought that they could be gamers. He had also noticed a large plastic box leaning against a wall nearby.

There was an access point to the tunnel only a few metres from the plastic box that he had seen. He thought that it was possible that he had been 'clocked' by the gamers, but we might still be able to make an arrest. Roger added a word of warning that some gamers became aggressive when tackled by police.

We agreed a plan of action and walked off along the street, where we split up. Roger would go in first, followed by me. The other two would follow me at a distance. We returned to the entrance to the tunnel about twenty minutes later.

When Roger reached the entrance, he ran down the stairs and into the tunnel at Olympic gold-medal speed, with me a short way behind – Olympic silver. Roger caught the startled principal with his three cards and a large bundle of banknotes. He told him that he was under arrest, and the man made no attempt to escape.

Catching gamers was a little bit like catching disqualified drivers, as the actual evidence was straightforward when you caught them, but the business of trying to catch them could be very time-consuming. The system definitely favoured the gamers. The maximum fine was only fifty pounds at that time, and the principal and his associates would each be making about five hundred pounds a day. It was hardly a deterrent.

All we could do was make their lives a little more difficult and drive them off our patch. When they went to court, principals were nearly always fined fifty pounds, but if a case were to be adjourned, the police officer would ask for bail conditions. A good bail condition was one to prevent them being anywhere in central London, such as being forbidden to enter an area within five miles of Hyde Park.

The first couple of weeks of our plain-clothes squad were a bit slow, but after that we brought in a regular supply of 'bodies'. We were 'feeling a few collars' – in plain English, we were making a good number of arrests. This was our objective, and while we were doing so, morale always remained high. If we went for two days without a crime arrest, we all became a little down, but as soon as an arrest was made, we all seemed to regain the momentum.

'All units. Walton Street. Burglary, suspect decamped.'

The call came over the PR, and shortly after that we were given the address. Two of my PCs who were very close answered the call, and I made my way towards Walton Street. By the time I arrived, my two PCs had spoken to the victim and had the basic story.

The householder, an American, had returned to his flat a few minutes earlier and disturbed a burglar, who had run off. The American had chased him for some distance, until the suspect had jumped into a car and driven off at speed. The victim had noted the make and registration number of the car and had written it down on a piece of paper. One of my PCs had circulated the information straight away.

Once the immediate action had been taken, we checked the flat with the victim, and found that some cash and items of jewellery were missing. Having the car number appeared to be a good start, and we held on to our five-star exhibit, the piece of paper. We should have consulted with the CID, but my plan was that this was something that our squad could get its teeth into. First of all, I was not impressed by the detective ability of some of the CID officers at Chelsea. Apart from that, there is the old saying: If you want a job done properly, do it yourself.

One obvious problem would be trying to identify our burglar. The victim had only had a brief glimpse of the man's face and had told me that he was unlikely to recognise him. This meant that the information about the car was crucial. However, dismay started to set in when we ran a vehicle check. The vehicle registration number was unusual, as there were three letters and then four numbers, followed by a fifth number, 8.

A check with the Licensing Department revealed that there was no vehicle with that number registered in the UK. We seemed to have hit a brick wall, one that could bring our enquiry to a full stop. There was a chance that the number could relate to a foreign registered car, I thought. That could mean that the enquiry was dead in the water, unless there was something else we had missed.

Then a possible explanation struck me. At that period of time there were large numbers of cars on the roads with a *B* suffix. The American had made a mistake when he wrote down the number, I decided. He should have written a *B*, not an *8*.

'Let's run a check on this number,' I said, writing down the number with a *B* at the end instead of an *8*. Bingo! This time the vehicle was recorded as a pale-blue Ford saloon, just as our witness had described. This looked promising, but we still had to trace the car, and after that we still had to find the person who had been driving it when the burglary took place.

It is easy enough to find out who is shown as the registered owner of a vehicle, but criminals have a nasty habit of doing things that make life difficult for police investigators. They tend to buy cars with cash and do not register ownership of them. In this case, a man living in the East End of London was shown as the registered owner. One of my PCs volunteered to contact Stepney, the station that covered the address given, and he asked for an urgent enquiry to be done. Within an hour, he received a reply from Stepney. The registered owner had sold it to another man in the Stepney area about three months earlier, and the new owner had written his name and address on a piece of paper for him. This did not help us a great deal, because the address given did not exist.

It appeared that we had come to another brick wall. I discussed it with the PC who had been in touch with Stepney and suggested that he contact them again and see whether their collator's records might have any useful information for us. It was then that luck turned in our direction. An interesting story unfolded.

Two days before the burglary, one of the PCs at Stepney had carried out a stop on the blue Ford that we were interested in, and the man driving it had been identified as a local criminal called Norman Beech. The officer had been thorough, and there was no doubt that he had correctly identified

Beech. The man was not shown as being wanted, but he had a number of convictions for burglary and theft.

The PC had noticed that the VEL was two months out of date and had reported Beech for this. Local records at Stepney indicated that Beech had given his correct home address when stopped. Although we did not have a good description of the burglar, it seemed that Beech fitted the general picture: white male, slim build, and about forty years of age.

We all realised that it was going to be a long day. In police parlance, we needed a search warrant and we needed to 'spin the suspect's drum'. Whatever we did, we had to do quickly. One of my PCs found the three things that we needed in the main CID office: two pieces of paper and a New Testament. One piece of paper contained the information, and the other was the actual search warrant.

I started typing and asked one of my PCs to find a list of JPs who lived on the division. The officer returned with a list of JPs and pointed at a name, Eric Miller, who lived in the Little Boltons. His wife answered when I called. She told me that her husband had been on a business trip to New York and was now on his way home from Heathrow.

We drove to the Little Boltons with the two documents and the New Testament. The address was a large, attractive detached house, and there was no doubt that whoever lived there was very wealthy. Mrs Miller told us that her husband would be home in about ten minutes. She produced two cups of coffee, and the three of us sat chatting while we awaited his arrival.

At that point in time, the name Eric Miller meant nothing to me. He was the chairman of Peachey Property Corporation and a director of Fulham Football Club. Eric Miller was close to Harold Wilson, the leader of the Labour Party who would soon be prime minister again. He was one of those people that political leaders seem to cultivate, a conduit into the business world and someone who can raise money for the party.

When Eric Miller arrived home, I told him about the burglary and why we needed a search warrant. It was probably the first time that anyone had come to him with an application for a warrant. This was obviously a very confident man and someone who was used to making decisions. He signed the warrant, and a short while later I was in a GP car with two PCs, heading for the East End.

We stopped briefly at Stepney police station, picked up one of the local officers, and then went to Beech's address. As we arrived outside the block of flats where he lived, I made the point of saying that it was unlikely that a burglar like him would keep any stolen property at his home address. At the same time, we all knew that we had to try. Beech answered the door, with his wife standing just behind him. I told him that we were investigating a burglary in Chelsea and showed him the warrant.

We then asked him when he had last been in Chelsea, and he claimed that he had not been anywhere near Chelsea for the past two years. Beech seemed slightly flustered, but it was interesting that he and his wife showed very little surprise that we had come to search their flat.

'Last time it was the Flying Squad,' said Mrs Beech. 'Where did you say you was from – was it Chelsea?'

I told Beech that he was under arrest on suspicion of burglary, and we started searching his flat. We took Beech with us as we worked our way from room to room. The flat was clean and tidy but poorly decorated. There were two bedrooms, and in one of them we found a large chest of drawers. Inside it, we found some pieces of jewellery in between the items of clothing. When they were shown to Beech, he said that he had bought them about three years before. They did not match the description of the items stolen in the Chelsea burglary, but I told him that we would seize them for enquiries.

There was nothing else of interest in the flat, so we took him downstairs and searched his car that was parked a short distance away. There was nothing in it that appeared to be stolen property so we took Beech back to Chelsea. By the time we arrived at the station it was about midnight, so I briefed the station officer, and Beech was put in a cell.

A residential burglary was one for the CID to investigate, and it was only fair that they should be informed of the arrest. It seemed unlikely that any of them would still be about, but as luck would have it, one of the DCs from our newly formed burglary squad was still on duty. He came over as shrewd and enthusiastic. He was impressed that we had brought a suspect in and was keen to be involved. We agreed that we would question him later that day.

The burglary squad DC came up with a suggestion for questioning our prisoner, which was to use a questionnaire. We sat down together and drew up a list of questions that we could ask him, all aimed at trying to put him at the scene of the burglary. When we interviewed Beech, we had a certain amount of success. He started by saying that he had not been in the Chelsea area for two or three years but ended up admitting that he had parked his car near Walton Street at the time of the burglary.

His story was that he had been invited to meet someone in South Kensington for a job interview. Strangely, he could not remember the name or the address of his prospective employer. We questioned him about the jewellery that we had found at his flat, and his answers were evasive. We were never able to find out where it came from, but we all felt sure that it had come from another burglary somewhere.

I wrote out the two charges for the station officer, who then dealt with the charging procedure. Beech was charged with one count of burglary and one of handling stolen property. The case was dealt with four or five months later at Inner London Crown Court. He pleaded guilty to the burglary charge and not guilty to the charge of handling stolen jewellery. The pleas were accepted by the prosecution, and Beech was sent to prison for six months for the burglary.

After this case, I tended to take an interest in what was being done regarding residential burglaries. It concerned me that nobody else was charged with a residential burglary at Chelsea for a period of about ten weeks following the arrest of Beech.

After my time in plain clothes, I returned to my normal duties with my relief, now on night duty. There were three sergeants on duty that week: Andy Norman, Peter Close, and me, and we took it in turns to be station officer. On the first night, Andy Norman was scheduled to be station officer, and he made a point of walking into the parade room and telling the PCs that he was the station officer and wanted a quiet night. He told them that he did not want anything that he described as 'rubbish' – such as arrests for drunkenness offences.

As I was the section sergeant that night, I was annoyed that he should do such a thing. It seemed unprofessional, but at the same time it was obvious that his psychology was all wrong. To my mind, telling a bunch of policemen not to arrest people would be like a red rag to a bull.

'Keep clear of the station,' whispered Peter Close to me a few minutes later, and we were both out on the streets fairly quickly.

Fifteen minutes later, the first arrest came in – drunk and disorderly – and after that prisoners came into the charge room at a rapid rate. We noted that Andy Norman could work fast, and that night he had little choice. On night duty, there was normally only one station officer, but Andy did not ask for any assistance in the charge room. Peter Close came in to cover Andy for his refreshment break, and things then went quiet. As soon as Andy Norman returned to the charge room, the arrests started coming in again. It did not take long for me to notice that Andy was often abrasive in dealing with people, and he had managed to upset a lot of our PCs.

Early turn on a Sunday morning was normally a quiet time. Often the station officer would ask one of the PCs to go out and buy some newspapers. I noticed that the two PCs in the reserve room had the *News of the World* and that they were chatting and laughing as they flicked through the pages. Then there was a gasp, and everything seemed to go quiet. Sometimes a sudden silence can be as bad as a scream in the night. As I looked over at the two reserve men, it was obvious that the news was not good, and a couple of minutes later one of them handed me the *News of the World* and pointed.

The article was not on the front page, but it was a big one with headlines about an illegal gaming club in Chelsea. It mentioned the names of the people who were alleged to be running the club. One of them was Harry Fraser, described as a police sergeant based at Chelsea. Bad news like that travels fast, especially in the police. The duty state showed that Harry was listed as annual leave for three days.

There was an ominous silence in the station. About thirty minutes later, the chief superintendent appeared in the front office and walked over to the duty state. He wrote a brief entry stating that Sergeant Fraser was now suspended from duty. This was now a discipline case that would be dealt with by CIB. I did not hear what happened to him, but he never returned to duty. I had been working with Harry Fraser a few days before, but I never saw him again. About five years later, someone told me that he was managing a pub in Wales.

Apart from what had happened to Harry Fraser, other people were on the move. Euan Hay, our station sergeant, was promoted to inspector and went to another division. Peter Close was transferred to another station, and Keith Savidge, a newly promoted sergeant, arrived. We now had a sergeant who was suspended and another one, Andy Norman, who always seemed to be somewhere other than Chelsea. Therefore, it was not surprising that Keith Savidge and I found ourselves in the charge room day after day. For a period of about twelve months, the two of us probably worked harder than we had ever done before.

In the past, I usually had a chance to stop and think about what I was doing but it seemed that thinking time was in short supply in the charge room at Chelsea. There was a constant supply of prisoners coming in, and we worked our way through formidable amounts of paperwork each day. It was a question of learning to sink or swim.

The age-old advice for station officers in the Met was to take particular care with the three *P*s: prisoners, property, and prostitutes. Prostitutes could make nasty complaints, and we had plenty of prostitutes in Chelsea. However, they operated from flats and houses, there was no problem relating to soliciting and therefore they rarely came to notice. But it was important never to forget the other two main problems. Working as a station officer, I was responsible for two sets of keys. There were the cell keys that I always carried, and there was a very large bunch of smaller keys, called the station keys. The assistant station officer usually looked after the station keys, and these keys gave access to numerous places where property of different types was held.

If a prisoner managed to escape, it was bad news for the station officer – but the news was even worse if a prisoner died in our custody. We might refer to prisoners as 'bodies', but we wanted them to be live bodies! In this respect, the most dangerous prisoner for a custody officer to deal with was a drunk or drug addict. All sorts of things might have happened to a drunk prior to being arrested. This could include being the victim of a serious assault or simply falling over and receiving a head injury. Then there was the chance that the supposed drunk had a serious medical condition and was not drunk at all. Apart from that, drunks could make life difficult in other ways for a custody officer. One of the first ones that I dealt with as station officer tried to hang himself while in a cell.

Property was always a problem, because we dealt with so much of it, and it was the station officer's responsibility. There was the personal property belonging to prisoners and the property taken from them that fell into different categories, such as drugs, stolen property, and items that were to become exhibits in court cases.

Then there were all the other categories of property that came into the possession of the police, such as dogs, firearms, property found in the street, and property found in licensed taxicabs.

On one of my first days as a station officer, I dealt with a shoplifting charge, in which the property stolen was a haunch of beef. The person who detained the thief was a store detective working for a private security firm. It was normal to ask the store detective to sign the charge sheet as the person preferring the charge. At that time, all property linked to charges was placed in brown-paper property bags, and so that is what I did. The sensible thing would have been to sign it over to the store detective, but for some reason I did not do so. The station was 'heaving', as it often was. The personal property belonging to the prisoner went into one bag, and the piece of beef went into another one.

The station may have been busy but the mistake was mine. The property bag containing the beef found its way into the station officer's safe, and from there it went into the main property store. About two weeks later, the PC who was in charge of the property store came to see me. He wondered why he had a large piece of rotting beef in his store. I submitted a brief written memo asking for the meat to be 'destroyed on division'.

A regular problem at Chelsea was dealing with women who had been arrested. A person detained at a police station could not be placed in a cell until he or she had been searched, and if the person was female, she had to be searched by a woman officer. It was a catch-22 situation. The women police office at Chelsea consisted of about four or five officers, and there were many times when none of them were available. This meant that we had to send an officer in a car to another division to pick up a woman officer, bring her to Chelsea to carry out the search, and then take her back to her own division.

During my first few weeks at Chelsea, a woman was arrested for being drunk and disorderly, and when brought into the charge room she wanted to fight all and sundry. The two officers involved in the arrest managed to sit her down on a chair in one corner of the charge room, but every ten minutes or so she wanted to stand up and fight someone. There was no woman officer available at Chelsea, and the saga with this female went on for over an hour until a woman officer arrived from another station to assist us.

In terms of using manpower effectively in a force that was about 5,000 below strength, the system did not make a great deal of sense. However, this particular problem was destined to be solved by equal opportunities legislation. Police Orders announced that women officers were now to be integrated into the Uniform Branch and would carry out the same duties as their male colleagues.

The world of policing was never going to be the same. In 1970, it would have been safe to assume that the faces you saw in the parade room would be white and male, but this was all changing before our eyes. Within the next ten years or so, the faces would be black, white, Asian, male, and female.

Inspector Woodhead left the division, and there was a period of several months when two or three different inspectors took charge of the relief for short periods of time. It usually works better if a relief has one particular inspector in charge for some time. After those months, a newly promoted inspector, Martin Murray, arrived. He had a good leadership style that was relaxed but always very professional, and within a short time of him taking charge of the relief there was a noticeable improvement in morale and enthusiasm.

20

One evening in March 1974 I was out in the duty officer's car with John Bond, the inspector who was in charge for a couple of weeks while Martin Murray was on leave. As we drove along Knightsbridge, we heard a sudden series of radio messages. Something was going on in the Mall, the road that runs from Trafalgar Square to Buckingham Palace. I found a place to stop at Hyde Park Corner, and both of us listened intently to the messages that were coming over the air.

It was difficult to understand what was going on, but whatever it was sounded serious. A large number of units had been assigned to the incident, and as we were close to the Mall, I called IR and told them our location. We were told to remain at Hyde Park Corner for the time being.

It was frustrating listening to the calls coming over the radio channel and not knowing exactly what was happening, but there were a few clues. The officers at Information Room were doing their best to avoid saying too much, but we soon realised that the incident involved royalty. We could hear that several ambulances had been sent to the scene, and there were references to at least one person being shot.

'Terrorists,' I said. Sitting in the car, the two of us started talking about an assassination attempt or a kidnapping, as they appeared to be the two most likely situations. We also decided that this incident might have been an attack by the IRA. This idea then led to the next thought: Maybe the terrorists had been successful in whatever they had done.

It took a little time to find out what had happened. Princess Anne and her husband, Lieutenant Mark Phillips, had left Buckingham Palace to attend a charity film screening in the West End. After the event came to an end, the royal party was returning to the palace. The car was driven by Alex Callender, one of the Queen's senior chauffeurs. Also in the car was Rowena Brassey, who was lady-in-waiting to Princess Anne, and Inspector James Beaton, who was Princess Anne's protection officer. As the car with the royal party made its way along the Mall towards the palace, it was forced to stop when a light-coloured Ford Escort car swerved across its path.

The royal party was confronted by a man called Ian Ball, who jumped out of the Ford Escort brandishing a handgun. Inspector Beaton drew his Walther PPK automatic and fired at the man, but his weapon jammed. The man shot Beaton three times, and the chauffeur, Callender, was also shot and wounded. Although seriously injured, Inspector Beaton climbed into the back of the limousine to try and protect the princess. Ronald Russell, a cleaning company manager who was driving along the Mall at this time, spotted what was happening and manoeuvred his car in front of the Ford Escort to block Ball's escape. He confronted Ball and punched him.

Brian McConnell, a journalist, was following the royal car in a taxi. When McConnell realised what was happening, he jumped out of the taxi and ran towards the royal car, but as he did so he was shot and wounded by Ball. A PC, Michael Hills was in the Mall a short distance away. He could see that there was an incident that involved a royal car, and he decided to find out what was happening. He was also shot and wounded by Ball but he managed to put out a call on his radio for urgent assistance.

The perpetrator of this crime was Ian Ball, a 26-year-old man from Hampshire who owned a house in Fleet. His plan had been to kidnap Princess Anne and hold her for ransom. His criminal history at that stage had been limited to burglary, but he must have spent some time planning what he was going to do – this involved building a dungeon at his house where he could keep the princess as a prisoner. Ball had written a ransom note addressed to the Queen, in which he demanded £2 million. One of the features of the incident was the courage and resistance displayed by Princess Anne. It was widely reported that when Ball told her he was going to hold her for ransom, her response had been, 'Not bloody likely – I haven't got two million pounds!'

One of the officers on duty at Cannon Row police station that night was Peter Edmonds. He was attached to the CID and based at Cannon Row. I knew Peter Edmonds well, because we had worked together on the same relief at Rochester Row. He heard the 'urgent assistance' call and must have realised the gravity of the situation. He immediately drove to the Mall in his own car as other police units were being directed to the scene.

Ball must have realised at that point that his kidnapping plan was not going to work. He then ran into St James's Park, with Peter Edmonds in hot pursuit. At one point, he stopped and threatened the officer with his firearm, but Peter threw his coat over Ball's head, managing to force him to the ground and arrest him. Ball was later charged with a number of offences, including the attempted murder of Inspector Beaton. He was sentenced to life imprisonment and later transferred to Broadmoor.

Inspector Beaton recovered from his injuries and received the George Medal from the Queen. PC Michael Hills and Ronald Russell were also awarded the George Medal. Peter Edmonds was awarded one of the first Queen's Gallantry Medals, as were Brian McConnell and Alex Callender. Ball's target, Princess Anne, was also awarded a medal by the Queen.

In the general election campaign a few weeks earlier, no party had gained an overall majority, and the Conservative PM, Edward Heath, stayed in office while he tried to negotiate with the Liberal Party led by Jeremy Thorpe. It looked at one point as if the Liberals might support Edward Heath's government, but there was no agreement, and Heath resigned. Harold Wilson became prime minister with the first minority government since 1929. He had a working majority with only three seats. Later that year there would be a second general election, and Wilson would be able to increase his government's majority. It was a bad period for the economy, and inflation was to hit 27 per cent by 1975.

1974 was destined to be a year of explosions. The first one was a huge explosion at the Nypro chemical plant at Scunthorpe. Twenty-eight people were killed, and about one hundred others were injured. A public enquiry pointed at an accident rather than a terrorist attack. A few days later, an

IRA bomb exploded inside the Palace of Westminster. Nobody was killed, but eleven people were injured. The explosion fractured a gas main, and a fierce fire spread quickly through Westminster Hall. One of the POW officers rescued a woman who was trapped by the fire. Improving security at locations such as the houses of parliament, in the face of a well-organised terrorist campaign, was an ever-increasing problem for the Government and the police service.

In Ireland, a Loyalist paramilitary group detonated four car bombs in Dublin and the town of Monaghan. This caused the highest death toll during the Irish troubles of that period with 33 dead and 258 injured. In England, the Provisional IRA continued their campaign, with certain parts of London, such as Chelsea, Kensington, and the West End being attacked time and time again. Bombings and shootings continued throughout the year.

Despite the serious terrorist campaign, there were signs that the Met Police was improving in its general effectiveness. A total of 98,326 arrests were made during 1974, and this represented an increase of 11 per cent over the previous year. In addition to the day-to-day policing, there were significant breakthroughs in the police response to armed robberies. The early seventies was the golden age for armed robbers in London, averaging one every four or five days. There was a perception amongst police officers that the abolition of the death penalty had changed the attitudes of many criminals and that their traditional reluctance to carry firearms was fast disappearing.

A specialist robbery squad was set up, with officers from the Flying Squad and the regional crime squads. At first it did not appear that the new squad was having a great deal of success. However, the arrest of one of the most active robbers, Derek Creighton Smalls, would prove to be a major breakthrough. Smalls, usually known as Bertie Smalls, knew that he was facing about twenty years or so in prison and told police that he wanted to negotiate a deal in return for information about other armed robbers.

Initially the police refused his offer, but Smalls later said that he was willing to give up 'every robber in London' in exchange for immunity. This was the beginning of what would become known as the age of the 'super-grass'. An agreement was drawn up between the Director of Public

Prosecutions and Bertie Smalls that gave Smalls complete immunity for all of the crimes he had committed in exchange for his help.

Bertie Smalls confessed to fifteen robberies and named thirty-two bank robbers plus a number of other associates. One of the most significant aspects of the whole episode was that Smalls went against the underworld code of silence, not only providing information but giving evidence against other criminals in court. It was rumoured that a contract had been put on Smalls; whoever killed him would receive £1 million. At one point when he was giving evidence, the defendants started singing the wartime song made famous by Vera Lynn: 'We'll meet again, | Don't know where, | Don't know when ...'

Bertie Smalls would always be a marked man, but he survived to die a natural death in 2008. Although Lord Justice Lawton later said that the deal struck between the Director of Public Prosecutions and Smalls should not be repeated, there were several more trials in which the prosecution made use of super-grasses. It had a significant impact on the number of armed robberies; in the short term, they declined significantly. However, after the initial shock wave created by the super-grasses, armed robberies started to increase dramatically. There were 734 in 1978 and 1,772 in 1982.

The era of the super-grass put the Flying Squad under the spotlight. There were some cases where the relationships between detectives and robbery suspects became a cause for concern. There were incidents that pointed at corruption and others in which it appeared that criminals had been given unauthorised immunity by CID officers in return for information.

An officer who had served on the Squad during that era told me about going to a Flying Squad Christmas dinner at one of London's best hotels. The officers in his unit within the Squad had been targeting a major robber named 'John Smith.' It came as something of a shock to them when they noticed that 'John Smith' was sitting at a nearby table as a guest of another Flying Squad team.

However, during this era many things were changing for the better throughout the police service, and the events that occurred then would lead to a more professional robbery squad. The methods used to protect Smalls led to the development of a well-organised witness protection programme in the Met.

Since my promotion to sergeant, I had been prosecuting at magistrates' courts, and the cases fell into three main categories. There were the drink-drive cases that I had dealt with as station officer, and there were minor crime cases that went to magistrates' and juvenile courts, especially if the arresting officers were inexperienced. As well as this, dangerous-driving and careless-driving cases were sent to me to deal with at court.

Nearly all the drink-drive defendants pleaded guilty, but when there was a plea of not guilty, the policy was to apply for legal representation to our solicitors' branch. The reason for this was that during the early seventies many defence solicitors were using the technicalities of the law to challenge police powers of arrest and procedures in breathalyser cases. Many court cases became enmeshed in legal arguments, and it made me think of Sandgate, where life seemed to revolve around definitions. Legal arguments arose over the meaning of a sentence, or two words, or maybe just one word. If the police officer was not wearing his cap, was he in uniform or not? It seemed that everything was in question.

In cases arising from accidents, summonses were often served for both dangerous and careless driving. Unless the evidence of dangerous driving was very strong, prosecutors were happy to enter into a plea-bargaining deal with the defence. Put simply, we accepted a plea of guilty to the careless driving summons and offered no evidence on the dangerous driving one.

There have always been some good, practical reasons for plea bargaining. By this time, defendants had lost their right to go to the crown court in drink-drive and dangerous driving cases, and it would have proved almost impossible to have large numbers of summary trials running at Marlborough Street. They needed to be pushed through magistrates' courts as quickly as possible, or there would have been a huge backlog of cases. Defence solicitors were happy, because they could tell their clients that they had talked the sergeant into a plea-bargaining deal, and the defendant would then tell his friends, 'My solicitor is absolutely brilliant! He managed to get the police to drop the dangerous-driving charge.'

When there were contested cases, I produced my witnesses, took them through their evidence, and cross-examined defendants and any defence witnesses. It proved to be very good experience for me.

I only lost two contested cases at Marlborough Street. In one of these cases, there were two summonses: careless driving and failing to stop. In that case, the defendant was represented by a very good barrister, who asked me to carry out a CRO check on my main witness. It was obvious that something was amiss, and on completing the check I discovered that my witness had a conviction for perjury, so it would be necessary for me to inform the defence about it. The defence barrister must have known, as there was no other reason for him to make the request. Naturally, the perjury conviction was mentioned. This put a different slant on everything, and I had great doubts about what my witness said in one part of his evidence that related to the defendant having failed to stop. You can only win or lose in court, but this was almost like a draw, as the magistrate dismissed the summons that related to the failure to stop but convicted him of careless driving.

During one contested careless driving case at Marlborough Street I clashed with the magistrate's clerk. As a general rule, lay magistrates do not have legal qualifications and rely on their clerks to advise them on procedure and matters of law. However, stipendiary magistrates are legally qualified, and in this case, Eustace Hatton, one of the senior 'stipes' was presiding. The defendant was a wealthy man, and he was represented by a very good solicitor.

The clerk was a grey-haired man aged about sixty, who I had never seen before. There were two prosecution witnesses for me to take through their evidence, and as this was happening I became concerned about the actions of the clerk. When my witnesses were giving their evidence, he started shaking his head and making quite loud huffing and puffing noises. It did not take long for me to start feeling hot under the collar.

When my witnesses had given their evidence, I provided additional information, describing the scene of the accident and giving details of measurements taken at the scene. This accident had occurred at the junction of a road and a square in a residential area of Chelsea, and the junction at the scene of the accident was exceptionally wide.

When I mentioned the width of the road, the magistrate's clerk suddenly shouted, 'Rubbish!' I then addressed the magistrate and told him that in my opinion the defendant had a very good legal representative, and that there was no need for the clerk to jump in and give him any further assistance. Eustace Hatton could see that I was angry, and it was obvious that he was embarrassed. He waited for a couple of seconds and then said, 'All right, gentlemen. Let's get on with it, shall we?'

For his part, the clerk of the court sat there scowling at me, his face white with anger. Later, one of the police officers attached to the court whispered in my ear that this clerk was likely to make a bad enemy and warned me that there could be problems when I applied for warrants. Thus I felt even more pleased than usual when Eustace Hatton found the defendant guilty. On my many visits to the court I kept an eye out for that particular clerk, but I never saw him again. It may have been that I was not the only person that he managed to upset.

The Government had concerns about the high rate of crime at Heathrow Airport, which had been nicknamed Thief Row by the press. The British Airports Authority had its own police force. Naturally, the primary concern of the airport authority was to keep the airport operating, and the perception was that this took precedence over the detection of crime, especially when arrests of employees sometimes led to trouble with the unions.

When police took an interest in the lifestyle of some of the baggage handlers at that time, it became fairly obvious that there was a web of organised crime at the airport. Generally speaking, they were on fairly average wages, but it was surprising how many of them owned large houses, drove expensive cars, and sent their children to private schools. The Government decided that the Met would take over the policing of the airport, and a new airport division was created that year.

In June 1974 there was serious public disorder at Red Lion Square in central London. A demonstration by the right-wing National Front resulted in a clash between their supporters and people belonging to a left-wing group called Liberation. There was a deliberate attack on the police by one of the groups taking part in the demonstration, called the International Marxist Group. A battle ensued in which several police officers were injured. A police inspector collapsed and died of a heart attack, and a young student called Kevin Gately was injured and fell to the ground. He later died of his injuries, and the leaders of the Liberation group accused the police of murdering him.

For many years the high rate of police casualties has been cause for concern. Recent figures from the Home Office for the year 2011–12 recorded more than 7,500 assaults on officers. Injured personnel can be off duty for several months, adding to the problems of forces which are already undermanned. Violence was never a major problem in Chelsea, but we had officers injured, as in every other division.

On night duty we worked seven nights in a row, starting on the Monday night. During one week of night duty, our relief had a total of five officers injured by the time we reached Friday night, and two of them had been placed on the sick list. I was guilty of throwing some gallows humour into my conversation with our inspector, Martin Murray, by suggesting that at the rate we were going we might not have anyone left by the time we reached Sunday night.

Apart from our usual day-to-day work, we had to remain vigilant about the terrorist threat. A bomb exploded inside the Tower of London at a time when it was packed with tourists. A woman was killed, and eight children were injured. No organisation was to claim responsibility for the bombing, but police believed that it was part of the IRA campaign.

As there was no canteen at the station, we took our meal breaks at the nearby Philip Game section house in Ixworth Place, now the site of a hotel. When we worked night duty the kitchen at the section house was closed, but we used the canteen to sit and eat our sandwiches. From about one o'clock in the morning on, one of the probationers would be given the job of making tea and coffee for everyone.

The standard times for meal breaks were at 1 a.m. and 2 a.m. It was difficult to stick rigidly to this, because the first few hours of night duty are usually busy and officers are dealing with incidents, making arrests, or writing their notes. Thus it was quite a common situation that by 2 a.m. most of the relief could be found in the canteen. On this particular night, the general conversation and banter was brought to a halt by the loud 'crump' of an explosion that produced two or three seconds of silence.

'That's a bomb!' someone shouted.

As the sound of the bomb reverberated across Chelsea, we were up and running to our parked vehicles, while a spate of messages started coming over the air. One included the location: 'Duke of York's Barracks'. The barracks that stood opposite Peter Jones department store was the home of a territorial army Special Air Service (SAS) regiment. An open day had been held a few days before, and this may have been the time when a bomb had been left inside the commanding officer's jeep.

The explosion had done considerable damage to the barracks, with Peter Jones and several small shops nearby being hit as well. Windows had been shattered for a considerable area, and there was broken glass everywhere. Inspector Murray asked that the chief superintendent be informed, and a few minutes later we received a message to say that Mr Pickford was on his way.

In this type of incident, casualties must always be the first consideration. There were three or four of them, and within a few minutes they were on their way to hospital. Two officers went with them to take their details and ensure that their next of kin were informed.

Shortly after our arrival at the scene, a phone call came in from a member of the public who had spotted something that he believed was a bomb in another part of the division. Inspector Murray went to deal with this and left me in charge of the bomb scene. Once the casualties were removed to hospital, my main concern was to keep the area secure until a forensic examination was carried out. I told the officers at the scene to make sure that nothing was touched or interfered with.

Eventually, a number of radio messages on the Chelsea PR system alerted me that Pickford was on his way to the scene of the bombing. The chief superintendent used the call sign Five One. As luck would have it, my shoulder number was also Five One. It was normally used over the radio, so it was not surprising that an element of confusion slipped into the situation as calls went back and forth on the Chelsea PR system.

'Bravo Delta from Bravo Delta Five One. Who authorised that?'

'Bravo Delta Five One from Bravo Delta, it was authorised by Five One.'

'Bravo Delta, what are you talking about? This is Five One speaking. I don't know anything about it.'

'Five One, it was authorised by Five One.'

I took a deep breath and smiled. It sounded as if Pickford was not going to be in a good mood by the time he reached the scene. It had to be something serious before we considered calling out our divisional commander. A couple of months before he had been called to one of our embassies when there had been an invasion by demonstrators, but that had been at a more civilised time of day. This was the first time that I recalled a chief superintendent being called in from home during the night.

By the time he arrived at the scene of the bombing, everything had quietened down. We were now waiting for officers from the Anti-Terrorist Branch and forensic personnel. Most of the members of the public who had come to see what was happening had drifted away. By this time, there were about six or seven members of the public and about twenty police officers standing close to Peter Jones.

'No point just standing here, sergeant,' said Pickford, walking up to me. 'You need to start deploying your troops to prevent looting.'

There had been no looting, and my naïve belief was that the small group of people on the pavement did not intend to rush forward, overpower the police, and ransack the damaged shops. However, I directed all the officers to spread out along the pavement outside Peter Jones and the nearby damaged properties in the King's Road. It certainly looked better. More tidy. One of my PCs winked at me and grinned.

For whatever reason, I never seemed to be in the good books of my chief superintendent. A couple of months later, I was walking through the police station when he spoke to me about one of the PCs on my relief who was the subject of a complaint. Mr Pickford then went on to make some adverse comments about sergeants in general and followed this up with an attack on me personally.

He informed me that he did not like my style of leadership and explained how good sergeants knew how to deal with their PCs. A good sergeant was one who shouted and swore at his PCs, and they soon knew who was in charge. My views on the subject of leadership did not apparently strike a chord with him, so he just turned around and walked away from me.

The Turkish invasion of Cyprus was one of the factors that added to public-order problems in London at that time. Not surprisingly, the invasion and fighting in Cyprus caused friction between the Greek and Turkish communities in London, and there were marches and demonstrations outside the two embassies.

The Provisional IRA announced that if they were to make attacks on political leaders or against the army there would be no warning. However, they added that if they were to attack civilian targets, a coded warning would be given in advance. Naturally, any such code would be top secret, but it was soon obvious that some sort of code-word was known to some of the senior officers in the Met. The IRA campaign in the UK continued, and towards the end of the year they carried out more attacks in Chelsea.

A London insurance broker, Allan Quartermaine, was a passenger in his chauffeur-driven car, travelling along the King's Road in Chelsea. The car stopped at traffic lights, and Quartermaine was shot. He died a few days later. The IRA has never claimed responsibility for the attack, but it was believed to be a terrorist attack, and it may be that Allan Quartermaine was mistaken for someone else. Nobody has ever been charged with his murder.

Apart from the attempt to bomb Scotland Yard, the IRA had not targeted the police. However, in November, the Tite Street bombing would show us how ruthless the terrorists could be. The Royal Hospital in Royal Hospital Road is famous for its residents, the Chelsea Pensioners. A short distance away is Tite Street, a quiet residential street. Close to the junction with Royal Hospital Road there was a letter box, and when the small bomb placed inside it exploded, it threw pieces of debris all over the immediate area.

I was the station officer that day, and one of my officers in the reserve room shouted out the news to me that there had been a bomb explosion. A large number of calls were coming over the air from officers at the scene, including the duty officer and Keith Savidge. A few minutes later, the explosives officer arrived at the scene. His driver parked the Range Rover in front of a building site on the opposite side of the road from what was left of the pillar box. What nobody realised was that a second bomb had been placed on that side of the road, and it had been timed to go off about fifteen minutes after the first device. The tactic of installing a second device had been used several times in Northern Ireland, but this was going to be a nasty new experience for us.

When the second bomb exploded, the Range Rover took most of the impact. This saved police and others from death or very serious injuries, but the blast knocked everyone off their feet, and some were thrown into the air. The explosives officer, six police officers, and two ambulance men were injured. They had cuts and bruises and ear injuries from the blast. Keith Savidge later told me about the sensation of feeling the blast lifting him into the air. At the start of the Provisional IRA campaign, some officers did not take all potential terrorist situations as seriously as they should have done. Nobody could have guessed that in a future terrorist attack on Chelsea division three police officers would lose their lives. However, the effect of the Tite Street bomb was to concentrate our minds on the dangers that we were facing. We were now on the front line in what was a sustained, ruthless terrorist campaign.

In December 1974 it seemed likely that the IRA would carry out more bombings during the Christmas shopping season. Clubs and hotels in the West End were attacked in a wave of shootings and bombings. On 19 December an IRA terrorist called O'Connell parked a car loaded with 160 sticks of gelignite outside Selfridges in Oxford Street. A warning message was phoned to *The Sun* newspaper, and police were able to evacuate the area. There was a massive explosion that caused a huge amount of damage to the surrounding area – but there were no deaths or injuries. Three days later, the IRA announced a ceasefire for Christmas.

Despite what terrorists were doing, the world still kept turning, and political news was dominating the media at the beginning of 1975. In January, Prime Minister Edward Heath told the House of Commons that a referendum would take place later in the year concerning UK membership of the European Union. Although Britain had been a member of the European Community since 1973, the decision to join had not been a popular one.

Heath's leadership of the Conservative Party was challenged by a rising star in the party, Margaret Thatcher. In February, Edward Heath withdrew from the leadership contest, and Mrs Thatcher became the new leader. She was the first woman ever to become leader of a major political party in Britain. As she lived in Flood Street, a few yards from the King's Road, we all knew straight away that our division was faced with another security problem. It was decided that the house in Flood Street would become an armed post, guarded around the clock, and that Chelsea division would be responsible for its security.

In June 1975, 67 per cent of those voting in the national referendum voted Yes to staying in the EU. All through the year the IRA campaign continued, with many attacks in central London. There were a total of 29 bombings and other terrorist incidents during the year, and this resulted in 10 deaths and 169 people suffering injuries. A Met officer, PC Stephen

Tibble, was shot dead while chasing an IRA terrorist along a street in Hammersmith. It would be many years before the man who killed him, an American, would be brought to justice.

On night duty in September, I found myself at the scene of the Spaghetti House siege. It was strange to see what had happened to Knightsbridge. At first glance, it appeared to be a massive traffic jam, comprising mainly police vehicles.

It took a little time to find out what had happened. A company called Spaghetti House Ltd owned a chain of restaurants in London. They had an arrangement that when they finished work on a Saturday night, the managers would all meet at the Knightsbridge restaurant and discuss business. The other important task was that the day's takings from all the restaurants would be paid into the night safe of a nearby bank.

During the early hours of Sunday, three men carrying firearms attempted to rob the nine Italians of their takings, a sum of about £13,000. They ordered them to walk down a flight of stairs to a room in the basement, but one of the Italians managed to escape through a door at the rear. He ran to a nearby hotel and dialled 999. The police response was rapid, and this resulted in the robbers and their victims finding themselves trapped together in a small basement room. The leader of the three gunmen was a Nigerian called Franklin Davies. He had just completed a sentence of ten years for armed robbery.

The three robbers were urged to surrender but refused, and we were facing a long siege. For several days, Knightsbridge became a completely different place. A wide area around the restaurant was sealed off, and armed officers covered every possible spot where the three gunmen might try to escape. It went on day after day, until the sixth day, when the robbers released their hostages and surrendered. Franklin Davies shot himself, but his wounds were not fatal.

A new chief superintendent, by the name of John Parris, arrived at Chelsea, and shortly after this Andy Norman was transferred to another division. It may be that the two matters were linked.

Parris had a different style to Pickford. He was strong but approachable, and he was soon well respected by officers on the division. We later heard that the superintendent on Andy Norman's new division was not happy that he had a sergeant who was often not available for operational work when needed. He made a number of efforts to clip Andy's wings but had to give up after receiving a phone call from a very high-ranking officer at CO with words to this effect: 'You will let Sergeant Norman do whatever he wants.'

Andy Norman left the Met a few years later, and by the eighties he would be regarded as the most powerful figure in British athletics He managed the careers of leading athletes such as Linford Christie and was in the foreground of the fight against what was called 'sham amateurism'. For many years, the athletics establishment tried to maintain a facade that all British athletes were amateurs, whereas the reality was that they were being paid. Andy Norman challenged the status quo and brought about radical change in the world of British athletics.

There had been many movements of personnel on the division, and it seemed strange to find that in terms of service I was now the senior sergeant on my relief. As 1975 was coming to an end, I was asked to take over the post of duties sergeant. Barry Smith, the sergeant who had been doing the job for about two years, was moving to another division. A week went by with me sitting in my new office with Barry while he showed me the way the system worked.

The main requirement of my new job was manpower planning and, at its most basic level, to ensure that there were enough PCs available to police the division around the clock. This might sound fairly straightforward, but in practice the job often proved to be complicated by a variety of factors.

The basic planning system could not be described as high tech. There was a large square plywood board for each relief, with a printed sheet attached to the front with Sellotape. Each sheet was a planner covering seven days; it showed every PC and what he/she was doing. Each officer was posted to a specified beat or duty for four weeks at a time, and my plan was to work at least one week in advance.

Generally speaking, postings were within the gift of inspectors in charge of reliefs. Inspectors and sergeants on reliefs usually discussed the key postings and decided who should do what. Many inspectors preferred to make those decisions themselves, but others might delegate this job to one of their senior sergeants. There could sometimes be rivalry amongst PCs about the postings that they received.

One of the first decisions was choosing the crew of the area car. In the early seventies, Met area cars were usually Jaguars, but as they were always high-speed vehicles, the person at the wheel had to be an advanced driver. The second crew member was a radio operator and, in central London divisions, a plain-clothes observer was also posted to the car. Generally speaking, most of the younger PCs were keen to receive a posting to the area car. This could be used as a carrot by inspectors, and if someone was not pulling his/her weight on foot duty, they were unlikely to find themselves on the area car.

Another key job was the reserve room. The two PCs there had to deal with the divisional radio communications and a large number of incoming phone calls. At least one of them had to be an experienced officer. The two officers in the reserve room were the centre of the division's system of communications. They were in charge of two handwritten message books, an in book and an out book. Every message sheet had to show a result, and this was done by writing in a crime book number or some other reference. Working in the reserve room at Chelsea was often quite stressful because of the large number of calls coming into the station. A sergeant would check the messages and ensure that all the necessary action had been taken.

Apart from the area car and the reserve room, we needed PCs to drive the van, GP car, and panda car, not to mention the Noddy bike. Once the key postings had been agreed, I tried to cover as many of the foot beats as possible. Chelsea had thirteen beats and six patrols, but we never came close to filling them all. Barry Smith had set up a T-card system with an individual card for each PC on the division. Each card contained symbols indicating the officer's qualifications for different duties, such as using firearms or driving different types of police vehicles.

Having a protection post in Flood Street was top of the list of problems that needed my attention. The PCs who were authorised to carry firearms were usually those with the most experience. Therefore, they tended to be part of the same small group of people on each relief who could be put in charge of the reserve room or drive the area car.

My opinion was that we needed a number of younger officers trained to use firearms, so I discussed it with the chief inspector (ops). He told me that he would do all he could to obtain the training courses we needed. Within a short time, we had a group of younger officers authorised to carry firearms.

The terrorist threat seemed to be always with us, and while I was still learning my new job, there was a deadly attack in Walton Street, Chelsea. In this one, an IRA man threw a bomb into Walton's Restaurant, killing two people and injuring fifteen others. One the PCs who was first on the scene gave me a graphic description of what he had seen there. The bomb had been filled with nuts and bolts and other bits of anti-personnel ordnance, which had caused absolute carnage inside the restaurant.

It seemed that the IRA unit that was operating in London was well organised. It carried out attacks and then quickly disappeared, always keeping a few steps ahead of the police.

The Met started planning a major operation in December 1975, with a large number of marked and unmarked police cars covering most of central London. The suggestion for this operation had come from a young detective sergeant who had been studying the MO of the terrorists. One feature he'd noted was that the IRA unit had sometimes attacked a specific target a second time. One of their previous attacks had been on Scott's restaurant in Mayfair. On 6 December, when the terrorists carried out a second attack on Scott's Restaurant, they were unaware that they were in the middle of an army of police waiting for them to do something. A PC had spotted a Ford Cortina driving very slowly around Mayfair and decided to follow it. His heart had probably missed a couple of beats when he saw the occupants of the Cortina open fire on the restaurant with a machine gun.

There were two police officers on foot nearby as part of this operation. They were Inspector John Purnell and Sergeant Phil McVeigh. They flagged down a taxi and went in hot pursuit of the Cortina. Within minutes, one of the most dramatic car chases in police history ended in Marylebone, where the terrorists abandoned the Cortina, together with their automatic weapons, and ran off. Several handgun shots were fired at Purnell and McVeigh, who were unarmed.

The four IRA men gained entry to a flat in Balcombe Street, where they held the two occupants hostage. This was the second major siege for the Met Police within a matter of weeks, but they had gained a great deal of valuable experience during the Spaghetti House operation. Police marksmen moved quickly into strategic positions, and the field of fire from the flat was clearly marked by tapes. Everyone settled down to a long wait. An SAS unit arrived, and the soldiers stood by, ready to attack if that action should be considered necessary.

The commissioner, Sir Robert Mark, was asked by journalists whether he intended to try and negotiate with the IRA terrorists who were holding the hostages. His reply was short and to the point. He said that the only place the IRA men would be going was to prison. A journalist asked him what he would do if a senior politician had been taken as a hostage.

'Ask them if they want any more,' was his curt reply.

It later turned out that this was all part of the psychology being used against the four IRA men, who had a television and a radio in the flat. The siege lasted for five days and eighteen hours before the terrorists surrendered. It was a major victory for the police, but there was a limit to how pleased we could be, as everyone knew that it was just a matter of time before the IRA sent another unit to London.

During 1976 the IRA decided on a strategy that they referred to as the Long War. They decided that in order to survive and win their war against the British state, they would have to prepare for a long campaign. The military wing started to develop political thrust through their political party, Sinn Fein, and they reorganised their paramilitary units into small cells which they called active-service units. Each IRA cell would have a quartermaster, responsible for supplying it with guns, ammunition, and explosives. The identity of the quartermaster would only be known to senior IRA officers in Ireland and the leader of the active service unit.

In my new post as duties sergeant, I shared a large open-plan office with another sergeant, Brian Mayes, who had responsibility for licensing. Also with us were three experienced older PCs known as enquiries officers, who worked in plain clothes. They dealt with administrative enquiries that came to the Chelsea division from other divisions or other forces. We also had a civilian clerical officer, who did her best to keep track of all our correspondence.

One of my enquiries officers told me that he had been to see Eric Miller on a routine enquiry, and I told him about the time I'd gone to him for a search warrant. Two or three weeks later, the officer told me that

Miller had invited him out to lunch. This caused me some concern, and I wondered what his motive might be. It might have been that Miller was under the impression that the officer's job was much more high powered than it actually was. I had a chat to my PC about it, suggesting that Miller might be trying to find someone in the Met who could supply him with confidential information. The end result was that my officer decided to decline the lunch invitation.

Eric Miller was chairman of the Peachey Property Corporation and in the early 1970s had been a generous contributor to Harold Wilson's private office. In 1976, he received a knighthood in Wilson's retirement honours list. However, by this time rumours were circulating about the financial dealings within Miller's companies, and it seemed that large amounts of money had been siphoned off from the Peachey Corporation.

After that, there were investigations by the Department of Trade and the Fraud Squad. In 1977, Sir Eric Miller committed suicide by shooting himself on the Jewish Day of Atonement at his home in Chelsea.

When probationers arrived at Chelsea, I read their files and decided what relief they should go to. I also had to arrange for each probationer to attend training classes two days each month. Each relief had about twenty-eight PCs, and an important part of my job was to make sure that the four reliefs all had a good balance of experienced officers and probationers.

Requests for me to supply manpower for public-order events, which were known as 'aid requirements', arrived on my desk virtually every day. The main manpower planning was done by the public-order branch at New Scotland Yard. Major events would always need a large number of serials, and each district would be told to supply one or more serials. 'B' District headquarters would decide how many officers each division would supply, and my job was to supply them.

Brian Mayes and I covered each other's jobs when one of us was away. Because of the nature of Chelsea, with its many bars, pubs, hotels, and restaurants, Brian was kept busy. My knowledge of liquor licensing was not extensive, but Brian was able to give me advice about how it all worked and the procedures at the local licensing court in Walton Street.

The requests to provide aid to other divisions came in thick and fast throughout the year. It seemed that I was forever putting together serials and sending them off to various parts of the MPD. At the same time, it was important to ensure that there were enough people left on the reliefs so that they could still provide a basic service to the public. In the Met Police, public order was always given priority over day-to-day policing, and sometimes my decisions drew the wrath of inspectors and sergeants on days when teams were stripped to the bare minimum.

When I'd worked on relief, I'd complained about the same things. I knew how they felt. It did not take long for Brian Mayes and me to develop our own cynical sense of humour when we saw all the requests for manpower that came in. There was a cupboard in the office where we kept our stationery.

Our private joke was that the cupboard was the place where our strategic reserve of manpower was hidden. When the demands for manpower arrived, we would say to one another, 'No problem – let's have a look in the cupboard. There must be a few policemen in there somewhere.' However, the cupboard was always bare.

On a couple of occasions when I was new to the job, I spoke to the chief inspector (ops) and told him my concerns about the shortage of PCs. He made it quite clear that it was my problem and I would have to sort it out. In fairness, he was in the same position as I was. The basic problem was that the Met was about 5,000 short of its establishment and faced with rising crime. Very often, all we could do was to cancel officers' leave.

Compared with many other divisions, Chelsea had a very large overtime budget available, but there were some officers who were going for three or four weeks without a day off. There was a group of six or seven PCs who were keen to earn overtime, and they tended to come into my office and volunteer for anything that might be available. There is a saying that it is better to have volunteers than 'pressed' men.

However, solving one problem can just lead to others. Jim Haynes was one of the officers who liked volunteering to earn overtime, but one day he failed to appear at court for one of his cases. When interviewed by his inspector next day, he pleaded exhaustion.

'I'm worn out. Sergeant Ramsay is always putting me on aid and cancelling my days off. I am just so tired I forgot about my court case.' Needless to say, his days of wine and roses had come to an abrupt end.

In my opinion, Haynes was a man of dubious character. A few months later he was in trouble after selling a car to another PC. Apparently, the car had a large amount of hire purchase outstanding, and soon after that he left the Met under a cloud. Haynes may have been weak or dishonest, but aside from that, there was a serious, underlying problem to all of this. The annual leave and sickness records were my responsibility, and I discovered that there were three or four officers who were working a lot of overtime and not taking the leave that they were entitled to. One had only taken five days annual leave in twelve months. I called them all in and told them to take the annual leave that they were entitled to. If they did not apply for it, they were going to be sent on leave whether they wanted it or not. They all started taking their leave.

The summer of 1976 has been called 'the long hot summer'. That year we experienced the hottest summer average temperature in the UK since records began. There was serious rioting at the Notting Hill Carnival, involving hundreds of black youths. The carnival was marred by a large number of street robberies, and several shops were damaged and looted. The police soon found themselves under attack, and there were many casualties. A total of about 400 police officers and 200 members of the public were injured.

Tension between the black community and the Met would remain high for years to come, and the problem was destined to get worse before it got better. Apart from that, what happened raised many basic questions about public order. We needed to be properly equipped and better trained for this type of fast-moving, violent situation.

Although on a much smaller scale, Chelsea division was the location of another type of disturbance that must have come as a surprise to all and sundry. One boiling hot night, a man was arrested near the Coleherne public house in Old Brompton Road, and for several minutes there was a street battle between police and men from the pub. After the initial violence, there was a confrontation that lasted for two or three hours between hundreds of gay men and a large contingent of police. Eventually, the duty officer, a young inspector, made the decision to withdraw police from the immediate area. It was a risky strategy to take, but it worked, and the situation soon calmed down.

The IRA terrorist campaign continued, although there were signs that the terrorists were trying to avoid causing as many casualties as they had done in previous years.

In the Met promotion system, sergeants who wanted to be promoted could apply to take the exam for station sergeant. The format was similar to the sergeants' exam, and promotion beyond station sergeant was by way of interview boards. Then a decision was made to abolish the rank of station sergeant, and it was announced that there would be a new competitive inspectors' exam.

Any sergeants who wished to sit for the new promotion examination in 1977 had to apply for a certificate of fitness from their district commanders. My initial reaction was that this had happened at a good time for me. However, there was little doubt in my mind that the competition in the exam was going to be fierce.

21

In January 1977 I returned to operational duties at Chelsea. A series of events had been planned across the country to mark the twenty-fifth anniversary of the Queen's accession to the throne. We were in the middle of a period of high inflation and wage restraint, and the Queen advised that spending should be kept to a minimum. The Labour Government had a series of confrontations with unions and, to make the situation worse, was also in conflict with the police over pay and the right to strike.

Some years before, as an MP, James Callaghan had been the political representative of the Police Federation. Now, as prime minister, he wished to avoid industrial action but was determined to prevent any breach of his incomes policy. The conflict between the Government and Police Federation became increasingly bitter, and James Callaghan threatened to resign over the issue, although this was not common knowledge at the time. It was later reported that he had discussed the dispute with chief constables who told him that nothing less than a 10 per cent rise would satisfy the Federation. It appears that the Federation did not realise the strength of its own position, and many of us were surprised when they settled for 5 per cent, well below the rate of inflation.

After my office job as duties sergeant, I was back on the front line and had to become used to night duty again. At three o'clock one morning, there was a call from a member of the public with information that two men were on the forecourt of a block of flats in Fulham Road and loading timber onto a lorry. Arriving at the front of the flats, we saw two men running away. I chased after one of them, who ran down into the underground car park of the building. My first thoughts were that the man would probably be trapped there. However, by the time I got near him, he was climbing up a pipe towards an open window.

He might have escaped if my speed had been two or three seconds slower, but I managed to grab a leg and hang on. Although I had a good grip on him, he kicked out at me a couple of times with the leg that was still at liberty, luckily not causing me any injury. A PC came running up and grabbed the other leg, so my suspect gave up the struggle, accompanied by a few comments of, 'Okay, guv, I'm not going nowhere.'

Gaylor was a man aged about forty who lived in Wandsworth. He was charged with theft of £2,000' worth of timber. He was remanded in custody, as there were warrants for him from two other courts, where he had jumped bail. One charge was burglary and the other charge related to an incident when he had threatened another man with a firearm in a south London pub. He was a typical South London criminal or as we might say 'Saf London Boy' with convictions going back over about twenty years. He pleaded guilty to all three matters, but the result was surprising. After being held in custody for a few days, he appeared at the three courts, where he was given the same sentence each time: six months imprisonment, suspended for two years. No action was taken for the two occasions when he had jumped bail.

The more knowledge I gained about the criminal justice system, the more obvious it became that many criminals played the system to their advantage and that the courts did very little to discourage it. Bearing in mind his criminal history, if Gaylor had been to court in the usual way and not jumped bail, he would have expected to be sent to prison for at least one of those three offences. In the 1970s everyone seemed to be receiving suspended sentences. It appeared that this was part of a policy to reduce the prison population, but so many criminals committed further offences when they were on suspended sentences that it had the opposite effect.

The courts had become very liberal in their approach to sentencing and bail. One of my PCs arrested a heroin addict for burglary, and this enquiry was taken over by the Burglary Squad. A CID officer went to court to oppose his application for bail. In police parlance, he was a 'heroin burglar', meaning that he burgled houses every day in order to pay for his drugs. The amount of money he spent on heroin was about three times his weekly income.

Burglary had always been treated as a serious offence by the courts. In the sixties, someone with previous convictions who was charged with burglary would expect to be remanded in custody and receive a prison sentence. However, I noticed that during the seventies there seemed to be a major change in the attitudes of courts, with burglary often being treated much less seriously than it had been in the past.

I had to be at court that day with another case, so it was an opportunity for me to see what happened to the burglar. The omens were not good. The first case listed was a bail application by three men who were charged with murder. My knowledge of the case was limited, apart from knowing that it was a gangland killing. The three smartly dressed defendants all described themselves as company directors, and each one was represented by an expensive-looking lawyer. I thought that the police objections to bail were strong. The defence applications for bail seemed fairly weak and followed a particular route, along the lines of 'My client is a businessman, and if he is remanded in custody his business will suffer.' The three JPs, appeared to be totally out of their depth and spent a lot of time whispering to each other. Eventually they decided that all three defendants should be released on bail.

When the burglar appeared, the CID officer gave objections to bail that were well thought out and logical. After this, the three JPs again spent a couple of minutes whispering together. My guess was that if they were going to grant bail to men charged with a gangland murder this application would probably fall on deaf ears. Unfortunately, this proved correct, and the burglar was given his freedom. He went on to commit a few more offences until he was arrested a second time, about two weeks later, and remanded in custody.

The new Bail Act had given all defendants the right to bail, irrespective of the offence, and objections to bail by police had been limited by the Act. In the past, a recognisance – in other words, bail money – had been involved, and a person released on bail could lose that money if he/she failed to attend court. Under the new act, generally speaking, all the person had to do was promise to attend court. They committed an offence if they jumped bail, but often no action was taken by the courts when they did.

Criminals played the system and committed further offences when released on bail, confident that no extra punishment was going to come their way when they were eventually sentenced. Put simply, this all fuelled the rise in crime. Through the sixties, reported crime in England and Wales rose year by year, and there were suggestions that it might hit one million crimes per year. However, many experts on the subject said that the idea of a million reported crimes in a year was ridiculous.

Police forces started keeping records of reported crime in 1876, and for many years the national total remained fairly steady, with about 100,000 offences being recorded annually. During the 1950s the crime figures remained low, but they were starting to rise. Statistics can be misleading, and I suspect that there was more crime in the forties and fifties than was recorded. Anyone who delves into this subject needs to know how these statistics are compiled. It can be a matter of comparing apples and oranges. Another factor is that during the past few decades parliament has created many more criminal offences than existed in the middle of the twentieth century.

However, the figures do provide a worrying story. During the 1950s there was very little crime, but over the next fifty years this changed dramatically, giving the UK one of the highest crime rates in the Western world. Worrying about a million crimes each year now seems quite quaint. The total in 2003 was 5,974,960, and the following year it reached 6,013,759.

During the 1950s, violent crime only represented 2 per cent of all recorded crime, about 7,000 offences. Now this category makes up 19 per cent of all reported crime, with an annual total of over one million, giving Britain the highest rate of violent crime in western Europe.

I would like to be able to provide some simple solutions to the problem of crime. However, this comes with a warning: Anybody who announces that they have all the answers to the crime problem is probably going to be wrong. The police and the different elements of the criminal justice system will always be ineffective to some degree when they try to tackle this complex subject. Criminals come from within our society. Social deprivation, bad parenting, family breakdown, not knowing right from wrong, poor schooling, greed, and envy are all factors that can play a part, but these are not issues that can be put right by other people. Individuals are responsible for their own actions, and many of them want to be criminals. In terms of the total value of property stolen in the UK, it appears that crime is a much bigger business than Tescos or Sainsbury's. The hours are flexible, and the villains don't pay tax.

Because of the high rate of crime in the first years of the twenty-first century, there must be a point at which the police service becomes much less effective. It simply becomes too busy to deal effectively with its rapidly rising workload. Nowadays, much of day-to-day police work can only be described as 'fire-brigade policing'. An incident occurs, and the police dash to the incident and deal with it. In other words, it is reactive rather than preventive. It has to be an understatement to describe the crime figures for 2003 and 2004 as 'worrying'. The police service may have reached saturation point in those years. One positive feature is that, after reaching a very high point during the first few years of the new century the crime rate started to fall.

In the summer of 1977, a prisoner died while in custody at Chelsea. When I arrived at 6 a.m. to take over as station officer, the weather was unusually warm and humid. Station officers always carry out a procedure referred to as 'handing over'. In this case, the night-duty station officer would tell me about the people we had in custody and explain why they were detained. The correct procedure was for the two sergeants to visit the cells or detention rooms together so that each person could be properly identified and to ensure that they were fit and well. After that, a similar procedure would be carried out so that all property held by the station officer was accounted for.

Although this was a bureaucratic procedure, in practical terms it was very important to me as the incoming station officer to know that everything was in order. John Barlow, the night-duty station officer, told me that we had five people in custody, and we checked them, one by one. That morning, the cells were several degrees hotter and humid than outside. In one of the cells I could see a young man lying on his back, apparently looking at the ceiling.

'A burglar,' said John. He went on to explain that two men had been arrested for burglary the day before, and this man, a heroin addict, was one of them. Earlier that night, John had noticed that the prisoner was showing signs of distress, apparently suffering withdrawal symptoms, and he had decided to call a police surgeon. The doctor had examined the prisoner and certified that he was fit to be detained.

I called out to the man and banged the wicket on the cell door, but there was no response from him or any sign of movement. John opened the cell door and we went in. The man did not appear to be breathing. We walked over to him, and John took hold of his shoulder and shook him. There was a gasp from John as both of us realised that the man was dead.

We contacted the duty officer, and he started the investigation of what was now a sudden death. Nobody wants a death in custody, especially the station officer. There has to be a coroner's inquest into all deaths in police custody, and there is always the danger that there could be criticism of police action. A quick look at the records confirmed that the police surgeon had been called several hours before and had examined the prisoner. The doctor had certified that the prisoner was fit to remain in custody at the station, and he had been visited regularly during the night by police.

A post mortem was carried out and an inquest held. The verdict at coroner's court was that the death had been from natural causes, and there was no criticism of police in this case. It was a sharp reminder to me of the potential risks involved when drug addicts or drunks are held in police stations.

A large number of people are detained at police stations every day, and among them there will always be people who are vulnerable in one way or another. Custody officers need to be very vigilant, but no matter how careful they are, the sad fact is that some people will continue to die in police stations.

The chief inspector (ops) asked me to start another plain-clothes crime squad. Our first case concerned two drug addicts who were stealing antique books from book dealers in the King's Road. We arrested them and recovered a large number of valuable books. While we were still busy trying to identify the books we received information that led us to arrest a man for the theft of a car. This case appeared to be simple but was not as straightforward as it should have been. A man hired a car from a hire company in Chelsea for two weeks but did not return it. The hirer provided identification and an address, except that this was a house that he had moved out of about three months before he'd signed for the car. The company brought in their own investigators, but they were not able to find the person concerned or the car.

Two years went by, and the car was still missing. Then, one day, a CID officer at Chelsea received some new information about it and passed it to me. The DC had been given an address in west London where the man lived, and it appeared that he still had it. We picked up an observation van, and three of us drove to Acton. After finding the address, we spotted the car parked in the street some distance away. We found a good spot to keep an eye on the car, and we waited. 'He has had it for two years,' I thought. 'Let's catch him actually driving it.'

Four or five hours went by before we saw a man walking towards the car. He sat in the driver's seat, started the engine, and started to drive away. As the car came down the street, I drove the observation van forward to block its path. We spoke to the driver, and he readily admitted that he had hired the car two years before and had been using it ever since. We told him that he was under arrest for stealing the car. It was then that the thought went through my mind that everything seemed too easy.

We searched his house and seized any papers that related to the car. When we returned to Chelsea, I discussed it with the two PCs who had come to Acton with me. There are times when police officers need to take a step back and think like lawyers, taking a cold, clear look at the law and at their evidence. I was interested to see whether they were thinking along the same lines as I was, but it was obvious that they had a different perspective.

'It's straightforward,' said one of them. 'He's had the car for over two years. That is evidence of his intention to permanently deprive the owner of the car. Mens rea – guilty intent – all that stuff, any court would convict him.'

'No. It's not straightforward,' I said, coming in as the devil's advocate. 'If you take the simple facts, it's actually only an overdue hiring. Suppose he had returned the car two weeks late – it would be an overdue hiring, wouldn't it? We would not have arrested him, would we?'

'Yes, but this is different. He has had that car for over two years.'

This is where police officers can go down the wrong path, because common sense and the law often travel along different pathways. The law is concerned with principles, definitions, and rules of evidence. Ideas that relate to common sense, or right and wrong, do not carry much weight in a courtroom. Evidence of guilty knowledge was going to be the key factor in this case. We then examined the letters and documents that we had found in the man's house. He had been involved in a traffic accident when driving the hire car. There were letters about the accident and a bill from a garage that had carried out repairs to the car.

After that, two of us interviewed the suspect. My questions were aimed at his use of the car and his intentions. He agreed that he had hired it and not returned it. He also admitted that he had used it virtually every day for two years. We showed him the bill from the garage and the other papers. After linking him to the different bits of paperwork, I told him that he had treated the car as if he owned it. He told us that he had paid to have the vehicle repaired and agreed that he had treated the car as his own. At no point did he mention that he was planning to return it to the car-hire firm.

He was charged with the theft of the vehicle and some traffic offences. At court, his case was adjourned so that he could be legally represented, and his solicitor told me that the charge would be strongly contested. When we returned to court, there was an opportunity for me to meet his solicitor and give him a summary of the evidence we had gathered. After that, he decided to advise his client to plead guilty. The man had no previous convictions and was fined £500 on the charge of stealing the car and another £100 for the traffic offences. Afterwards, I thought about the case. The defendant had had the free use of a car for two years; he must have come out of it making a profit.

While patrolling in plain clothes one Saturday afternoon, I was assaulted – and managed to receive a complaint for my troubles. I was with a young PC called Alan Shillingford, walking along the Fulham Road and mingling with the crowds of supporters as they headed westwards towards Chelsea Football Club. It was a bad time for football; whenever it was mentioned, the next word in the conversation was usually 'violence', but that day everyone seemed friendly and relaxed. However, this did not include the two young men just ahead of us. It seemed obvious to me that they were trouble. As we followed them, they deliberately knocked into other people on the pavement or forced them to step out of their way.

In this situation, it is always best to be wearing a uniform. I told Alan Shillingford that we were going to speak to them but advised him that that we needed to be careful about how we dealt with them. Apart from that, we would both produce our warrant cards as soon as we stopped them. Shillingford had about three years' service. He was strong and fit but had a slight build and looked very young. Because of this, most people would say that he did not look like a policeman.

Up ahead, there was an alley to the side, and we both thought that this would be a good place to speak to them. Neither of us had any thoughts about arresting them. It was more a question of doing a stop and searching them for weapons. They both stepped into the alley with us when requested; I told them that we were police officers, and we produced our warrant cards so that they could see them clearly. It was obvious that the two of them had been drinking heavily.

We did not have the opportunity to complete whatever we were saying to them. One man, who was the larger of the two, put both hands around Shillingford's throat and rammed him up against the wall. I grabbed the Strangler and managed to pull him off Shillingford. The second man made a half-hearted effort to help his friend but did not cause us much trouble. I found myself rolling around the ground with the Strangler, while Alan used his PR to call for urgent assistance. A van with three PCs from my relief arrived within a couple of minutes. We put the less-aggressive man in the van without any trouble, but the Strangler started shouting abuse and struggling. We had to virtually lift him off the ground and throw him in.

The van headed off to the police station, and the two of them seemed to have quietened down. There was the old adage in the police, 'Don't take your eye off a prisoner.' I suppose that I must have done because it took me by surprise when the Strangler suddenly punched me in the side of the head. The force of the blow knocked me across the van, and I slid sideways onto the floor. For a few seconds I felt dazed, but I soon became aware that there was a battle going on around me. The Strangler had made a bad error of judgement. It's not a good idea to attack a policeman in the back of a van, especially when you are outnumbered. The Strangler came out of it second best, and by the time we reached Chelsea police station he was lying spread-eagled on the floor with two policemen sitting on him.

The station officer put both prisoners in the cells and called for a police surgeon to examine everyone. Shillingford had developing bruises and scratches all over his face, neck, and arms. The doctor noted that I had reddening on my face that was consistent with receiving a blow to the head. Both prisoners were examined, and the Strangler told the doctor that he had been punched several times in the face and body, and this was all noted. The second man had no injuries.

The Strangler was charged with two counts of assault on police and criminal damage to Shillingford's shirt, which was badly ripped. Both prisoners were charged with being drunk and disorderly.

At court, the Strangler entered pleas of not guilty to all the charges, but his friend pleaded guilty to being drunk and disorderly. The case against the Strangler was adjourned for trial at the magistrates' court, and a couple of days later I was informed that a complaint of assault had been made against Shillingford and me.

The Strangler must have complained, I thought. However, it turned out that the complaint had come from a member of the public who had been walking along the Fulham Road when we put the two men into the van. He had made a phone call to Scotland Yard, stating that he had seen a man being roughly handled by police and thrown into a police van. Any complaint of that nature is always treated as an allegation of assault, and a chief inspector at Kensington was assigned to investigate the case.

As this was a court case, the chief inspector had to inform the man who made the complaint that the matter was *sub judice* and the complaint investigation could not be started until the charges had been dealt with. It turned out that the complainant had been staying at a hostel in the East End. The chief inspector discovered that the man had only stayed there for two days, had since moved, and nobody knew his current whereabouts.

The Strangler was a railway worker, and his union paid for a solicitor who was very good. The defence was that the two had been drinking heavily but were not aggressive. Their solicitor said that the police had operated in what he called a Starsky-and-Hutch style. We had grabbed his clients without any warning; they had thought that they were being attacked and had only acted in self-defence. They had no idea that we were police officers. The defence solicitor produced the official police photograph of the Strangler, and this showed that he had received a number of blows to the face. We were quite open to the court about his having been punched during the struggle in the van.

The defence solicitor asked me if a member of the public had made a complaint about us, and all I could do was agree that this was true. It could be argued that the complaint was anonymous, but the damage was done. The court dismissed all the charges against the Strangler except that of being drunk and disorderly. I then read out his previous convictions to the court, which included three for offences of violence and from the look on their faces, the JPs realised that they had made a mistake.

The complaint made against us seemed to have a life of its own. The chief inspector who was dealing with the complaint investigation was unable to find out where the complainant was living and decided that the complaint file should be marked up as 'no further action'.

A few months before that, Sir Robert Mark had retired, and a new commissioner, Sir David McNee, had been appointed. Sir David had decided to inspect complaint files personally so that he could satisfy himself that they were being dealt with correctly. Thus each month a sampling of these files were selected at random and sent to him. As luck would have it, the complaint against Shillingford and me was one of those that found its way to the commissioner's office. Sir David read the file, which stated clearly that the complainant could not be found. His decision was to send the file back to the chief inspector, saying that he wanted the Strangler to be asked whether he wanted to make a complaint against Alan Shillingford and me. It can only be said that we were both shocked and angry when we learned of this. There has to be a complaints system, granted, but I did not think that the commissioner should be encouraging hooligans to make complaints against his officers. The chief inspector was obviously embarrassed about it but explained that he would have to comply with the commissioner's directions. He had a meeting with the Strangler, who said that he did not want to complain about anyone, and eventually the complaint file was laid to rest.

While all of this was going on, our squad spent some time in and around Harrods, looking for pickpockets. Harrods and the surrounding area will always attract pickpockets and shoplifters. A couple of weeks before, an Arab woman had had her handbag stolen while shopping in Harrods. It had contained £50,000 in cash. Professional pickpockets can make a lot of money, and it is not surprising that they target areas such as Knightsbridge, where they know that they will come across people carrying large amounts of cash.

Two of my officers, working in plain clothes, were watching people going in and out of Harrods. They noticed a couple of youths aged fourteen to fifteen years alighting from a taxi. One of the boys produced a wad of banknotes and paid the taxi driver with the words, 'Keep the change, mate.' The two PCs decided to follow the youths around the store and soon had the impression that they were not there to go shopping. After about fifteen minutes or so, they stopped and searched them. One of them was carrying a large amount of money, and his friend had three different wallets in his pockets that belonged to other people. Both of them were arrested.

One of the PCs called me on the radio and told me about the arrests. It turned out that the two youths were already well known to police, and they obviously saw themselves as hardened, professional criminals. At the police station, one of them thrust a solicitor's card in my face. 'We know our rights. We want our money back, and we're entitled to see a brief. We shall take legal action against you if you stop us seeing our brief.'

A few years earlier, this would probably have earned him a slap or a kick in some police stations, but we just told him to shut up. They were juveniles, and we needed to contact their parents before we could interview them. After the interviews, the station officer decided that the two youths should be released while we made enquiries and sent a file to Juvenile Bureau for a decision as to proceedings. Within the next couple of days, we were able to identify the owners of the three wallets. We found that they had been stolen during a period of about four hours prior to the time when they had been spotted by my two PCs.

Two weeks later, the two police officers involved saw the same two youths again near Harrods. They were stopped and questioned and found to be in possession of property that they had stolen in a Knightsbridge shop. We went through the whole procedure again at the police station. We had been told that they came from a couple of well-known criminal families in North London. When the parents came to the station, the father of one of them set the tone for the meeting. 'My boy is a good lad, but you bastards keep picking on him. You're determined to turn him into a criminal.' Needless to say, the parents were not that cooperative. The only good news was that we never saw the two of them on our patch again.

It was about that time that we went to the assistance of one of the Harrods store detectives who had followed a couple of shoplifters out of the store. The two men that were stopped were of Arabic appearance but said that they were French. They both spoke French and produced French identity cards. After they were arrested, we took them back to their flat in Earls Court and carried out a search. We found two Algerian passports hidden inside a cushion.

They eventually admitted that they had travelled from Algeria to France, where they had stolen French identity cards from people who were similar in appearance to themselves. The identity cards were useful as it gave them access to all the countries in the EU. In London, they passed themselves off as Frenchmen. It seemed obvious to me that they were living by theft – and doing well at it until they were caught. They were both sentenced to three months imprisonment and deported.

There was an unusual postscript to this story. About twelve months later, the arresting officer was in uniform patrolling Sloane Street, when he noticed a man walking along the other side of the road and recognised him as one of the two Algerians we had arrested at Harrods. He crossed the street and arrested the man on suspicion of being illegally in the UK. The Algerian admitted that he had simply applied for another passport in Algeria under a fictitious name and returned to London. He was handed over to the Immigration Service and deported again. For all we know, he may have come back again at some later date.

One of the Jubilee events was a visit to Brixton by the Queen, and hundreds of schoolchildren had been given the day off to welcome her. Serials from all over were being sent to assist the local division with crowd control, and a serial from Chelsea was among them. The only noteworthy incident that day occurred on the actual journey. We knew that the Met was having difficulty providing transport for the large number of events that had been planned, and we were amused to find that we would be travelling in a double-decker bus provided by a seaside town a short distance from London.

The serial, including me, left Chelsea, and within a few minutes we were south of the river. In Battersea, our route would take us under a railway bridge. The bus driver – very sensibly – uncertain about the height of the bus slowed down and then stopped. The inspector in charge of the serial seemed very unhappy about this. 'Of course you can get through,' he shouted.

Looking at the bridge, I had a feeling of unease about it. The inspector's words would soon be written in that well-known book *Famous Last Words*.

The bus continued, and there was a loud crash when the roof came in contact with the superstructure of the bridge. The bus stopped moving, and there were a few gasps and some nervous laughter. 'What about the people upstairs?' I thought. I ran up the stairs, wondering if I might find a few decapitated bodies lying there. Luckily there were no casualties, but the front part of the roof had been ripped off. The accident meant that we arrived late at Brixton, but the event itself was a very happy, friendly affair.

During the previous year I had started studying for the inspectors' exam that would be held in April. There was no doubt in my mind that it was going to be hard going. The competition for the first exam under the new system had been particularly fierce, with more than 300 sergeants battling for about twenty places. There were two separate papers; the first one dealt with theoretical matters, whereas the second was designed to test the candidates' practical knowledge and the law. It soon became obvious that to stand any real chance of success it was necessary to achieve very high marks in the first paper. Because of this, any sergeant who was a serious candidate was busy reading pages and pages of General Orders and trying to memorise the most important parts.

During 1977 I was asked to assist the superintendent at Chelsea with a number of complaints that he was dealing with. The superintendent had been given five complaint files about officers in the Kensington and Notting Hill divisions. If an official complaint was logged against an officer, the investigation had to be carried out by a senior officer from a different division. My main job was to see the complainants and take written statements from them.

Some complaints seemed amusing to me but not, apparently, to the complainants. A PC at Kensington had stopped a man who had driven through a red traffic light and reported him. The man had his wife with him, and she started to give the policeman a hard time, which included,

'Why don't you go and find a burglar? We pay your wages. Why are you picking on my husband?' It seems that she went on and on and on.

The policeman's sense of humour made the situation even worse when he warned the man that he was committing a serious criminal offence, as he was 'in possession of an offensive person' and he might have to arrest him. Anyway, I have to confess that it made me smile.

Then it was time to take the promotion exam, which I entered as a competitor, having few illusions about what was facing me. In April, I passed the exam with a high mark, but to my frustration, it was not quite good enough to push me into the group of thirty or so candidates at the top of the list who would be promoted. I needed to take a break from studying for a few months but decided that I would try again the following year.

As part of the response to the IRA terrorist campaign, the Met started a new initiative in which each district provided a car with a sergeant and two PCs to deal with bomb incidents. I was posted to the newly named 'bomb car' with a PC from Notting Hill and another one from Kensington. As a team we had a good knowledge of every part of 'B' District. The Met was receiving large numbers of calls about suspected bombs, and we knew that some would prove to be the real thing. We needed to take every call very seriously.

A car bomb was one of the most deadly terrorist attacks that we were likely to face, as it would throw bits of metal all over the place and could be lethal over a considerable distance. Whenever we decided that we were unhappy with a vehicle or any other object, we had to seal off the surrounding area. The first few minutes were always difficult, as there was often only the three of us at the scene. We would tape off the immediate area, and once we were satisfied that there was nobody within that area we would do our best to extend our perimeter. In most parts of central London, this was not as easy as it may sound.

Assuming that we had enough manpower, it was essential that we carry out measures to avoid casualties. The public had to be warned and directed away from the immediate area. The people we noticed who were busy watching everything from the windows in the office block across the road needed to be directed to the other side of their building. Those inquisitive people on the street, who wanted to find out what was happening, had to be sent on their way.

It never failed. Just when you were satisfied that you had done a pretty good job and the area was clear, people would suddenly pop up, apparently from nowhere. They would emerge from alleyways and rear doors of shops and restaurants, deep in their own thoughts, not realising that they might be walking into danger. They would often walk up to officers and ask them what was going on. This tended to be annoying and frustrating, especially at the beginning, when we did not have enough manpower and we were desperately trying to clear the area.

Apart from the long-running terrorist situation, I found myself involved in the policing of the most high-profile industrial dispute of the 1970s. Grunwick's was a small film-processing plant, owned by a man called George Ward. It was situated at two sites in Willesden, north London, and had a workforce that was mainly Asian. A strike started in 1976, when six of the workers were sacked. The following week, the six sacked workers returned to Grunwick's with placards and a petition that demanded union recognition. Many of the workers at Grunwick's said that they wanted to join a trade union, and sixty of them joined APEX (the Association of Professional, Executive, Clerical, and Computer Staff).

Soon there were 137 workers on strike out of a total workforce of 480, and management sacked all the striking workers. Central to the dispute was the fact that the strikers wanted the company to recognise the union, and they wanted their jobs back. The union view was that working conditions at Grunwick's were poor. It was said that workers were only paid twenty-eight pounds for a forty-hour week, when the national average was about seventy-two pounds per week. It was also alleged that white workers were paid more than their Asian colleagues. APEX tried to negotiate with George Ward, but he refused to enter into negotiations with them.

The whole dispute started to escalate when other trade unionists became involved. At the same time, George Ward was offered assistance by a right-wing group called the National Association for Freedom. Grunwick's was soon being picketed around the clock, and the Post Office unions refused to deal with their mail. One night at 2 a.m., a commando group of twelve people from the Freedom Association outsmarted the night pickets and removed 80,000 postal packages. All of this post was removed in two lorries to a secret location in Gloucestershire, where £7000 worth of stamps were used, and the packages were then posted all over the country.

Large numbers of police were on hand at Grunwick's when there was mass picketing, and I was there with a Chelsea serial on three occasions. The main principle of picketing is that it should be peaceful. It is not illegal for pickets to ask the workers to join the strike. A basic question has always been how many pickets should be allowed for this purpose. Many people would consider that two or three pickets would be enough but the workers at Grunwick's were often facing a picket that numbered several thousand. Our serials would be there early so that we would be in position for the crucial time when the workers arrived in a hired bus.

The policing of the dispute had developed into a daily routine. The pickets would try and prevent the bus from reaching its destination, and the police would do their best to assist the bus to reach the factory entrance. At that point, police would stop the bus, and a senior officer would speak to the passengers inside. They would be asked whether they wanted to speak to the leaders of the trade union pickets and they always said that they did not wish to. Once they said that, the bus would be allowed to continue into the factory.

My first two visits to Grunwick's were peaceful. There were several hundred pickets on both occasions, but everything remained good-natured. It was my first experience of this type of dispute. On my third visit to Grunwick's, it started to become clear that the situation was different. There were several thousand pickets, and the atmosphere was unfriendly and ominous.

A number of serials, including the Chelsea contingent, formed a cordon across the road. Some distance from us we could see pushing, shoving, and shouting going on. I saw that some of the serials were from the SPG, and their officers arrested three or four pickets. The level of tension started to rise, and suddenly the pickets charged our line. We were hit by a tremendous impact, and the police lines broke. For a few seconds I felt a sense of shock. They had broken our lines! It was the first time that I had been in a public-order situation where it appeared that we had lost control of the situation.

For a few minutes everything seemed to be total chaos. I was aware that someone had punched me, but I was not sure who. Blows hit my right arm and chest. Someone or something struck my helmet, and it came flying off. I saw a large, strong-looking man charging forward in my direction. He pushed one PC out of his way and punched another one. Then he tried to push me out of the way. We exchanged a few blows, and he tripped over something or someone and fell to the ground. The situation had degenerated into a large-scale brawl between police and pickets, while a number of senior officers had plunged in to try and restore our cordon.

None of us were using our sticks. Then I saw one of my probationers run past me, waving his truncheon. There was a wild look on his face, and he appeared to have lost it. At this point, I was standing close to Terry Hobbs, one of the home-beat officers at Chelsea. The two of us must have had the same thought at the same time, for we both went after the footloose probationer. Terry Hobbs reached him first and took his truncheon away from him.

There are several types of pressure, and every police officer reacts in a different way to each one. What surprised me about this incident was that the PC concerned was fairly young but would be described as mature for his age. The chaotic scenes that I describe probably only lasted a matter of a few minutes. Somehow or other we managed to restore the cordon, and the situation started to calm down.

A few aches and pains would not kill me, but I guessed that there were parts of me that would soon have bruises to remind me of my time at Grunwick's. My tie had been ripped off, and my watch was missing. A number of helmets were lying on the ground, and I eventually found mine; it was in a dirty, battered condition. Travelling back to Chelsea, I must have looked pretty battered myself. There seems to be a wag in every serial, and one of the PCs was soon amusing everyone by linking me to the famous American television series of the time, *The Six Million Dollar Man*.

'Sergeant Ramsay, a man barely alive. We have the technology. We can rebuild him.'

Flood Street was still our responsibility, and the duty officer would make at least one visit during a tour of duty. One of my fellow sergeants gave me his account of a 2 a.m. visit to the house with the duty officer.

They had parked in Flood Street and walked to the house, but they soon became concerned when there was no sign of the PC who was posted there.

The officer looking after Margaret Thatcher was PC Lucerne, a large, friendly man who often worked in the reserve room, usually with a smile on his face and a cigar in his mouth. The inspector and sergeant did a second circuit to try and find the missing officer. There were lights on in the house, but there was no sign of PC Lucerne. They walked around to the back door of the house for a second time. The door opened, and Dennis Thatcher emerged, a glass of whiskey in his hand. 'You must be looking for your officer,' he said.

The inspector and sergeant were invited into the house, and Dennis Thatcher took them through to the lounge, where they could see Maggie Thatcher sitting on a sofa. PC Lucerne was sitting on the floor, holding a glass of wine in one hand. His firearm was lying on the floor next to him. A conversation was in full swing, and PC Lucerne seemed to be doing most of the talking. 'Look, Maggie, if it was me, this is what I would do—'

His advice to the future prime minister was cut short by the arrival of the duty officer and sergeant.

'Good evening, sir. I was just telling Mrs Thatcher ...'

PC Lucerne's advice was probably excellent. Maggie Thatcher managed to win three general elections after that.

On night duty that year, we dealt with a serious, unprovoked attack on a man in the street. A smartly dressed 42-year-old businessman had been walking through South Kensington when he was attacked by three men in their early twenties. There was no obvious reason for the attack, and there was no attempt to rob him. It may be that they just did not like the look of the man because he was smartly dressed. One of my colleagues called it a *Clockwork Orange* attack, after the book and film bearing that name. The victim was punched several times, knocked to the ground, and kicked repeatedly while he was lying on the pavement. His injuries included a broken rib.

The three attackers ran off towards Fulham Road, and a member of the public dialled 999. We caught them a short distance away, but all three denied that they had been involved in the assault. One of them was arrested by the duty officer, one by me, and the third man by one of my probationers. I questioned my suspect and managed to obtain an admission from him that he had been involved in the assault. All three pleaded not guilty and chose to go 'up the road'.

The trial at Inner London Crown Court lasted a whole day. They were all individually represented by counsel. Two of them, including the one that I had arrested, were found guilty and fined thirty pounds each. The judge may have believed that a stiff penalty like that would probably deter them from attacks on other innocent people in the street. However, the victim left court obviously upset at the result.

22

1978 was a good year for the police. The Labour Government had set up an enquiry into police pay and conditions, with Lord Edmund-Davies as chairman. The Edmund-Davies report to the Government recommended that police officers should receive a large pay rise and included an amount, written into the award that would compensate them for not having the right to strike. The pay rise would be 42 per cent, and the Government said that the increase would be awarded in two annual instalments. The leader of the Conservative Party, Margaret Thatcher, went one step further, saying that if she were elected prime minister the police service would receive the pay rise in one lump.

In April that year, I sat the promotion exam for the second time. After putting in much more study than the previous year, I actually received a lower mark on this occasion. It was very disappointing and made me wonder whether it was worth trying again.

Knightsbridge and Brompton Road were being plagued by a group of men operating the three-card trick. There had been several attempts made to arrest them but none had been successful. The chief inspector (ops) asked me to pick a plain-clothes squad and deal with the problem.

We knew that this team of gamers came from the East End of London and that their leader was a man called Henry Hunt. Everything indicated that they were highly organised and would be difficult to catch. The maximum fine had been increased to £500, but the gamers were making lots of money, and as long as they could avoid being arrested too often, they simply treated their fines as acceptable business losses.

My plan was to choose three PCs who fitted certain criteria for this particular job. All of them needed to be fast runners, but I did not want anybody with a distinctive appearance, being tall or looking too much like a policeman. Once I had found the three best people for the job, we met to discuss tactics and then went into action.

The gaming was taking place outside shops in Brompton Road, a short distance from Harrods, and we spent three days trying to reach the principal. There were a number of tactics that we thought would work. One was the bus-ambush plan. This was nothing new, as it had been used by police in the West End quite often in the past. One or two officers would travel on a bus that passed the location where the principal was, jump off the bus, and grab him. We tried it a few times with no success. Another tactic was to act like shoppers and drift in and out of shops and then suddenly sprint out of a shop doorway, taking the man with the cards by surprise.

Our plans may have sounded very good in theory, but they all came to nothing. It seemed as though we were watching some kind of magic trick, where the principal could disappear into a cloud of smoke at the drop of a hat. Our lack of success during this time soon became an embarrassment. I spoke to two of the PCs on my relief and asked them to help us. Louis Nwaegbe was a young black PC with about three years' service. Janet Goodyear was a woman officer with about the same length of service. She was slim and attractive, with long blonde hair.

The rendezvous point next day was South Kensington tube station, and they turned up as arranged in plain clothes, smartly dressed. My master plan was for them to saunter along Brompton Road together as boyfriend and girlfriend, and if they saw the principal, they were to hang onto him and wait for us. The four of us in the plain-clothes team split up but stayed within striking distance. One officer followed the couple along Brompton Road but kept a good distance behind them, with me a little further back. My thinking was that if the gamers were to recognise anyone it would probably be me, and thus I could be the weak link in the team.

Louis and Janet spent some time walking around as bona fide shoppers but found no sign of the principal. We could only surmise that one or both of them had been recognised. A job that had seemed fairly straightforward was now starting to present a real challenge. I thanked Louis and Janet for their help and sat down with my team to talk it through. We had seen two or three people who might have been lookouts, but there had been no sign of a principal and no sign of Henry Hunt.

It looked as though we were dealing with a team consisting of a principal and at least five or six lookouts. Henry Hunt, known to be a shrewd operator, would have been there somewhere. If we had the evidence, the lookouts could be arrested for obstructing police in the execution of their duty, but that would smack of desperation. Our real target would always be the man with the three cards.

Police officers working in plain clothes usually wear casual clothes and feel that they are doing a good job at not showing out. However, professional criminals will usually spot them however cleverly they dress. We had information that Henry Hunt's team included men with some serious form, and later we discovered that armed robbery, burglary, and GBH all featured on their records.

It seemed they would always spot us. We had no photographs of the people we were looking for, but it was likely that they knew who we were. Another problem was that in some parts of London, like Brompton Road, most people looked smart or fashionably dressed, and the plain-clothes officer in T-shirt and jeans stood out like a sore thumb.

Our failure to make any arrests had left me feeling very frustrated. All four of us discussed the various tactics that we had used and the clothes that we had been wearing. We were running out of ideas fast, and my suggestion was that we needed a change of image and a change of pace. Next day, there was an unusual sight at the police station – it looked like a wedding party. They may not have reached the heights of sartorial elegance, but there were four men in their best clothes and ready for action. This time, the sergeant was in the vanguard, with a PC following some distance behind. The other two travelled from South Kensington to Knightsbridge by underground.

It was the usual route, starting near South Kensington tube station and then east along Brompton Road, where I stopped at a shop to buy an Italian newspaper and put on my sunglasses. It is my habit to walk at a fairly fast pace, so it was necessary to tell myself to slow down. A foreign tourist would not be rushing anywhere. He would saunter along, looking into shop windows and thinking about nothing too serious. It was a good state of mind for a holiday. Was there any point in worrying about gamers or anyone else? After I'd passed Harrods, I could make out a small group of people standing around a man who appeared to be showing them something. Each step brought me closer and closer, but it seemed too easy. I had the feeling that the group of people ahead of me might suddenly evaporate like some sort of mirage in the desert.

The man with the cards was using a large plastic bread container as a table, and I could see three cards lying on it. I moved closer and closer and soon found myself standing next to the principal as he encouraged people to put their money down. It did not take long for him to turn to me.

'Do you want to put something on, guv? How about fifty quid?'

'How about this?' I replied as my warrant card landed on top of the cards. The man's mouth opened, and he just stood there looking at me as if he were in deep shock and had lost the ability to speak. I could see a couple of men running across the road towards me. 'Lookouts,' I thought, wondering if we were going to have a fight on our hands. At the same time, it was reassuring to see two of my PCs running in my direction from Knightsbridge tube station.

Then I spotted Henry Hunt, who just seemed to appear from nowhere. Someone had pointed him out to me one day when I was at Marlborough Street Court. Henry Hunt was then a man in his fifties, and on this occasion, he was not happy. His anger was directed at his two lookouts, both of whom were now standing looking at me with worried expressions on their faces.

'What's wrong with you?' he shouted at them. 'Don't you know who that is? That's sargee from Chelsea nick,' he said, pointing at me. 'Sargee,' he said, repeating it a couple of times in a tone of great frustration while shaking his head. He then turned to me. 'You've caught our best bloke. 'Ow about you take one of these other blokes instead? They'll plead guilty, no worries.'

'I'm quite happy with what we've got,' I said.

Henry Hunt stood there shaking his head sadly, and then he turned his head towards me and spoke to me in almost a whisper. 'You know what the trouble is, Sarge?' he said. 'You just can't get the staff these days!'

The principal pleaded guilty and was fined £500. It was a turning point in our luck. Maybe it was because we had developed the necessary know-how for dealing with gamers. Whatever the reason, we just kept arresting them every day after that. We used different approach routes and took it in turn to arrest the principal. If a court case was adjourned, we asked for the bail condition that they hated, the one which banned them from being anywhere within 5 miles of Hyde Park Corner.

There can be disadvantages to being a short police officer. On one occasion, the principal was a particularly large man and the arresting officer was probably one of the Met's smallest. The gamer was not violent, but he ran off across Brompton Road with the PC hanging onto him. It was a bit like policemen in the Met's early days hanging onto runaway horses and gradually bringing them to a halt. If the gamer had decided to fight, it was unlikely that my PC would have held onto him for long. Luckily there were two of us running along the other side of the road to intercept the struggling pair before anything happened.

One of the older stipendiaries at Marlborough Street was known to hate anyone involved in the three-card trick. One of my PCs told me that he had been off duty, walking along Oxford Street, when he had seen this magistrate chasing a gamer along the street, hitting him repeatedly with his walking stick. This same magistrate was presiding at court when one of our arrested gamers was due to appear, and when the defendant heard who it was, he ran out of the courtroom. So we found that we had a warrant to execute.

A message was sent to him via another gamer, telling him that we wanted him to report to Chelsea police station at a specified time so that we could arrest him. He turned up as agreed. Eventually we notched up a total of about seven or eight arrests, and each principal received a £500 fine.It must have had some effect, because Henry Hunt and his team suddenly moved off the Chelsea division to go elsewhere. The actual result was displacement rather than a real victory. All that the arrests had done was make life a little bit difficult for them and dent their profit margins.

My time at Chelsea had widened my experience in all sorts of ways, but I was aware that it could be a mistake to stay in one place for too long. During the previous year or so I had twice applied for specialist posts at

Scotland Yard but had not been successful. Various thoughts went through my head. Was I becoming part of the furniture? Even the gamers knew who I was, it seemed. Eventually I put in a written application for a transfer to another division.

A couple of years earlier, a routine enquiry had taken me to a very large house in the Boltons to see a wealthy Danish count. One afternoon while I was station officer, the count appeared at the front counter at the station. He recognised me and explained that he had to produce his driving documents. The count had been involved in an accident in Surrey, and the local police had asked him to produce his documents at Chelsea. Everything was in order except for the MOT certificate that he should have had.

In theory, this could not have been more straightforward. He had been driving a car that was not covered by an up-to-date MOT certificate, and I would have to report him for that offence. There was very little paperwork; it went to our process section, from where everything would be forwarded to Surrey. It was a minor matter, and I quickly forgot about it.

A few days later, at 7 a.m. while patrolling the division, there was a call over the PR asking me to return to the station. There had been a phone call directing me to report to the Complaints Investigation Branch at Scotland Yard as soon as possible. Everyone knew that CIB investigated serious complaints against police, and my first thought was that it could be someone's idea of a joke. There were a few jokes from colleagues, but they assured me that the message was genuine, so I asked one of the PCs to drive me to Scotland Yard. When I arrived at the CIB office, there appeared to be only one officer on duty there. Naturally, I tried to find out what I could, but he said that he had no idea what it was about and directed me to take a seat in the waiting room.

The first few minutes ticked by with me telling myself that there was nothing to worry about, but the longer I sat there the more worries flashed through my mind. Soon my memory went into overdrive, working its way through all my activities over the past few weeks. First of all I considered assaults. It had been several months since I had been involved in anything that could be described as a violent incident. So this probably ruled out any allegations of assault.

Then my thoughts moved on to the gamers that we had been dealing with a short time before. As far as the world of vice is concerned, street gaming may fall at the lower end of the spectrum but maybe Henry Hunt or one of his friends had made an allegation against me alleging corruption of some sort. Maybe he wanted to hit back at me after being driven out of Knightsbridge. However, East End characters like him had their own code and their own ways of doing things, and my feeling was that it would have been out of character for Henry Hunt to do something like that.

The fact that someone wanted me to be at the CIB office at such an early hour was also puzzling, but I tried not to worry about it. Then Detective Superintendent Churchill-Coleman arrived. He apologised for keeping me waiting and explained that he had wanted to get me away from Chelsea as quickly as possible that morning. The mystery continued to deepen. He invited me into his office, and I took a seat in front of his desk.

Churchill-Coleman produced a file and handed me a sheet of paper. It was the official form completed at police stations when people produce driving documents; I must have completed a thousand or more by then. It was in my handwriting with the name of the Danish count at the top. I could see that there was some writing along the side of the form, made with blue fountain-pen ink.

Chief Superintendent Fuller was the third divisional commander during my time at Chelsea, and his handwriting was familiar to me. The detective superintendent asked me to make a brief statement relating to my conversation with the count and the production of the driving documents. He made it clear that he was not going to tell me anything about the enquiry and instructed me not to talk to anyone about it. That ended our conversation.

My arrival back at Chelsea was greeted with some amusement by one of my fellow sergeants, who asked me whether I would now have to comply with bail conditions. I soon had a picture in my mind of what had happened. It was known that the chief superintendent and superintendent had been invited for dinner at the count's house in Chelsea on more than one occasion. It turned out that the superintendent had gone to the house in the Boltons the day after the count had been to the police station with his driving documents.

It appeared that Fuller had endorsed my report with a handwritten note, stating that he had seen an MOT test certificate that covered the Count for the day in question. However, it seemed that someone in Surrey had rightly been suspicious and had been in contact with CIB. It was a serious complaint, because it could be seen as an attempt to pervert the course of justice. In any event, my position at Chelsea had become uncomfortable, as a prosecution witness against my superintendent and chief superintendent in any future proceedings. Within two days of my visit to Scotland Yard, an entry appeared in Police Orders announcing my transfer to 'V' District.

Divisions in the suburbs cover very large areas compared with those in central London, and 'V' District took in the boroughs of Kingston and Merton plus parts of Surrey that included Esher and Cobham. I went to Kingston for a meeting with the commander, who informed me that he was posting me to Wimbledon. The idea of working there pleased me. Although I had lived in several different parts of the country, Wimbledon was probably the only place that I thought of as my home town. On my mother's side of the family, four generations had lived there, and my grandfather had been a well-known builder in Wimbledon.

Travelling to work would be easier, as my home was only 4 miles away. Part of New Malden was within the Borough of Merton and therefore part of the Wimbledon Division. I reported to the chief superintendent at Wimbledon, who seemed to be pleased to see me. It was a different type of greeting than I'd received from Pickford in 1972. He was a man in his fifties who had served as an army officer in an infantry unit during the Second World War, and his tunic bore an impressive number of medal ribbons.

The relief that I was to join was posted late turn that day, so I had lunch in the canteen and took a quick look around the police station. One of the first people that I came across was one of the Kent PCs who had been in my class at Sandgate. It turned out that he had transferred to the Met some years before. Late turn started at 2pm and I decided to find my inspector and introduce myself. One of the PCs told me that there had been a disturbance at a pub, and the inspector was involved in an arrest.

Looking back, I see that my walking into the charge room at that particular point in time was not well timed. My new inspector, Gary Miller, and one of the sergeants, Brian Burton, had arrested a man for drunk and disorderly. Like most drunks, the prisoner changed his mood erratically from friendly to violent; he would appear to be docile for about a minute and then go into fighting mode. At first sight, he appeared to be behaving himself, but as soon as I spoke, he decided that he wanted to fight everybody. It seemed as though the environment for introductions was not quite right while the three of them were rolling around on the floor in front of me.

Sitting on the bench in the charge room after two or three minutes of struggle, the drunk appeared to have calmed down, so I tried again to introduce myself. This was the point at which the drunk jumped up and took a swing at Brian Burton, so Gary Miller and I grabbed him and sat him back on the bench. Then the man jumped up again and there was another brief struggle. The station officer appeared on the scene about this time, looked at the three of us and grinned. He decided that the safest option would be to search the prisoner and put him into a cell before anyone was seriously injured. After that, conversation became that bit easier.

Arriving at a new police station will always mean confronting new situations, and much of what I found at Wimbledon seemed very strange. The magistrates' court was opposite the police station. My first thoughts were that this was quite useful, but I soon discovered that there were no cells inside the court building. This meant that prisoners who were in custody were brought to the police station and had to be escorted across the road to court. After that, they had to be guarded by the officer in the case in what was a public area within the court.

While working as station officer a few days after my arrival at Wimbledon, I heard some shouts and looked through the front window to see what appeared to be a large brawl outside the court. Suddenly, it seemed that every police officer in the station was sprinting across the road and into the general melee.

A PC had been walking a defendant across the road to the court, where the man's friends and relatives were gathered. Emotions started to run high, and the officer thought that he was going to lose the prisoner.

Luckily, the arrival of reinforcements brought the situation under control. It turned out that this sort of incident was fairly common.

The charge room is the operational hub of a police station, and it goes without saying that it needs to be the most secure part of the building. Nowadays, this secure area is referred to as a custody suite. A modern custody suite will include a charge room, detention rooms, cells, and rooms for medical examinations, interviews, fingerprints, and photographs. In nearly all cases this will be on the ground floor, but the other parts of the station can be designed in much the same way as any other office building.

'Who on earth designed this police station?' I wondered while looking around on my first day as station officer at Wimbledon. On more than one occasion there had been blunders when stations were planned. There was the famous case when Brixton police station was built without a charge room, but there were many other stories. It was not always possible to tell what was true, false, or exaggerated in Met folklore.

The charge room at Wimbledon was positioned so that many people at the station had to walk through it to reach other places, and there were five doors leading in and out of it. One door led into the reserve room, which was an annexe next to the charge room, and police officers and civil staff were continually walking through the charge room to reach it. Another door was a few paces from the front door to the station. The door had a bolt on it but this was always unbolted by the people who needed to walk through. Every station has its own myths and legends, and there were several Wimbledon stories about prisoners escaping from the charge room. In the event of an escape, it would always be the station officer who would be the first in the firing line when it came to any official enquiry.

At this time new technology was starting to make its mark on the police service, with the development of the Police National Computer. The PNC had two databases, the Nominal Index and the Vehicle Index. All the relevant information held at CRO was transferred to the Nominal Index, and it streamlined stops on the streets.

Reserve rooms at police stations were gradually having computers fitted although Wimbledon did not have access to the PNC at that time. When one of our officers took details of a vehicle that had been reported stolen, the information had to be passed immediately to Kingston or Esher so that the Vehicle Index could be updated. Details of all vehicle owners could be provided in a matter of a few seconds. The police service was moving into the computer age, and to me the speed at which information could be accessed seemed quite amazing.

My relief at Wimbledon was much smaller in numbers than its equivalent at Chelsea. The average PC was older and more experienced, and many of them had worked in central London divisions before coming to Wimbledon. There were two or three probationers on the relief, and I became the reporting sergeant for one of them.

One of the first aspects that surprised me was the high level of crime within the Wimbledon division. Offences involving violence were quite common, and the rate of motor-vehicle crime was exceptionally high. The Broadway at Wimbledon was a busy area for entertainment, with its theatres, cinemas, and night clubs. There was a general perception that the shortage of public transport at night was one of the main reasons for the high rate of vehicle crime.

The division was made up of two subdivisions, Wimbledon and Mitcham. At that time, Mitcham had a certain amount of autonomy, with its own chief inspector in charge. If Mitcham had a serious incident, their chief inspector would be called out to take charge, and if he was not available, the inspector who was his deputy would deal with it. If neither were available, then the duty officer at Wimbledon would be responsible for taking action.

The police station had a large number of dogs handed in by members of the public, and kennels were located at the far end of the yard. Dogs, of course were another of the station officer's many responsibilities. If dogs are not happy, they bark, and this annoyed residents living near the station. About the time of my arrival, local people had decided on legal action, and the chief superintendent had been served with an injunction ordering him to make the dogs stop barking (or at least to reduce the noise). The engineering branch of the Met Police was called in, and they designed soundproofed kennels. The whole thing cost a small fortune.

This sort of problem led to some research being done into our procedures. We were supposed to look after found dogs for seven days and then send them to the Battersea Dogs and Cats Home if they had not been claimed. The responsibility for checking the Dogs Found Book against the information in the Dogs Lost Book fell on the shoulders of the station officer, who generally had a few more important things to worry about than dogs. From time to time a dog would be destroyed when it should have been restored to its owner. In theory, dogs should have represented the least of our policing problems, but in reality they resulted in many complaints against police, not to mention the litigation that kept our solicitors' branch busy.

It seems highly unlikely that there would be links between found dogs and organised crime – but truth can often be stranger than fiction. While I was sitting in the front office and writing an entry in the Occurrence Book, my attention drifted from the book to the man who had appeared at the front counter holding a small dog in his arms. 'A big man,' I thought. What was he? A professional wrestler, maybe? He was conversing with the PC who was my assistant station officer.

'I found him in South Park Road,' the big man said sadly. The tone of his voice suggested that he might burst into tears very soon. 'It really upsets me when I see a little dog that is lost.'

The PC glanced quickly in my direction as if there were something wrong. I was a bit mystified and sat watching as the dog was handed over. As I looked at the man at the counter, I thought about going into dark alleys and the people that you did not want to come up against while you were there. 'Better add that man to the list,' I thought.

'Joe Pyle,' said the PC quietly as the man walked out of the police station. Although his face was new to me, everyone knew that Joe Pyle was someone who had been at the centre of organised crime in south London for many years. Part of the reason for his success was that he had managed to maintain good relationships with the Krays and Richardsons, the other two large crime firms that had emerged in the sixties. He had even been best man at Ronnie Kray's wedding. It would be a mistake to underestimate him, because Joe Pyle was very shrewd and had nearly always managed to stay one or two steps ahead of the police. In fact, many of the people in the Kray and Richardson firms were behind bars at this time, while Joe Pyle was walking through the streets of Wimbledon.

Pyle's crime empire was based mainly on gambling and protection rackets. Fights would break out in south London pubs, and shortly after this Pyle would speak to the publicans and offer them protection, a classic criminal operation. In the 1980s, police who were becoming increasingly frustrated at their inability to convict him resorted to objecting to his applications for liquor licences. Senior detectives gave evidence to magistrates that he was a major international criminal with Mafia links, but they admitted that they did not have enough evidence to bring charges against him.

The FBI had information that linked him to two of the most important Mafia families in the United States. In 1987, police and customs uncovered a plot to import drugs worth about £5 million. Pyle was charged, but a key witness refused to give evidence against him, and he was acquitted. In 1992 he was convicted of masterminding a multi-million pound drug ring. He was sent to prison for fourteen years after being convicted at his second trial on this indictment. The first trial had been stopped when three jurors claimed they had received death threats if Pyle was found guilty.

When Pyle died in 2007, there was a huge gangland funeral in Sutton. About one thousand people arrived at the church, including well-known names from the underworld and show business. Members of the Kray and Richardson firms were there to pay their last respects to a man who, against the odds, died of natural causes at the age of 69. Pyle wrote a book in the last few years of his life. The title was *Crime Doesn't Pay ... But the Hours Are Good.*

The winter of 1978–79 was a period of bad industrial relations and the notorious Winter of Discontent. There was a series of confrontations between employers and trade unions, and the strike at Ford at the end of 1978 was the most serious of these. The main claims by the unions were for a 25 per cent pay rise and a thirty-five-hour working week. In July 1978 the Government announced that wage increases should not exceed 5 per cent. Two months later, all 57,000 workers in the twenty-three Ford factories in England stopped work.

Many political commentators believe that this strike led to the fall of the Labour Government. The claims made by the Ford workers set the tone for about six months of industrial unrest that included a strike by lorry drivers. Petrol stations ran out of fuel when tanker drivers joined the strike. The industrial unrest carried on into 1979 and seemed to become a giant unstoppable snowball, growing larger by the minute. Ten workers in a car factory in Scotland brought all production to a halt when they refused to move to a new location a few metres away.

Gravediggers were even refusing to bury the dead, and the newspapers hinted at revolution or some sort of new class war. A snowstorm unleashed a strike by the workers who were employed to clear and grit the roads. There were incidents when lorries carrying food for the elderly were attacked and their contents stolen.

In January 1979, *The Guardian* newspaper went against its normal liberal principles and called for the Government to declare a state of emergency. This is something that the Government was considering, but the fact that nine of its members were sponsored by unions made this outcome seem unlikely.

The prime minister, James Callaghan, referred to the strikers' methods as 'free collective vandalism'. One factor that helped the Government was that two powerful groups, the miners and dockers, who had caused so many problems for Edward Heath's administration a few years before, did not go on strike at this time. However, everything that happened made the Government look weaker and weaker as the months went by.

The IRA campaign continued. A bomb went off in the Blackwall tunnel under the Thames. An attempt was made to detonate a bomb at the vast complex of oil-storage containers at Canvey Island in Essex, but the device failed to detonate. There was an Islamic revolution in Iran, and the shah fell from power. It seemed that few people were aware of the importance of what happened in that country, and it now appears that Iran was just the tip of the iceberg.

The saga involving the MOT test certificate finally came to an end when the chief superintendent and superintendent at Chelsea were both brought before a discipline board at Scotland Yard. I was called to give evidence against them. Chief Superintendent Fuller was known to be a very influential Freemason, and someone told me that three high-ranking officers who were all Catholics had been chosen to sit on the discipline board. After being found guilty, Fuller was reduced in rank to superintendent. The superintendent was reprimanded.

In April 1979 I took the promotion exam for inspector for the third time. Working unsocial hours and studying was not easy, and I had been doing this for three years. It had put me under a certain amount of strain, but I knew that it had been just as difficult for my wife and daughters. My social life had been reduced to the minimum, which seemed unfair to the three of them, as they spent a good deal of time keeping quiet when I needed to sleep or to study. In 1979 Amanda was eleven and Emma was seven. It was not an easy situation for any of us, but they had all done their best to help me.

On the day of the exam, as I travelled by underground to Hendon, I was thinking about the situation. It was unlikely that I could face doing it again, and I decided this would be my last crack at it. However, after I read the examination papers, it seemed that there was a glimmer of hope. Apart from one question, they were all on my (long) short list, and I went home feeling reasonably happy about everything.

After I sat the exam, it seemed strange to have spare time to do mundane things such as watching television or visiting friends. While I waited for the result of the examination, there was a general election. It was a victory for the Conservatives, who had a working majority of forty-three, and Margaret Thatcher took office as Britain's first woman prime minister. The new prime minister stood by her promise about the pay rise for the police, and we received it in one large lump.

In many ways this was a good year for me. One of my colleagues at Wimbledon phoned me at home to tell me that I had been successful in the promotion exam. Of course I was pleased with this news, and I felt as though a heavy weight had been lifted from my shoulders.

Effective policing needs very good methods of communication. The ownership of telephones had increased at a rapid rate, and more and more people were making calls to Scotland Yard or to police stations. Year by year the number of calls increased, and a system based on countless thousands of handwritten messages could only be seen as antiquated and inefficient.

The new system being planned was called Computer-Aided Dispatch, usually referred to as CAD, and this would revolutionise the Met's communications; each division would have its own control room equipped with computers.

Here's a simple example of how the system would work. A member of the public dials 999, stating that two men are breaking into a shop.

The officer at IR would type a few words onto the computer. The system would automatically identify the division, the location of the informant, and the call sign of the nearest area car. At the touch of a button, all of this information would appear on the computer screens in the divisional control room, where local officers would take control of the incident.

I was to attend a course for supervisors who would be in charge of the new-style control rooms; it was my first experience of using computers. The plan was to have a sergeant in charge of a control room, which was good, but we would need more sergeants. However, it was going to take a long time before the new system could be rolled out over the whole of the Met.

Shortly after the course, I was pleasantly surprised to receive a posting to the District 'Q' car. There was always a sergeant in charge of a 'Q' car, and each district had a CID crew and a Uniform crew working alternate weeks of day shifts and late shifts. The two cars would cover the period from 10 a.m. until 2 a.m., with the officers working in plain clothes across the whole district. We would have a high degree of freedom in respect of how we worked. There was an element of rivalry between the CID and Uniform crews to see who could make the highest number of crime arrests. The two PCs who had been assigned to work with me, Mick Mountain and Frank McConville, were both very experienced officers.

On my first day, I went to district headquarters at Kingston to be briefed by the detective superintendent. He asked me to see one of the CID officers at Kingston, who needed some help in finding someone. Two weeks earlier there had been a smash-and-grab raid on a shop selling televisions and radios in Wandsworth, and information had been received that the suspect was living in the Kingston area. The CID officer at Kingston believed that he knew where the man lived.

Our first arrest was a percher. We went to the address, spoke to the man there, arrested him, and took him to Kingston police station. Our car was a powerful yellow-coloured Rover that was not easily identifiable as a police vehicle. We had the freedom to go wherever we wanted, within the district and beyond. We kept a log to record the hours we worked and the arrests that we made. On most days we had crime arrests. Some of these came from stops and some from incidents that we were called to. We found it was useful to maintain frequent contact with the CID office at Wimbledon, who supplied us with information about wanted people or suspects.

CID officers at Wimbledon were investigating a series of burglary artifice offences. These crimes are sometimes referred to as distraction burglaries, and in most cases the victims are elderly. The key feature is that the offenders steal property after gaining entry to the victims' houses by some form of trick. There were two men living in Mitcham who had become the main suspects, and I said that we would arrest them.

The two men were brothers, and we found one of them at his home and arrested him. When we saw him, we must have all been thinking the same thing. Mick Mountain, our driver, later made comments comparing him to a brick outbuilding, and this was pretty accurate. The man could only be described as huge, and we realised that if he became violent we would have our hands full. When told that he was under arrest he just grunted, and we put him in the back of the 'Q' car, with me sitting next to him.

As our man was coming quietly, we thought that we would look for the other suspect, who lived in the next street. He was at home as well and turned out to be the same size as his brother. Neither of them caused any problems, but it was difficult fitting the two of them plus me in the back seat of the Rover. Once the doors were closed, I felt as though I were being crushed by the sheer weight of the men on either side of me.

At Wimbledon, the two brothers were questioned by detectives investigating the burglary artifice offences, but both of them refused to answer any questions. The next logical step was to try and see whether witnesses could identify them. Identification parades must be organised by an officer not below the rank of inspector who is not directly involved in the investigation. It was arranged that the inspector on duty that day would organise one in two weeks' time. Identification procedures take up a large amount of police time and manpower, so I volunteered to help with it. The two suspects were released on bail and were to return to the station for the identification parades.

Three or four hours before the identification parades were due to start, I received a phone call telling me that everything was cancelled for the time being. The next day I found out what had happened. One of the two suspects had been at home in Mitcham with his wife, watching television, and his neighbours next door had been having a party that was becoming noisier and noisier. His wife had gone to see the people next door and asked them to keep the noise down, only to receive a large amount of abuse for her trouble.

The giant must have grunted a few words to his wife before setting forth to speak to the people next door. As he walked out of the house, he picked up an axe, as you do. The sequence of events is not totally clear, but about twenty 999 calls were received. The wording was similar in all calls; it referred to a large number of men fighting in the street, with weapons being used, and it sounded like total mayhem. About fifteen mobile units were sent to the location, but when the first officers arrived, they found that everything was mysteriously quiet.

The situation made no sense until one of the officers found a body in a nearby builder's skip. It appeared that the battle had raged for several minutes in the street. The men at the party had picked up weapons and attacked the giant with everything that they had. I guessed that he probably managed to do some damage himself but had been outnumbered, beaten unconscious, and thrown into the skip. He had been taken to hospital seriously injured and was in no fit state to appear on an identification parade the following day.

My work was important to me but it was also important for my wife and me to have a social life. Maureen and I had a long-standing invitation to see some friends one evening when I was due to be on the 'Q' car working a late shift. I asked one of the older, experienced sergeants at Wimbledon to cover me for that night. As luck would have it, the 'Q' car crew found themselves in a bizarre situation that nobody could ever have predicted.

A local company owned a secure unit in an industrial estate in Kingston, where they kept a large amount of copper and other valuable metals. In addition to a high security fence around it, they employed a security guard at night, who spent most of his time sitting in a hut with a phone so that he could ring for help if needed. There was only one gate that gave access to the unit, and this had an alarm system.

The night security guard was about twenty years of age and nervous. A couple of months earlier he had spotted two men trying to cut their way into the secure area. He had dialled 999, and the two men had been arrested. After the two men were released on bail they'd threatened him, saying that they would kill him if he gave evidence against them. It appears that he did not report the threats to police.

The security man had found a place where he could climb over the fence and had started to make trips to a local pub. He would go off for a drink and then return by the same method. His timing on this occasion could not have been worse. As the 'Q' car cruised along slowly through the industrial estate, the headlights picked up the shape of a man on the security fence. The young security man had a quick look at the three men in the yellow-coloured car and decided that his worst fears were about to be realised. He dropped to the ground and sprinted away at high speed. The 'Q' car driver, Mick Mountain, slammed the brakes on and ran after the fleeing figure. After him went Frank McConville, the radio operator, followed by the sergeant.

Mick Mountain was a man in his thirties who had been an amateur boxing champion and was very fit. He started to gain on the 'suspect', who came out of the industrial estate and ran along a street with terraced houses on either side. Halfway along the street there was an elderly man sitting on a chair in his front garden smoking a pipe. The front door to his house was open. Sheer terror must have been gripping the security man by this time, for he sprinted past the elderly man and into the house. The man with the pipe must have been totally shocked when four men ran past him and into his house in rapid succession.

The man being pursued ran right through the house, opened a door at the back, and ran into the small garden. As he did so, he slammed the door behind him. Mick's speed and momentum meant that he was unable to prevent himself hitting the door, and his arm smashed through the glass panel. The broken glass sliced open his arm, and there was blood everywhere. The second running police officer, Frank McConville, thought at first that Mick Mountain had been stabbed.

The security man was trapped in the garden and arrested by Frank McConville. An ambulance was called and Mick Mountain taken to hospital. It must have been about this point that the sergeant had time to regret his agreement to cover the 'Q' car for me. He said that it had taken some time to sort out exactly what had happened.

To drive a 'Q' car or a Flying Squad car you have to be a Class One, the top echelon of advanced police drivers, and Mick Mountain, our Class One, was going to be out of action for some time. Mick Mountain eventually returned to work and went on to become the Met's longest serving officer. We needed a new driver, and Vic Gambie, a very experienced PC who had previously worked on the Flying Squad as a driver, took over for our last two weeks.

My time on the 'Q' car came to an end, and a few days later my family and I were off to Canada. The weather was hot as it had been on our first visit and it was fun for our daughters to go swimming or paddling in some of the many lakes that we visited. My mother had a friend, a woman who came from Lancashire and she worked as a secretary for the superintendent in charge of the Barrie District of the Ontario Provincial Police. The province of Ontario is at least four times the size of the UK, and the OPP is responsible for all of it, with the exception of Toronto and some other cities that have their own forces. I met George Miller, an inspector in the OPP who lived in Barrie and worked at OPP headquarters. He invited me to visit their HQ, which was then in Toronto, close to the Lake Ontario waterfront.

He picked me up at 7 a.m., and we drove into Toronto. I had expected heavy traffic, but the road system was very good, and we reached the OPP headquarters by eight o'clock. He introduced me to several police officers, who told me about the work that they did. One of them was an Englishman, the superintendent in charge of the training department. Much of the training was similar to police training in the UK, but one aspect that was different was the training of Native Canadians, often called Indians, to work as police officers on reservations.

There are several tribes in Ontario, including the Cree and Ojibwa, with a number of native police forces under the umbrella of the OPP. These officers are responsible for the day-to-day policing of their own communities and can call on the OPP for assistance if they need to.

Dealing with missing-person enquiries took on a whole new meaning for me when I considered the vast areas of the 'north country'. People who want to get away from the stress and strain of modern life can hire a float plane, and the pilot will drop them off on a lake in the middle of nowhere. Anyone who does this can arrange for the pilot to pick them up at an agreed time and place, but in the meantime they are on their own in the wilderness.

A lot of people like to do this, and it is possible to spend two weeks or more in northern Ontario without seeing another human being. If one of these modern-day adventurers is reported missing, it can cause the OPP a lot of trouble. A police search party has to be flown into the area with their equipment, and because of the distances involved, they may be left on their own for a week or two. Again, because of the huge areas involved, police radios do not always work.

The OPP is proud of its forensic science laboratory which must be one of the best in the world. One piece of equipment I looked at was a scanner that was used for finding marks at the scenes of serious crimes. Many crimes are solved when fingerprints or other marks are found and identified, and this is usually done by the human eye. However, there are cases when the human eye cannot see marks that are there, even with magnification.

Their scanner uses nuclear technology to bombard a surface in order to find marks that would normally be invisible. The OPP had been investigating a case where a child had been murdered. An unusual feature of this crime was that the naked body of the victim had been washed following the attack, and this had apparently destroyed all chances of finding any useful forensic evidence. In a secret operation, the body of the child had been brought into the laboratory early on a quiet Sunday morning. Using the atomic scanner, the body had been scanned and a thumbprint found. This resulted in the murderer being arrested and convicted.

As we returned from Canada, we heard the news that Lord Mountbatten and members of his family had been killed by an IRA bomb while sailing off the Irish coast. The news that day was destined to become even worse. An attack on the army at Warrenpoint, on the border with the Irish Republic, had left eighteen soldiers dead and several others seriously wounded. It was the highest number of deaths suffered by the army in Northern Ireland. On holiday in Canada, it was almost possible to forget that there was a major terrorist campaign going on in Britain.

At this time, Wimbledon Football Club was busy fighting its way up the football ladder, league by league. When they had an away game at Aldershot, there was a serious disturbance involving the fans. Hampshire police asked us to arrest several named individuals living in Wimbledon.

When nine Wimbledon fans were arrested, I was the station officer and found myself busy compiling custody records for them. Hampshire police collected all nine, and they were taken to Aldershot.

Two weeks later, during our week of night duty, there were only two sergeants on duty: Brian Burton and me. We took it in turns to be station officer, but Brian had been invited to a wedding on the Saturday and asked to take the night off. Going down to two sergeants was seen as the bare minimum, and the inspector asked me whether I would be happy to be the only sergeant on duty on a Saturday night. There was no problem as far as I was concerned. One of our PCs was awaiting promotion, and the inspector decided to make him an acting sergeant for that night.

At about eleven thirty, there was a disturbance at Morden Underground Station, the southern end of the Northern Line. Two rival gangs of young people, mainly teenagers, bumped into each other near the tube station. The result was that one group ran into the underground station, pursued by the other group, which was much larger. As they charged through the station, they knocked over an 80-year-old woman, who struck her head and suffered a fractured skull.

We received two or three 999 calls, and within a few minutes there were officers at the tube station. A train was about to leave, but the driver was asked to hold it at the station. Initially there was some concern that the youths might take advantage of the fact that police were outnumbered and charge out of the station using the same method that they had used to enter. However, one of the first police officers to arrive was Ray Guy, an experienced dog handler, and he positioned himself on the stairs with his dog. None of the troublemakers seemed happy to try and run past the police dog.

All the youths involved in the incident were arrested in batches and transported to the police station. We knew it was going to be busy in the station but did not realise at first how busy. A quick count of the arrests coming in from Morden brought the total to twenty-eight and included five juveniles. The inspector, the acting sergeant, and I had a quick meeting and then the three of us started writing. It was best to deal with the juveniles first, and messages were sent to their parents asking them to come to the station.

There were three girls involved, and they were put in a cell together while the other cells were probably crammed with six or seven apiece. Three of our patrolling officers were called in to act as gaolers, and within a few minutes virtually every Wimbledon officer was involved in what had now become a paperwork battle. I stopped for a few minutes to eat my sandwiches, but apart from that I worked towards one thing: trying to complete the mountain of paperwork in front of me. My first job was to make sure that all the custody records had been completed. It was important to ensure that the arresting officers interviewed each person and to check that the questions and answers were recorded. The three gaolers were busy fingerprinting, photographing, and running CRO checks.

The inspector and I agreed that we were talking about a joint offence of threatening behaviour under the Public Order Act. Three of the accused were also in possession of offensive weapons. We realised that we had an aggravating factor in the injured woman; if she were to die, the matter would have to be treated as a suspected homicide. We worked on through the night and into the morning. All the young people were charged and bailed to appear at magistrates' court in two weeks' time, and I decided it would be best to take the case to court myself. By nine in the morning we had completed the paperwork, and I placed it in my correspondence locker.

The inspector who was duty officer that morning had previously seen me writing up the records for the Wimbledon football fans who had been arrested. He joked and suggested that I was obviously trying to become a specialist in dealing with mass arrests.

'With a bit of luck, never again,' I said.

A few days later the injured woman was discharged from hospital, and I went to see her. She had only a vague memory of what had happened, but she was adamant that she did not want to go to court and give evidence. I took a witness statement from her to that effect. After that, it was necessary to send a report to our solicitors' branch with details of the case, asking their opinion on whether police should be legally represented. Their advice was for me to take it to court and to have all the defendants bound over. When the day came, one of my defendants failed to appear, and a warrant was issued. The other twenty-seven were all bound over. This was a practical way of dealing with the case, although I felt that it was as an easy way out for the defendants.

The chief inspector (ops) decided to give me the rank of acting inspector for several weeks in order to give me experience as duty officer. I still wore my sergeant's uniform but received an 'acting up' allowance for taking on the job of duty officer.

Customs officers were involved in a major investigation into a number of people who were suspected of smuggling drugs into the UK from the Far East. Some Met officers had come under suspicion. A highly secret surveillance operation had been set up and one of the targets was a police officer based at Wimbledon. When the officer was arrested, it sent shock waves through the Met.

The officer was working in plain-clothes at the time of his arrest and all police officers working in plain-clothes have to keep a diary. In this case, the diary entries would be of interest to the investigators. For example, an entry might state that he was in Kingston on a certain date – but if customs officers had him under surveillance in Singapore that day, the suspected officer had a problem. It is not easy for anyone to be in two continents at the same time.

The officer went on trial at the Old Bailey and was acquitted. He remained suspended for many months while an internal enquiry took place into a number of disciplinary matters. This led to his dismissal.

The whiff of scandal lingered on the division when an allegation of corruption was made against two Wimbledon CID officers. There was an investigation which resulted in both officers being charged. The case went to a magistrates' court in south London, and proceedings were held to have them committed for trial at the crown court. However, magistrates held that there was not enough evidence to justify sending them for trial. Both of them later found themselves facing disciplinary charges that would lead to their dismissal.

At Christmas I was duty officer covering the division for night duty. When I called in at Mitcham police station on Christmas Day at 3 a.m., one of the sergeants thrust a glass of whiskey into my hand.

'Merry Christmas,' he said.

The seventies were coming to an end.

23

The years went by, and I lost touch with most of the officers I had worked with in Hampshire. Gathering information for this book gave me the opportunity to make contact with two of my classmates from Sandgate: Mick Lyons and Peter Spencer. During the seventies, Peter Spencer worked on Hampshire's South East Area drugs squad, and this led to his involvement in Operation Julie. The story behind this famous police investigation started in November 1974 and went on into 1978.

Nothing would have happened without the determination of Detective Inspector Dick Lee, the head of the Thames Valley Police drug squad. Although he had no specific information, Lee began to suspect that LSD was being produced in large amounts in the UK, but this went against the official view that the use of LSD was restricted to a small number of people in the country. Lee started to receive many small bits of information that made him think that this could not be true. A picture was starting to emerge that LSD trafficking was on a much bigger scale than anyone had thought possible. It was well organised, and there were links all over the UK. Dick Lee knew that a large police operation was necessary to unravel it all, but he soon came up against many problems. He had to deal with bureaucracy, inter-force rivalry, and apathy from some high-ranking police officers.

However, eventually Lee managed to obtain authority for a task force to be set up, with twenty-eight officers drawn from eleven forces, including two DCs from Hampshire: Steve Bentley and Peter Spencer. Setting up a large drug squad for a task of this nature was something new to the UK and even after it had been established Dick Lee would still have to deal with a number of bureaucratic problems in order for the squad to function effectively.

Peter Spencer worked undercover during this operation, soon earning the nickname 'the bionic man'. This was due to his ability to work very long hours and get by with only four hours' sleep. Over a period of about two years, the Operation Julie officers built up a picture of the organisation that they were up against. Many of the people in it were very intelligent and well educated. Some of them produced the LSD, others made it into tablets, and there were others who distributed it to various locations, such as Jersey or Birmingham. The criminals involved had links to the United States, Germany, Holland, Australia, and Israel. It has been estimated that they produced at least 50 per cent and perhaps as much as 95 per cent of the world's LSD.

In March 1977 the arrests started. More than eight hundred officers took part, and in the initial wave of raids, 120 suspects were arrested. Officers seized LSD with a street value of £100 million, along with large amounts of cash. Eventually, the Operation Julie suspects stood trial, and twenty-six people were convicted on a number of charges. The ringleaders would receive sentences that ranged from eight to thirteen years' imprisonment.

There was a dark side to all of this. Although they were delighted with what they had achieved, Dick Lee and others would soon face disenchantment when the operation came to an end. Operation Julie had been functioning as what could only be described as a national drug squad for about two years. During this time, a huge amount of information had been gathered on many people in organised crime and the drugs business in a number of countries.

Dick Lee wanted to follow up these leads but was forbidden to do so by the officer who had been appointed as executive commander of the squad. Lee also believed that this would be a good time to set up a national drugs agency. His argument was that a national squad could identify problems when they arose and react swiftly to deal with them, as Operation Julie had shown. However, it seems that high-ranking officers within the police had other ideas. The Operation Julie team was disbanded, and its officers returned to their own forces. Dick Lee was promoted to chief inspector in the Uniform Branch and given a job which he described as 'supervising traffic wardens'. Within months, Dick Lee and five of the men in his team had resigned from the police service.

Shortly after his work on Operation Julie, Peter Spencer was promoted to detective sergeant and worked on another major drugs investigation, Operation Wrecker. During 1978 there were rumours circulating in Hampshire of a plan to import a very large amount of cannabis. It was also rumoured that the people who were financing this drug smuggling were top-level London criminals.

The town of Fareham is on the coast between Portsmouth and Southampton. A drugs squad officer spotted a shipping container inside a car repair garage in Fareham that was owned by a man named Eddie Watkins. Surveillance was carried out, and it soon became clear that work was being done to fit the container with a false bottom. It was also known that Watkins had close connections with organised crime in London. Some of his associates were under observation near Fareham Creek, where they were seen practising their shooting skills with Stirling sub-machine guns.

This is what led to Operation Wrecker, a joint investigation involving Hampshire drugs squad officers working with the Regional Crime Squad and HMRC. It was believed that the container would be used to import a large quantity of drugs, and RCS officers followed it when it was taken to a port on the east coast of England.

The container went to Pakistan with a legitimate cargo of domestic goods, and for several months nobody knew where it was. However, Customs officers were able to identify the container when it arrived in Felixstowe from Rotterdam in October 1979. It contained a consignment of shoes that were on their way to a major British supermarket chain.

A mobile surveillance team of police and customs officers kept watch around the clock on the container as soon as it was taken off the ship. The consignment of shoes was removed by a freight company. The officers kept watch until Eddie Watkins arrived with a lorry and drove away with the container. They followed Watkins from the port as he drove to a farm in Kent, where one of the suspects, Billy Cullen, had a scrap-metal yard. Cullen was later arrested by Peter Spencer. The officers believed that Watkins planned to cut open the container there. Professional criminals are very aware of police surveillance methods, and such operations are extremely difficult, especially when they go on for a long time. There was now growing concern that Watkins realised that he was under surveillance.

He then started driving towards London but parked and spent the night in his lorry. During the morning, he drove into London but stopped several times to use public phone boxes. There were signs that he was becoming more and more agitated. Intelligence suggested that Watkins and his associates had access to firearms, and several of the RCS officers involved in this operation were armed. However, they did not receive authorisation to carry firearms when they were inside the Metropolitan Police District.

One of Peter Spencer's colleagues from the drugs squad was DS John Harvey, who was working with a customs officer, Peter Bennett. Watkins drove his lorry into the East End, and when he reached Commercial Road he jumped out of the lorry and used a phone box to make another phone call. He then walked to a nearby bus stop. This was the point when the senior officers controlling this operation needed to make a quick decision.

Orders went out to the surveillance team that Watkins had to be arrested and the container seized. John Harvey and Peter Bennett were the nearest officers to the suspect, and there was an RCS officer, DS John Mosely, available to back them up. None of the officers were armed. Harvey and Bennett approached Watkins. Harvey told him that he was under arrest and made a move to handcuff him.

Watkins backed away from them. He was wearing a parka and had both hands in the coat pockets. Suddenly, there was the sound of a firearm being discharged, and Peter Bennett fell to the ground. Watkins had fired a 9mm pistol that had been concealed in a pocket of his parka, and he then ran off along Commercial Road. John Harvey did not realise that Peter Bennett had been mortally wounded and gave chase.

After running about 100 metres, Harvey caught up with Watkins and brought him down with a rugby tackle. During the struggle, Watkins turned his gun on Harvey and fired. The bullet grazed his own stomach, causing a slight wound, and went through John Harvey's coat. Watkins tried to fire again, but the gun jammed. As John Harvey was struggling with Watkins, John Mosely reached the scene and managed to take the gun away from him.

Peter Bennett was taken to hospital but died of his injuries. Watkins was later charged with the murder of Peter Bennett and the attempted murder of John Harvey. His container was searched and over one ton of cannabis was found inside it. Several people were arrested and charged with conspiracy to contravene the Drugs Act.

At Winchester Crown Court, Watkins was found guilty of the charges against him and was sent to prison for a minimum of twenty-five years. He died in prison a few years later. The other people who were convicted received prison sentences that ranged from two to twelve years. Peter Bennett was posthumously awarded the Queen's Gallantry Medal. John Harvey and John Mosely were both awarded the Queen's Gallantry Medal personally by the Queen.

In January 1980, Robert Mugabe returned from exile to Rhodesia, and everyone knew that this would be followed by a general election. There seemed little doubt that if there were a free election, Mugabe's party would win. A number of British police officers went to Rhodesia to cover the planned elections in a country that would soon be known as Zimbabwe.

Naturally my thoughts were on my forthcoming promotion and the six-week pre-promotion course that started that month. At Hendon there were about fifteen of us, all from different backgrounds in the Met. One aim of the course was to broaden our horizons, and we had the opportunity to meet and sometimes work alongside people from organisations outside the police service, such as social workers.

My promotion was scheduled for June, so I returned to Wimbledon. While on night duty, I was patrolling with John Holden, one of the most experienced PCs at Wimbledon, when we received a call to a block of private flats where a young woman had been attacked. The call had been made by a man in one of the flats, and he explained that the victim had banged on his front door, injured and suffering from severe shock.

There are times when something makes you speechless, when you just stop and stare. The woman's nose was missing, and it stopped us in our tracks for a moment or two. John Holden put up an urgent call for an ambulance, and I asked her if she had any idea where her attacker might be. 'Next door,' she said.

'He lives next door,' she repeated. John Holden and I exchanged glances. We had not expected that answer. It sounded too easy, but I pointed at the door to the flat next door, and she nodded. My knock on the door was answered by a smartly dressed young man, and both of us must have been thinking the same thing: Mr Respectable. He did not look like someone who had done something like this. Maybe the victim was wrong, I thought. She is in shock and gave us the wrong address.

I told him that we had been called to a serious assault on a young woman, and he made no attempt to deny it. All he said was, 'I don't know why I did it.' He was arrested and taken to the station. The attacker was a quiet-spoken, well-educated man with a good job, who had never been in trouble before. He had met the victim through a dating column in a well-known magazine. Their first and last meeting had taken place that evening, and he had asked her to return to his flat for coffee. Initially she had not wanted to go there, but he had assured her of his good intentions. However, at some point he had launched into a savage attack on her and tried to tie her up.

I found the severed nose, placed it inside a clean piece of paper, and handed it to one of my PCs, who went with the victim in the ambulance. It seemed the only thing that I could do, but I was told later that the hospital would not be able to use it and they would have to carry out plastic surgery to rebuild the woman's nose. The man who attacked her was sentenced to life imprisonment.

In April 1980, the Met Police was suddenly faced with one of the most dramatic stories in its history, when six armed terrorists seized the Iranian embassy. They overpowered PC Trevor Lock of the Diplomatic Protection Group, who was on duty there, and they held him hostage, together with twenty-five other people within the embassy. Trevor Lock was an experienced officer who appeared to remain calm and professional throughout the ordeal. He had a police firearm that was hidden from view; the terrorists never found it because they did not search him. Within a short time, armed police with rifles had taken up hastily prepared positions at strategic points all around the embassy.

The situation inside the embassy was complicated by the public-order situation in the surrounding streets. A group of people who were supporters of Khomeini, the Iranian religious leader, arrived at the embassy to demonstrate in favour of the Iranian regime, where they were confronted by another group, who were opposed to Khomeini. Stuck in the middle, the police were doing their best to keep them apart. Each day, there were large numbers of people chanting and waving placards. It must have been the commissioner's worst nightmare suddenly becoming reality.

Met officers who were trained negotiators, were in constant communication with the terrorists, who were from an Arab ethnic group living in the south of Iran. When speaking to Trevor Lock, the negotiators used a number of phrases that were 'police speak', as they guessed rightly that the Arab terrorists were unlikely to understand the complete meaning of these phrases. The terrorists made several demands. The main one was the release of ninety political prisoners being held in Iran. They also wanted an aircraft so that they could fly themselves and their hostages out of the UK.

It was clear that these demands were never going to be met. On the sixth day of the siege, fatigue and tension had taken their toll on everyone involved. The terrorists were becoming increasingly frustrated as they started to realise that their demands were not likely to be granted. They murdered one of the Iranian hostages.

The body of the dead man, Abbas Lavasani, was pushed out of the front door. This was a tragic development and altered the whole situation at the embassy. Prime Minister Margaret Thatcher decided that the operation should be handed over to the army, and a short while later television programmes were interrupted and viewers saw live pictures of the SAS attacking the embassy. Some of the most dramatic live footage ever filmed suddenly appeared on television screens throughout the UK and the world. A number of television viewers complained, especially the ones tuned in to BBC One who were watching a western starring John Wayne.

At 7.23 p.m., an explosive charge was lowered into the stairwell of the embassy from a skylight. The explosion and confusion that followed was the signal for the SAS to storm the embassy. Eight soldiers abseiled down ropes from the roof at the rear of the building, but there was a problem when one of them became entangled in his rope. The others could not use their explosive charges for fear of hitting him, but they managed to smash their way in and used stun grenades inside the building. At the same time, another SAS team used explosive charges to blow in the windows at the front of the embassy. The room at the front caught fire, and people watching television saw one of the hostages being hauled to safety over a neighbouring balcony.

At this point, Trevor Lock was on his own with Salim, the leader of the terrorist group. An SAS man appeared at the window, and Trevor Lock did a rugby tackle on Salim to prevent him firing his weapon at the soldier. The SAS man shouted at Trevor to get clear and then shot Salim. In the general panic and confusion, the gunmen on the second floor opened fire on the male hostages, killing one and wounding two others. With the exception of one, all the terrorists were killed within a few minutes. The building was on fire, and the hostages were tossed down the stairs from soldier to soldier.

One of the PCs from Wimbledon who was involved in the operation told me that all the hostages who were rescued were kept together in a garden at the rear. Terrorist Number 6 was among them, trying to pose as a hostage, when the genuine hostages pointed him out to police. My Wimbledon officer thought that the SAS men seemed disappointed that one of the terrorists was still alive and I had an image in my head of the police and SAS trying to pull him in opposite directions. But he lived long enough to face trial at the Old Bailey and be sent to prison for a long time.

In May 1980, there was news of my promotion and transfer to 'A' District. Reporting to the district HQ at Cannon Row seemed to me like a repeat performance of what had happened ten years before. I had a meeting with the commander, during which my main concern was what division he was planning to send me to.

Gerald Road was the division that covered Belgravia and part of Knightsbridge, an affluent part of London with a large number of embassies. As I had worked on 'A' District as a PC, I had a good knowledge of the three divisions. Cannon Row was not a station that appealed to me. Rochester Row was the one I would have preferred, as it had a bit of everything. There were some streets where it cost a fortune to buy a house, but there were large council estates, businesses, and a number of important Government buildings.

The commander decided that he wanted me at Rochester Row. I had some slight concerns about going back to a station where I had worked as recently as eight years before. However, I did consider that 'Roch' was the best of the bunch. I walked to Rochester Row and went to see Ray Heath in the administration office. He grinned when he saw me. 'No escape,' he said, laughing.

Ray Heath introduced me to the chief superintendent. We spent some time in conversation, and he told me that he had a relief that had not had a regular inspector in charge for some time. He said that they were on night duty that week, and he wanted me to join them the following night. The next day I made a point of arriving about an hour early, so I could introduce myself to the inspector who was the duty officer on late turn.

It felt strange to be walking into the parade room shortly before ten o'clock and seeing the night duty gathered there – a sergeant and ten PCs, all of them probably wondering what sort of inspector they were going to be stuck with. I carried out an inspection of the PCs, and they headed towards their beats. After chatting to the sergeants at the station, I asked one of the PCs to drive me around the division. It was interesting to see how little everything had changed. There were some new building developments, especially in Victoria Street, but Alfa Romeo Division looked much the same as it had in 1972.

Geoff Woolgar, the PC who was driving, had about three years' service and told me that he was keen to join the CID. After driving for about an hour, we found ourselves in Vauxhall Bridge Road. There was a man walking along the footway, and I glanced at him as we drove past. It was one of those moments when something instinctive clicked in.

'Do you want an arrest?' I asked.

Geoff Woolgar looked at me with some surprise when I pointed at the man.

'Drugs,' I said. 'He's got drugs on him.'

Geoff turned the car around, and we stopped the man. Geoff searched him and found that he had a small plastic container containing heroin. Five minutes later, we were in the charge room. Each police station had a book to record details of people who were stopped in the street. If a stop resulted in an arrest, it was written in red ink. I was pleased that we could write up a red-ink stop on my first night as an inspector at Rochester Row.

On my second night, one of my officers was called to a sudden death and asked me to come to the scene. There were circumstances that made it a little unusual, and I decided that it should be treated as suspicious. I was the duty officer, it was the middle of the night, and the decision was mine to make. There was nothing that we could do at that time, but an officer was given the task of guarding the scene, and it pleased me that all the PCs involved dealt with everything in a professional manner.

I passed the enquiry on to the CID to follow up later that day. In many sudden-death cases like this, after witnesses are seen and there is a post mortem, it becomes clear that the death is not suspicious. That is what happened in this case. Being aware of several murder cases that had been handled badly in the initial stages, my instinct was always to treat sudden-death cases very carefully. When our week of night duty came to an end, I was able to meet many of the senior officers and administrative personnel who worked on the division.

The canteen was on the first floor, and it was open from 8 a.m. until 8 p.m. every day except Sundays. Next door was the senior officers' dining room, which anyone holding the rank of inspector or above was entitled to use. I met the chief inspector (ops), Ray Purnell, who had won the George Medal for his actions during the operation when the IRA men were arrested at Balcombe Street.

The key role of the chief inspector (ops) was overseeing the duties of inspectors and sergeants. Another important role was ensuring that public order events were dealt with correctly. There were important buildings on the division, including the Home Office, Department of Trade, Passport Office, and Scotland Yard. Because of their status, some buildings would always attract people with particular concerns, and small demonstrations frequently occurred on the division, often without any advance warning.

All day-to-day operational decisions were in the hands of the duty officers, the relief inspectors. From time to time, there might be exceptional circumstances when inspectors would need to go higher up the chain of command, but this was rare. The next few months gave me the opportunity to ascertain the strengths and weaknesses of my sergeants and constables. In terms of the age of its PCs, Rochester Row was a young division. At full strength, I had five sergeants and twenty-five PCs, and this included at least seven or eight probationers.

Adjoining the police station was a building that had once been a court. This was where Scotland Yard's cheque fraud squad was based, and the building had its own cell block. It was often used for holding suspected terrorists, and more than a few IRA suspects had been held there. Other countries in Europe were facing their own terrorist campaigns from left-wing and right-wing groups. Italy was going through a phase in its history known as *Anni di piombo* – Years of Lead. In August 1980, Italy suffered one of the worst terrorist attacks in modern times, the bombing of Bologna railway station. It resulted in 85 deaths and 200 injuries.

A few months after my arrival at Rochester Row, I was in the duty officer's car with one of my sergeants. We heard a radio call from a Special Branch unit calling for assistance to stop a car that they were following through central London. The driver of the car was an Italian terrorist wanted for murder in Italy. Two area cars were called in to help halt the vehicle, and we listened to the messages as they came over the air. Eventually the car was stopped, and the man was arrested.

'Good,' I said. It had slipped my mind, but my sergeant reminded me that the Italian would probably be coming to Rochester Row. He was wanted for the murder of a police officer in Italy. The information we had was that he had forced a policeman to kneel down on a street and then shot him in the back of the head. The wanted man arrived at the station a few minutes later and I wrote up the custody records for him. He was eventually extradited to Italy.

Nearly all of my time was taken up with the day-to-day management of the relief. This included dealing with the appraisal, training, and welfare aspects that cropped up every day. My sergeants were good supervisors, but all were relatively inexperienced. Two or three came to our relief from the CID on the interchange system. 'Interchange' meant that all detective constables who were promoted to sergeant spent at least twelve months in the Uniform Branch. Their expertise was very useful when we had crime arrests.

As with any team of police officers, my relief was a mixed bunch. There were two or three older PCs who were dependable but did not always show a great deal of enthusiasm. If called to an incident, they would deal with it, but they did not show much initiative or effort when it came to catching criminals or anything else.

There was another group of PCs who worked hard and were continually making good crime arrests, and there were a number of others that I would describe as inexperienced men and women who were doing their best. We had a good number of probationers and they tended to be productive because their work was under continual review by their sergeants. Records were kept of all the work that they did, much of which was traffic process.

From my perspective as an inspector, a major problem was that the system did not encourage officers to work hard. To me, it seemed that once police officers completed their period of probation, they could cruise along for the rest of their service and do very little. This was not true if they wanted to be promoted or transferred to a specialist branch, but there were many without any particular ambition. At any police station there are likely to be a small number of officers who cruise along doing the bare minimum in terms of work.

All police officers were appraised by their line managers each year and assessments made covering a number of qualities and skills, such as vitality, professional ability, written work, oral expression, detective ability, judgement, and leadership. Each quality or skill was given a grade, ranging from outstanding to unsatisfactory.

My opinion was that officers often received higher grades than they deserved. The two bottom grades were 'not entirely satisfactory' and 'unsatisfactory'. At least three of my PCs should have received some of these low grades in relation to some of their qualities – and they received them from me.

However, a previous inspector had taken a different path and awarded a large number of officers with grades that described them as 'outstanding' and 'very good'. I was quite shocked, as these 'outstanding' officers included at least two who always did the bare minimum of police work. The inspector concerned may have thought that this would improve the morale of the relief, but the problem was that the comments were not accurate. I believed that personnel reports should always be as balanced and accurate as possible. Some of my officers seemed to be very resentful when they saw what I had written about them.

One morning I spent a few minutes talking to the detective inspector about the system of appraisals, and he laughed. 'Everyone in the CID is a brilliant detective,' he said. 'You just have to read their appraisals – they say so!'

There were five or six young officers on the relief who were all good workers and who had applied for specialist posts. One had been accepted to join the Mounted Branch. There were two or three waiting to go to the CID and one who was going to Special Branch. Within six months or so of my arrival at Rochester Row, we started to lose them. In a period of a few weeks, five of our best officers left. It was damaging to the team and would make my job more difficult.

In January 1981 a house fire in Deptford, South London, killed thirteen people attending a birthday party, all of whom were black. This tragic incident became an issue that increased tensions within the black community, where many believed that the fatal fire had been caused by a racial attack. During the early part of the investigation there was the suggestion that a petrol bomb had been thrown into the house.

A lengthy police investigation followed, aimed at establishing whether the fire had been started by accident or arson. However, despite all the enquiries and forensic work that was done, the result was unsatisfactory; there was no compelling evidence to reach a conclusion either way.

This did not prevent some community leaders announcing that they knew it was a racist attack and that the Met had deliberately covered up the facts. Two months later, a protest march was organised in support of the Deptford fire victims. A number of people taking part in the march attacked and looted shops in Fleet Street. The symbolic significance of the fire went far beyond the actual tragedy. Black people were angered by their perception of what they saw as lack of interest shown by the police, the Government, and the press.

The investigation was hampered by conflicting stories told by some witnesses. Two young men who were at the house gave witness statements to police stating that the fire had broken out inside the house but later said that police officers had forced them to say this. In 1981 the first inquest resulted in an open verdict. The Met started a second investigation in 1997. Using the most recent forensic techniques, it showed that the most likely place where the fire started was in an armchair next to a television set in one of the rooms. In a second inquest in 2004, the coroner pointed at the forensic evidence available and a second open verdict was recorded.

In April 1981, we arranged a family party at our home in New Malden for the Saturday night of my long weekend. Our daughters were now aged thirteen and nine, and we had invited about twenty guests. Our television and radio were switched off, and therefore we were blissfully unaware of what was happening in the outside world.

While our family party was in full swing, there was trouble in Brixton. Two police officers arrived at an incident where a young black man had been stabbed by another black youth. One of the officers made a call on his radio asking for an ambulance. A crowd of young men gathered at the scene of the stabbing. The two policemen were giving first aid to the injured youth in the face of a hostile crowd who believed that the police were about to arrest him. People at the scene overpowered the two police officers and 'rescued' the injured youth, whether he wanted to be rescued or not, it seems. Other youths started throwing bricks and bottles at the two officers, and police who came to their assistance were attacked. The disturbance went on for over an hour, during which six people were arrested and six officers injured.

Within the next few hours, rumours started to circulate around Brixton. The first story was that police officers had attacked and seriously injured a young black man and refused him first aid or any medical treatment. These rumours started to escalate quickly, and it was soon being reported that not only had the police beaten up a young black man but he had died of his injuries. The Brixton riots were about to start.

The background to all of this was complicated. The relationship between the police and the black community in Brixton had never been particularly good. A major concern of the Met for some time had been the large numbers of street robberies committed by young black men in Brixton. A major operation was launched in Brixton to tackle this problem, and this was given the name Operation Swamp. Not surprisingly, this resulted in large numbers of black men being stopped and searched – and this increased the level of tension.

While our family party ran its course, we had no knowledge of what was happening in Brixton. The first we knew that anything was going on was when my peaceful Sunday morning was disturbed by someone ringing our front doorbell. Standing at the door was a policeman from our local division of Kingston.

'Are you Inspector Ramsay?' he asked. 'I have a message for you, sir. We have had a phone call from your division. They want you to go to Rochester Row as soon as possible.'

He must have wondered why I was standing there looking at him with a puzzled expression on my face. It suddenly went through my head that something terrible had happened at Roch, and I could only look blankly at him, wondering what had happened.

'Brixton,' said the PC as though that would take care of any question that he might be asked. However, all I could say was, 'Brixton … what's happening?'

The PC was starting to look at me strangely. He must have wondered why he was talking to the only police officer in the country who did not know what was going on in south London.

'Brixton,' he said again, with some emphasis on the word. 'There are serious riots in Brixton.'

Initially, the fast-moving events of Saturday night had taken the Met by surprise, but the Public Order Branch at CO had started organising their response to the disorder. When serious rioting started, divisions were ordered to put together serials at short notice and send them to Brixton. The units that were deployed in Brixton on the Saturday night faced one of the worst riots in this country's history, and a large number of officers were injured.

On my arrival at Alfa Romeo, I noticed a police bus parked outside the station. My serial contained a mixture of police officers from Gerald Road and Rochester Row. No female officers had been included. We set off towards Brixton, stopping at Battersea to pick up another serial. The inspector in charge of the Battersea contingent was able to tell me something about the rioting, which he had picked up from officers who had been to Brixton the previous night. A radio message directed me to take my serial to Brixton police station, and on the way we dropped the Battersea serial off at their location – known in public-order jargon as 'ground assigned'.

Looking around the area that was ground assigned for the Battersea serial, I was shocked. It could only be described as a war zone. Most of the surrounding buildings had been set on fire the previous night, and the smell of smoke hung in the air. There was a feeling of unreality about the situation. As we headed towards the police station we saw family groups of black people on their way to church, all dressed in their Sunday best.

At Brixton police station I found the superintendent who was in charge of our sector. He told me that he wanted my serial to guard the police station, and within a few minutes my officers were positioned around the outside of the building. I also met the senior officer who was second in command of our sector. It turned out to be Chief Inspector Beaton GM, who had won his medal protecting Princess Anne in the Mall a few years earlier.

Brixton had set up its own control room. I later discovered that Prime Minister Margaret Thatcher had turned up there suddenly during the Saturday night. At one point, one of the phones had been ringing, with nobody available to answer it, so Mrs Thatcher had decided to answer it. 'Prime Minister speaking, may I help you?'

The superintendent who told me the story had been sitting nearby, speaking on the phone, when he realised what was happening. He told me that he had stopped speaking and froze for a moment. It was not so much that the prime minister was answering the phone but more a case of wondering what comments would be made by the police officer on the other end of the line. 'Don't be a silly bitch – this is important. I need to speak to Superintendent Smith urgently.'

No, this did not happen. The officer making the call must have sensed that it really was Margaret Thatcher and addressed her as Prime Minister. I am not sure what he would tell his colleagues later. 'It must be a really bad situation in Brixton. The prime minster is covering the phones in the control room.'

It was logical to divide my serial into two halves comprising of one sergeant and ten PCs. I then asked the sergeants to divide PCs into pairs. I stressed that, whatever happened and whatever they were doing, they should stay in their allotted pairs at all times. There must have been about thirty or forty people hanging around at the front of the station, but none of them was causing any trouble. We created a 'sterile area' for a few metres around the front of the station. In plain language, that meant keeping an area free of people, cars, and any other objects.

After we had been outside Brixton police station for four or five hours, another serial was brought in to cover our job, and it was time for us to take our refreshment break. The Met Police Catering Service had set up a mobile canteen unit near the police station and supplied us with sandwiches, coffee, tea, and soft drinks. They appeared to be very well organised, but we barely had time to eat before we received a radio message sending us to a new location. We were needed at Stockwell Park Road, where there was trouble.

As we headed towards Stockwell Park Road, the coach was hit by a number of missiles. Suddenly broken glass was flying all over the place, and couple of bricks ended up on the floor of the coach, but nobody was hurt. We did not stop, and when we reached our ground assigned, we found that there were already two serials waiting there. I jumped out and spoke to the other two inspectors. From our position, the road sloped at a slight downhill angle towards some high-rise council flats. Standing in front of the flats was a group of sixty or seventy youths, and several of the youths were throwing bricks and bottles in our direction. This was no major problem for us, as we were just out of range.

It was difficult to estimate the exact distance between the three serials and the people who were throwing things in our direction. It was probably something like 100 metres. During the ten minutes that we stood there, other youths were arriving, and there was a gradual build-up in the numbers facing us. A number of ideas went through my head. There was a good chance that a police charge would send the rioters into a full retreat. It seemed unlikely that they would stand and fight us, but as soon as we started to move towards them we would come within the range of their bricks and bottles.

One of the basic factors relating to serious public order is quite simple. There will be two opposing groups of people facing one another, police and rioters. If one of those groups (rioters) has missiles and the other group (police) has not, you don't have to be a brilliant strategist to work out which one is going to take most casualties. I thought that a police charge was a good idea but we needed to be aware that the rioters might be planning to lure us into an ambush. If there were people on the high-rise flats above with bricks and bottles, we would be in a very vulnerable situation. Another aspect was that none of us had any protective clothing or equipment. As far as I know, all the police officers dealing with the riots in Brixton were wearing ordinary police uniforms. At the same time, it did not make sense for us to just stand there while the rioters gathered in strength.

The other two inspectors and I had a quick discussion about what we should do. A couple of minutes later, all three serials lined up across the width of the road, facing the rioters in front of the flats. I pulled out my truncheon. In terms of weaponry, an inspector's stick is much smaller than the ones carried by sergeants and constables; it must have looked quite pitiful. For two or three seconds we started moving forward slowly, and then there were shouts of 'Charge!' from all of the inspectors and sergeants. After that, everyone shouted, 'Charge!' All three serials suddenly took off at speed towards the rioters.

There are probably not many people who have seen a police charge. There were about seventy of us, and we were likely a more frightening sight than we could have imagined. As we pounded down the street, I could see that there were a lot of people throwing things in our direction. One of my Rochester Row men was hit and fell to the ground. I saw a bottle arcing into the air in my direction. It whizzed past my shoulder. Most of the rioters took to their heels, but there were still five or six stone-throwers ahead of us. Then they suddenly broke and ran back into the estate behind them.

There seemed little point in chasing them into the housing estate where they had retreated. None of us knew the local geography, and it might have been a serious mistake to go in there after them. Our serials had taken control of the other end of the street where the rioters had been, and we all felt a sense of elation. At the same time, some of our officers were injured. My serial had only suffered one casualty, the PC from Rochester Row who had gone down during the charge. He had been hit by a brick, and his right arm was broken.

The other two serials had a total of five or six injured officers. Most of their injuries consisted of bruises, and the injured men were insistent that they did not need treatment. We could see that one of them had a head wound and his inspector told him that he needed to have medical treatment. An ambulance was called for him and the injured Rochester Row officer.

We spread out across Stockwell Park Road and prepared for whatever might happen next. This became our ground assigned, as we received orders to stay there. Two or three hours passed by without any sign of rioters or any further trouble in our area. We stayed where we were until relieved by night-duty serials. My serial was told to stand down, and we returned to our coach. We had to pick up the Battersea serial, and so we made our way to the spot where we had dropped them off.

The Battersea officers looked totally exhausted. The only real comparison would be to a platoon of soldiers worn out by battle. The inspector in charge of the serial told me what had happened and described how they had been attacked on two or three occasions by large numbers of rioters. Each time they had fought off their attackers, but five or six of their PCs had been injured. Our coach made its way to Battersea and then to Rochester Row. We had been on duty for about thirteen hours in difficult circumstances, and by comparison the streets of south Westminster seemed quiet and peaceful.

The Government asked a senior judge, Lord Scarman, to conduct an urgent enquiry into what had happened in Brixton. Lord Scarman drew attention to a number of factors. In the area where the rioting took place, half of those in the age group of 19 to 21 were black, and the rate of unemployment for young black men was as high as 50 per cent in some parts of Brixton. The amount of money spent on social services in the Borough of Lambeth was the highest per capita in England.

Lord Scarman was concerned that the rioters had taken control of some streets, such as Railton Road, before the police had assembled sufficient numbers to regain the initiative and quell the disorder. The arrival of police reinforcements in Brixton had been slow, and they had not built up a sustained momentum until after 8 p.m. on the Saturday night.

On many occasions, the police had faced attacks by rioters throwing petrol bombs at them, and sometimes police uniforms had caught fire. Lord Scarman was concerned that much of the police equipment did not offer the protection that it should have done. He also identified problems with communications and the command structure during the riot.

Lord Scarman commented that there had been no loss of life in the suppression of the riots and praised police for their restraint. However, he blamed the police in Lambeth for failing to achieve the degree of public approval and respect that they needed to carry out their duties. He criticised police for being inflexible, saying that some junior officers were guilty of harassment and racial prejudice, which had played a part in the background to the trouble. Lord Scarman declared that police methods and attitudes had not responded in the proper way to the policing of a multiracial society.

The following month, the conflict in Northern Ireland was centre stage again, with the deaths of Bobby Sands and nine other Republican prisoners who had taken part in a hunger strike. The Republicans blamed the British Government for the deaths, and there was a rapid rise in tension in Northern Ireland. As a piece of propaganda, it had proved to be an amazing success for the IRA and their allies, the Irish National Liberation Army, or INLA.

Brixton did not suddenly become peaceful. There were a number of aftershocks, but these could only be described as mini riots. However, serious rioting broke out in some other cities such as Liverpool and Bristol, where there were substantial black communities. We realised that there needed to be fundamental changes in the way that police reacted to serious public-order situations. The Met had been taken by surprise by the rapid escalation of violence in 1976 at the Notting Hill Carnival. Brixton had thrown up issues that were subsequently pointed out by Lord Scarman – and all of this called for new ideas.

Our methods of thinking and reacting to serious public-order situations would need to change. A British police officer is trained to work on his/her own and make decisions as an individual, but when he/she is faced with serious public disorder this may actually be a weakness. When there is a serious breakdown in public order, large numbers of police will always be needed. Good tactical decisions need to be made quickly by senior officers, and their serials must move speedily and effectively, in the same manner as military fighting units.

The Special Patrol Group had been given public-order training and had always been effective when deployed in those situations. However, the SPG was regarded as 'very robust' in its policing style and by 1979 had many critics, especially among London's politicians. In April 1979, during disturbances in Southall, a man called Blair Peach was found unconscious, and he later died. Peach was an activist and member of the Socialist Workers' Party, who took part in demos against far-right groups such as the National Front. A lengthy police investigation followed his death, and the evidence suggested that Peach had been struck by a police officer. The enquiry soon started to focus on a number of SPG officers who had been deployed in the street where Blair Peach had received his injuries. One of the officers was arrested and held at Rochester Row for three days.

The commander who was the senior investigating officer considered that the most serious aspect of the case was that some officers had obstructed the investigators in the execution of their duty. He strongly recommended that proceedings be taken against two police officers for conspiring to pervert the course of justice and conspiring to obstruct the investigating officers.

Later that year, the DPP wrote to the commissioner, stating that he had decided that there was insufficient evidence to justify criminal proceedings against any police officers. Not surprisingly, the death of Blair Peach raised a number of questions about the style of policing and management of the SPG. The political repercussions would go on for some time.

The SPG was a CO unit and it had critics within the Greater London Council and in parliament, who complained that the SPG lacked any local accountability. Eventually, the commissioner decided to set up a large support unit that could be available at short notice to deal with serious public disorder. The SPG was disbanded, and new support units were created within each police district. These district support units would each have two teams with an inspector in charge. The 'A' District Support Unit was based at Cannon Row. One team would be on duty from 8 a.m. until 4 p.m., and the other team would normally work a late shift, from 4 p.m. until midnight.

A worrying new development was the use of petrol bombs by rioters; this seemed to have spread from Northern Ireland to the British mainland. Missiles – whether bricks, bottles, or anything else – had resulted in many officers being injured, and research was necessary into this issue. We needed to evaluate all items of uniform and equipment for public-order use, and our training had to become more sophisticated.

The Met built a public-order training centre on some land alongside the Thames, near Greenwich. It was necessary to give all the new DSU officers public-order training, often referred to as shield training. Looking back, it was surprising how little had been done in the past to train officers to deal with serious public-order situations.

Later that year, the Home Office arranged for the Met to be given three water cannons, made in Germany. When they were tested, a number of problems regarding their use soon came to light, and they were never used in public-order situations.

It was always a bad sign when the IRA went quiet. On 10 October 1981 there was an attack on the Irish Guards at Chelsea Barracks. The target was a coach carrying soldiers from the Irish Guards who were returning to the barracks. Two people were killed and thirty-nine were injured. Five years later, the IRA planned a second attack, and this is covered in Chapter 1 of this book.

The press were taking an interest in the developing romance between Diane Spencer and Prince Charles. It turned out that she was working on our division, at a nursery school in Pimlico. Suddenly, the press turned up there. It was not the worst disaster in the world, but it must have come as a shock to her, a young woman with no experience of being tackled by journalists.

It caused me some embarrassment, as I was duty officer that day. Someone at Scotland Yard contacted the chief superintendent, who was a bit put out because I had not briefed him about it. The problem was that I had been involved with another incident, and the chief superintendent heard about it before I did.

In April 1982, Argentina's military forces invaded the Falkland Islands. The following day I found myself in charge of a serial outside the Argentine embassy. We stood by while the diplomats moved all of their documents and paperwork from the building. We were there to protect them, but it was surprisingly quiet. There were a few bystanders but no sign of a mob of angry British people gathering to attack the embassy.

The invasion had not come out of the blue. There had been many clues that an attack was imminent, but they seemed to have been ignored by senior Government officials. A British intelligence officer based in Argentina had submitted a report which gave details of a large military and naval build-up by Argentine forces. He had stated that the only logical target for them was the Falkland Islands. When his report reached London, someone of high rank had written the words 'What rubbish!' in red ink across the report.

The Americans became aware that something serious was happening when their surveillance satellites showed a large Argentine naval force heading towards the Falklands. This information was passed to the British Government, who realised that they were now powerless to do anything about it. The only British military presence in the Falklands was a force of eighty marines, based at Port Stanley.

The Argentines landed their special forces, followed by other units, including armoured vehicles. The position that the Royal Marines found themselves in was hopeless, but they put up fierce resistance. In the fighting that followed, five Argentine soldiers were killed and several others wounded. The marines surrendered when asked to do so by the governor of the Falklands.

In the weeks immediately after the invasion, everyone wondered what would happen. From the start, my opinion was that Margaret Thatcher would take military action to regain the islands. However, they were 8,000 miles away, and it would take some time to organise a naval force and point them in the direction of the South Atlantic. A task force that included an aircraft carrier and ships carrying soldiers and marines was soon on its way.

While our relief was on night duty, we heard that the first clashes were taking place in and around the Falklands. Years later, a lot more information came out about the intelligence war that was going on in the shadows. Argentine secret agents were trying to purchase missiles in various countries that could be used against British ships. Dummy companies were set up by both the British and Argentine intelligence services. These 'companies' were used by the Argentines as a means of purchasing missiles and used by the British in order to mislead the Argentines. It seems that the Argentines believed that they had found genuine arms dealers that would sell them what they wanted. As far as I am aware, they were never able to purchase any missiles.

During May 1982, the big news was the visit of Pope John Paul II to the UK. This was a historical first, and there was considerable controversy about it. It was going to be a very large public-order event, and the Met had set up one of its largest operations to ensure the safety of the Pope and the public. The year before, the Pope had been shot and seriously wounded by a member of a Turkish terrorist group in Saint Peter's Square.

When we were night duty in May, I posted a sergeant and a PC to patrol in plain clothes. This is something that I did from time to time when we had enough personnel available. These were two very good officers for that type of work. In the early hours, they stopped a young Frenchman who was walking along a street that ran alongside Westminster Cathedral. He was questioned about his movements and he seemed nervous. It seemed to the officers that there was no reason why he should be in that street at that particular time. They searched him and found that he was carrying a loaded .357 Magnum revolver. He was arrested.

The Frenchman lived in a flat in central London, and I decided that the arresting officers should carry out a search of it. When they returned to the station, we discussed what they had found. They described how they had had noticed a religious picture hanging on a wall in the flat but someone had made a number of stab marks or bullet holes in it. It might have just been a coincidence that this suspect had been found outside Westminster Cathedral, where the Pope would be in the next two or three days.

Of course, we were all thinking the same thing. Was he an assassin? Was he stalking the Pope? He admitted that he did not have a firearms certificate but did not give us any reason why he should be carrying a .357 Magnum, a weapon regarded by many as the most powerful handgun in the world. There was nothing further that we could or should do at that stage. I briefed the inspector who took over from me that morning, and he later discussed it with a senior CID officer.

A man who was planning to murder the Pope would not be likely to admit it, I reasoned, but it was always possible that some clever questioning might reveal something. We knew that unless we could find something more substantial we would have to fall back on the offences under the Firearms Act. CID officers questioned the Frenchman, but he did not disclose anything that might link him to any type of terrorist plot or assassination attempt.

We were certainly left with a feeling that there might be something sinister going on, but there was no evidence to support this. The Frenchman was charged with possession of a loaded firearm in a public place and the illegal possession of a firearm. We managed to have him remanded in custody for a few days. After that, he pleaded guilty and was fined fifty pounds. The good news in this case was that by the time the Frenchman was released from court the Pope was back in Rome.

In June 1982, the Israeli ambassador to London, Shlomo Argov, was leaving the Dorchester Hotel in Park Lane where he had attended a function. He was accompanied by a police protection officer. Three men from the Abu Nidal terrorist group were standing in the street near the hotel. They approached the ambassador, and one of them fired a shot that hit Argov in the head. The three assailants then ran off, chased by the police officer, who opened fire. He hit and seriously wounded the man who had fired the shot, Hussein Ghassan Said.

The other two terrorists escaped but were arrested by police the next day. Shlomo Argov was very seriously injured; he died from his wounds many years later. There was great anger within the Israeli government about the attack, and four days later the Israeli army invaded Lebanon. Israel's plan was to eliminate the Palestine Liberation Organisation (PLO) and its headquarters in the capital of Beirut.

This campaign would last for many years. Many people lost their lives, and much of Beirut was destroyed. Israeli troops did not finally withdraw from Lebanon until May 2000.

A new chief superintendent arrived at Rochester Row, and within a couple of months he had announced that he was going make some changes. At that point, there were four inspectors in charge of reliefs and another three doing administrative work and filling in as duty officer when needed. As part of the changes, I was moved from my relief to an administrative role.

In July 1982 the Met Police faced one of the most embarrassing moments in its history, when a man named Michael Fagan gained access to Buckingham Palace. This would have been bad enough, but he managed to enter the bedroom where the Queen was sleeping and engage her in conversation. A senior official in the Home Office suggested to the commissioner, Sir David McNee, that he should consider resigning. The subsequent investigation showed that some officers at Buckingham Palace had been organising their duties to fit their own agendas rather than what they should have been doing, namely, guarding the Queen.

It turned out that one officer who was responsible for an important post inside the palace had gone home early without authority. He was sacked, and the district commander was transferred to an administrative position at Scotland Yard.

Newspaper articles appeared about the commander in charge of royalty protection, who was 'outed' as a homosexual. It smacked of a witch hunt. There did not appear to be any evidence that his sexuality had caused any of the security failures that marked this unfortunate incident. However, the Michael Fagan break-in was a major news story and it ran and ran for some time.

The year 1983 did not start well for the Metropolitan Police. Officers were looking for David Martin, a dangerous criminal wanted for a number of offences, some involving firearms. Martin was well known for his ability to disguise himself, sometimes in women's clothes. On one occasion, police officers were called to an office block in central London where Martin was committing a burglary. He provided a plausible explanation to them as to what he was doing in the building. Then, when there was only one PC with him, Martin produced a handgun, shot the officer – wounding him – and escaped. In another incident, when approached by an officer he put his pistol to the policeman's head and pulled the trigger. Luckily, the gun misfired.

Armed officers were watching a car in Kensington, and eventually a man they believed to be David Martin was seen to drive the car away. It turned out that the driver was a man called Stephen Waldorf, and the wanted man was not in the car. However, police forced the car to a stop and fired a number of shots. Waldorf was shot five times and seriously wounded. He was also struck on the head with a firearm, and his skull was fractured. The only glimmer of good news in this story was that Waldorf was taken to hospital and eventually recovered from his injuries.

The shooting of Stephen Waldorf was investigated as an attempted murder, and the DPP made the decision to take proceedings against two of the police officers involved. Arrangements were made for them to come to Rochester Row, and one of my fellow inspectors was asked to deal with the charging procedure. The officers concerned were angry and obviously believed that they were being treated unjustly.

The hunt for David Martin continued. Some weeks later, when cornered by police, he shot himself. The two officers who were charged with attempted murder were acquitted.

24

In 1982 the newly formed district support units had proved successful in dealing with public disorder in London, and during 1983 I spent some time working with our district unit. Based at Cannon Row, the unit was divided into two serials. I was in charge of one of them, with two sergeants and twenty PCs. At that time, there were no women officers posted to the DSU on 'A' District. To my mind, not allowing women officers to work in public-order situations went against the official line that they did the same work as their male colleagues.

As public order was our number-one priority we spent several days training at Greenwich, working together as a team. Physical fitness was an important element of our training, and part of this was a run where we had to complete a circuit of a mile and a half. This in itself did not sound like a major problem, but my concern was that I would probably be the one who came in last.

The two sergeants were both about 30 years of age, and the average age of my PCs was somewhere between 24 and 29. As I was at least nine years older than any of them, it would be no disgrace to come in last, but I managed to keep up a fairly fast pace. At the halfway mark we had a panoramic view of the newly built Thames Barrier as we turned and headed back towards the training centre.

There were shouts of 'Well done, guv' as the old man reached the end. We stood watching as six of my PCs struggled in after me; it seemed that my level of fitness was a bit better than I had thought. At the same time, it was a matter of concern to me that many young policemen were finding it difficult when they had to run.

At Greenwich, we worked with shields and other protective equipment on a number of different simulated public-order situations. Our favourite was probably the 'nutter room.' One of our trainers, a very big man, would stand inside a room brandishing a large piece of wood. Our job was to disarm him without getting injured. Three of us would enter the room, carrying our shields, and we would immediately be attacked by the lunatic inside – who obviously loved his job. He battered our shields with his piece of timber while we used them to trap him in one corner of the room. Once we had him firmly pinned in the corner, he would surrender. It was hot, tiring, sweaty work. Afterwards, we all had showers and headed back to Cannon Row.

There was an office at Cannon Row called the ceremonials office. The staff consisted of an inspector, sergeant, and constable, and they worked on the planning for all the many public-order and ceremonial events that took place on 'A' District. Their work was very important and brought them in daily contact with high-ranking police officers and Government ministers.

The ceremonials office sent me requests each week to cover a number of small-scale public-order events on the district. It reduced the amount of time available for patrolling and could be frustrating for everyone in the unit. When we were not needed for these events, we patrolled our three divisions, going to places where there were particular crime problems. We organised training days in Hyde Park, and this usually involved playing football or running around the Serpentine a couple of times.

We had to be ready to move into our public-order role at a moment's notice. Our two carriers had protective grilles that could be pulled down over the windows to give us protection if a public-order situation went pear shaped. There was a sergeant in charge of each carrier, and I would take turns to travel in each one. Within a few years, the DSU evolved into what is now the Territorial Support Group.

One afternoon when we were patrolling Pimlico, a call came over the radio to a burglary in the Jungle, where the suspect had been disturbed and run off. There was a vague description, but the suspect's face had not been seen. All we knew was that he was a young white male with a slim build. As we drove towards the scene, one of the Rochester Row PCs spotted a young man of about 19 walking along the street. I heard the name Jimmy Randall.

My sergeant pointed him out to me, saying that he fitted the description. 'So does virtually everyone else,' I thought, but then it clicked as to who it was. Jimmy Randall was one of our local criminals who had a couple of previous for burglary. I had not seen him for some time and did not recognise him straightaway. We stopped, and my sergeant jumped out to speak to him.

Jimmy Randall denied everything but seemed nervous. After some further questions, he was arrested and taken to Rochester Row. The sergeant seemed quite confident that he had the right person, but I was not totally convinced. Randall was surprisingly calm. 'If he did it, he's a first-class liar,' I thought. However, my sergeant was very persistent. But after about an hour of questioning, we were making no apparent progress and it seemed likely that we had the wrong man. There was one basic problem - we did not have any evidence. Then the sergeant sat down with me in the inspectors' office, and we talked it through. We both realised that we had done things back to front. Normally at a burglary, the first police action would be to examine the scene. In this case, the property was a basement flat, and two of our PCs had been there to obtain a description of the suspect. However, it did not appear that they had checked the scene for any marks or clues so the sergeant decided to go back and have a look. It had rained earlier that day, and he found a small wet patch in the basement area, quite close to the front door of the flat. Between the wet patch and the steps leading to the street there was a clear shoe print with an unusual design.

The day was starting to warm up, and the marks would not stay there forever. The sergeant asked the person living at the flat whether she had a camera, and she fetched him a Polaroid. He took a photograph of the shoe print and returned to the station. Randall was asked to remove the trainers that he was wearing. We looked at the design on the bottom of the trainers and saw that it was an exact match. Once he saw the photograph, Randall admitted that he had broken into the flat. Case solved. I congratulated my sergeant for the persistence and initiative that he'd showed.

A call to a street robbery took us to Knightsbridge, where we spoke to the victims, two Italians. We asked the two men to come with us as we drove slowly around Hyde Park – where they spotted the robbers and we arrested them. Several other crime arrests were made by our unit and I was pleased with the way that things were progressing.

Following the IRA bomb attack on the Irish Guards at Chelsea Barracks, wanted posters appeared all over London with Photofit pictures of people suspected of being involved. One evening when we were patrolling the Pimlico area, we received a 999 call with information that one of the suspects in the bombing was drinking in a pub in Vauxhall Bridge Road. A member of the public had seen a man in the pub who appeared identical to one of the men on the wanted posters.

One of our PCs was in plain clothes, so I sent him into the pub to take a look. He soon spotted the man concerned sitting at a table drinking with three other men. He told me that the man bore a striking resemblance to one of the people in the Photofits. Two or three issues went through my mind straight away. We could arrest that particular man on suspicion of murder. However, what about the three men with him? They could all be IRA men. If they were, could they be armed?

We were not an armed unit, so it was necessary to carry out a quick risk assessment. I decided to take eight officers into the pub with me and just grab all four of them and put them in the carrier. We went in fast and 'swooped' on them, as the press later reported. I arrested the main suspect, who was from Northern Ireland, and the other three were arrested by my PCs. The second man was English but of Irish descent; he lived in north London. A third man was English, living in east London, and the fourth man was Scottish, living in west London. It made me wonder if it could be an IRA unit who came together in central London. All four were searched for weapons, but none of them was armed.

We took them straight to Rochester Row, which was only about a quarter of a mile from the pub. James Clancy, the man I had arrested, seemed remarkably relaxed. When I took a close look at the Photofit, the likeness to him was quite remarkable. I spent a short while chatting with him and it came as a shock when he casually admitted that he was an IRA man.

'I'm a Stickie,' he said. 'You've got the wrong man if you think I'm a bomber.'

Clancy then told me about his time in the Official IRA when they had been involved in a feud with the Provisionals. He had been walking along a street in Belfast when a car had pulled up next to him and he'd been dragged into it at gunpoint. He had then been 'taken for a ride' by three Provisional gunmen. He'd realised straight away that this was a ride for which there was no return ticket; he would have to escape or be murdered.

The next time the car slowed down, Clancy made his escape by jumping out. He then ran away as fast as he could, with the three Provisionals in hot pursuit, firing at him with automatic pistols. He felt the bullets hit him, and he fell to the ground. His attackers would have probably put a bullet in his head but for one thing. A British Army patrol suddenly came around the corner, and his attackers ran off. It was a happy coincidence for Clancy that the army hated by Irish Republicans had appeared just at the right moment and had saved his life.

Clancy pulled his shirt off. 'That's what they did to me,' he said. There were the scars from four or five bullets on his chest and stomach.

The situation was strange. On the face of it, he was an obvious suspect for the Chelsea Barracks bombing. He was an IRA man who appeared to know the area, he'd been drinking in a pub about a mile away from the bombing, and his face seemed a perfect match to the wanted poster. At this point, we handed the case over to the Anti-Terrorist Squad and the suspects were detained at Rochester Row. The following day, on my way to Cannon Row, I bought *The Evening Standard*. The banner headlines on the front page announced the arrest of a suspected IRA bombing team. It stated that armed officers had 'swooped' on a pub in Vauxhall, where they had arrested four suspected terrorists. I thought that if we had arrested an IRA bomber, or maybe a whole terrorist unit, that would have been an amazing result. However, this was not destined to be the great arrest of the year. Officers from the Anti-Terrorist Branch questioned all four men, and within a few hours they were all released. It was not surprising that Clancy had been so relaxed.

After completing my tour of duty with the DSU, I returned to Rochester Row, where the chief superintendent asked me to take over a relief. The role of inspector in charge of a relief is always a challenging one. Looking back, there were a number of things that I probably could have done better in my first couple of years. My leadership style had improved considerably since then. As I started again as a relief inspector, an important part of my strategy was to hold regular meetings with my sergeants, to develop an effective management team for the relief. We all worked hard to turn our team into what the chief superintendent would later describe as a first-class relief.

The previous year there had been an incident in Holloway Road, north London, in which five teenagers had been assaulted by police officers attached to the local DSU, but in the lengthy investigation that followed it had proved impossible to identify those responsible. It was quite clear that there were other officers who knew the identity of the culprits, but it appeared that everyone had closed ranks. The newspapers ran stories about the incident and the lack of progress in the investigation. This would become a running sore in the side of the Met for some time. Eventually the officers who were involved in the assault were charged and convicted.

The shooting of Stephen Waldorf was an incident that would cause problems for the police service for many years. The Home Office quickly imposed new guidelines regarding the issue and use of firearms. Under these new rules, firearms could only be issued by an officer of the rank of superintendent or higher, and the reasons for issuing them were restricted.

It seemed to most operational officers that the new guidelines had been issued in haste and did not make a great deal of sense. When it came to the decision to shoot someone, the responsibility was always going to be on the shoulders of the officer who had a finger on the trigger. Put simply, if the commissioner was the only person with the authority to issue firearms in the Met, would this prevent officers from making mistakes in future incidents?

On some divisions, there were regular movements involving large amounts of cash being moved by private security firms. In some places it had become the practice to have a couple of armed officers in a car following the security van as it travelled to its destination. This practice stopped as it was not considered to be within the new guidelines relating to the issue of firearms. There were some places where the system continued but with two unarmed officers keeping an eye on these types of cash movements.

Police officers tend to be cynical at the best of times. There was often the perception of 'them and us' when PCs on the streets talked about their senior officers. Some held the view that an ambitious superintendent might worry about something going wrong and have concerns about how this might affect his/her future career. I had confidence in the judgement of the superintendents and chief superintendent at Alfa Romeo but there were a number of worrying stories about decisions made on other divisions regarding firearms.

Some senior police officers have what I call a negative decision philosophy. This is summed up by the following attitude: 'If I don't make a decision, I can't be blamed if something goes wrong.' Sadly, it often proved to be a good philosophy for those who used it.

When drugs raids were being planned there were cases when we needed to consider using armed officers. In the 1970s, many search warrants related to people who had illegal drugs for their personal use. However, by the 1980s, raids were mainly targeting people who were suspected dealers and more and more firearms were being found during searches. Drug dealers are worried about their goods being stolen, and they often keep guns as a defence against other criminals rather than police. However, there is always the danger of a police officer being shot in these situations.

When planning to carry out that type of search, it is very important to assess the level of risk involved. The speed of entry needs to be fast, and the drug dealer may be known to be violent. When everything is considered, the officers involved are often facing a potentially dangerous situation. My opinion was that if we had reliable information that a drug dealer had a firearm, we should always have armed officers involved in the search. The problem was that there were some senior officers who did not think that this was enough. 'Can you obtain some further information in order to corroborate the first bit of information that you have?' they might ask.

A basic question has to be considered in these cases. 'Is it worth a police officer or anyone else being killed or seriously injured?' Authority to issue firearms was not always granted in these cases. This sometimes resulted in the officers involved deciding to cancel the search that they had planned. It sounded as if the so-called War on Drugs was becoming a bit one-sided – and the police did not appear to be on the winning side.

As Christmas 1983 approached, an IRA car bomb exploded outside Harrods, killing six people and injuring seventy-five others. It was a terrible tragedy for all the victims and their families, and for the Met, who lost three officers. Chris Stanger, a sergeant at Chelsea, was on duty near Harrods when a coded message was received from the IRA about the bomb and he was seriously injured in the blast. Chris was an ex-army officer who had served in Northern Ireland.

The phone call from the terrorists had been made to a well known charity. The words used were misleading – 'Two bombs inside Harrods. Car bomb outside.' However, there were no bombs inside the store. Later, there were reports that the registration number of the car containing the bomb had been given to the police by the terrorists but this was untrue.

When the car bomb exploded, Chris had been standing quite close to it, but he was not conscious of actually hearing it. His memory was of being in darkness and his first thought being, 'So there *was* a bomb.' He had been to a number of bomb incidents where nothing had happened. His second thought had been, 'I'm dead.'

He'd felt a burning sensation to his face and a moment of acute pain as his trousers caught fire. The pain in his legs lasted for a very short time; the nerve endings must have been destroyed. His third thought had been of his family. 'Who is going to look after my wife and daughters?' He had twin daughters who were thirteen months old.

The suddenly, he had been able to see. 'I'm still alive,' he'd realised. He found himself lying in the road between two parked cars. He looked at the bloody mess that was his left hand, which had been hit by shrapnel. He did not look at the rest of his body at that point and did not know the extent of his injuries. They were extensive. His legs had been badly burned and hit by shrapnel, and his stomach had been sliced open.

Inspector Stephen Dodd was Chelsea's duty officer who had arrived at the scene to take charge of the incident at Harrods. Chris had been talking to him when the bomb detonated. He could see Stephen Dodd's body in the road a few metres away. Stephen Dodd died from his injuries. Chris later realised that the duty officer had been standing between him and the bomb when it exploded.

He was disorientated for some time but realised he needed to get up and go for help. As he walked unsteadily towards the Harrods security office, a man approached him looking horrified. Chris recognised him as one of the regular street traders, who asked him, 'Are you all right?'

Chris replied 'No, I'm not.'

He may have used words that were a bit stronger than that but cannot be totally sure. Chris remained conscious at the scene and was still conscious when he arrived at hospital. It was several days later when he started to realise the extent of his injuries. Apart from everything else, he had a large wound to his stomach, and this must have been a horrifying sight to everyone who had seen him staggering down the street. Luckily, there were no injuries to any of his internal organs.

On his arrival at the hospital, Chris still had his PR with him, which was switched on. The constant radio traffic must have been disturbing the medical staff as they were busy trying to deal with people even more badly injured than he was. One nurse came over to Chris and did her best to find the 'off' button on his radio. After struggling with it for a while, the nurse asked Chris for help. She held the radio up in front of him, and he was able to switch it off.

While waiting in the casualty unit, he asked to use a phone so that he could contact his wife. The two of them were planning to go to a police Christmas party that night, and Chris thought that he should tell his wife that he was still alive but would probably not be able to get home that night. The problem was that everyone else was busy ringing their loved ones, and the phone lines became jammed. Eventually he managed to speak to his wife, who had not been aware of what had happened.

In the aftermath of the explosion, the Met's communications system was under tremendous pressure due to the thousands of extra phone calls that had to be dealt with. At Chelsea, Stephen Dodds, Jane Arbuthnot, and Noel Lane were dead and several others injured, and the division started doing whatever it could to help. Sergeant Mick Bell and the other Police Federation reps at Chelsea played an important role in organising help and support for the relatives and families of those who had been killed or seriously injured.

The day after the bomb, a police officer and his wife arrived at Chris Stanger's home. The officer drove Mrs Stanger to the hospital while his wife looked after their two young daughters. Chris spent a long time in hospital, but eventually he returned to duty. The scars on his body and legs are there for the rest of his life, and the events of that December day will always loom large in his thoughts.

On 17 April 1984 a small, peaceful demonstration took place outside the Libyan embassy in St James Square. In Libya, two students had been executed for criticising the president, Muammar Gaddafi. About seventy demonstrators came to the embassy to protest about this. Gaddafi loyalists informed the police that they wished to carry out a counterdemonstration. Thirty police officers were in the square to deal with this event, and their task was to ensure that no demonstrators were able to come close to the embassy building and that both groups were kept apart. It was a typical policing operation of its type, dealing with a peaceful demonstration. Then, suddenly, there was a volley of shots. Someone inside the embassy had opened fire on the demonstrators with an automatic rifle.

Thirteen people were shot, and this included PC Yvonne Fletcher, who was hit in the stomach. Her fiancé, a police officer who was also policing this event, was by her side when she was wounded. Yvonne Fletcher was removed from the scene by ambulance but died a short time later at Westminster Hospital.

Armed police quickly surrounded the embassy, and the area was sealed off. Now the Met had another high-profile siege on its hands that would go on for some time. Edgar Maybanks, who had been my chief superintendent at Rochester Row in 1970, had been promoted to DAC – Deputy Assistant Commissioner – by this time, and he took charge of the incident. Colonel Gaddafi blamed the British police for what he described as an attack on their embassy in London, and he ordered his troops to surround the British embassy in Tripoli. Eighteen of our diplomats were then trapped inside the embassy.

The day after the shooting, I was at the scene near the embassy. All the streets leading into St James Square were sealed off, and sandbagged gun positions were in place at every strategic point around the embassy. Police riflemen were in position, covering all likely exit points from the building. On 23 April the British Government severed diplomatic relations with Libya. The Libyan diplomats inside the embassy were entitled to immunity from prosecution, and much to everyone's anger, they were allowed to leave this country and return to Libya.

In 1999, the Libyan Government admitted that it bore a general responsibility for the death of Yvonne Fletcher and paid a large amount of money in compensation to her family. Everyone knew that the investigation into her murder would be difficult and protracted, but the matter has been kept under review, and it is hoped that the person responsible will eventually be brought to justice.

March 1984 saw the start of the miners' strike, one of the largest and most difficult industrial disputes faced by the police service. All the forces that had coal mines in their areas were soon under enormous pressure, and a system of mutual aid was developed. This meant that police forces provided assistance to other forces, and in many ways we started to act like a national police force. The Public Order Branch at Scotland Yard would send requests for Met districts to provide serials to aid other forces for a week at a time.

In July that year, I was selected to take charge of a serial assigned to assist the Humberside Police. Prior to leaving, we were addressed by one of the district commanders. He gave us a briefing about how we should police an industrial dispute and stressed that officers must always remain neutral and be impartial when dealing with people involved in the dispute. We then travelled to an army camp at Driffield in East Yorkshire where I shared a hut with three other inspectors. Once we had settled in, we reported to the chief inspector in charge of our four serials. He told us that the job for two of our serials, which included mine, was to guard the Humber Bridge and that we would need to be out of bed by four the following morning.

In the morning, my breakfast was huge, even by northern standards; it appeared that the catering contractors had been given a large budget to feed us. The Humberside Police provided a Traffic Division motorcyclist to guide us to the bridge, and soon our small convoy was gliding through the quiet countryside of East Yorkshire. We pulled in when we reached the control centre on the north side of the bridge. The motorcyclist told me that the duty officer would be coming to see us, and then he roared off in the general direction of Hull.

The other inspector and I spent about ten minutes walking up and down in front of the control centre and talking. We knew that we were there to guard the bridge, but it seemed strange that there was nobody there to brief us or give us any background information. We decided that we would probably not be able to find out much until the duty officer arrived. It seemed that this would probably be someone from Hull. We could not imagine who else it might be.

Suddenly, a man wearing a uniform emerged from the control centre and approached us. He introduced himself and turned out to be the mysterious duty officer we had been told about. We had been expecting a police officer but he was the duty officer for the bridge control centre. He gave us a quick tour of the surrounding area. The three of us walked around the side of the control centre and the land alongside the north end of the bridge. The duty officer revealed that two weeks earlier a number of cars full of striking miners had arrived and blocked the north side of the bridge which caused a very big traffic jam.

We wondered how the problem had been sorted out, and someone later told me the story. A couple of units from the Manchester Special Patrol Group had arrived at the scene and asked the strikers to remove themselves and their vehicles from the approach to the bridge. The miners had refused and locked themselves in their cars. We were told that the Manchester SPG tended to be very big men who were not used to their requests being ignored. After a couple of polite requests had been ignored, they produced their night sticks, smashed the windscreens of the cars, and dragged the occupants out.

The other inspector and I both felt that we should have had more of a briefing. However, we knew that our job was to guard the bridge, and so I sent a sergeant and five PCs to patrol the immediate area. There was no sign of any trouble. The day was becoming hot and sunny, and we moved to an open grassy area overlooking the River Humber that was a suitable place for everyone to sit down. It was out of sight of the public, and soon everyone was lying or sitting on the grass, enjoying the sun.

After two or three hours, a chief inspector from the Humberside Police arrived. He was a very friendly man and told us how pleased he was to see us all there. He then went on to inform us that his chief constable was keen to 'get his K'. We told him that we would hold the bridge against all odds and do everything we could to ensure that the chief constable received his knighthood. After a brief conversation, the chief inspector jumped into his car and drove away. We still had not received a proper briefing, but maybe there was not a great deal that could be said about guarding a bridge, aside from, 'Make sure that nobody steals it, damages it, or obstructs it.'

Soon afterwards the Met chief inspector arrived at the bridge and gave us a short briefing about the importance of the bridge to local transport. He asked us both how long we had been inspectors. The other inspector had only held his rank for two years, so the chief inspector told us that he was putting me in charge of both serials at the bridge. Each day we travelled to the bridge, where we stayed from 5.30 a.m. until about 7 p.m. The weather stayed hot and sunny every day, and there was no sign of anyone who wished to create any problems for us.

It is not possible to fully appreciate the length of the Humber Bridge unless you walk across it. One day, I crossed over to the other side with one of my sergeants. After reaching the other side, we had a panoramic view of the river and the houses below us. We spotted a woman coming in our direction who was walking her dog. She realised that we were not from the local police force and started talking to us. The woman seemed quite amazed to think that we had come all the way from London. 'We haven't had this much excitement here since 1943, when the Americans were here,' she told us.

On the Friday morning, we arrived at the bridge as usual, but after we had been there a few hours we were told to go to the British Steel works at Scunthorpe. A large number of flying pickets had arrived in an attempt to blockade it and prevent coal being delivered. When we arrived, we were told that there was great concern about the steel works. The furnaces needed to stay hot, and without coal they would go cold. If this happened they would be permanently damaged, and the damage to the economy would be huge. The costs of repairing the furnaces would run to millions. A number of Met serials, including mine, were being held as a strategic reserve close by. There were hundreds of striking miners at the steel works, accompanied by a lot of shouting but no violence. After about four hours we returned to Driffield.

A few weeks later, I found myself heading north again on aid to the Staffordshire Police. We were billeted in army barracks on the outskirts of Nottingham. We knew that Nottingham had a high crime rate and we were told that there were many robberies in the city centre. What surprised me was that when we were given a briefing by the local police, they warned us not to go into the centre of the city on our own, saying that it was too dangerous.

Each morning, three or four Met serials went to assist a Staffordshire serial at Shirebrook Colliery. On our arrival in Shirebrook, we all picked up on the atmosphere of the place. The only comparison would be a country where there was a civil war. The problem at Shirebrook was that there were a number of working miners living there, and every person who lived in the area was either backing the strikers or supporting the working miners. This pattern must have developed in many other parts of the country. The bitterness divided communities and families and was often a case of father against son or brother against brother.

We were given a good briefing before we arrived at the colliery. For the past few weeks there had been a series of attacks on working miners in Shirebrook, and there had been at least one assault on a striking miner by working miners. There had been some serious assaults, but most incidents had involved damage done to the homes and vehicles of working miners. Bricks had been thrown through windows, and cars and caravans had been set on fire. During the week that we spent there, a working miner had been walking along a country lane just outside Shirebrook when he'd been attacked and badly beaten up by four men. It did not make a great deal of sense to me when people such as Roy Hattersley, the deputy leader of the Labour Party, stated that the police should not be involved in policing an industrial dispute. Who else was going to do it?

Each day we went through the same routine at the colliery. We made sure that we were in position early, a couple of hours before people started arriving. If there were to be a flashpoint, it was likely to occur at about eight in the morning, when the working miners arrived at the colliery. The two buses that carried them had been specially fortified with protective grilles to protect the occupants from whatever missiles might come their way. It reminded me of the Grunwick dispute a few years before, except that the miners' strike involved the whole country. For about an hour before the arrival of the buses, striking miners would start appearing, and eventually there would be about three hundred or so gathered there. As the buses appeared, there would be a big rise in tension and noise as the pickets shouted abuse at the people in the buses.

'Scab, scab, scab, scab!' they shouted, among other things. The two buses would enter the colliery, and then everything would suddenly go quiet. After that, the pickets would start walking away. It appeared that not everyone was there to support the strike. On our first day there, a local man in his sixties walked up to me and pointed contemptuously at the pickets.

'That lot couldn't fight their way out of a paper bag,' he said, shaking his head.

After that, we would spend the rest of the day waiting for something to happen, but everything stayed surprisingly quiet. The only positive aspect for the police was that we were receiving a lot of pay in overtime. Because of this, there were many officers who let it be known that they wished to volunteer their services. It was easy for us to return to London after a week in the north and forget about what was happening, but at the same time, the strike was resulting in real hardship for the striking miners and their families and difficulties for local police officers.

There were some violent confrontations between police and striking miners, and it was natural that these incidents would be given wide publicity by the media. However, these represented only a small part of what was happening overall, and my experiences were probably typical for most Met officers who were involved in the policing of the strike.

After my two trips up north, it was back to my usual duties in charge of my relief at Rochester Row. There had been occasions in the past when I had failed to see the wood for the trees. The business of managing a relief is always challenging, but now it was becoming easier. All the experience gained over the previous four years was starting to pay off, and I felt I had become a better leader and manager.

One day in October 1984, I switched on my television to be confronted with a view of the Grand Hotel in Brighton that had been devastated by an IRA bomb during the night. The Conservative Party conference was taking place in Brighton, and I knew that the Met had sent a number of serials to assist the Sussex Police. I could see two of the PCs from my relief standing at the front of the hotel. Their serial had been held in reserve during the night, and the officers were sealing off the area around the hotel, which had now become a very large crime scene.

The bomb had exploded at three in the morning, and the IRA had come close to wiping out the cabinet. The explosion had ripped open the front of the hotel and sent masonry crashing down on the guests sleeping below. Five of the guests had been killed and thirty-four injured. The prime minister and her husband had narrowly escaped with their lives; part of the suite they were staying in had been wrecked by the bomb.

We knew that the terrorists had some highly skilled bomb makers. The man who had planted the bomb was Patrick Magee; he had stayed at the hotel under an alias. During the three days that he stayed there, he'd primed a bomb containing thirty pounds of explosives and hidden it in a bathroom wall. Using the same technology that was being used by people who were recording television programmes on video, he created a timing device that was set to detonate twenty-four days later.

The investigation by Sussex Police tracked down every guest who had stayed at the hotel for many weeks prior to the explosion. Eventually they found that there was only one person who they could not account for, a man who had given his name as Walsh. A fingerprint belonging to Magee was found on the hotel registration form completed by Walsh. This led to the conviction of Magee, who was sentenced to thirty-five years in prison. He was released in 1999 under the Good Friday Agreement.

The following month, in Wales, a taxi driver named David Wilkie was killed by striking miners. The victim had been taking a working miner to the job site when a block of concrete weighing forty-six pounds and a concrete post weighing sixty-five pounds were dropped on the taxi from a bridge as the car passed underneath it. It was the last thing that the union would have wanted to happen, and not surprisingly, it resulted in a huge amount of negative publicity for everyone who supported the strike.

Two of the people involved were convicted of murder and sentenced to life imprisonment. Following this, union members started a campaign to raise funds for an appeal. Later, the murder convictions were reduced to manslaughter, and the sentence was set at eight years in prison. Figures produced at the end of the year showed that the costs of policing the strike had risen to £200 million.

All of the inspectors at Alfa Romeo had been given other roles in addition to their day-to-day responsibilities, and one of mine was liaison with the Royal Military Police. Their London headquarters was in Rochester

Row, opposite the police station. In 1980, when I first arrived on the division, we had held suspected terrorists, although this practice had soon ended when more secure accommodation was found for them. The more I thought about it, the more concerned I became that the IRA might see us as a good target. An explosion in the street, possibly a car bomb, could hit the police station and the Military Police.

I crossed the street, introduced myself to the major and captain who were based there, and we discussed our security concerns. Using Rochester Row and Military Police personnel, we carried out a couple of exercises to see how effectively we could react to a terrorist incident. We had two simulated bomb threats, wherein we noted everything that happened and how quickly everyone responded to the threat. It all looked very efficient, but the IRA never carried out an attack in Rochester Row – so, happily, we never discovered how well we would have done in a real-life situation.

25

The Police and Criminal Evidence Act 1984 was very important new legislation. Before long, we were all referring to it as PACE. There had always been laws that affected our style of policing, but with PACE, parliament initiated something that would have a significant effect on police working practices.

The Codes of Practice contained in Section 66 of the Act were of particular interest to all operational police officers. This section covered powers of stop and search; searching of premises; seizure of property; the detention, treatment, and questioning of suspects; and identification procedures. The traditional role of a station officer would be replaced by someone called a custody officer, and the new title was more of a change than it appeared. Under PACE, custody officers would have a legal responsibility to ensure that people in police custody were treated in accordance with the law. The first thing to give me cause for concern was the amount of information that had to be recorded on custody records. The hardest-working man or woman on a division tends to be the custody officer, and it looked as if the amount of writing that they had to contend with was about to double.

A decision was made that the Met Police would start complying with PACE in 1985, so that we could become familiar with it all prior to 1986, when it became law. This involved a huge amount of new stationery being required by every police station. It also meant that all officers, irrespective of rank, needed training so that they would have a good knowledge of the Act.

In March 1985, a working party was being set up for the City of Westminster to look at the problem of criminal damage. The working party would be a multi-agency group, and they wanted a police officer as a member. The chief superintendent decided to nominate me, and I went to the meetings each month. After the first meeting, I realised that my contribution was going to be important, as many of the people on the working party had very little knowledge of the basic factors relating to this problem. We all agreed that we would never be able to come up with a strategy that would effectively combat criminal damage, but we produced some initiatives that improved the environment for Westminster residents.

During that month, the miners' strike finally ended. The policing of the strike had put considerable pressure on the police service in terms of the huge manpower demands and the financial cost. There had also been a human cost. The striking miners and their families had faced hardship, and police action had often caused bad feeling in mining areas. The repercussions would be felt for some time.

In April that year the Met published a book called *Principles of Policing*, and a copy was given to every officer. It laid down a number of ethical standards that police officers should be guided by. One of its more controversial sections dealt with Freemasonry and advised police officers against becoming Masons.

The following month, a very serious fire at Bradford City's football stadium suddenly pushed the question of football safety high up the priority list for the police service. There were many football grounds, even some of those belonging to wealthy clubs that were dingy and antiquated. What occurred at Bradford was that an old wooden stand at Valley Parade caught fire, and within about four minutes the whole of the roof and the wooden stands below were on fire. In all, 56 spectators lost their lives and 265 were injured.

We can always be wise in hindsight and say that this looked like a disaster waiting to happen. Over many years, piles of rubbish had built up under the stand. A small event, such as the dropping of a match or a cigarette being stubbed out in a polystyrene cup, could have ignited the wooden stand. It was the worst fire disaster in British football history. The death toll would have been higher had it not been for the courage of several police officers and twenty-two spectators who were responsible for saving a number of peoples' lives and were later honoured with bravery awards.

Racial tension was high during 1985. In September, rioting broke out in Handsworth, Birmingham, in which two Asian shopkeepers were murdered. During a police raid in Brixton, a woman called Sherry Groce was mistakenly shot by a police officer, and although she was not killed, she was paralysed. This sparked rioting in the Brixton area.

A week later, there was rioting in the Broadwater Farm Estate, Tottenham. This started when officers carried out a search of a house looking for a wanted man. The woman living there, Mrs Cynthia Jarrett, suffered a heart attack and died. It was reported that she had been pushed to the ground by one of the police officers. Broadwater Farm was the scene of one of the worst riots in London's history. Although police were better trained and equipped than they had been in the past, this was a particularly savage and violent event. They were under sustained attack from people armed with all sorts of weapons, including petrol bombs and firearms. One of the police officers, PC Keith Blakelock, was murdered, and many more were injured.

What occurred at Broadwater Farm caused serious damage to morale within the Met. When I spoke to officers who had been there, it was obvious that they were angry about some of the things that had occurred before and during the riot. They complained that, for some time before the riots, local senior officers had adopted a laissez-faire attitude towards criminal elements within Broadwater Farm.

Many officers complained about what they believed were failures in leadership by some high ranking officers during the rioting. Apart from anything else, there was a strong feeling that police needed to use plastic bullets or other types of defensive weaponry in serious riot situations such as Broadwater Farm. It may not have been true but there was a widely held belief within the Met that many officers of ACPO rank were desperate not to use plastic bullets whatever happened. Apart from anything else, it seemed that little was being done to raise the flagging morale of Met officers.

The following year, a sergeant submitted a report to the Police Federation alleging that senior officers had failed to act after they had been provided with information about the situation at Broadwater Farm and the problems that had been building up there for some time.

The year ended badly for the Met with the violent death of another police officer. The Brink's-Mat Robbery had been described by the press as the 'crime of the century'. Three tonnes of gold, together with diamonds and cash had been stolen. At the time, the value of the stolen property was estimated to be about £26 million. DC John Fordham was taking part in a surveillance operation that was targeting suspects believed to be involved in the Brink's-Mat Robbery and was killed by one of them, Kenneth Noye. In the court case that followed, Noye stated that he had acted in self-defence and was acquitted of murdering John Fordham. In a later trial, he was convicted of being involved in the robbery and received a sentence of fourteen years. In 1994, he was released from prison after serving eight years. A civil action was taken against Noye by the loss adjusters of Brink's-Mat insurers, and £3 million was recovered from him.

Just over a year after being released, Noye was involved in a road-rage incident in Kent with a 21-year-old motorist by the name of Stephen Cameron. Cameron was stabbed to death, and a major police hunt was launched to find Noye, who had fled abroad. While this was going on, it was suspected that a Met officer had been passing on confidential information to Noye about police operations. There was a lengthy investigation, and the officer concerned was later sent to prison for eleven years.

In July 1986, the Met published a public-order review relating to the Brixton Riots in 1985 and what had happened at Broadwater Farm. The report was critical of some senior officers for allowing what was described as 'no-go' areas to develop on the two divisions concerned.

This was a time when I had started to think about a change of direction in my career. My work as an inspector in charge of a relief seemed to be going well. My chief superintendent had given me very good appraisals and recommended me for promotion. At the same time, all my work had been operational, and I had never worked at CO or in any specialist unit. So it was probably a good time to move on and do something different.

The Directorate of Management Services (DMS) at Scotland Yard was responsible for research and development work within the Met. A notice appeared in Police Orders saying that they were looking for inspectors and chief inspectors to work on a wide range of projects. It sounded interesting. My application was endorsed by my chief superintendent with a very positive recommendation, and two or three weeks later I received an invitation to visit DMS, which was in Aybrook Street, close to Marylebone High Street.

There were three or four other inspectors there, and we were introduced to some of the people who worked at DMS. After that, we were asked to sit down in one of the offices and tackle some written tests. Some involved looking at a strange array of numbers, symbols, or shapes and putting them into a logical order. A lot of it appeared very odd, but I did my best to make some sort of sense of it.

We were told that we should not think about these tests as a form of examination because there was no such thing as a pass or a failure. At this point, there were a few quiet murmurs, indicating some cynicism on our part at the idea that the tests served no purpose in the selection process.

A couple of weeks later, I was one of those selected for interview. The interview board consisted of two senior civil servants and a detective chief superintendent. I did not normally do well in this type of formal interview process, but on this occasion my mood was fairly relaxed and this probably helped.

The questions in the interview all related to matters that I could answer with a good degree of confidence. One of them was about public order, and I was able to talk about my experience on 'A' District and the miners' strike, even describing myself as an expert on the subject. This was something that would come back to haunt me in the future.

A few days after the interview, my chief superintendent told me that I had been successful, and my transfer to DMS would take place in three weeks' time. It seemed that it was the right time for me to leave Rochester Row, but at the same time it surprised me that I felt quite sad when it was time to go. What also surprised me was the number of presents I received from officers in Uniform and CID at Alfa Romeo.

Apart from the people, one of the aspects of operational police work that I would miss was the humour. Many of the incidents that police get called to can only be described as bizarre, and this leads to some very funny stories. One of my favourites arose from something that happened in Birdcage Walk a few weeks before I left Roch.

Birdcage Walk is the road that runs along the south side of St James Park, which at that time was the divisional boundary between Cannon Row and Roch. At night it was quite a dark area, and one of the Cannon Row PCs on foot patrol at about 2 a.m. was surprised to hear a man in a parked car calling for help. The officer must have grasped the situation very quickly. A Mini is a good little car, but is not the ideal vehicle for what the man and woman inside were doing. It appeared that the man had slipped a disc and was in great pain.

It was a tricky situation. The man said that he could not move, and the woman found herself trapped because she was underneath him. The PC must have scratched his head and decided to call his sergeant. Soon after that, the duty officer arrived. At some point, a Rochester Row officer came along and informed Alfa Romeo about the incident. An ambulance was called, and before long there was a large crowd consisting of paramedics and police gathered around the car.

The first rescue attempt ended in failure. Police and paramedics attempted to lift the man out of the car as gently as they could, but he started screaming in pain. Then someone thought that it would be a good idea to call the fire brigade. So eventually, there was a summit conference of all three emergency services in Birdcage Walk. The senior firefighter present said that there was only one solution to the problem. The brigade had cutting equipment, and they could slice off the roof of the Mini and lift the man upwards and out of the car.

The brigade went to work, and within a short while the roof had been cut away. A joint task force then lifted the man upwards out of the car and placed him in the ambulance. My colleagues described the woman in the story, an attractive blonde with a mini skirt, who stood chatting to the inspector from Cannon Row for a few minutes. She pointed at the car, and her words will be remembered forever by those who were present.

'Oh my goodness! My husband will go absolutely mad when he sees the state of the car.'

At that time there were four main departments at Scotland Yard, each one headed by an assistant commissioner. DMS was part of Management Support Department, and the Director of DMS was Dr Norman Hand, who was responsible to Assistant Commissioner Management Support, known as ACMS.

Dr Hand was a scientist, and there were two deputy directors, one a scientific officer and the other a civil servant. DMS was staffed mainly by scientific officers, civil servants, and police officers, but there were others, such as psychologists and work-study experts. It made for a very interesting mix of experience and viewpoints. The two most senior police officers there were a detective chief superintendent and a detective superintendent.

When people mention Scotland Yard, they tend to think of the main building, then based in Broadway, SW1. However this was never large enough to house all the branches that are part of the Met's headquarters. DMS had five or six people working at Scotland Yard, but everyone else was in the DMS building at Aybrook Street, which had started life as a section house for women officers.

My office was on the first floor at Aybrook Street, part of a spacious, open-plan area where eight of us were based. Sitting at a desk next to mine was Ian Tolley, a SEO (senior executive officer) who had worked in a number of Met civil-staff branches and had a great knowledge of admin matters. He gave me much useful advice in my first few weeks at DMS; he was someone who could find his way through the dark tunnels and recesses of the Met Police bureaucracy.

Ian thought that it would be helpful for me to read a sampling of files, which would give me some idea about the wide variety of projects that were taken on at DMS. He also suggested that I meet other project officers and find out what they were working on.

The deputy director who would have overall responsibility for my work was John Tubb, who had been on the board that had interviewed me. Although he was a senior civil servant, one of my colleagues told me that he had a background in naval intelligence and spoke fluent Russian. He had a habit of sending notes to people from time to time that were in English but written in Cyrillic characters. My knowledge of the language was limited to two or three words, but some years before I had learned the Russian alphabet, so when one of his notes landed on my desk it did not take me by surprise.

John Tubb thought that a good place for me to work was the branch that dealt with O&M research – Organisation and Method. During my second week, he invited Ian and me to a meeting in his office to discuss a new project that he wanted us to take on. The Metropolitan Police Training School at Hendon carried out the initial training course for Met recruits. There were also seven or eight training schools in different parts of England and Wales providing standardised training courses for all the other forces. The Met style of training was different to the rest of the country, and DMS had been asked to carry out a study showing how the two systems compared.

Later that day, Ian Tolley and I sat down together to discuss how we were going to tackle this project. John Tubb had given us a deadline to complete it, and Ian explained how that was something that rarely happened at DMS. Project officers were normally able to work at their own pace, as long as they produced a good report at the end of it.

In this case, we had ten weeks to complete a preliminary report on this study. Coming from a world where operational police officers are constantly under pressure from deadlines of one sort or another, this did not concern me unduly. Ian and I set up a plan for gathering all the information that we needed in order to complete the project. One of the main factors was that it would involve a lot of travelling.

We made contact with the person we referred to as the sponsor, the senior officer who had asked for the work to be done, and we agreed on terms of reference for the work. After that, I spent a lot of time travelling around the country visiting police training centres. My first thoughts were that things might have changed since my time at Sandgate and that the training of recruits had probably become a national system. However, it soon became clear that there were two distinct methods of doing things. There was the Met system and then there was another system for everyone else.

One of my visits was to the training school at Pannal Ash, near Harrogate, where I stayed overnight. It had been several years since my last visit to North Yorkshire, and I had forgotten what a beautiful county it was. On my arrival, I was introduced to the commandant, who was a Met commander. He was keen to catch up on news from the Met and find out about my work, so he invited me to join him and his wife for dinner.

My project seemed like a good excuse for me to visit Hampshire and find out something about their training methods. It was a hot, sunny day when I arrived at the Hampshire training school at Netley, near Southampton. It was a large, modern building that looked a bit like an air terminal, in marked contrast to the red-brick buildings of the old Victorian military hospital a short distance away. After parking my car, I enjoyed a panoramic view of Southampton Water, the sun glinting off sparkling water seen through a fringe of pine trees.

During my visit, I was taken to see officers doing public-order training. At one point, one of the men walked over to see me and told me he recognised me.

'Remember that time I was struggling with that man in Winchester High Street, and you came to help me?'

I was taken aback at first, because I had no memory of him. Then the penny dropped, and I remembered him but could not recall the incident that he was talking about. It would have happened in 1965 or 1966, and many years had gone past by then. He then went on to tell me that he had just received his Police Long Service and Good Conduct Medal. This reminded me that I would be receiving mine that year. It was something that made me reflect on how quickly the time had gone by. I was now a veteran with twenty-two years' service.

At DMS, the reports that we submitted on projects required a completely different style to anything else in my previous experience, so it was good to have Ian Tolley giving me advice. Eventually, we had a lengthy, untidy-looking handwritten report several pages long that went to the word-processor operator.

After that, our report spent two or three weeks travelling around DMS between various senior officials and ourselves. Although I always tried to maintain a high standard when it came to paperwork, the world of operational policing was not one where you could spend weeks trying to make reports look like works of art. The important thing was that they were speedy, accurate, and functional. Working with civil servants was a whole new experience.

The principal who had overall responsibility for the project spent an amazing amount of time checking the written style of the report and the quality of the English in it. Naturally, I could appreciate that the reports coming from DMS needed to look professional. Most would go to high-ranking police officers, senior civil servants, and sometimes Government ministers. However, I must have lost count of the times that my reports went back to the word processor to be amended. Eventually John Tubb gave it his blessing and we sent it to our printing branch with a request for thirty copies.

I received my Police Long Service Medal while I was working on my first project at DMS. One side shows the head of the Queen, and the other side shows the figure of a woman who represents Justice and bears the words 'for exemplary police service'.

Maureen was invited to the ceremony at the Training School, and when we arrived there were about 100 officers gathered there, together with members of their families. The commissioner, Sir Kenneth Newman, presented me with my medal, and the next day Maureen sewed the medal ribbon to my tunic. There were weekly meetings at Aybrook Street, when project officers took it in turn to give a presentation relating to one of the projects that they were working on. In one of our meetings the project officer explained that he was involved in testing equipment for public order. John Tubb looked in my direction, and his face lit up in an evil grin.

'You had better speak to Richard Ramsay,' he said. 'He tells me that he is an expert on anything to do with public order.'

26

During January 1987, large crowds gathered at Wapping for the anniversary of the *News International* Dispute. The concept of peaceful picketing seemed to have been forgotten by some of the people there who described themselves as pickets. Many of them had gone there prepared to fight the police, and this resulted in a full-scale battle on the streets. As part of their tactics, protestors used trip wires to bring down police horses. It was one of the most violent episodes arising from a trade dispute and resulted in 163 police being injured. Sixty-seven people were arrested, and there were complaints from many pickets and demonstrators that police had used excessive force to deal with the situation.

There was no doubt that my life at DMS was much more comfortable than that of officers on the streets. Within the first six months of my arrival at Aybrook Street, I had been on courses within the Met, the Civil Service College, and a private management services college in Wolverhampton. This was all aimed at helping me to develop my skills dealing with information-gathering and analysing problems.

Not having to work unsocial hours was good for my general health and well-being. The fact that DMS did not have an overtime budget had a good side to it. Operational police work and overtime had always been part of my life. However, in my new role I had a plain-clothes allowance and did not work any overtime. Working regular hours and having all my weekends free made it possible for me to plan my life in a more ordered manner than in the past.

An added bonus was that I always available at weekends to spend time with my family. As history had always been a particular interest of mine I enrolled at the Kingston College of Further Education to start an A-level course on nineteenth century British and European history.

The Metropolitan Police has its own suggestion scheme. All police officers who have ideas that they believe will increase efficiency or save money are encouraged to put their ideas in on paper and send their suggestions to DMS. One of the police officers at Management Services was the Secretary of the Suggestion Scheme and had the responsibility of administering it.

The officer in charge of the scheme was a detective chief inspector who had decided to retire, and John Tubb asked me to take over the job. This meant that a lot of my time would be taken up with the suggestion scheme, and this would eat into the time available for working on projects.

The most important part of the job was to carry out an assessment of all the accepted suggestions each year. After that, a report would go to the commissioner, giving a list of the best ten or twelve suggestions. It would include details of the officers who had made the suggestions and an analysis of the benefits.

Any officer who made suggestions that resulted in the Met reducing costs was given a monetary award, and this was based on a percentage of the first year's savings. In any case that led to significant savings, the officer could receive a large sum of money. It was my job to select the three or four best suggestions. I would arrange for the officers who had made these suggestions to meet the commissioner, who would hand them their cheques.

At first sight, the way that the Suggestion Scheme worked sounded straightforward. However, within a couple of weeks something happened that gave me cause for concern about the system. An officer phoned me and stated that he had sent in a suggestion but nobody had contacted him to inform him whether it had been accepted or not. I asked him when he had sent us his suggestion, thinking that he would probably say something like four or five months.

'Three years ago,' he said.

This would have been followed by me repeating, 'Three years ago?' in a puzzled voice.

'He must be exaggerating a bit,' I thought. 'How could it be three years?' I assured him that I would look into this. The first thing to do was to find out the name of the project officer who had responsibility for that suggestion file. That was easy enough, but the person concerned had been transferred from DMS about two years before my arrival.

The suggestion related to equipment, and the file had been sent to the Met Engineering Branch three years before, with a request for their opinion on the merits of the idea. It would involve someone at Engineering Branch stating whether they thought this was a good idea or not. Often, when equipment was involved, technical evaluation tests would need to be carried out, but in this case the suggestion related to something simple and straightforward. My guess was that the response could be covered in a couple of paragraphs.

My fear was that the file had been lost somewhere in the system. Engineering Branch could not have the file three years down the line, could they? Looking through the Met phone book, I found a suitable person to contact, one of the senior managers in Engineering Branch. I have to confess to adding a little 'spin' to my story but believed that this was justified in order to get something done quickly. In my phone call, I explained that the PC who had made this suggestion was very upset about the delay and the fact that he had not been informed about what was happening. In fact, he was so upset that he wanted to put a complaint in writing about what had happened, but I had done my best to talk him out of this by telling him that he would receive an answer very soon.

The next day, one of the managers in the Engineering Branch phoned me to say that the file had been found, and two days after that the file arrived on my desk. Inside the file was a report dated two days before, which consisted of about sixty to seventy words. It concerned me that something so straightforward could have taken so long.

Not surprisingly, this episode suggested to me that there could be other suggestion files lying on desks, gathering dust in the four corners of the MPD. As secretary of the scheme, it was not my responsibility to check what had happened to 'live' suggestion files. This was the responsibility of the project officers and the principals who had given them the files to deal with. However, I had a nagging feeling that it might be a good idea to take a look at what was actually going on.

Although police officers at DMS were not on the front line, we were always aware of important operations taking place within the Met area. In July 1986, hundreds of police took part in Operation Trident. The strategy was to provide saturation policing and clear drug dealers from certain parts of Notting Hill in advance of the annual carnival. Local residents said that they welcomed the police operation but said that they feared retaliation from gangs of youths when the carnival started.

At the 1986 carnival, one person was murdered and there were attacks on police by gangs of youths. One of the evenings was marred by running battles in the streets but the overall level of violence was not as serious or well organised as it had been in previous years. The Trident name would be used some years later for a project aimed at tackling gun crime within the black community in London. This initiative started in 1995 in response to what were referred to as black-on-black shootings, mainly in the boroughs of Brent and Lambeth.

At first, Trident acted as an intelligence-gathering project, but as the killings continued, the Met set up a specialist unit to investigate shootings within London's communities and all gun-related murders within the black community. This unit became known as the Trident Operational Command Unit (OCU). In May 2004, Trident was expanded; by 2011 it had a total of about 460 police officers and support staff.

The work by Trident officers has led to the disruption of the activities of many criminals responsible for gun-related violence. A major success has been the conviction of people who were supplying firearms and the seizure of a large number of weapons.

Trident now has its own independent advisory group that assists its aims by harnessing the support of the community and ensuring the public is aware of the work that is being done by the police to make their lives safer. The group does its best to encourage members of the community to provide information about gun crime in London.

During the late 1980s, police were becoming increasingly aware of the activities of the 'Yardies' and other criminals involved in organised crime within the black community. Yardies was a name applied to Jamaican-born gangsters operating in Britain, and the name refers to the impoverished backyards of Kingston in Jamaica, where many of them came from.

Yardies tend to drive top-of-the-range BMWs, wear expensive designer clothes, sport gold jewellery, and carry firearms. 'Image' and 'respect' were the two key words used within their criminal culture, and they had a fearsome reputation for ruthless violence. The killing of Mark Burnett in 1991 in the middle of a night club was an example of their casual attitude to murder. Mark Burnett was shot dead because he had accidentally stepped on the toe of a Yardie gangster. At the time that the shooting took place, there were about 2,000 people in the club, but they all claimed that they had seen nothing out of the ordinary.

The Sicilian Mafia has always been admired by other criminal organisations, who copy their style and methods. Although the number of Yardies in the UK is small, probably no more than 300, their activities and style are admired and mimicked by large numbers of young black men and teenagers in Britain.

Yardies make their money mainly from selling drugs, robbery, and arms dealing. Unlike many other criminal organisations, they tend to operate with a total lack of structure or discipline, and this is a problem for police who investigate their crimes. A major difficulty for the police is the climate of fear that surrounds them and the reluctance of witnesses to give evidence against them. They believe in a live-for-the-moment philosophy, and one senior police officer who spent some time investigating them states that the life expectancy of a Yardie is about thirty-five years.

In 1993, Yardies were suspected of the murder of PC Patrick Dunne, who was shot dead in Clapham when he came across a shooting incident while on patrol. This crime is still unsolved. During 2011, in a period of six weeks, Yardies were the main suspects in five London murders where the victims were all black.

In August 1987, a new commissioner arrived. This was Sir Peter Imbert. He had a reputation of being a practical police officer with a wealth of operational experience. His career had started in the Met, and he had become well known for his work as the commander in charge of the Anti-Terrorist Branch.

My time at DMS coincided with the era when more and more police information systems based on handwritten records were being transferred to computer systems. An obvious target for change was the crime-reporting system in the Met, which consisted of handwritten crime reports.

A team had been set up at Aybrook Street to plan a computer system for recording crime; it would be called CRIS – or Crime Reporting Information System. The CRIS team consisted of a number of scientific officers from DMS, IT consultants, and Stewart Hull, a detective chief inspector.

The development of CRIS would be one of the most important events in the history of the police. Apart from recording reported crime, CRIS would enable us to produce statistics necessary for policing purposes and for the Home Office. It soon became apparent that the research involved to develop CRIS was complex, and by 1987 the project was running about three years behind schedule.

It was interesting for me to see how civil servants dealt with problems in their work, which was quite different from my style of doing things. Generally speaking, members of the Met civil staff were not under serious time constraints, and this led to a different style of decision making. The nature of police work calls for quick decision making, and most police officers like to think that they have the ability to do this, although in fairness, many do not.

A civil servant who was faced with a problem would spend some time thinking about it and would often make a point of discussing it with another colleague. Decisions were made in a style that was thoughtful but very slow.

Police officers need to make quick decisions in order to sum up situations or people, sometimes based on very little information. It made me think about the whole concept of making decisions and the psychology that went with it. There is a negative side to making decisions quickly. Because officers become used to making decisions rapidly, they sometimes do so when it is not necessary, and this can result in poor decisions.

Some senior police officers make fairly quick assessments about the character and style of junior officers based on very little information. This can be due to straightforward prejudice because the man or woman is a bit different from the picture of 'a good police officer' that they have in their heads.

In police work, time to stop and think is a luxury, and I counted myself lucky to have that luxury in my work at DMS. Generally speaking, the operational police officer is too busy trying to prevent the animals from taking over the zoo and rarely has time to sit down and think about how policing methods could be improved.

My new role did not give me the opportunity to prevent or detect crime, but project officers like me had the opportunity to investigate aspects of policing itself. It was necessary for me to develop completely new attitudes when looking at the way things were done. In the past it had been important to gain knowledge on the procedures we used to tackle specific problems. Now I had to become used to challenging accepted procedures. One question was all important: 'Could this be done in a more effective way?'

In Hungerford in Berkshire, Michael Ryan, who was an unemployed gun enthusiast, went on a shooting rampage, killing sixteen people and wounding fifteen others. One police officer was among the dead. It was the worst incident of its kind in British criminal history. There were complaints made about the time it took the Thames Valley Police armed support unit to reach the scene and pinpoint Ryan's location. There were also complaints that in the general confusion some officers had allowed members of the public to go into areas in the town where the gunman was, and this had, apparently resulted in at least one of the deaths.

Ryan had been armed with an automatic rifle, a handgun, and a grenade. One major problem was trying to find where Ryan was and where he was going as he walked through the town shooting people as they came into view. When cornered in a school by armed officers, Ryan shot himself.

The Hungerford shooting raised a number of questions. One basic issue was having officers on patrol who did not carry firearms becoming involved in an incident like this. Unarmed police were the first on scene at Hungerford, and one of them lost his life when Ryan riddled his police car with a burst from his automatic rifle. Hungerford is at the extreme western end of Berkshire, and the armed unit had to travel some distance to reach the scene.

Bill Ibbotson, one of the inspectors at DMS, had spent many years in Traffic Division. He had acted as an advisor to the Government on policing aspects relating to the M25 motorway during its construction. Because of his experience with the M25, Bill had been asked to go to Phoenix in Arizona in an advisory capacity when a decision was made to build an orbital motorway around the city.

Bill had started work on one of our most important projects, which was an assessment of the Crimestoppers programme. He was then given the news that he was to be promoted to chief inspector and would be transferred from DMS within the next few weeks. John Tubb asked me to take over the project from him.

For many years, police have had great success in using the media to appeal for witnesses in criminal cases. An example of this is the long-serving BBC television programme, *Crimewatch*. This uses cooperation between journalists, the public, and police in order to solve crimes that might otherwise remain undetected.

Crimestoppers takes a completely different approach to solving crime than do initiatives such as *Crimewatch*. The basic idea of Crimestoppers is to gather information rather than to find witnesses to specific crimes. The project began in Albuquerque, a city in the American state of New Mexico, and within a few years it had been copied by many police forces in the United States.

It proved successful, and before long it had crossed the Atlantic, and several British police forces had set up Crimestoppers schemes. The way it works is quite simple. Members of the public make phone calls to a Crimestoppers office and give information, naming people who have committed specific offences or are involved in criminal activity. The caller remains anonymous but is given a reference number.

Informants can receive cash rewards for information that leads to serious crimes being solved. The unit based at Scotland Yard was linked to a charity, and if police recommended a reward it would be paid in cash by someone working for the charity. Police officers were not involved in paying money to informants.

The Crimestoppers unit at Scotland Yard started operating in January 1987. My job was to follow the work of the unit for its first twelve months, looking at the results they achieved measured against how much it cost the Met to run the unit. After collecting all the necessary information, I would recommend whether or not the scheme should be allowed to continue. The final decision would probably be taken by the assistant commissioner, who had responsibility for crime and specialist operations.

Bill Ibbotson had set up a computer system at Aybrook Street that kept records of all the calls that came into the Crimestoppers unit each day. This was new territory for me, as I had never used a computer before, but Bill showed me how it worked, and it seemed quite user-friendly. We had details of all the calls coming into the Crimestoppers' office, and we broke them down into categories. After that, we recorded a list of all the calls that resulted in arrests and charges.

There was no doubt in my mind that this was likely to be the most important project that would come my way at DMS. My first port of call was the Crimestoppers Unit at Scotland Yard, where I introduced myself to the officer in charge, Detective Inspector Bill Gent. After that, I met the other members of the team, a DS and three DCs.

Each week the unit would send me a report that acted as a record of their work and summed up all the calls received. The calls were then divided into categories, for example, (1) Murder and Serious Assaults, (2) Rape and Indecency Offences, (3) Drug Dealing, and (4) Robbery. I also kept records of each case when information was received that led to an arrest. It soon became clear that the Crimestoppers Unit was responsible for clearing up a great deal of crime including some very serious ones.

27

Not surprisingly, there has always been concern within the police service about the level of violence faced by officers on the streets. This became even more relevant during the eighties, a very violent period of time, when more police officers were murdered than in any previous decade. A total of 42 police officers were murdered in Britain and this figure did not include the many officers murdered in Northern Ireland.

In a typical year, thousands of police officers are injured as a result of assaults. Comparisons with other countries indicated that British police had one of the highest casualty rates in the western world. In terms of crime and other issues, London is often compared with New York, as both cities have populations of a similar size.

During the eighties, some research was done to compare policing in both these cities. Information was gathered over a period of five years, and this included looking at the risks faced by police. There had always been a general assumption that police work would be much more dangerous in New York. However, during those five years, four officers had been murdered in New York and five in London.

At that time, another topical issue was the rapid growth of the private security industry. The rising crime rate and the fear of crime had created a climate of opinion in the UK that boosted business for private security companies. In Government circles, there was increasing talk of privatisation in the public sector of some services, including policing, prisons, and the National Health Service. The Met had become involved in the controversy over private security when an announcement was made that enquiries into cheque fraud and credit-card fraud would be privatised.

DMS had started a project into police overtime, to evaluate how well it was supervised by sergeants and inspectors. The project was given to one of my fellow inspectors, Bob Gordon, who asked me whether I could assist him for a week or so. He had chosen a busy police station in south London where there was a lot of overtime being worked.

Every division has its own overtime budget, and the amount varies considerably between divisions. The general rule is that overtime should only be claimed by officers for operational work, such as making an arrest or carrying out specific crime enquiries. Overtime is also authorised for officers who attend court on days when they are on leave or should be off duty.

Given the nature of police work, it can be difficult to certify that every hour of overtime claimed is always justified. If an officer makes an arrest shortly before his/her tour of duty ends, this might mean three, four, or five hours of overtime. That would normally be regarded as a good example of justifiable overtime.

However, there are always going to be cases that fall into a grey area. Good detective work has always involved officers working additional hours in order to obtain the necessary evidence to support a charge. The CID was founded because of the need for a force of detectives available to investigate serious crime. Investigating an offence can result in an officer working flat out without a break for many hours. Some crimes may take months or even years to investigate properly.

When we arrived at the police station in south London on the first day, we talked with one of the detective sergeants. He had returned to divisional CID work after spending a number of years working on the Flying Squad. The DS said that coming back to a division had been quite a shock to him.

He noticed that crime had increased significantly during the time that he had been away. Arriving on his first day, he'd found that his DI and several other people in the CID office were absent, mainly involved with court cases. He soon discovered that there was only one other CID officer on duty with him that day.

Picking up the major crime book, he noted that there were a large number of reported crimes to be allocated to CID officers for investigation.

There were only two officers available to investigate, do the paperwork, and answer the phones in the CID office. And, of course, the custody officer might call on them at any time to give advice on incoming crime arrests.

He told us that his case load that day came to a total of twenty-nine reported crimes, twenty-eight burglaries, and an indecent assault on a woman. In practical terms, it meant that if nothing else happened that day, he would be hard pressed to do anything other than contacting the victims and writing some brief information about his actions in the crime reports. This could easily take about ten hours, so that he would be on overtime without actually being able to do any proper detective work.

After a few days working our way through overtime claims, we noticed that there was another DS who claimed two hours overtime every day that he was on duty. The significance of this would not be lost on any police officer. Working for ten hours means completing a normal tour of duty (eight hours) plus two hours overtime. Police Regulations stipulate that an officer who works ten hours or more is entitled to a refreshment allowance.

The reason for the 'refresher' is that the officer will need to have something to eat, and the allowance is to cover food that he or she buys. At one time, receipts had to be produced for the food purchased. However, the Police Federation took the view that it was wrong to expect police officers to provide paperwork for what was a small amount and fought a campaign against receipts. Eventually the commissioner accepted this argument, but it soon became standard practice for everyone to claim the maximum.

We examined the workload of this DS, and it did not appear to be particularly heavy. After that, we checked station records to see when he had last made an arrest and found that he had charged someone with burglary about three weeks before. Further reading revealed that the arresting officer had been a Uniform PC, but the DS had taken over the investigation.

This was a case where the CID officer concerned worked ten hours every day but we were doubtful whether all of those hours were necessary. We would refer to this as 'institutional overtime', which suggests that overtime was not being properly supervised.

This was not just a problem involving CID officers, as we soon came across another case where a Uniform PC was making frequent overtime claims. It seemed that he worked overtime several times each week, whatever his scheduled hours of duty were. The records showed that he booked on duty for a variety of reasons, including attendance at court and carrying out crime enquiries.

At every station there are Uniform officers who are known as 'thief takers'. These officers seem to have a natural ability to 'sniff out' people who are committing crime. There had been several occasions during my service when I'd stopped people I just 'knew' had committed offences without having the slightest piece of evidence to support it.

However, as far as this division was concerned, we were outsiders. We had no idea about the reputation of this officer, whether he was a genuine thief taker or not. If you have to go to court, you go to court, but other types of overtime, such as crime enquiries, can fall into something of a grey area.

Overtime has to be authorised by a supervising officer, who writes and initials a written record of it. Later, it is initialled when the period of overtime is completed. As we looked through station records, it appeared that this PC was a hard worker, but we were concerned about all the overtime that he'd claimed.

After doing some calculations, I told Bob Gordon that the officer must be earning at least £10,000 each year from overtime. We were at the station to see how well or badly overtime was being supervised and not there to investigate individuals. There was no evidence that the officer concerned had done anything wrong. However, we were not totally happy that his overtime was being supervised correctly. Bob brought it to the attention of the chief superintendent, and we continued working on the project.

For about a week that project took up most of my time, but it will not surprise the reader to learn that during 1988 there were other events occurring that were even more important than police overtime.

During August, there was a meeting between three men at Peshawar in Pakistan, two of whom were Egyptian militants. They were Ayman al-Zawahiri and Sayyid Imam al-Sharif, also known as Dr Fadi. The third man was a wealthy Saudi Arabian named Osama Bin Laden.

They decided to set up an organisation that would rid Muslim countries of western influence and destroy Muslim regimes that they considered corrupt. They planned to work for a future when they could do away with national boundaries and set up a caliphate, a huge empire consisting of all the Islamic countries in the world.

Dr Fadi wrote a book setting out the case for war against the West, and in 1991 Osama Bin Laden moved to Sudan, where he organised a number of terrorist training camps. Bin Laden's strategy was that Sudan would become the base to plan and launch attacks on Western targets. The organisation that developed from this would become known as al-Qaeda.

A company of management consultants, called Wolff Olins, was hired to carry out a management review of the Metropolitan Police. As an organisation, the Met was described as sound, but their management and communications were pronounced to be in poor shape. Wolff Olins also stated that the absence of clear goals for the Met was damaging to morale. A few months later, the President of ACPO, Roger Birch, chief constable of Sussex, called for an urgent Royal Commission to examine the role of the police service.

In January 1989, the Guardian Angels, an American vigilante group, sent some of their members to train British recruits to help control violence on the London Underground system. Their arrival on the scene was not welcomed by the British Transport Police or the Met.

My visits to the Crimestoppers office were always interesting. On my arrival one day, I became involved in a discussion about one of the calls that they had received. Two weeks earlier there had been an armed robbery at a jeweller's shop in a city in the north of England, where the manager had been shot and seriously injured.

The officers who were investigating this offence were having great difficulty in identifying suspects. They knew that the two men involved were black but not much else. Shortly before my arrival that day, a call had come in from someone who said that the day after the robbery one of the men involved had fled the country.

Our informant had received a phone call from the suspect, who'd told him that he was in another country and had run out of money. The suspect had not said what country he was in but had provided a phone number and asked if his friend in England could arrange for funds to be sent to him. It appeared that the first part of the phone number had been written down wrongly. The DS showed me the number and asked me if I had any ideas about where the place might be.

Two or three people present, including me, made a few suggestions but it turned out that we were not on the right track. Then one of the officers in the unit picked up a phone directory and sat reading through it for a few minutes. Eventually he spoke. 'I think that it must be Turkey,' he said.

The DC amended the country code, and we all went quiet while he dialled it. A man answered the phone speaking in a strong Jamaican accent. I did not know whether the officer was a skilled linguist or not, but he suddenly starting speaking in a strange language that could have been a mixture of Brazilian Portuguese and Latvian. Both parties attempted to carry on some sort of conversation for about a minute, and then the line went dead. Three hours later, the Turkish police arrived at the place where he was staying. They knocked on his door but did not receive a reply, so they kicked it down. They found the suspect and arrested him. A few weeks later, he was extradited to the UK.

The most important part of my project, as mentioned, was to look at the cost of Crimestoppers and see whether the arrests made justified the cost of running the unit. Was it cost effective to have a team of experienced detectives answering phone calls at Scotland Yard, or would it be better to employ them investigating crime on division?

The results obtained during the first twelve months were impressive. Many serious crimes – such as murder, rape, and armed robbery – had been solved. Information had been provided about all sorts of other crimes, and in particular, a considerable amount of information about drug dealers had come in.

One of the aspects that surprised me was that very few of the people who had provided useful information leading to the detection of serious crimes wanted to receive a reward. Each day the unit received a number of hostile or malicious calls, but it was interesting to note that the majority of people who contacted Crimestoppers seemed to have a genuine wish to help remove criminals from the streets. My report on Crimestoppers included a breakdown of all the costs involved in running the scheme and ended with a recommendation that the scheme should continue.

Another of my projects was to examine the physical fitness of officers who were authorised to use firearms. An officer carrying out protection duties can be faced with all sorts of situations – such as the shooting of Shlomo Argov, the Israeli ambassador. In that case, the protection officer had chased and shot one of the terrorists. My opinion was that all police officers should have a good level of physical fitness, and one of my recommendations was that officers carrying out protection duty should have regular physical training.

When prison officers working at Wandsworth Prison went on strike, Met officers went in to help run the prison. It was another period of time when there was friction between the police and government, with the Federation becoming more and more vocal in its criticism of some government policies.

One spokesman mentioned the frustration felt by officers working in drugs squads in major cities who were not allowed to carry out surveillance operations on drug dealers because of financial constraints. There was also the problem of hundreds of prisoners being kept in police cells.

A Federation representative pointed out that the Conservative Party had always prided itself on its strong approach to law and order. He underlined the comparison between the huge sums of money available to the police service during the miners' strike and the lack of resources that were now hindering the police so that they were not always able to provide a high quality service to the public.

One of my projects was to develop a system where handheld computers could be used to issue fixed penalty notices for parking offences. Our FPNs were handwritten, and most of them were issued by traffic wardens. However, a number of cities in the United States had moved to a system in which a FPN could be issued by a handheld computer.

It was necessary for me to do some research as I needed to have a thorough knowledge about the system of parking enforcement in London. As I did so, more and more problems came to light. For example, the Met was paying thousands of pounds each year to people who made complaints about their cars being clamped or towed away.

When this type of complaint was examined, it was often the case that there was no evidence to support the action that had been taken. The police copy of the FPN was simple enough. The front page had the details of the alleged offence, and if you turned it over, you could read the evidence of the traffic warden or police officer who had written it. This sounds easy enough, but when some of these FPNs were examined there was a problem. The evidence page was completely blank.

In fairness to traffic wardens, many of these problems were caused by police officers. Traffic wardens were trained to write FPNs and they did so methodically, but there were a number of officers who had a cavalier approach to writing tickets. Their attitude was sometimes, 'This is easy', and it was – especially if you forgot to complete the section that read Details of Evidence.

Whether or not motorists really deserved to receive a FPN or be towed away became irrelevant in these cases. If there was no evidence about the offence that they were alleged to have committed, we had to pay them compensation.

I needed to have a look at what actually happened on the streets, and part of this involved me spending two days with the crew of a removal unit in north London. There were two people working together, a TD officer and a civilian removal officer. The two of them appeared to be at war with a local shopkeeper who had decided that he would park his car every day on the yellow line outside his hardware shop.

The shopkeeper seemed to be very well organised. As soon as the removal truck came anywhere near his shop, he would come running out, jump into his car, and drive off. This situation represented a serious challenge to the forces of law and order – the fast-moving shopkeeper had managed to defeat them each time!

However, about three weeks earlier, the removal team had been successful for the first time, when they'd managed to hitch up his car and remove it in a very high-speed operation. A few days later, they struck again and removed his car for the second time. Every war consists of a number of battles, and each side can win or lose.

The next phase of this campaign came a few days after the second successful car removal. The two of them swooped one morning and started to hitch up the offending car, but stopped in their tracks when they came up against a large, vicious-looking dog, barking and snarling at them through a half-open window. They decided that this one would have to be chalked up as a victory to the shopkeeper, who was standing at the front of his shop, grinning.

'All's fair in love and war.' I later heard that the shopkeeper was not totally happy in his efforts to prevent his car being removed. One day, there was a mysterious incident when a bar of chocolate laxative was pushed through the open car window. As they say in France, 'C'est la guerre.'

It was interesting to see what was happening on the streets of north London, but there was a serious side to all of this. It became increasingly obvious that there would be many advantages to switching to handheld computers. One important factor was that the system could prevent an FPN being issued until every necessary action had been completed. There were often problems of legibility with handwritten documents, but a computerised system would produce a neat, professional-looking ticket every time.

As Christmas 1989 approached, I wondered whether it was time for me to go back to operational policing. My work at Management Services was interesting, and my senior colleagues had told me that I had very good analytical skills. It appeared that the senior management at DMS would be quite happy for me to stay there, and my working conditions were good. Another aspect in my decision was promotion. Although I'd been recommended for promotion to chief inspector, being in a formal interview situation was not one of my strong points. Operational policing was something that I had always enjoyed, but by this time there was an element of 'seen that, done that' when I thought about working on division. It was not an easy decision to make.

There were dramatic changes taking place in the outside world. The most symbolic event was the fall of the Berlin wall. It meant the end of a divided Germany, and it was a sign that the communist system was breaking down. A crucial weakness in communist Eastern Europe was a poor economy that failed to provide a high standard of living for its people. After many years of conflict and tension, it appeared that the West had won the Cold War.

28

Once I had made the decision, my return to operational policing took place in January 1990, and it took me to Staines. My new division covered the Borough of Spelthorne, just outside what would later be known as the Greater London Area, the GLA. It seemed strange in some ways. Staines was part of the old county of Middlesex, which was now little more than a postal address. However, politically, it was a Surrey borough that took in Staines, Ashford, Sunbury, Stanwell, and Shepperton. The division also covered part of Heathrow Airport where the cargo warehouses were situated.

A few days after my arrival on the division, we were faced with a serious situation that was totally different to anything that I had experienced before. Hurricane-force winds hit us on 25 January 1990; the occurrence was given the name The Burns Day Storm by the press. By the time that the storm abated, thirty-nine people had lost their lives in England and Wales and large numbers of people been injured.

The division had just updated its planning for major incidents, and they seemed to be strongly influenced by memories of the accident in 1970 when a British Airways airliner had crashed on some open land at Staines. It had been estimated that if the aircraft had continued flying for an extra three or four seconds it would have come down in the town centre.

Our major-incident plans were activated, and the chief inspector (operations) took charge of the divisional control room, with two extra officers being brought in to deal with incoming calls. A control centre was also set up at the Spelthorne Borough Civic Centre, where there was a team of council employees and police working together.

In this case, what we spoke of as being a major incident was quite different from the sort of event that we had imagined, such as a railway accident or aircraft crash. This did not involve something happening at one location but, rather, a large number of small, dangerous incidents occurring one after the other all over the division. People were being injured, and there was considerable damage to property.

It was very similar to what had happened in October 1987 when the country had been hit with hurricane winds. Across the division, dozens – if not hundreds – of trees were falling. They were hitting houses, crushing cars, and knocking down walls and fences. Advertising hoardings, scaffolding, and roofs of buildings were being torn loose by the ferocity of the wind. Within the first thirty minutes or so, reports started coming in of roads being blocked and people injured.

The police, fire brigade, and other services were soon under great pressure. They were doing all they could to reduce the risk to the public. Police officers were spending much time sealing off roads and dangerous buildings. The fire brigade were busy using their equipment to cut through fallen trees and clear roads that were blocked.

We identified some dangerous situations in Staines and Sunbury that needed to be given priority. I discussed the situation with one of my fellow inspectors, and we decided to divide the area into two sectors. My colleague looked after the problems in Staines, while I drove to Sunbury. The most serious situation there involved a six-storey building that was under construction.

It came as quite a shock to me when I saw the building. The only way to describe it was a disaster waiting to happen. All six storeys of the building were covered in scaffolding. It had not collapsed, but all the scaffolding had moved and shifted to one side. One more puff of wind would probably mean disaster, and something needed to be done fast. This building was part of the shopping area of Sunbury and close to a block of flats.

I thought that the scaffolding was likely to come crashing down at any moment, and I directed officers to seal off the surrounding area. One of the sergeants went to the flats to advise people to evacuate. Looking back on it, we were probably all too close to the area of danger. As luck would have it, the scaffolding did not move, and twenty-four hours later it was still holding together. We were never quite sure how they managed it, but the scaffolding company started work next day and managed to take all the scaffolding down without anyone being killed or injured.

After several hours of mayhem, the storm winds started to abate. Within the next few days we had the opportunity to discuss what had happened and how we had responded to this emergency. On the division, at least twenty people had been injured, including four police officers who had been hit by flying debris. Nobody had been killed or seriously injured, and the major incident plan had worked quite well.

My role for the first three or four months at Spelthorne was to act as the deputy to the chief inspector (ops) and also provide cover as a divisional duty officer. The chief superintendent knew about my work at Scotland Yard and asked me to carry out a study in order to improve our system for dealing with people suffering from mental illness.

The Metropolitan Police had its own long-standing system for dealing with mentally ill people. They were not arrested unless it was thought that they could be a danger to themselves or other people, but Section 136 of the Mental Health Act provided the authority to detain them and take them to a police station. An officer holding the rank of inspector or above had the power to sign a form to have the person taken to a mental hospital. This procedure was referred to as the person being 'deemed'. They could be detained at the hospital for up to three days in order to be assessed.

In most cases, the person who had been arrested would be held at a police station for no more than about an hour before being taken to hospital. This system, involving all the London boroughs and the Met, had worked well for many years, but Spelthorne was not a London borough. Surrey boroughs did not have their own social services departments; this function was the responsibility of the county council.

The law stated that a person who was mentally ill could be taken to a 'place of safety', and this definition included police stations. However much service I had as a police officer, it was never going to be possible to escape from definitions! The problem was simple. It arose because Surrey's social services held the view that a police station was a suitable place for detaining people who were mentally ill and a good location for their mental-health workers to carry out an assessment. There was a large general hospital within our area, but its staff would not accept people who were mentally ill. The chief superintendent was concerned about how long people suspected of suffering from mental illness were being detained at Staines. My first task was to go through all the custody records for the previous year and see what had happened in these cases. It did not take long for me to come up against the practical problems that officers were facing. While sitting in the charge room making notes, I was approached by a frustrated-looking custody officer, who started telling me about a case she had been dealing with earlier that day.

Police had been called to a disturbance at about ten o'clock the previous night, and this had resulted in a man being arrested who was violent and appeared to be mentally ill. A phone call went to Surrey Social Services requesting that they send someone to Staines so that the man could be assessed. We were told that they did not have any staff available, but they would have someone at Staines by 9 a.m. the following day.

This meant that the custody officer on night duty was responsible for a person for eight hours who appeared to be mentally ill, someone who was a potential risk to himself and any officers who might have to deal with him. We would need to visit this person regularly and watch him carefully. If the man died, it would be a death-in-police-custody case.

What had upset the early turn custody officer was that nobody from Surrey Social Services had arrived by nine. She waited until about ten o'clock and then contacted them. By this time the man had been in police custody for twelve hours. She was told that they knew nothing about this matter and had no record of any communication with the police station. Eventually, two social workers turned up at 1 p.m. The whole situation was summed up by something that the custody officer said to me. 'If a police officer comes across a man lying in the street with a broken arm, would he arrest him, take him to a police station, lock him up in a cell, and then call for a doctor?'

I could not fault the logic of her argument. The division had a total of about twenty mental-health arrests the previous year, including about four cases where people had been detained for twenty-four hours or more – in one case for forty-eight hours. My personal opinion was that the system was not in the best interests of those who were mentally ill. However, in fairness to Surrey County Council, I need to point out that their policy defining police stations as places of safety was correct as far as the law was concerned.

My report had a number of recommendations, the main one being that we came to an arrangement with our local general hospital, Ashford, with a view to the hospital holding mentally ill people for assessment. It was agreed that I should enter into discussions with hospital administrators in order to move this initiative forward. This led to a number of meetings over about twelve months, but at the end of this there was no agreement.

In February 1990, the big news was from South Africa, when Nelson Mandela had been released from prison. By 1990, Mandela had become the deputy president of the African National Congress (ANC); he had been in prison since 1964. Now, television screens all over the world were showing him walking away from prison as a free man.

Everyone knew that there would now be momentous change in South Africa, but we were surprised at the peaceful transition of power that was taking place. Much of this came about because of the character and personality of Mandela.

While South Africa seemed to be coming together, it started to look as though British society was falling apart. The government had decided to make changes to the system of local taxation and came up with a new concept known as The Poll Tax. Essentially, this meant that every adult person in the country would pay the same amount of money, irrespective of their wealth or the value of any property they owned. This was the trigger for serious rioting in March 1990 which became known as The Poll Tax Riots. In London, the area around Trafalgar Square was soon looking like a war zone, with damaged buildings and fires burning. The political backlash to the poll tax and the resulting riots were factors that would lead to the fall of Prime Minister Margaret Thatcher.

There were three police buildings within the Spelthorne division. Staines was a very old station, and its working facilities were quite poor. Some of the station's offices were in prefabricated buildings, and the divisional headquarters occupied part of an office block a short distance away. There was also another station at Sunbury, although all charges were dealt with at Staines.

It appeared to me that nobody seemed quite sure what to do about Sunbury police station. It was a small, old fashioned Victorian building in a residential area, cut off from the main shopping area of Sunbury by the M3 Motorway. There were two long-serving PCs there who looked after the front office, and the station was open to the public for a few hours each day.

The chief superintendent told me that he wanted to improve the quality of policing in Sunbury. He lived there and was aware of all the local problems. He wanted me to work at Sunbury and take responsibility for a number of policing aspects there. One of my tasks would be planning and managing the policing of events at Kempton Park Racecourse.

For some time, most of the day-to-day supervision at Sunbury had been in the hands of John Simons, a very experienced sergeant. The home-beat officers in Sunbury and Shepperton were all based at Sunbury. John supervised them and made sure that the station ran smoothly. I called in at Sunbury to meet him, and he took me for a drive around Sunbury and Shepperton.

John produced a map of Spelthorne, pointing at the various places that made up the division. Looking at a map made me realise how interesting the local geography was. The River Thames made a good natural boundary, with the Surrey Police area on the other side. There seemed to be water everywhere. Spelthorne division was covered in lakes, rivers, and reservoirs, and there were a number of small islands along the Thames. There was also a considerable amount of open countryside, much of it farmland.

Sunbury, Lower Sunbury, Sunbury Common, Shepperton, Upper Halliford, Charlton, Littleton – these were all villages that had grown larger and larger over the years. Shepperton film studios stood on what was almost an island, a strip of land with the huge Queen Mary Reservoir to the north and the River Ash to its south.

I spent two or three weeks with John Simons, exploring the area and meeting the home-beat officers and local residents. It seemed that the policing of Sunbury had been given a low profile for many years. At Staines, as elsewhere, one sergeant would be custody officer and one would patrol the division. If there was a third sergeant on duty, he/she would be posted to Sunbury. Sometimes one, or even two, PCs might be posted to Sunbury, dependent on the manpower situation.

John Simons went with me to Kempton Park Racecourse and introduced me to some of the key people who managed the race meetings and other events. We planned the policing for the next race meeting and carried out an estimate of how many officers we would need. After that, I completed a report and then went to the chief inspector (ops) with my recommendations and request for manpower. It was the first time that I had been in charge of policing a race meeting, and everything went smoothly.

Britain was about to go to war. In August 1990 Iraq invaded Kuwait, and there was mounting concern about this in the West. There was the danger that Iraq's next move might be an invasion of Saudi Arabia. The United States, Britain, and several other countries formed an alliance in order to protect Saudi Arabia and force the Iraqis out of Kuwait.

In November, former cabinet member Michael Heseltine announced that he intended to challenge Margaret Thatcher's leadership of the Conservative Party. This led to a series of events, and within a short time, Margaret Thatcher had decided to resign as prime minister. A ballot would see John Major emerge as the new party leader.

During 1991, there were more and more signs that the Soviet Union and Communist Party political structure that had dominated Eastern Europe since the Second World War was starting to disintegrate. Later that year, Boris Yeltsin became the first freely elected president of Russia, and ten of the countries within the old Soviet Union were given their independence.

On 7 February 1991, the IRA carried out an attack on Downing Street. The attackers used a Ford Transit van, with a hole cut into its roof so that a mortar could be fired from it. Whitehall and the immediate area were probably the most heavily patrolled streets in the UK, so any attack like this would need to be exceptionally well planned. An IRA man had driven the van to a pre-planned location in Whitehall, set three mortars to fire and left the scene on a motorcycle.

As a PC walked towards the parked Ford Transit to investigate, the three mortars detonated and hurtled towards Downing Street, each one of them with a warhead of twenty kilograms of Semtex. Two of the mortar bombs overshot the target and failed to explode, landing on grass at the edge of St James Park. A third bomb landed in the rear garden of Number 10 and exploded while a meeting of the war cabinet was taking place.

Prime Minister John Major had called a meeting to discuss the Gulf War, and when the explosion took place, those present took cover under the Cabinet Office table. It was reported later that John Major said to colleagues, 'I think that we had better start again – somewhere else.'

Peter Gurney, the Met's senior explosives officer, reached the scene within two or three minutes of the mortars being fired. He commented on the audacity and speed of the attack, pointing out that the van had been positioned in an area that was always well guarded by police. Someone would have had to park the van, set the mortars to fire, and flee the area in less than a minute. Linked to the firing mechanism was a second device that set fire to the van, in order to destroy any forensic evidence that there may have been.

Peter Gurney was also surprised at how accurate the mortar had been considering that the person who'd fired it had had no line of sight. What was sobering was the knowledge that if one of those bombs had been fractionally more accurate, the prime minister and the other members of the war cabinet would all be dead. Four people, including two police officers, were hurt, but none of them had serious injuries.

During my time at Staines, my duties sometimes took me to Twickenham when there were important rugby matches taking place. It was a long-standing operation with a contingent of police inside the stadium and others posted outside. For many years, Spelthorne Division had assisted Twickenham division, patrolling in two or three carriers to provide public-order support on the streets of Twickenham.

Having policed football matches in the past, I knew that you had to be prepared for anything. It made me recall one incident when I was a sergeant. I had been with two or three PCs when we found ourselves caught between two armies of football fans who were at war. Both sides pelted each other with bottles and anything else that was to hand. Luckily for us, it appeared that they did not want to hurt us, but it was scary being caught in the middle with everything flying over our heads for a couple of minutes. At Twickenham, it came as a pleasant surprise to see how well behaved the rugby fans were, and it was rare that we had any trouble.

During 1991, less and less of my time was being spent at Sunbury. There were seven inspectors on the division, but one of these was the community liaison officer, who did not normally do operational work. There was always a requirement for a duty officer on a twenty-four-hour basis, and we seemed to be continually short of inspectors. There were many public-order commitments, which added to the problem. There was one period of four weeks when I was only at Sunbury for two days.

At divisional meetings my senior officers often referred to me as 'our man at Sunbury', and this suggested that I was the officer in charge of a subdivision who knew everything that was going on there. My attitude was that it was only fair that I took my turn as duty officer, but the whole concept of me being in charge at Sunbury did not make much sense if I was hardly ever there. I mentioned this to the chief superintendent, and he nodded as if in agreement, but it seemed that he did not wish to come to any decision at that point. He was close to retirement, and I sensed that he did not want to tie the hands of the next divisional commander by making any major changes. Another good reason to leave the matter up in the air was that we had all heard rumours that the Met was planning to move to a new system, to be called sector policing.

Sector policing would be an important new strategy for operational policing within the Metropolitan Police, and it would mean major upheaval and change. The plan was that the territory of every division would be divided into two or three sectors with an inspector in charge of each one. Every sector would have several teams with a sergeant in charge of each team. The underlying philosophy was that the Met would move from time-based policing to territory-based policing.

A new chief superintendent arrived, and at our monthly inspectors' meetings we started to discuss sector policing. It was decided that a small working party should be set up that would consist of a sergeant, a PC, and myself to do the initial planning. We met regularly and discussed every aspect of it. We soon agreed that there was one crucial question: whether the division should be divided into two or three sectors.

For many years, a key strategy of the division had been to develop a strong partnership, binding together three main elements, namely the borough council, the people living in the borough, and the police. This was not a concept that was unique to Spelthorne, but the fact was that community relations in the division were particularly good.

One of the benefits to the police was the strong support of the Spelthorne council, which included money to finance some policing projects that we had developed. We knew that sector policing was not simply a matter for the police and that it had become an important local political issue. There was a strong feeling in the community that Ashford should have its own police station or office.

We already had a station at Sunbury, so we developed two models for sector policing. The first plan was the most simple; this would involve dividing the division in half. The northern half would take in Staines, Stanwell, and Ashford, and the southern part would cover Sunbury and Shepperton. In terms of manpower and buildings, this would not be too difficult.

Our second model was to divide the division into three sectors. This would mean building a police office at Ashford or having an Ashford sector based at Staines. A three-sector division was good politically and our relationship with the council was very important to our whole strategy; it was something that had taken years to build up.

At our working-part meetings, all three of us saw one obvious problem with having three sectors – manpower. There would be six teams to each sector, with a sergeant in charge of each one. We played around with the figures in various ways, but we had to accept the fact that there would be a maximum of six PCs to each team, although we all felt that eight would be better.

Staines police station needed to be kept open and manned on a twenty-four-hour basis, and there were several roles that would be divisional rather than sector based, such as the control room and the area car. Officers would need to be brought in from sectors to cover these posts. We calculated how many PCs would actually be on duty on each sector for an eight-hour shift. On most days, there would be no more than two. However, we realised that with three sectors we would have to accept this situation.

29

The Met still had serious manpower problems, and on my arrival at Staines one Sunday morning as duty officer, I got a sharp reminder of it. As usual on a Sunday, there were two sergeants, one taking over as custody officer and the other patrolling the section. The section sergeant and I walked into the parade room together and stood there, feeling slightly bemused as we looked at an empty parade room for two or three minutes.

Then a PC appeared and hurriedly mumbled some apologies for being late. Where were the others? We soon discovered that the lonely looking officer in the parade room was the only one we had. The other four or five who should have been there were on public-order duty in central London. We had two for the area car and the inside staff for the station, but apart from that, we had one PC to patrol the division.

Sadly, we had become used to working without the manpower that we needed, but I could not recall a previous time when we'd only had one PC available to patrol a division. In this case, with the population of the Borough of Spelthorne being about 90,000, we were definitely outnumbered that day. Luckily for us, it was a very quiet day, and somehow we managed to deal with everything.

The media appear to become obsessed with certain types of offences from time to time, and in 1992 it appeared that the only crime that was 'fashionable' and worth mentioning was 'ram raiding'. The modus operandi was fairly simple. Three or four young criminals would steal a high-powered car and then use it to ram a shop window or warehouse door. They would move as fast as they could through the building, stealing property, and then leave the scene as quickly as they had arrived.

As they were usually masked, the evidence from security cameras was of limited value. The people involved were not bothered about setting off alarm systems, because they were probably only inside the premises for about two minutes and would be on their way before Old Bill arrived. In the event of a chase, they would drive at exceptionally high speeds, often followed by police cars that could not keep up with them. The extremely fast speeds of the bandit cars produced a situation that was dangerous to the offenders, the police, and other road users. Police took the view that it was better to let them escape than to have an accident in which people lost their lives.

Sometimes it seemed as though the drivers of these high-powered cars were so high on adrenalin that they were not bothered about losing their own lives, especially when they drove at police vehicles. On one occasion, a Ford Cosworth was driven straight at the Staines area car head-on. Faced with a car coming straight towards him at about 90 mph, the area car driver swerved off the road to avoid what would have been certain death.

Information came in that one of the gangs involved in ram raiding was based in our division. It appeared that they were not committing any offences close to home but were operating mainly in the Surrey Police and Thames Valley Police areas. The suspects were all living in Stanwell, just north of Staines, and our divisional crime squad was tasked to catch them.

By this time, each Met Division had its own crime squad, and at Staines there were six or seven officers with an experienced DS in charge. PCs who were interested in joining the CID were posted to crime squads to test them and give them the experience that they needed.

The subject of the ram raiders came up at our monthly inspectors' meeting, and we made suggestions about how to tackle the problem. However, it was one of the PCs on the crime squad who came up with a cunning plan, as they say. He thought about the road system in and around Stanwell and reasoned that our suspects were likely to drive along one particular stretch of road.

Two or three nights later, four PCs from the crime squad, dressed like council workers, travelled to the agreed location in a pick-up truck. They got to work, and soon a large pile of soil and rubble appeared on the road surface. Official-looking Road Works signs were put in position, and by the morning it looked very realistic. A special camera was set up amongst the bits and pieces on the road-works site. It was crucial that the obstruction forced all the traffic to stop or slow down at one particular point, where each vehicle was photographed. It was equally important to obtain clear pictures of the driver and any front-seat passenger. Within a few weeks, our local ram raiders had been arrested and charged.

The Spelthorne Division, together with our neighbouring divisions, was being plagued by burglary artifice offences. I had not come into contact with this type of offence much since my time at Wimbledon. In this wave of offences, the victims were nearly always very elderly and vulnerable, and the classic MO involved two people. In a typical scenario, one person would come to a house, telling the victim that he/she was from the council and needed to check the water supply urgently.

While the victim was being distracted with talk about the terrible damage that water can cause to the house, an accomplice would slip in and steal property. It appeared that the suspects were Irish tinkers, and eventually Staines CID officers arrested two people, a 32-year-old Irish tinker and his 25-year-old girlfriend. It turned out that the young woman came from an upper middle class family in Ireland but had been living in a travellers' community for two or three years.

When questioned, both of them refused to answer any questions, and the investigating officers knew that the only way forward would be to try and have them identified. There were a large number of witnesses, many of whom were frail and in poor health. There was a male suspect and female suspect, which would mean two separate sets of identification parades. We soon realised that this was going to need a considerable amount of planning if we were to do it effectively.

The identification procedures were likely to take two or three days, and we decided that the best plan was for one inspector to deal with all of it. One of the inspectors volunteered to organise everything, and within a few days the identification parades started. Finding suitable volunteers for the parades involved a lot of work. Most of the victims were men and women in their eighties and nineties, and it was a slow, painstaking process. Some of the people who took part in the parade as volunteers found it very distressing, and two of the women started to cry when they saw the victims and realised what had been happening.

The inspector who carried out the identification procedures did a very thorough job, and the suspects were identified time and time again as the people responsible for committing offences. They went to crown court, where they both received long prison sentences.

About the same time as this, a large public-order situation in central London had gone 'pear-shaped', and afterwards there were complaints made against some of the officers who had been involved in policing it. The chief inspector (ops) at Staines was given the task of investigating some of these complaints. The chief superintendent told me that he would be gone for three or four months and asked me to cover his job while he was away.

The chief inspector (ops) had a large, comfortable office on the first floor of the station. After I moved in, my first job was to go through the paperwork in his in-tray to check that there was nothing urgent. One of the basic functions of the ops job was to ensure that there were enough inspectors and sergeants on duty each day to cover all the operational needs of the division. The ops chief inspector also had to be aware of all the events taking place on the division and assess whether or not there was a need for a police presence.

There were seven inspectors on the division, including me. As I was now doing the chief inspector's job, it meant that we were one inspector short. This was not a problem, but within a few days of me taking over as acting chief inspector (ops) a number of things happened that made my job a little more challenging than I had anticipated.

One of the relief inspectors was involved in a traffic accident and suffered a serious back injury. He was going to be out of action for some time. Two or three days after this, the superintendent walked into my office and told me that a serious complaint had been made against one of the other inspectors on the division. He went on to say that the inspector would have to be suspended.

An inspector being suspended was something that was new to me, something that had never happened anywhere else where I had worked. The superintendent did not tell me much about the complaint, but he officially suspended the officer concerned from duty that day. We now had a difficult problem on the division, a shortage of inspectors. The inspector who was suspended was eventually cleared of wrong-doing and was reinstated.

Each day was going to involve quite a lot of juggling and creative thinking on my part. Thinking back to the mythical cupboard at Chelsea where we kept a few PCs in storage made me smile. It seemed that we needed one like that for inspectors at Staines, but the cupboard would always be empty, as it had been at Chelsea.

Mick O'Neill, the Acting Sergeant (Duties) was in an adjoining office, and the two of us held regular meetings to try and sort out our manpower problems. Requests to supply inspectors for public-order events in other parts of the MPD continued coming in, but Met policy was that every division must have an inspector as duty officer 24/7. This was now my problem to sort out.

There were some obvious problems looming up, as there were going to be many days when there would only be two inspectors available during a period of twenty-four hours. I tried to improvise day to day. One officer might work from 8 a.m. until 6 p.m. and the other from 6 p.m. until 2 or 3 a.m. Then there were days when there was only one inspector available for twenty-four hours. Sometimes I worked for five or six hours as chief inspector (ops) and then worked for three or four hours as duty officer.

Nick Wood was one of the best sergeants on the division, and he had recently passed the inspectors' exam. I decided to give him a temporary promotion, and he became one of our duty officers as acting inspector.

As I was usually covering two jobs at that time, it kept me busy. One evening while sitting in the ops office and working my way through some paperwork, I was interrupted by a phone call from the custody officer. It was not good news. One of our detective sergeants had just been arrested on suspicion of driving with excess alcohol.

An operation had been underway for some weeks to arrest someone suspected of being a receiver of stolen property, and the DS in question had been in charge of the operation. Earlier that day, the suspect had been arrested, and the officers had recovered a considerable amount of stolen property. The detective sergeant had supervised everything, and once he was satisfied that everything had been done correctly, he had driven back to Staines police station. At some point, he had been followed by a

Traffic Division car, and the two TD officers later stated that he had been speeding.

Upon arrival at the police station, he'd parked the car in the station yard and gone into the CID office. The two Traffic PCs had spoken to officers at the station and asked them whether they knew who the driver of the car was. Some time had gone by between the moment when the DS had parked his car and the point at which the two traffic officers spoke to him. They told him that they wanted him to provide a breath test, and he agreed. The breath test showed positive for alcohol, and the DS had then been arrested.

I decided to sit in with the custody officer and keep an eye on the procedure at the station. Given the circumstances, there were some concerns in my mind about the case. However, it would have been wrong for me to show any favour towards either our CID officer or the two PCs from Traffic Division. The most important aspect was to ensure that everything was done to the letter of the law.

The breathalyser system had changed since its early days in the late sixties. Police stations now had machines with the capacity to measure the amount of alcohol in someone's breath, and the machine showed a reading that was slightly higher than the legal limit. The DS was then charged with the offence of driving with excess alcohol. This provoked a great deal of anger and argument within the station, especially in the CID office. The canteen at Staines police station had been a popular spot for TD officers, but suddenly they became conspicuous by their absence.

The CPS decided to prosecute, and the DS appeared at Staines Magistrates' Court, where he pleaded not guilty. He was convicted, but then he appealed, and the case later went to the appeal court at Kingston. At the appeal hearing, the presiding judge ruled that the conviction was unlawful; the DS's appeal was successful.

It was about this time that I met a colleague who had a background in combating terrorism, and we chatted about some of the IRA terrorist attacks that had occurred in the last few years. It surprised me when he commented that Irish Republican terrorism was no longer the main threat facing this country. He then went on to say that the most serious threat now came from Islamist terrorists.

In December 1992, al-Qaeda carried out its first terrorist attack. A bomb at the Gold Mihor Hotel in Aden killed two people and injured several others. Two months later, a massive bomb concealed in a lorry exploded under the World Trade Center in New York City. The intention was to collapse the twin towers, and although this did not happen, six people were killed and over 1,000 were injured.

During 1992, the home secretary announced an independent inquiry into policing that would include pay and conditions. Sir Patrick Sheehy, the chief executive of British American Tobacco, was chosen to head the inquiry. He had a number of people working with him, but surprisingly, none of them had any policing experience. Police staff associations were not involved with any of this, which led the Federation to be concerned about the motives of the Government.

The inquiry examined the way that police forces were structured and looked at the management skills of all officers with managerial roles. Sheehy soon attacked what he described as antiquated management practices and stated that senior officers were good at giving orders but many had never learned the skills needed to counsel, teach, lead, listen, and manage.

Any outsider who took a look at management within the police would be concerned by many of the issues that came to light. For example, when it came to days lost through sickness, some forces had sick rates of twenty to twenty-four days per head. Some officers had been on the sick list for two years without anyone enquiring about the situation.

In many forces, sick visits by supervisors were rarely carried out, even when malingering was suspected. Another aspect that caused concern was that many officers facing discipline hearings used medical retirement to escape punishment.

The Sheehy report was published in 1993 and made 272 recommendations. The most hard-hitting of these urged that police numbers should be reduced, that the housing allowance should be abolished, and that the starting pay for a PC should be reduced by £2,000. There was criticism of the rank structure and a recommendation that the ranks of chief inspector and chief superintendent should be abolished. It was also recommended that in the Met the rank of DAC (deputy assistant commissioner) should go.

There were some very controversial ideas regarding performance-related pay and pensions. New recruits would have a ten-year contract, and this would be renewable for five-year periods at the discretion of their chief officer of police. Officers would have to serve for forty years before they were eligible for a full pension.

The Sheehy Report contained some very good ideas. Its political weakness was that it was brutally truthful and criticised all levels of the police service. Thus, Sheehy would be attacked by the Federation and the Superintendents' Association, which represented divisional commanders. It also antagonised ACPO, the organisation that represented the highest-ranking police officers in the UK.

The reaction was swift, and the firepower aimed at Sheehy was enough to sink most of the report. Some good will always emerge from this type of inquiry. There was some agreement that the number of inspectors and of senior officers above that rank could be reduced. It was also agreed that the police service needed more sergeants.

Lurking in the shadows behind all of this was the fact that there were police officers who were lazy or incompetent. All PCs come under a certain amount of scrutiny and pressure to work hard during their first two years as probationers. If they do not show the necessary enthusiasm and commitment, they risk failing their probation. But generally speaking, the pressure comes off after that. An officer who is lazy can do the bare minimum of work for the next twenty-eight years and cruise along until it's time to retire. We joked that some officers had decided to retire after working for two years. It might only relate to a small percentage of officers, but it was a problem nonetheless.

Compared with many other jobs, the starting pay for a police constable was quite high. Any intelligent man or woman should be able to become an effective police officer by the time that he or she had completed two years' service. Police Regulations stipulate that if someone is not likely to make an effective officer, he/she can be dismissed during or at the end of their probation. However, it has often proved difficult to sack unsuitable officers.

As far as the rank structure was concerned, the police establishment seemed determined to keep the edifice looking like a pyramid. The House of Lords decided to save the rank of chief inspector, and twenty years on, the ranks of chief superintendent and deputy assistant commissioner appear to be alive and kicking.

Sir Patrick Sheehy was an experienced and successful businessman, and much of what he said made sense. His ideas could have been explored in more depth and used as a platform to modernise management of the police service and make it a more effective organisation. However, the Sheehy report was a hot potato, and the Government probably felt that it might be safer to throw it into the long grass rather than run with it.

30

We were still grappling with the logistics of sector policing, and it was necessary to come to a decision about the first basic question – would the division be divided into two or three sectors? Feedback from the public revealed that local people wanted to have a police station or office at Ashford. Although we had concerns about manpower, our working party recommended that there should be three sectors.

It was soon clear that there was likely to be great competition among inspectors for sectors. They would be treated as subdivisional commanders, with a certain degree or autonomy and the chance to work their sectors in their own style. The process was started to find the best candidates for the job.

Whatever system was adopted, the bottom line would be that the police service was facing an increasing demand from the public for policing services but the manpower situation was not likely to improve. All categories of crime had increased at a rate that would have been unimaginable to the police or public during the 1950s. Citing just one serious crime as an example, the rate of robbery had become forty-eight times higher than it had been during the fifties.

There were concerns about one of our local magistrates' courts because of the high proportion of cases being dismissed when people pleaded not guilty. One of my fellow inspectors was chatting to one of the local JPs about this and was baffled by his approach to the criminal justice system. The JP explained his attitude by saying that if someone pleaded not guilty, this was a strong indication that the defendant was innocent.

It concerned me on one occasion when magistrates dismissed a charge of assault against a burglary suspect who had struck one of our officers with an iron bar. However, he did tell the court that he'd been frightened that she might hit him and was just acted instinctively, as you do.

Officers often grumble about things that happen at court, and some cases can be lost because of lack of preparation by police or the CPS. However, this did not appear to be an issue in these cases. Apart from anything else, penalties for serious offences usually seemed very lenient. I started to look through our charge records, and noted some of the more serious cases in which I would have expected defendants to receive custodial sentences. This included drug dealers and people who had carried out serious unprovoked assaults.

One drug dealer was arrested in possession of a large number of ecstasy tablets. I noted that the sentence was a conditional discharge for twelve months. I did not feel that this was a sentence that could be seen as a deterrent to other criminals.

If every criminal that deserved to go to prison received a custodial sentence, the prison system would soon buckle under the sheer weight of numbers. The courts need to think of non-custodial sentences that do something to deter offenders. For example, someone who is a drug dealer and is convicted as a first-time offender could be fined but it would need to be a heavy fine. However, there is no point in courts fining offenders if the system of fines is not enforced effectively. Figures show that about half of all fines are never paid.

Every town and city in this country has a hard core of offenders. As we move into the twenty-first century, it is not uncommon for a 30-year-old criminal to have thirty previous convictions, for offences such as burglary, theft, assault, or receiving. This means that the defendant has appeared at various courts on at least thirty occasions to be sentenced. Why has he or she been allowed to carry on committing crime without anybody seriously addressing the issue?

My simple definition of a good criminal justice system is one that makes members of the public feel safe on the streets and secure in their homes because they have confidence in the system. At the same time, criminals fear that they may be arrested and worry about what is likely to happen to them at court.

Nowadays, a great deal of evidence suggests that the criminal justice system tends to have the opposite effect. Victims and their concerns are often not seen as important, and police officers note that criminals have little respect for the courts and show little sign of being worried when they appear as defendants.

Anyone who has a good knowledge of the court system and knows what actually happens can see the problems. They notice the lack of enforcement in relation to many issues, including fines, compensation orders, and breaches of community service orders. There appears to be no central plan or structure that binds it all together.

During 1992, my thoughts were turning towards my approaching retirement. My thirty-year service mark in January 1994 was now in sight, and after that I could retire or carry on for two or three more years. The idea of being in charge of a sector appealed to me, but it would take time for any inspector to develop his or her team, and it did not seem practical unless I decided to make a firm commitment to stay for an extra couple of years.

Maybe I was guilty of thinking that the world of policing had no new challenges for me, but I was mistaken. Keith Bateman, one of my fellow inspectors at Staines, held the position of community liaison officer. The chief superintendent told me that he planned to make some changes and that he wanted me to take over Keith's role. My new job would have two main aspects to it.

Firstly, as police liaison officer, I would maintain links with the Borough of Spelthorne and the local community. My second role, which was closely linked to this, would be managing the division's crime-reduction strategy. I would take over what was known as the Community Involvement Office, a small group of officers who worked on several projects each year, all aimed at the prevention of crime.

The office had two experienced sergeants, Tony O'Sullivan and Janet Dorey. It was important for me to review the projects that had been started over the previous twelve months as well as any new ideas that were being explored. I met with the two sergeants for a briefing. After that, we had a general discussion about our contacts within the community and what we were trying to achieve. It was clear straight away that both sergeants were very committed to the work that they were involved with.

The PCs in the unit were all experienced and had been chosen for their ability to work on their own with little supervision. Each officer had a specialist role, but everyone's work related to community relations and crime prevention. One officer was responsible for firearms licensing, and another managed the division's Neighbourhood Watch schemes. There were three crime reduction officers, all experienced in the field of crime prevention and another who worked as schools liaison officer.

Some years before, the Met had decided that crime detection and prevention would be the responsibility of the senior CID officer in each division. This meant that the DCI, Alan Jude would become my line manager. The two of us met to discuss the various crime problems faced by the division and the projects that I was now responsible for.

Alan Jude believed that these projects always had an important role to play in the traditional heartland of policing – the prevention and detection of crime. Some of the projects that we had been running within the Spelthorne division were aimed at reducing residential burglaries and motor-vehicle crime. We had also carried out 'diversionary' projects. In plain language, we set up schemes to attract young people so that they became involved in a range of activities, and this diverted them from committing crime or being involved in antisocial behaviour.

Working as a police officer in Spelthorne had a number of advantages. The borough council was very supportive of police efforts to reduce crime. There was a very active crime prevention panel within the borough that was willing to finance most of our schemes, and its members were happy to work alongside us on many of our projects.

31

On 22 April 1993, at about ten thirty in the evening, something happened in south east London that would become one of the most controversial events in the history of modern policing. This was the murder of Stephen Lawrence. Two black teenagers, Stephen Lawrence and Duwayne Brooks, had been standing at a bus stop in Eltham, hoping that a bus might come their way. Brooks noticed that there was a group of five or six white youths standing on the other side of the road.

Duwayne Brooks heard one of the white youths shout out, 'What, what, nigger?'

The white youths quickly surrounded the two black teenagers, and Stephen Lawrence received two serious stab wounds. Brooks shouted to his friend to run for it, and both of them ran off down the street. Stephen Lawrence must have been a fit young man. Although he was bleeding to death, he managed to run for about 120 metres before he collapsed. He was dead within a few minutes.

The attack probably lasted no more than fifteen to twenty seconds and was witnessed by three people who were standing at the bus stop. However, afterwards, none of them was able to identify the attackers.

The Met had moved away from its old structure of districts and was now made up of areas, which were split into divisions. Each area had a squad to deal with serious crimes and an investigation team was set up within a few hours of the killing. A detective superintendent was in overall charge, with a detective inspector as his deputy, and a team of investigators.

The murder squad soon had five prime suspects, and within a matter of weeks they were arrested and interviewed, although none of them made any admissions. In July 1993, the CPS decided that there was not enough evidence to support a charge of murder against any of the suspects.

The tragedy that had befallen the Lawrence family was made worse by the fact that the police had failed to bring the matter to a satisfactory conclusion. The victim's parents believed that the investigation had not been as thorough as it could have been and were upset because they felt that some of the investigating officers acted in a patronising manner towards them. They believed that if the murdered boy had been white the police would have done more to bring the killers to justice.

Later that year, a decision was made at Scotland Yard to carry out an internal review of the investigation, and this was done by Detective Chief Superintendent Roderick Barker. It would have been difficult to find a more experienced senior detective than Barker; he had been head of the Flying Squad and had been involved in more than 200 murder enquiries.

Barker's review supported the work that had been carried out by the area investigation team and found no serious defects in the way the investigation had been conducted. However, he later admitted that he had not wanted to be too critical of their work, as it could have been damaging to CID morale.

In May 1994, the Met decided that a second murder enquiry should be started. Detective Superintendent William Mellish was appointed to head the investigation, and he came up with some fresh ideas to start the murder enquiry moving again. One of the prime suspects was David Norris, the son of Clifford Norris, a man well-known to police in south east London. Clifford Norris was wanted by Customs for his involvement in smuggling cannabis into the UK. He had been on the run for several years.

Many officers believed that he represented a particular threat to the investigation. Information suggested that Clifford Norris was keen to protect his son, and police thought that potential witnesses would be frightened to provide information, knowing that Clifford Norris was on the loose.

A BBC television programme raised the question of corruption, and a retired officer alleged that a detective sergeant involved in the murder enquiry had been protecting Clifford Norris. The Stephen Lawrence murder had become a massive news event and a major PR disaster for the Met.

Mellish decided that one of his first priorities was to find Clifford Norris, and as part of this operation, officers started keeping watch on a cottage in Sussex. On 10 August 1994 at 5 a.m., Mellish was at a police station in Sussex, where he briefed a team that included officers from Sussex Police, the RCS, and a specialist firearms unit.

Later that morning, Clifford Norris and another man were under police surveillance. They stopped at a café for breakfast, and it was there that they were arrested. Both of them were found to be in possession of loaded handguns. After this the cottage was searched, and a machine gun and a large amount of ammunition were found. In 1995, Clifford Norris was convicted of smuggling cannabis worth £1.3 million into the UK and for possessing a machine gun. He received a sentence of nine and a half years.

The arrest of Clifford Norris was good news, but the hoped-for breakthrough in the case still seemed far away. In September 1994, the Lawrence family decided to bring a private prosecution for murder against the suspects. Superintendent Mellish gave advice and assistance to the legal team that represented the family. In April 1996, three of the prime suspects appeared at the Central Criminal Court.

The prosecution at the Old Bailey was not successful. The trial judge drew attention to a number of weaknesses in the prosecution case. The result was that the three defendants were acquitted upon the judge's direction before going to a jury.

In 1997, the parents of Stephen Lawrence made a complaint against a number of Met officers, saying that the original murder investigation had been handled in an unsatisfactory manner. The Police Complaints Authority took over the supervision of the complaint and asked Kent Police to conduct an enquiry into the way the Metropolitan Police had handled the murder investigation.

The Kent enquiry was led by Robert Ayling, deputy chief constable of Kent, who had a team of eighteen police officers. They spent about a year reviewing the original investigation. All the Met officers who had been involved in the original investigation were interviewed, as were a number of people who were potential witnesses.

The Kent report was given to the PCA in 1998. It contained 459 pages and described a large number of failures by officers during the original investigation. It also stated that there had been a lack of leadership and initiative shown by the officers called to the scene within a few minutes of the attack on Stephen Lawrence. The same criticism was made of the investigation team. The report stated that they had not found any evidence of racism in the way the investigation had been carried out, but it mentioned that bad decisions had resulted in opportunities to gather evidence being missed.

The Labour Party announced that if it should win the 1997 election it would set up a public enquiry into the Stephen Lawrence murder. The general election in 1997 resulted in a major victory for the Labour Party and its new leader, Tony Blair. Jack Straw was appointed home secretary and ordered a public enquiry, with Sir William Macpherson of Cluny as chair.

Public hearings started in 1998, and the Macpherson enquiry soon amassed a vast array of papers relating to the case. The paperwork would eventually total about 100,000 pages of reports, statements, and documents. A large number of witnesses were called before the committee to give evidence, and several police officers were criticised for their actions.

The Macpherson Report was published in February 1999, and the following words were used in the conclusion to the report.

'There is no doubt that there were fundamental errors. The investigation was marred by a combination of professional incompetence, institutional racism, and a failure of leadership by senior officers. A flawed MP review failed to expose these inadequacies.'

It was probably the most damning report made about a police investigation since the Met was founded in 1829. The seventy recommendations made by Macpherson were the only positive things to emerge from this tragic event. At the public enquiry, the Commissioner, Sir Paul Condon refused to accept the charge that there was institutional racism in the Met, but the statement itself was very damaging.

For many years, the parents of Stephen Lawrence had campaigned to do everything possible to bring their son's killers to justice, while maintaining that serious mistakes had been made by the investigating officers. The question about racism and whether it played any part in the attitude of investigators is something that is likely to remain controversial for some time to come. However, the enquiry carried out by Kent Police discovered that a large number of errors and failures had been made by the original investigation team.

The Macpherson Report became a historical marker that was aimed at a range of organisations apart from the police. It called for reforms in the civil service, the education system, local government, the NHS, and the criminal justice system.

The PCA recommended disciplinary action against five senior police officers. This included Roderick Barker, who had carried out the flawed Met internal review in 1993. The most junior officer of the five was Detective Inspector Ben Bullock, and he was the only one to face a discipline board. The other four had retired before the PCA was able to bring discipline charges against them.

Bullock had decided to retire when he reached thirty years' service. To his credit, he decided to postpone his retirement and announced that he wanted to appear on a discipline board so that he could clear his name. In July 1998, Bullock was found guilty of two counts of neglect of duty but was cleared of several similar counts. He received a formal caution.

In English law, the rule of double jeopardy means that someone who has been acquitted of a crime cannot be put on trial a second time for the original offence. This principle dates back hundreds of years to when the death penalty was in force for most serious crimes. The Macpherson report recommended that there should be exceptions to this rule in extraordinary circumstances, such as the murder of Stephen Lawrence. As a result of this, the rule of double jeopardy was changed.

In 2002, one of the prime suspects, David Norris, was arrested following an incident in which he shouted 'Nigger!' and threw a drink at an off-duty black police officer. He was sent to prison for eighteen months. This incident took place in the same street where Stephen Lawrence had been murdered.

In 2006, Detective Chief Inspector Clive Driscoll took charge of a new investigation into the murder. His strategy was to start afresh and work his way through all the potential suspects that were recorded on the system – 187 of them. Eventually officers were able to eliminate all of these people except nine men.

The eventual breakthrough in the case came when clothes worn by the suspects were examined using new techniques not available in 1993. LGC Forensics, a private analysis company, was contracted to mount a review of thirty items of clothing gathered by the police during the original investigation. The clothes were examined using a low-power microscope, a task which would, in most cases, be thought of as too time consuming.

This involved a meticulous search by the forensic scientists. They spent hundreds of hours examining the items of clothing. Eventually, they found some marks. One was a tiny speck of Stephen Lawrence's blood, measuring no more than 0.5 mm, found ingrained in the weave of the collar of a jacket worn by Gary Dobson. Two pieces of hair were found on a pair of jeans from the bedroom of David Norris.

In recent years, there have been dramatic advances in DNA testing, and this led to a strong scientific identification that the two pieces of hair came from Stephen Lawrence or a close relative on his mother's side of the family. A forensic expert was able to say that the probability that it had not come from Stephen Lawrence was about one in a billion.

Some years after the murder, two of the suspects, David Norris and another man, had been in touch with Scotland Yard and asked to have their clothes returned to them. At that point, it had seemed unlikely that they would ever be on trial for murder again. However, someone in the Met made the sensible decision not to return them. Had the clothing been returned, David Norris would not have been convicted.

Gary Dobson and David Norris were charged with the murder of Stephen Lawrence. When their trial started, unknown to the jury, Gary Dobson was already serving a five-year prison sentence after being caught in an operation organised by agents from SOCA – the Serious Organised Crime Agency. Another man had been the focus of this operation and was under close surveillance. Dobson had been seen handing over nearly 50 kilograms of cannabis, worth £350,000, to the target criminal.

On 3 January 2012, Gary Dobson and David Norris were found guilty of the murder of Stephen Lawrence. When the verdicts were read out, Dobson shouted at the court, saying that they had found an innocent man guilty. For his part, David Norris just smirked as he was led to the cells. They were both sentenced to life imprisonment. After the verdicts in the case, detectives revealed that several other men had not been eliminated from the investigation.

On 24 April 1993, the IRA detonated a huge lorry bomb in Bishopsgate, within the City of London. The bomb killed a journalist, Ed Henty, and injured forty other people. Apart from the death and injuries, there was damage to the value of £1 billion. The insurance payments that followed were very large, putting Lloyds of London under serious financial pressure and causing a major crisis within the London insurance market.

The move to sector policing would mean major changes in how Spelthorne was policed, and the option of having three sectors was chosen. A new station was opened in Ashford, and the three sector inspectors were appointed.

Each sector would have six teams and each would consist of a sergeant and six PCs. An important part of the planning was to ensure that there was a proper balance of experience on each team. About this time, a new divisional headquarters was established on the fourth floor of an office block across the road from Staines police station. The three sector inspectors set up their new bases at Staines, Sunbury, and Ashford.

One of my concerns about sector policing was that the inspectors in charge of sectors would need some admin support, but the chief superintendent made it clear that there was no finance available to cover this. It seemed obvious that these three inspectors were going to be faced with a considerable amount of routine administration and paperwork.

The Community Involvement Unit moved from the police station to a new office in the divisional headquarters. We were all in a large open-plan office that was not suitable for meetings, so the two sergeants would come with me to a local pub or coffee bar to discuss planning ideas. We soon had a list of projects that would take us through the following twelve months.

We ran a regular police column in one of our local newspapers, and this was financed by Sony, a large multinational company with a major presence in Staines. I normally wrote the articles and found the column a useful tool to warn the public about local crime problems and also to advertise our crime-prevention projects. Another of my jobs was to brief the local press every Friday morning, when I met journalists from three or four different newspapers.

One of my roles was to monitor any racial incidents that occurred on the division. In comparison with other Met divisions, there was little racial tension. However, I did become involved in several of them. One was a case where some white teenagers were making life difficult for a local Asian shopkeeper. One of them was charged with threatening behaviour and went to court.

Something that has always concerned me is the manner in which victims are often treated within the criminal justice system. I went to court to keep an eye on the shopkeeper, and it was easy to see how people could be intimidated.

Although it was a modern court building, there was no easy way of separating witnesses, victims, defendants, or anyone else. The defendant in this case came swaggering in and made a point of sitting down next to the victim. I walked over to the defendant but did not actually say anything to him. My right thumb did the talking, and it seemed that he knew what this meant. He scurried away to another chair some distance away.

Within a couple of months of me taking up my new position, I had a visit by one of the PCs who had been assigned to the Staines sector. 'Did you know that the Ku Klux Klan is in Staines and is recruiting?' he asked me.

No, I didn't. Before I could reply, he handed me four or five of their leaflets. It was interesting to see how they had been written. Every word seemed to have been carefully chosen, and there were three or four references to the KKK being a 'Christian organisation'. Nothing sinister or unlawful was suggested, but I asked the officer to keep me informed of any further developments.

After this, I did some research on the Klan. It appeared that the Ku Klux Klan was founded in Tennessee, shortly after the end of the American Civil War. The founders were six educated, middle-class men who had all served in the Confederate Army. It started as a social club, with its own secrets and rituals. However, it did not take long before its members were involved in a number of violent incidents in which black people were attacked. In the next few years the Klan became more violent, killing black people and also white people who they saw as their political opponents. It announced that Catholics and Jews were among its enemies.

Over the next hundred years or so, the popularity of the Klan rose and fell a number of times. Its political influence in the United States was probably at its strongest level in the years that followed the First World War. Some historians believe that as many as one man in five of the white population may have been members at that time.

In the first few years of the twenty-first century, the membership of the Klan within the United States fell to about three thousand. Very little is known about their activities in the UK, but in 1996 the *News of the World* had a scoop when one of its journalists went undercover in Birmingham and became a member. He soon found that the Klan had two main enemies in this country, Muslims and black people. He revealed a sophisticated system of identity checks and screening in order to keep out potential spies, such as police officers or journalists.

In Britain, the Ku Klux Klan has developed links with other extreme right-wing groups, such as Combat 18. It takes its name from the first and eighth letters of the alphabet – A and H – the initials of Adolf Hitler. This gives a strong clue as to their political orientation. Police action against members of C18 has resulted in the seizure of firearms and other weapons. It was reported that Gary Dobson, one of the two men convicted of the murder of Stephen Lawrence, had been to Combat 18 meetings.

As far as Spelthorne was concerned, we heard no more about the Klan. I suspected that their recruiting technique was probably to visit a town and distribute a few leaflets, gather a few potential members, and then move on quickly.

Over many years, a crime-prevention strategy had been developed in Spelthorne that was regarded as one of the best in the Met. Our unit came up with a wide range of ideas, all aimed at the reduction of crime in the borough. One aspect involved the planning process for new building projects.

As part of the process, the council would send the police the plans for proposed new buildings. The design of a building can make it vulnerable to burglary, and our crime-reduction officers were given the opportunity to comment on these factors. An important aspect of this was our strong relationship with the local council. Once we had commented, the council would draw our comments to the notice of the architects and builders concerned. In police jargon, we referred to this as 'designing out crime'.

For many years, the residents of Sunbury had worried about using the pedestrian subway that ran underneath the M3 motorway. In the Community Involvement Office, we would have regular team meetings, and this was one of the first issues that I took an interest in. My crime-reduction officers had a number of ideas to make the subway look less threatening and more pedestrian-friendly. One of the points we all agreed on was that if someone was walking though the subway tunnels and was attacked, the layout and surrounding landscaping were such that the attack would not be seen by anyone else. Our recommendations on the subway were passed to the council, and work was carried out to alter the landscaping design and decorate the interior in a different style. After the work had been finished, I took a walk through the subway, and it was obvious how different it looked. More importantly, there were many more people walking through it.

We worked closely with the Spelthorne Crime Prevention Panel on a wide range of crime-reduction schemes. We had a crime-prevention caravan, and we set this up at Kempton Park Racecourse in a project aimed at reducing motor-vehicle crime. This event was given wide publicity in advance, through the press and the distribution of thousands of leaflets. An important attraction of this scheme was that the first one hundred Spelthorne residents would receive free anti-theft steering wheel locks. We also advertised vehicle windscreen marking, and this was carried out free of charge by Autoglass, a company who specialised in that type of work.

One well-established project was the fitting of security locks on residential properties to reduce burglaries. All residents in the borough who were aged sixty or over could apply to the police for these locks to be fitted to their front doors. One of my officers monitored all the applications and then forwarded them to the council. After that, the work was contracted out to professional locksmiths, and the costs were paid by the council.

Our largest project was called Summersafe, and this was aimed at schoolchildren. The scheme ran for several weeks in the summer holidays, and every day there was a range of activities for them, such as football, canoeing, and rock climbing. This was one of our diversionary projects, designed to attract them to our activities and thus divert them from antisocial behaviour or crime.

It is not easy to measure the effectiveness of this type of scheme, so it was necessary for me to develop some performance indicators. My research was fairly rough and ready, based on feedback from shopkeepers in Staines about shoplifting. Most thefts from shops are minor and are rarely reported to the police, but they mount up, and shopkeepers are very aware of the financial losses that they are suffering. A survey of shops showed that there had been a significant drop in shoplifting during the weeks that Summersafe was running.

Some years before, Spelthorne had entered into a twinning arrangement with Melun, a town in the outer suburbs of Paris. Over the years there had been a number of exchange visits by different groups within the two towns, such as councillors, business people, and schoolchildren. I discussed this with my colleagues, and it seemed that there had been no links between the police in Melun and Spelthorne.

I made contact with the French police at Melun, and shortly after this we received an invitation for our officers to visit them. They also invited us to send a team to Melun to take part in a football competition. A tournament had been organised which had the title 'Le Challenge Christophe Larcher'. Larcher was one of their officers who had been shot dead by armed robbers, and his colleagues had wanted to do something in his honour. He had been a very keen footballer, and the officers in Melun felt that a police football tournament would be a good idea.

The visit and football tournament went ahead in May 1993, and the police in Melun showed great hospitality to everyone who went. There were sixteen teams in the football tournament, which was a knock-out competition. The Spelthorne team fought its way to the final, where it was defeated by one of the French teams. The visit was a great success, and I would have liked to go with our contingent, but the dates clashed with an important family occasion. However, the police officers at Melun sent me a letter of thanks for helping to organise the trip, as well as souvenirs of the day.

32

Although computers had become important tools in the police service, as everywhere else, my knowledge of them was very limited. I cannot comment on what other forces did, but in 1994 the Met was still mainly a paper-driven organisation. During my time at Management Services, the introduction of CRIS had seemed far away, with the project several years behind schedule. Therefore, it came as a surprise when I found out that CRIS would soon be coming to Spelthorne.

The Crime Reporting Information System – usually known by its acronym, CRIS – would be used in the future for recording all reported crime in the Met. The crime books that had been used for many years would soon be history. It appeared that initially three or four divisions would go 'live', while its progress was monitored. Eventually CRIS would cover all of the Met.

Everyone on the division had to be trained, and there were the usual rumours, arguments, and complaints about CRIS, typical of what always happens when the police service faces any major change. There were people who said that it was an amazing system and those who grumbled about how slow it was.

Wandsworth had gone live already, and some of the feedback we received about what was happening there was not encouraging. Several officers from Spelthorne, including me, went to a meeting where we met a couple of Wandsworth officers. One of them told us that he had been called to a burglary in a large house that had been divided into a number of flats. The burglar, or burglars, had gone to each flat to check that there was nobody at home. The MO had been simple enough. They had started on the third floor and worked their way down to the ground floor, kicking down each front door and stealing anything that appeared to be valuable.

The officer who was first to arrive at the scene soon had a long list of stolen property, and he complained about the length of time it took him using CRIS. There were eight victims, and it took him eight hours to complete the crime reports and the details of stolen property. To me, this sounded slower than the handwritten method. Computers were obviously the way of the future, but it sounded as though it might take some time to make the system more user-friendly.

The chief superintendent and I went to regular meetings with the Police Consultative Group at the Spelthorne Civic Centre. Our relationship with the council and the local community was very good, and it was our intention to keep it that way. I made a point of briefing them about the projects that we were running and mentioned incidents where good police work had led to arrests. It was an important factor that nearly all of the projects that we ran were financed by the council. Without this financial assistance, the division's crime-prevention strategy would have been mainly one of ideas rather than deeds.

We ran a work-experience scheme, and several older pupils at local schools spent a week working with police officers on the division. When we talked about projects, we sensed that there was a 'gap in the market', and this led us to think about something aimed at sixth-form pupils. This was all about motor cars and aimed at young people who were keen to buy one.

Traffic Division was asked to help, and they agreed to provide some officers to work with us. We set the project up at a local school, and we were pleased when the young men and women who would soon be school-leavers started arriving in large numbers. They were taken through a number of modules, each one related to cars. The first module gave them advice about buying a car. What things did they need to look at? How would they avoid buying a vehicle that might not be roadworthy?

There was a module that covered the 'nuts and bolts' of motor cars. How did the engine work? How would you look after your car? Another module dealt with the legal obligations that came with owning a car, and we were surprised at how many had no idea that they needed to have insurance cover. One module dealt with safe driving and advice about trying to prevent cars being stolen. They were all encouraged to enter a written competition about what they had learned, and those who received the highest marks were given prizes.

We received several letters of thanks from those who took part, their parents, and teachers from local schools. All the indications were that the local community saw it as a great success.

The last day of January 1994 was an important day for me, because it was thirty years since I had been sworn in as a constable at Winchester. It also marked the point at which I could retire. Maureen had organised a surprise party for me at our home in New Malden, and I was taken by surprise when my superintendent and chief superintendent arrived at our house, followed by Gil French and Roy Ramsier, two of my friends from Hampshire.

This was, of course, a reminder that my time as a police officer was coming to an end, and thoughts of retirement were very much on my mind. The only question now was when. I could carry on for at least another two years, if I wished to. On the other hand, when I had first thought about becoming a police officer, the idea of being able to retire at a fairly young age had been one of the job's main attractions.

Many retired officers had taken jobs in the private security industry, and this was something that initially appealed to me. At the beginning of the year, I started doing some research and developing contacts, most of which were people who owned companies or were senior managers in private security. My experience in crime-prevention work was something that proved very useful when I had job meetings with potential employers.

It did not take long for me to develop a picture of the private-security sector. There were a large number of positions available, but most of them held little interest for me. During the next few months, two job offers with good salaries and company cars came my way, but neither of them felt right for me. Eventually, my decision was to take a long break after retirement before making any major decisions. As it turned out, I never did work in the security industry, but that is another story.

In May 1994 I informed the chief superintendent of my intention to retire in August. Two weeks later, I went to the Area HQ at Kingston to complete some paperwork relating to my retirement. Each area had a DAC in charge, with two commanders, in many ways a similar command structure to some county police forces. It turned out that I was to see one of the commanders.

It went through my head that there might be some conversation or small talk on the agenda. I imagined the commander saying, 'Thank you for your service, Mr Ramsay,' or something of that nature. However, it appeared that a fireside chat was not on the cards, and talking seemed too much of an effort for him. He looked totally bored, and it made me wonder why it was necessary for someone of his rank to be involved with an admin task such as this. He did manage to say at least six or seven words, which included 'Sign these papers, please.' I was in and out of the building in about fifteen minutes.

My official date of retirement was to be 7 August, but there were some leave days owing me, so my last working day would fall towards the end of July. There was the usual printed list on the noticeboard in the inspectors' office showing everyone's duties. My name was there, showing me as duty officer for one day, followed by four days doing my job as Community Liaison Officer. The day after this, it just said 'handing in uniform'. This was followed by several days listing me as annual leave, and then my name simply disappeared from the list.

As police officers, we were always walking into situations that were different or just strange in some way or another. So, in a way, I was expecting something to happen the last time I was duty officer. The weather was hot and sunny, and everything seemed fairly quiet. During the afternoon I took a drive across the division. Whatever thoughts were going through my mind at that point were interrupted by the sudden crackle of the main set coming to life with a call to our area car.

'A316, near the end of M3 motorway – London-bound side – man seen to jump from the back door of a white van while vehicle on the move. Appears to have run off onto nearby land.'

Several units answered the call and were on their way, and I headed off in the same direction, wondering what on earth was happening. A white van could be a police vehicle, but if so, we should have received a bit more information about it. A more interesting story might be a kidnapping with the victim making a break for freedom. Or maybe it was just an LOB call? At the same time, it did not have the feel of a bogus call.

From the large roundabout at Sunbury, two or three minutes driving along the M3 would bring me to the end of the motorway. During this time, numerous calls were going back and forth over the PR. I could see two or three police cars in a lay-by a short distance further on.

Everyone, including me, was asking the same question: 'What is going on?' On my arrival, one of the PCs was calling our control room with a request to contact the person who had made the call and see if he could give us any further information. However, then we received another 999 call, from the remand centre in Feltham, about 2 miles away. Two Kent officers had been taking a prisoner there in a white police van, and it had only been on their arrival that they realised that he had escaped. The description of the man given in this call matched what we had been given in the first call.

At the lay-by where we had gathered, there was a large expanse of open countryside alongside the A316. From the road, we were looking into a jungle. Stretching out for some distance in front of us was an area that was totally overgrown with shrubs and bushes. He must have gone in there, I thought.

There was a rough pathway leading into the jungle, and I decided that this is where we should start our search. I started walking along the path, with two of my PCs. There were others spread out to the left and right of us, but they were making slower progress. After walking for about five minutes, we reached a bridge that crossed a river. Actually, it was more of a stream than a river. At this point, my two PCs started running as if they had seen something up ahead. However, I decided to stop there, because the bridge was a good place to stand quietly and look around. As I made a 360 degree turn, my eyes took in the view all around. All I could see was the surrounding vegetation and no sign or sound of movement.

Then, for some reason, I looked down, and I saw a young man in the water almost directly below me. He looked up at me for a moment and then started swimming towards the bridge. It seemed that he did not like my suggestion that he should give up, for he carried on swimming.

In this case, the word 'swimming' may not have been totally accurate, as the deepest water in the stream was probably no more than one metre. He then disappeared under the bridge and, a few seconds later, emerged on the other side. Whether the fugitive had planned it or not, he had just outsmarted us. Running alongside the path on his side of the bridge there was a tall wire fence, and he was now on the other side of it. I called my two fast-moving officers and told them to come back to the bridge. When they reached me, I pointed at the fugitive, who was standing a short distance away at the side of the stream, looking a bit forlorn. Then I pointed at the wire fence and suggested that one of them needed to scale it.

This was certainly a job requiring a younger person than I, and the PC who volunteered tackled the fence with some enthusiasm. However, the whole thing started to buckle under his weight, and it seemed that policeman and fence would come crashing down together. It did seem to take a while, but he finally heaved himself over the top and dropped down on the other side. The escaped prisoner appeared to have given up his dash for freedom and just stood looking at us.

My officer on the other side walked back with a wet-looking young man, and then both of them had to carry out the high-wire act, much to everyone's amusement. Our recaptured prisoner was taken to the remand centre, and about two hours later my last day doing operational police work came to an end.

About two weeks before this, one of my colleagues had brought an artist called Marek into Staines police station and introduced him to me by telling me that he was a friend of his, a scientific officer who wanted to visit the station. The real reason for his visit was that Marek could look at my face. When he went back to his studio, he made a sketch of me wearing my uniform in a BBC *This is Your Life* setting. He must have known what he was doing, because everyone in my family tells me that it is very accurate.

My colleagues were all very generous in giving me retirement presents, including the picture of me by Marek.

All my farewells had been completed, and I would be travelling to Canada three days after my last day at Staines. We had received an invitation to a wedding in Ontario, but Maureen had decided not to go with me because her father was in poor health.

On my last day, I cleared my desk and then removed all my uniform and equipment from my locker. It was a strange experience to be dropping each item into a large plastic bag; I had the feeling that thirty years of my life was now being wrapped up. Picking up my truncheon made me think of the some of the negative factors relating to police work, but I recalled that I had never struck anyone with my stick.

The truncheon and everything else went into the bag, and I sealed it. After that, I attached an identifying tag to the bag and placed it on the floor in the inspectors' office near my desk. The office was empty apart from me. A couple of minutes went by, during which I stood looking around and wondering whether there was anything that I had forgotten to do.

Then my thoughts were interrupted by the noise outside, the sound of a police car on a call. Looking out of the window, I had a brief glimpse of the area car flashing past, and I wondered where it was going. It seemed strange to think that it was not my business anymore. As it moved further away, the sound of its siren started to fade. It was time for me to go. I walked out of the police station and into the street.

33

People and Places

In life, one constant theme is change. The harsh fact is that places change, and we all get older. Andover is now bypassed by the A303, and the days when traffic trundled slowly through the centre of it have become a distant memory. The small market town of the 1960s was destined to grow and grow. Business development was rapid, with many companies making the decision that Andover was a good location to move to. Opportunities for employment and new housing attracted more and more people, and by 2001 the population of the town had reached 52,000.

When I made a visit to Andover in 2009, it was difficult to picture it the way that it had been. It was good to see that the High Street remained very much the same as it had been in 1964. The police station and South Street looked familiar, but the surrounding town bore virtually no resemblance to the Andover of the early sixties. Some streets looked as though they had been cut in half by a giant saw, and it was difficult to remember what the missing parts or new parts had looked like before.

Hampshire has always had close links with the Armed Forces. In 2010 the British Army officially opened its new headquarters at Marlborough Lines, Andover. The cost of the new headquarters was £44 million, and now there are 2,000 military and civilian personnel based there.

Winchester's population has risen, as in most places in Hampshire, and now stands at over 41,000. In that respect, it has been overtaken by Andover, but it remains the attractive cathedral city that it always has been. It has an interesting history, going back to Roman times, and in its time has been the capital of Wessex and England. Because of its history and atmosphere, it continues to be a major attraction for tourists from all over the world.

Hartley Wintney has been through a number of changes since the sixties. Nowadays the M3 takes most of the traffic away from it, and the A30 has become a much quieter road. This has given Hartley Wintney a more relaxed feel to it. The police station was closed some years ago, and Yateley has taken over as the local station, taking in a large area that covers HW and Odiham. In recent years, Hampshire in common with all other police forces is going through a period of serious financial cutbacks. Several police officers are based at Yateley but the station is not open to the public.

There have also been many changes affecting the Metropolitan Police since my retirement. Rochester Row and Gerald Road were amalgamated to form the Belgravia division, which is based at a new station in Buckingham Palace Road. The two old station buildings were sold and developed for private housing. The Met now takes in all the London boroughs that make up the Greater London Authority, and Surrey Police has taken over the policing of Spelthorne.

Mick Lyons served on the Havant division for the rest of his service, working at Leigh Park for fourteen years, and he describes his time there as being very busy. He says that there were always plenty of good people living in Leigh Park, but officers were kept so busy dealing with the people who caused problems that they rarely had time to meet anyone else.

Mick says that the main problem was never having enough police to deal with the workload that confronted them each day. His time at Leigh Park came to an end when it was decided to centralise police operations at Havant. The police station was left with an office and a skeleton staff, and then, after some years, the building was sold to Social Services. During his time as an operational officer on the Havant division, he was involved in two separate incidents during which he tackled suspects who were in possession of loaded firearms. In both cases he'd received commendations from the chief constable. At the same time, following one of the incidents he'd been ticked off for going in on his own and not waiting for back-up.

As he parked his police car outside a block of flats in Leigh Park, he'd heard a woman screaming out, 'Please don't shoot me!' Mick had passed startled residents as he ran up three flights of stairs to where the noises were coming from. He'd noticed a door that was slightly ajar and peered inside. He'd seen a man holding a rifle – aimed at the woman's chest. Mick had kicked the door open wider and at the same time thrown his uniform cap into the room, which had distracted the gunman for a few seconds.

He'd charged at the man, knocking him to the floor, and after a short struggle had managed to wrest the rifle out of the man's grasp and throw it beyond his reach. Within a few minutes, other officers had arrived. The weapon was found to be loaded and ready to fire. Mick told me that he had become angry when he saw that a man was about to shoot a defenceless woman, and so he had gone straight for him, as you do. In Mick's own words, it all happened so fast that the man with the gun did not know what hit him.

Mick's mother, Grace Lyons, had died of cancer, and this made him decide that he needed to do something that would help to combat this disease. In 1983 he started a personal campaign to raise money for Queen Alexandra's Hospital in Portsmouth, a hospital that specialises in cancer treatment. With funds that Mick raised, the hospital was able to set up a new unit for a CT body scanner.

There was an official opening ceremony for the new unit, and Mick was invited to attend. He was asked to pull a cord to unveil the name of the unit: The Grace Lyons Unit. Mick was totally taken by surprise when he saw that the unit had been named after his mother, and he broke down in tears.

At the time I am writing this book, Mick has raised the staggering sum of £14 million. In 1989, while still a serving police officer, he was awarded the BEM – British Empire Medal – for his charity work. He retired in 1994 and now has his own office at the hospital, where he continues to raise funds. His latest campaign is to raise enough money to purchase a da Vinci Robot for the hospital. The da Vinci Robot has proved to be an amazing success in the fight against many cancers. The internal anatomy of a patient can be seen in 3D, high definition, and colour. It has revolutionised surgery, being so minimally invasive; afterwards the patient only remains in hospital for one day and one night.

The da Vinci Robot does not come cheap. It is made in the United States and costs £2.4 million. Its running annual costs are about £184,000. In 2014, there were only fourteen of them in the UK. It is hoped that hundreds of patients in Portsmouth, the Isle of Wight, and the Channel Islands will benefit from its use. Mick's appeal is now halfway towards its target.

Peter Spencer was a detective for nearly all of his service. He went on to become Hampshire's longest serving officer and retired in 2003 with thirty-nine years' service. This does not include the two years that he spent as a cadet. Peter's links with Israel are important to him, and he has fond memories of his first visit. As a result of winning a scholarship, he spent some weeks living on a kibbutz 3 miles from the River Jordan, where he worked in its orchards, cotton fields, and fish ponds. He has maintained his links with Israel ever since and has made about twenty visits over the years.

Peter lives in Bedhampton in the south east corner of Hampshire. Some years ago, he set up the Bedhampton Volunteers, a group that works to improve the environment and visual features of the area. A major project for them is the planting of 30,000 daffodil bulbs each year. Places that have been overgrown with brambles and other foliage are cleared, and hanging baskets are arranged to make the area look more attractive.

******

In 2010, I went to Enbrook Park at Sandgate, where the police training school had been. The site is now the company headquarters of the Saga organisation, and a very modern-looking building stands in the centre of a large green expanse of well-manicured lawns. The buildings that were there in 1964 have all been demolished, and it was difficult to remember where everything had been. The only thing that remained the same was the view of the sea through the trees and the water sparkling in the sunlight.

About the Author

Richard Ramsay was working in a London bank when he decided to do something different. From his first day in the Hampshire Police as a new recruit, he realised that he had started doing a job that would be unlike anything that he had experienced before.

This was a world where he and his fellow probationers would be continually tested and would need to prove themselves. It was also a place where they might face danger or high drama in the middle of a mundane, routine patrol. Horror, humour, and tragedy all made frequent appearances.

The author describes the process of learning how the world of policing works, which he describes as a giant jigsaw puzzle. As time goes on, a picture emerges as the pieces of the jigsaw start fitting together.

People seem to have an insatiable curiosity and interest in police fiction in written form, radio, television, and cinema. However, the author believes that, overall, the portrayal of police work in the media is not authentic.

After six years in Hampshire, the writer transferred to London and spent the rest of his service in the Metropolitan Police. In central London he faced a whole new series of challenges, including plain-clothes work combating street crime, dealing with urban rioting, and keeping the capital safe from terrorists.

Later, he spent four years at Scotland Yard, where he worked on a number of projects that examined policing methods and researched more effective ways of doing things. He retired from the police service in 1994. The author has a wife and two daughters and lives in the London area.

About the Book

The story starts with a terrorist bomb at Chelsea Barracks. Then the author takes us back to his first days as a trainee constable, learning the basics: Do the trainees know the legal definitions of the crimes that they will be faced with? Do they know whether there is a power of arrest?

This is a fascinating story of the world of policing, which starts in the 1960s and jumps forward to the twenty-first century. Working in urban and rural parts of Hampshire, Richard Ramsay does his best to prove himself as a young constable. He soon finds that police work can be a place of high drama and that police officers can be pitched into situations of danger. There is plenty of humour, but horror and tragedy also make frequent appearances.

Although Britain has a high crime rate, its police officers normally patrol the streets unarmed, something that usually surprises visitors from abroad. There is some historical perspective, with politics and social change in the background.

After nearly six years in Hampshire, the author transferred to the Metropolitan Police, and in central London, he was destined to face a whole new series of challenges. This would include working in plain clothes combating street crime, facing major urban rioting, and keeping the capital safe from terrorists. Later, as an experienced inspector, he worked at Scotland Yard, carrying out projects aimed at improving policing methods in the Met.

Towards the end of the book, there is some 'catching up' to be done when Richard Ramsay meets up with two of his classmates from the class of '64 and adds some of their experiences to the story. This is an accurate account of events through the eyes of someone who was there when things happened.